Praise for
WHITEY

"*Whitey* is the definitive word on the whole sordid saga of the Bulger mob. Expertly crafted, beautifully told." —Dennis Lehane, author of *Live by Night*

"Having first uncovered the terrible Bulger story, Gerard O'Neill and Dick Lehr have now brought it full circle—a true circle of hell. Exemplary journalism, high drama, and, for Bulger's victims, an ongoing tragedy: rarely has a book mattered more." —James Carroll, author of *An American Requiem*

"*Black Mass*, also by Lehr and O'Neill, was the definitive book on the corrupt relationship of the Boston office of the FBI and the notorious gangster Whitey Bulger. *Whitey* will stand right next to it as the most in-depth portrayal yet of the life of the man who ruled the South Boston underworld by terror and duplicity. In this groundbreaking, intimately researched work, we learn how he became the person who was feared by so many. Once you start reading, you won't want to put it down."
—Bill Bratton, former Boston and NYPD police commissioner and LAPD police chief

"Lehr and O'Neill have outdone themselves. *Whitey* isn't just a chilling biography of a monster—it's also a vivid portrait of Southie, a blood-spattered history of Boston mob wars, and a searing indictment of the corrupt FBI agents who literally gave Whitey Bulger a license to kill. Full of new information about Whitey's prison stint as a young man and his life as an elderly fugitive, this is the definitive account of one of weirdest and most sordid chapters in the history of American crime."
—Tom Perrotta, author of *The Leftovers*

"*Whitey* is a masterpiece of investigative reporting that unravels a tension-filled tale of murder, treachery, and abuse of power."
—Ronald Kessler, author of *The Secrets of the FBI* and *In the President's Secret Service*

"Dennis Lehane and Martin Scorsese: take a seat. Nobody knows the twisted saga of Whitey Bulger and his gang, covered this story of criminal savagery and official corruption with more courage, or tells the tale now with such élan as Gerard O'Neill and Dick Lehr."
—John Farrell, author of *Tip O'Neill and the Democratic Century*

"So much has been written about Whitey Bulger, including by Lehr and O'Neill, but this book is different. It is comprehensive in its scope, tracing Bulger's family, his own journey from Southie, to Europe, from Leavenworth, and, finally, to the Princess Eugenia Apartment in Santa Monica, California. Lehr and O'Neill have culled material far and wide—transcripts, old prison records, official documents, interviews, books, and clippings. But best of all, they've woven it all in a narrative that is extraordinary, compelling, and impossible to put down."
—Nancy Gertner (Retired, U.S.District Court judge), author of *In Defense of Women*

WHITEY

The Life *of* America's Most Notorious Mob Boss

Dick Lehr and Gerard O'Neill

CROWN PUBLISHERS

New York

CROWN and the Crown colophon are registered
trademarks of Random House, Inc.

Library of Congress Cataloging-in-Publication data
is available upon request.

ISBN 978-0-307-98653-5
eISBN 978-0-307-98654-2

PRINTED IN THE UNITED STATES OF AMERICA

Book design by Donna Sinisgalli
Jacket design by Kristen Haff
Jacket photographs: Inmate case file AZ-1428 (The
National Archives at San Francisco)

10 9 8 7 6 5 4 3 2

First Edition

To my wife, Karin; my sons, Nick and
Christian; and my daughters, Holly
and Dana.
Nothing happens without them.

—Dick Lehr

To my steadfast wife, Janet O'Neill; my
sons, Brian and Shane, who make me
proud; my prized daughter-in-law, Patty;
and my grandchildren, Kylie and Jack.

—Gerard O'Neill

CONTENTS

NOTE TO THE READER

The arrest of James J. "Whitey" Bulger in June 2011 gave us the opportunity to reunite to write Whitey's life story—making *Whitey* the final part of our trilogy about Whitey Bulger, the Boston Mafia, and the FBI.

The Underboss, the first book in the trilogy, reconstructed the 1981 FBI bugging of Boston Mafia boss Gennaro Angiulo in the city's North End, an operation that crippled the Angiulo crime family.

Then came Whitey Bulger—who has long overshadowed the Mafia. Whitey's harnessing of a corrupt FBI Organized Crime Squad for nearly twenty years resulted in the reign of terror that we chronicled in *Black Mass.*

Now, in *Whitey,* we are able to place that unholy alliance into the context of his long life, from the streets of South Boston to the sunsets in Santa Monica, California. *Whitey* is a full accounting of the damage done as well as an excavation into the past to uncover the making of America's most notorious mob boss.

Dick Lehr and Gerard O'Neill
Boston, January 2013

WHITEY

September 17, 1981

Debra Davis

At mid-afternoon on a dying late summer day, the stunningly beautiful Debra Davis climbed into the snazzy, two-seat Mercedes convertible that her boyfriend had bought for her and drove away from the home they shared in the suburb of Randolph, Massachusetts. She headed north, her destination South Boston—East Third Street, to be exact, to a house located on the eastern side of the compact neighborhood shaped like a finger sticking out into Boston Harbor.

Her boyfriend, Stevie Flemmi, wanted to show her something—at least that's what he'd said on the telephone. He wanted to give her a tour of the Cape-style house he'd bought for his parents. The closing was earlier that very same day, and Stevie had paid the full purchase price of eighty thousand dollars, an act of generosity so that his parents would not be saddled with a mortgage.

Debbie exited the interstate. She began snaking her way through the streets of a community known as mostly Irish-American, insular and famous for its "Southie Pride." While she was familiar with the neighborhood, able to navigate the grid of narrow streets, many of which were one-way and dizzying to outsiders, if Stevie had been at the wheel he would have been able to make his way blindfolded. Stevie Flemmi had grown up in another part of Boston but Southie was now a key venue for his business interests—ever since 1974, when he signed on with a gathering force in the city's underworld: the legendary boss of Southie's Irish mob.

Debbie and Stevie had been together for that long, too. She was a teenager in late 1974 working behind the counter at a jewelry store on Beacon Street in Brookline when he'd spotted her. Stevie was significantly older: Debbie was nineteen; he was forty. Stevie had liked what he saw—the flowing blond hair, the blue eyes, the glamour of a ravishing young thing—and decided she was for him. He paid for her divorce from a brief mistake of a marriage, and the two were off and running. But at her age seven years was a long time to be in a relationship. Debbie had met someone else and wanted out. Stevie didn't think so; he wanted in, now and forevermore. An unmistakable tension had surfaced between the two.

Making her way down East Third Street, Debbie pulled up to the curb outside the house numbered 832. She could see that the one-and-a-half-story Cape Stevie had bought was positioned oddly. The front of the house did not face the street the way most houses do; it sat sideways. And it stood opposite another house that was its mirror image—two houses facing each other with only a small, shared yard separating them. Someone standing at the kitchen sink of one house could practically reach out to hand a cup of sugar to the neighbor standing at the window of the other.

The houses were in fact built as a pair in 1965. A year later a thirty-two-year-old state representative named Bill Bulger bought one. Ever since, Bill, his wife, and their growing family had lived at 828 East Third Street. When the twin house came on to the market in 1981, Stevie made his move. He'd talked to Debbie about wanting his parents to be nearer to him and to be safe. They'd recently been mugged in Boston. The house for sale at 832 East Third Street, situated in his South Boston stomping grounds and next to the home of Bill Bulger, a rising power in Massachusetts politics, certainly satisfied Stevie's idea of a safe haven.

Debbie Davis waited in her Mercedes. The day that began in bright sunshine was now mostly cloudy, with cooling temperatures and a quiet breeze. Soon enough Debbie saw Stevie's car coming down the street. She saw that Stevie was not alone. Stevie had arrived with the older brother of neighbor Bill Bulger.

James J. "Whitey" Bulger. The city's most menacing and beguiling gangster, a crime boss who embraced the role as slayer-in-chief, in large measure because he understood that hands-on viciousness created the footing for him to rival leaders of the larger, more organized La Cosa Nostra. That Whitey Bulger also seemed to find pleasure in the terror only added to his monstrous aura.

Debbie Davis should have run for it, but she did not.

When Debbie and Stevie Flemmi first began dating in 1974, Debbie's father complained angrily to her mother, Olga. In particular Edward Davis did not like their difference in age. But Olga basically ignored her husband's concerns; they'd separated that year and relations were not friendly. "He had a terrible temper," Olga said. The next year, 1975, Edward drowned in a boating accident.

For her part, Olga thought Debbie was "of age" and old enough to make up her own mind. "She said she'd met a nice guy who wanted to take her out to eat," Olga said about Debbie's first mention of Stevie. Besides, once Debbie began bringing Stevie around, Olga liked him. "He was always very polite." Olga knew one other thing about Stevie, that he was "a bookmaker," but that was all she wanted to know, and Debbie never talked to her about her boyfriend's business interests.

Instead, Olga appreciated that her daughter seemed happy. Stevie paid for everything, including one apartment after another the couple shared. He lavished Debbie with money, and she built up a wardrobe of expensive clothes, shoes, and pocketbooks. He'd bought her a Jaguar, a Corvette, and now the Mercedes. They socialized with Stevie's associates, be it at fancy restaurants downtown or Triple O's, the bar in Southie, with its nickname the "Bucket of Blood," that served all of his gang's needs, whether for business or pleasure. They traveled to faraway places, and earlier in 1981 Stevie had even paid for a one-week vacation to Acapulco for just Olga and Debbie. It wasn't as if Debbie was looking to meet someone, but, ironically, during this mother-daughter getaway, paid for by Stevie, a new man did enter Debbie's life.

"He met us," Olga said. "He approached us while we were at dinner." Debbie was enchanted by the suave, millionaire son of a Mexican oil baron, and the two spent enough time together that a smitten Debbie did not want to go home when the week ended. She did go home, but soon after returned to Acapulco to be with him again. "He was a very nice gentleman," Eileen, Debbie's older sister, said. "Treated her like a lady, a princess."

By summertime Debbie was telling her mother that this was the guy, and she was going to break up with Stevie. By then Stevie had discovered something was up. He'd gone through her things, found her address book, and discovered a new entry for the man from Acapulco—name, telephone number, address. "I told her she was crazy," Olga said. "Why did she leave it around? I would have kept it for her."

Olga had a front-row seat to the widening chasm. Debbie, on the one hand, was talking more and more about leaving Stevie Flemmi for the new love interest, while Stevie was suddenly and excitedly talking about marriage. In August, Stevie had stood up right there in Olga's living room, put his arm tightly around Debbie, and, in full denial, announced, "We're going to get married in September."

It was as if by squeezing Debbie Davis and issuing his marital declaration, Stevie was reasserting his claim on the young woman who'd long been such a delight to him. She belongs to me, he was saying—even if his woman was thinking otherwise, to the point that come the afternoon of Friday, September 17, 1981, when she agreed to meet Stevie in Southie, she had a secret plan to fly on Monday to Acapulco.

Stevie Flemmi was no longer trusting of Debbie Davis. But he was not alone. Whitey Bulger did not trust her, either. In the beginning Whitey might have made fun of Stevie for bringing his new young thing around to Triple O's, saying she was underage and could not be served, but very quickly he came to detest her. "She had a lot to say and was very loud about it," Lindsey Cyr, one of Whitey's girlfriends, recalled.

Lindsey was at Triple O's one night waiting for Whitey, and over the drone of the crowd she could hear Debbie Davis's voice at the other end of the bar. Debbie was bragging to a group of hovering men that her boyfriend controlled the city's underworld. When Whitey arrived, Lindsey chided him. "This lady down the bar is going out with the head of the underworld. Here I thought that was you."

Whitey took it in. He saw a woman who was noisy and reckless, a woman who, from his perspective, was a risk. And increasingly she got in the way, between him and Stevie. "Bulger kind of resented the fact that I didn't spend enough time with him in our business," Stevie said, "and that I was kind of like not being available as often as I should be." The two associates had a policy of not talking on the telephone—a Whitey rule to avoid possible electronic surveillance. The way it was supposed to work was that Whitey would signal Stevie on a beeper; Stevie would leave his house to find a "clean phone" and then call Whitey back. But too often Whitey dialed Stevie's beeper, waited for the call back, but the call never came. Stevie was with Debbie and didn't want to be bothered, which left Whitey staring at his beeper.

"He was very upset about it," Stevie said.

In March, for Debbie's birthday, Stevie had taken her out to an expensive restaurant in Boston, and right smack in the middle of dinner his beeper went off. Whitey was trying to reach him. "I called him back and he said that he wanted to meet." Stevie balked, explaining the situation. "I'm having a birthday party."

Whitey was apoplectic. He told Stevie to send Debbie home. Tell her he'd take her out another night. "You got to be here," he ordered Stevie. So on that night, Stevie did what he was told and reported for duty.

By mid-1981 the matter of Debbie Davis had become untenable. Stevie had admitted to Whitey he'd shared certain information with her—extremely sensitive information that was closely held and vital to their business survival. Stevie tried to explain to Whitey why he did it—that his frequent leaving her, and his refusal to say why, had strained the relationship. "She probably figured it was another woman, you know," Stevie said. The tension between them built to where, in frustration and worry, Stevie told her, "Listen, we have to meet someone."

That someone—a person whom Whitey and Stevie often met to talk strategy and all manner of underworld affairs—was an FBI agent named John Connolly. "We have a connection," Stevie told Debbie. "John Connolly, FBI agent."

This was bad. This was a connection that went to the heart of Whitey's world, one that in 1981 was operating at full throttle, was responsible for much of Whitey's success, and was fruitful for the trio involved, meaning the two crime bosses and their FBI agent. While only Whitey and Stevie knew the full contours of the special relationship, the mere disclosure of a "connection" was radioactive. In Cold War politics, it would be like leaking secrets about nuclear-bomb making.

Instantly, Whitey knew what had to be done. If Whitey needed justification for Stevie beyond the shocking breach of security, he could play off of Stevie's jealousy. Whitey, as always, was up-to-date; he knew about Debbie's new gentleman caller in Acapulco. This was a no-brainer. This was business.

The front door of the Cape-style house was unlocked. Whitey and Stevie stepped inside first. Debbie was behind them. She saw a kitchen off to the left. Directly ahead a set of stairs led to the second floor. To the right of the stairs, a hallway ran toward the rear of the house, past a living room and a bedroom. Stevie headed down the hall, where Whitey, already ahead of them both, was in the bedroom.

Debbie Davis followed Stevie. She had little time to look around, and when she approached the back bedroom Whitey stepped out into the hall. His attack was lightning fast. Whitey seized her by the throat with his hands and began to shake her like a rag doll.

Debbie, gasping for breath, was dying—although blocking her airway was not the actual cause of death. Death from manual strangulation results from what is known in the field of forensic pathology as the occlusion, or obstruction, of blood vessels supplying blood to the brain. The pressure of a strangler's hands against the neck is so powerful and profound that it crushes the neck's internal structures. And because the strangler has to alter his grip as the victim struggles, the degree of pressure varies—resulting in a roller-coaster ride of terror in those final moments as waves of blood course in and out of the victim's head.

Exactly how Whitey strangled Debbie Davis—and how long it took—will forever be in dispute, a discordance resulting from two differing accounts. Whitey later told a confederate that the young woman was still alive when he hauled her downstairs into the cellar and deposited her into a chair. In this version, Whitey likely questioned Debbie as to whether she'd told anyone about the "connection" at the FBI. Following that, her mouth was sealed with duct tape and Stevie leaned over her, kissed her forehead, and said, "You're going to a better place."

Stevie Flemmi repudiated that account. He insisted that Whitey finished killing her upstairs in the hallway, where Whitey "grabbed her by the throat and strangled her." Stevie denied kissing her on the head or uttering the line about her going to a better place. "This happened very quickly," he testified in court years later about a cold-blooded murder he said was "traumatic" given his relationship with Debbie.

Despite the conflicting accounts, what is not in dispute is that Whitey Bulger strangled a woman who had come to know too much and posed a risk to him as long as she lived. So she died. Then, confronted with a corpse in the house that would soon be Stevie's mother's, a house where Whitey, Stevie, and FBI agents would eventually hold secret meetings—meetings that at least once included a drop-in from neighbor Bill Bulger—Whitey was still not done with the ghastliness. He handed Stevie a pair of pliers and instructed him to yank the teeth from the lifeless Debbie Davis to hamper authorities from ever being able to identify her through dental records. Making Stevie pull the teeth from the woman he said he loved was yet another way for Whitey to impose his primacy and authority.

Whitey and Stevie wrapped Debbie in plastic, then dragged her body upstairs and out into the late afternoon light. They threw the bundle into the trunk of a car and drove off. Later in the evening they headed to what would one day become known as the Bulger burial ground—a stretch of marshland along the Neponset River, beneath a bridge connecting Boston's Dorchester neighborhood to the city of Quincy. It was a bridge that Debbie Davis would have seen as she drove north on Interstate 93 from Randolph to meet Stevie at 832 East Third Street. Months later, Whitey had Stevie obtain Debbie's dental records from her dentist so they could be destroyed.

But for now, during Debbie's burial, Stevie was left to mull over what he was going to say to Olga Davis when they next talked, what the excuse would be for why the gangster and his girl had not been able to make it to her house for dinner.

Stevie Flemmi said afterward that the reason he told Debbie about the FBI "connection" was to ease the strain in their relationship. He said he thought he was entitled to make that decision given his standing with Whitey. Two of Whitey's women knew about the FBI agent. Why couldn't his?

"So I told Debbie," Stevie testified later. "I felt justified."

But to stake out that position Stevie failed to appreciate the difference between his women and Whitey's. Whitey's women were in control, and they accepted Whitey's dictum about discipline, or else. In contrast, Stevie's involvement with Debbie Davis had been a mess. Looming larger than the issue of women, however, was Stevie's failure to understand the core difference between him and Whitey. Though they were partners, they were not equals, not by any stretch. Whitey Bulger was in charge, and this was how it had always been. In any gathering it was Whitey's outsized persona that filled the room. His brother Bill once commented that Whitey as leader "was the only role he would tolerate."

The strangulation of Debbie Davis was not Whitey Bulger's first killing, or his last. He strangled and shot upwards of two dozen victims. In September 1981, when the nettlesome problem of Debbie Davis needed a final solution, Whitey was at the threshold of a decade that would see him soar as a crime boss, to the zenith of his underworld powers.

He was not about to let a girl get in his way—and, as was his custom, the fact he took the Debbie Davis matter into his own hands reflected both psychological makeup and criminal genius. Whitey had an intense need for control, and so to get things right he often did it himself—which meant the empire he was building was more a cult of personality than an outfit with built-in lines of succession. Whitey also understood the message his free-killing ways sent through the city's dark underworld, a political statement of cold terror.

But as horrific as the killing of Debbie Davis was, this is not a book about one Bulger murder. This is Whitey Bulger's life story, the story of the most notorious crime boss in twentieth-century America, a story that cannot be told without also telling the story of Boston and, more specifically, South Boston, of the Irish in America, of organized crime, and of the Federal Bureau of Investigation. It is a story that includes his politically prominent brother, Bill Bulger, and the documentable instances where the two, forever loyal, looked out for each other, across the arc of their lives and mutual success in their chosen fields.

In the annals of crime in the United States, Whitey Bulger today stands at the front of a line that includes John Dillinger, Al Capone, Bonnie Parker and Clyde Barrow, and, more recently, John Gotti. His list of victims matches or exceeds that of any other crime boss, but

Whitey has achieved a distinction that no other major crime figure can claim: he brought the nation's top law enforcement agency—the FBI—to its knees, with FBI agents working in service to him. In his book *Public Enemies*, Bryan Burrough provides an excellent historical account of the FBI's War on Crime in the early 1930s—against Dillinger, Bonnie and Clyde, and many others. Burrough documents that for a young FBI, the early 1930s was when "the FBI became the FBI," a period when it evolved "from an overmatched band of amateurish agents without firearms or law-enforcement experience into the professional crime-fighting machine of lore."

Three decades later, the FBI underwent a second major shift, when it announced in the 1960s that its new priority was to fight organized crime, specifically La Cosa Nostra. But this time the effort went horribly awry, as a secret new FBI program where agents teamed up with underworld informants resulted in rank lawlessness: agents lost their compass, broke the law, and, ultimately, became gangsters themselves. The corruption became a way of life and continued to the end of the century, with Boston seeing the worst of it, a scandal of historic proportion. And at the center of the madness stood the master manipulator, Whitey Bulger.

This biography of James J. "Whitey" Bulger will explain the evolution of Whitey from a juvenile delinquent in the 1940s to stone-cold killer in the 1960s, from unchallenged crime boss in Boston in the 1980s with the blessing of a corrupted FBI, to fugitive from justice in 1995, and, finally, to his capture sixteen years later in June 2011 at age eighty-one. Other works, including our own *Black Mass*, have covered portions of his gangster life, most notably his years as an FBI informant, but they have left unanswered such fundamental questions as what created Whitey Bulger. What were the forces at work in the making of the monster? In *Whitey* we aim to answer those questions, and in the process reveal a man whose dark pathology and obsession with self-preservation, whose taste for blood, and whose criminal genius all combined to create a larger-than-life crime figure who single-handedly rivaled the Mafia as a criminal enterprise, who caused at least one Boston mayor to worry about his own safety, and who, most recently, was second only to Osama bin Laden as the nation's most-wanted fugitive.

2

Riverhead

*The Bulgers lived around the bend above
the church*

A half century after the American Revolution, the Bulger clan started out in the New World on one of the bleakest promontories the North American continent had to offer: Newfoundland.

William Bulger, Whitey's great-grandfather, arrived toward the end of the most lasting migration to North America in history. He came as a young man from County Wexford in Ireland, looking for a new start in a rough-hewn place that had better-paying jobs for the strong.

He had been born a year after the English put down yet another Irish insurrection, this one famously involving a secret alliance with France that was betrayed and became a too-little, too-late fiasco.

The high hopes of the Rebellion of 1798 yielded only a deep gash in the national psyche. It had been the most sustained country-wide uprising in Irish history and its last stand was in Bulger's home county. The Battle of Vinegar Hill became a turning point, followed by massacres of insurgents and civilians by English troops in Enniscorthy and New Ross. The bitter aftermath was the execution of rebel leaders and another century of ruthless rule from London and by Anglican Protestants.

By the time William Bulger was born in 1799, his village had glumly resettled into utter subjugation. The country once again turned inward, largely oblivious of momentous events in America and Europe. George Washington died at Mount Vernon and Napoleon became dictator of France. Within a year, Thomas Jefferson beat John Adams in one of the most drawn-out and hard-fought presidential elections in American history.

But Ireland was a medieval world away, subsisting in backwater repression. A quarter century later, it had little to offer William Bulger. His immigration fit the pattern of the day. He was in the prime age category of eighteen to twenty-five, and a single male on board a ship that had few women. Nearly all left behind slim prospects in a stifled society and an agrarian economy in hard times.

Bulger embarked at the tail end of a historic passage that began two centuries earlier when intrepid Irishmen first left Waterford Harbor for seasonal work in the Grand Banks fisheries. The trade was driven by English merchants from the port city of Bristol, with ships stopping in Ireland for better and cheaper salt provisions. Immigrants were added as another commodity.

Eventually, cyclical migrants became permanent settlers. As more "winterovered," a small Irish colony became a beachhead. In the first third of the nineteenth century, Newfoundland became a turnstile to new beginnings.

The immigrant wave turned the provincial seat of St. John's into a small city that grew haphazardly along the coast. Its steep streets and colorful houses peered over one of Canada's better harbors, which lies between two bluffs besieged by wet fog and fierce winds. In spring, massive icebergs from Greenland slide by its entrance. It has remained a bare-knuckled town of many pubs and tumble-to-the-street brawls. The raucous barrooms and Gaelic music are as indelibly Irish as a failed rebellion.

But the pioneers still felt the tug of home as they arrived with deep roots in their villages, most going back generations. Unlike the later emergency evacuation of Irish families to America in the 1840s, the newcomers to Newfoundland usually walked up the wharf in St. John's all alone, with no kin waiting for them. Ahead was a lifestyle and work world that shifted sharply from the agrarian to the maritime. Cod was king as much as Victoria was queen of England.

For the most part, the Irish stayed put in St. John's, with few venturing into the logging camps of the interior. The sea diluted the old ways and became the harsh rhythm of daily life. One study of the refugees found that most had worked on large estates, but not merely as tenant farmers. They had a variety of occupations that made them more adaptable to the New World—stonemasons, plasterers, painters, carpenters, thatchers, boatmen. The best credential was fisherman, though most of the Irish had worked on interior rivers and not the frenzied Atlantic.

According to an 1836 census, St. John's had 15,000 residents, or 20 percent of the provincial population, making it one of the largest Canadian cities of the day. Three out of every four Irishmen lived in the city or on the adjacent coast, which is still known as the Irish Shore.

The journey of the Bulger founding father surely resembled the peregrinations chronicled by John Mannion, of Memorial University in St. John's. An authority on immigration, he focused on residents who departed the village of Inistioge in Southern Kilkenny, next door to Bulger's County Wexford, over a fifty-year period.

The Inistioge contingent were generally passengers on the return trip of St. John's ships that carried cod and oil to Ireland. The émigrés embarked under arrangements made by a local trader who guaranteed fares that fell due after passengers got jobs in Newfoundland. The traders were part of a Protestant clique of Scottish ancestry who represented several vessels and booked passengers who traveled down the riverways on ferries to New Ross in Wexford, a bustling way station en route to the main harbor. Mannion found that during the nineteenth-century migration, Kilkenny ranked just ahead of Wexford in sending young men to St. John's.

William Bulger likely made a day's journey to the port on foot, carrying his aspirations in a seabag, to the quay of New Ross and then down to Passage, on Waterford Harbor, where he may have boarded one of the thirty ships that cleared the inlet each spring, bound for St. John's and its fishery. Or perhaps one of the twenty ships that left later in the year with more priority, since they carried provisions for the fall and winter.

Bulger caught the second and final immigration wave in the early nineteenth century that flooded St. John's with Irish refugees. Between

1810 and 1815, 14,000 came ashore, and a similar number disembarked between 1825 and 1831. The benchmarks of the era would have Bulger arriving at St. John's around 1825. According to Mannion, the pattern was for male Irish émigrés to take at least seven years to get enough money together to set up a house and start a family. It was more than tentative Irish bachelorhood. It was an economic necessity.

Newfoundland was a patriarchal society even as late as the 1830s, when William Bulger began courting Mary Myer, who was likely the native-born daughter of an immigrant from County Tipperary. In her day, men outnumbered women by two to one and she probably had several suitors.

Myer fit the marriage pattern of the era better than Bulger. He was almost an old-timer at thirty-four when they married, but she was twenty-one, a typical age, as nearly all Irish women wed in their early twenties.

They married on November 20, 1833, at the only Catholic church in St. John's at the time—the Old Chapel on Henry Street. Because of its expanding congregation, it evolved into the Basilica of St. John, which required both stone and stonecutters be imported from Ireland. It appears they were the rarest of Irish families, in that they had only one child—a son, James, who would be James "Whitey" Bulger's grandfather, as well as Whitey's namesake nearly a century later, in the generational Irish tradition of naming firstborn sons after the father's father.

Both family names were Gaelic but both were rare in New-foundland. Mannion found that in the nineteenth-century migra-tion, there were only sixteen Bulgers who listed Irish places of origin. Only three were from Wexford. Most were from Kilkenny. There were just three Myers, and they were from southern Tipperary County, also contiguous to Waterford Harbor, with its link to Newfoundland.

The Bulgers became a fishing family in the uniformly Irish West End of St. John's. Mannion thought it likely Bulger would have fished inshore, a few miles from town on an inlet from skiffs with a crew of up to four men. Or possibly as a "shoreman" curing fish. Mannion said that if William Bulger had taken a merchant's job as a shopkeeper or tavern proprietor, he would have left a larger footprint.

While the Irish populated St. John's in the early nineteenth cen-tury, the province was dominated by Protestant English merchants, who held tight the reins. For most of the migratory surge, the Irish had been denied full civil rights and could not hold office or enter certain professions, restrictions similar to the infamous penal laws in Ireland itself. But all that started to change within a few years of Bulger's arrival, a gradual amelioration that still took place faster than was the case in Irish Boston, and far more rapid than in Ireland itself. Newfoundland, perhaps because of its smaller scale, moved tentatively but surely toward assimilation, but not integration. Fishing villages were and remain English Protestant on one side of an inlet and Irish Catholic on the other.

James Joseph Bulger was born on August 25, 1844. Whitey Bulger's grandfather was baptized at the Basilica of St. John. But he arrived as an ill wind came in from across the Atlantic. Catastrophe leveled the Irish homeland before James Bulger's first birthday. The staple crop of Ireland—the ubiquitous potato—turned foul from fungus in the fields, beginning a savage starvation that the English ignored while peasants ate grass and died where they fell. One-third of the potato crop rotted in 1845 and the plight steadily worsened each year until 1850, a vicious iteration that decimated tenant farmers, especially on the west coast.

Only 1 percent of the famine refugees docked in St. John's, the old trade route from Waterford having been abandoned. But the sustained diaspora from Ireland meant pandemonium fifteen hundred miles away, in Boston.

With a small but growing Irish population, with kin and neighbors to offer helping hands to refugees, Boston became a major destination for immigrants. The city leadership was virulently hostile but there was shared misery in what became America's first urban slum, in the North End. The early immigrants were hemmed in along the waterfront, a miasmic place of overcrowded tenements and backed-up sewage. By 1855, Boston was one-third Irish, with fifty thousand immigrants sprawling across the north and west ends, Charlestown, and South Boston.

The tenfold increase became the impetus for a long-lasting anti-immigrant backlash in Massachusetts. Local nativists became part of a national movement that quickly evolved into a paranoid sect steeped in secret handshakes and passwords. They became the "Know-Nothing Party" because of their pledge to evade all questions about their purpose: "I know nothing."

Famine and bigotry influenced all nineteenth-century Irish immigrants, setting the contentious agenda in Boston for a half century. It would hold true even for late arrivals from Newfoundland like the Bulgers, who endured the mild stigma of being "two boat" Irish. In the petty pecking order of the day, descending from a stay up north was less pure than immigrating directly from County Cork.

As the unlovely Boston story boiled over at mid-century, before settling into one of edgy coexistence, the Bulgers made a meager livelihood in the Irish enclave known as Riverhead, in the West End of St. John's. But if there was no famine or cholera, there was plenty of hardship and heartache.

Like his father, James Bulger was a fisherman who married in his thirties, exchanging vows with Alice Gardiner at the basilica on November 25, 1875.

Whitey Bulger's grandmother was the right age for marriage at the time—twenty-one. She also came from an Irish immigrant family that had deep roots in the fishing trade, hailing from Harbour Grace, near St. John's. It was a busy village that serviced the Labrador cod industry farther north.

Alice Gardiner's family had immigrated from New Ross, the river town and transfer station for Waterford Harbor, where émigrés embarked for Newfoundland. The Gardiner lineage went back deeper into Newfoundland history than the Bulgers' and revealed the relatively rare intermarriage of English and Irish. The wedding probably took place before the Catholic Church became established in Newfoundland, and Alice's grandmother Eleanor Pippy brought an Anglican English surname from Devon to the family tree. And a long-distance reverberation for Whitey Bulger: because of her, the jingoistic gangster who helped smuggle guns to the Irish Republican Army has a drop of English blood.

The newlyweds lived with his parents at 128 Lazy Bank Road, in the West End. It's highly likely that James got work in the Labrador fishery through his wife's family—a fatal circumstance, as it turned out. Tragedy followed the best of prospects and intentions—a steady job for James. He drowned in a fishing accident in June 1883 at L'Anse-au-Loup, on the shores of Labrador Straits, an area known for its deadly shipwrecks. Alice Bulger was five months pregnant with her second son when her husband died.

Whitey Bulger's father, James J. Bulger, was born on November 25, 1883, and baptized in St. Patrick's Church, a couple of blocks from Lazy Bank Road, fatherless and the youngest of three. He would be the end of the line for the Bulgers in Riverhead, and the family's waning coincided with the ebbing of the Irish altogether in St. John's. When William Bulger and Mary Myer were courting, the Irish made up half of the province, but over the century, their portion fell to 20 percent as the general population rose from 60,000 to 202,000.

The Bulgers spent seventy years in Riverhead, experiencing all too well the region's bitter, endless struggle with the wild North Atlantic. The province would grow but never really prosper. Its natives remain known in Canada for doing the brawny jobs few will do and for being too stubborn for their own good. Like when they overfished the cod to virtual extinction.

The St. John's to Boston immigration route was well established by the time the Bulgers took it. One study found that a contracting job market and a bad fire in St. John's in 1846 sparked a mini-migration to points in Canada and New England and a sustained passage to Boston. The Bulgers took the Boston boat toward the end of the nineteenth century, when the clan petered out amid death and departures.

On April 15, 1879, the founding father, William Bulger, died at home in the Riverhead neighborhood; he was buried at St. Patrick's. It had been two years since the birth of his first grandson, William Michael Bulger. His other grandchildren were born after his death—Mary Maud in 1881, and James in the fateful year of 1883. (It appears the grandchild William did not survive.)

Five years later, on July 14, 1884, the matriarch, Mary Myer Bulger, died at seventy-two, also at home on Lazy Bank Road.

Five years after that, the widow from Harbour Grace, Alice Gardiner Bulger, her familial infrastructure gone, decided the sea and hard life had taken enough of a toll. At age thirty-five, she left her children behind and set out for Boston, arriving in 1889. It seems likely that she traveled with an old friend from the inlet town where she grew up. In any event, she and Michael Kelley, also from Harbour Grace, were married in Boston in 1892 and lived in Charlestown.

Three years later, young James, twelve years old, joined his mother and stepfather in Massachusetts. Perhaps with Bulger piquancy, he later listed his arrival date as the Fourth of July, 1895. His naturalization papers stated his occupation as "seaman," a vestige of the life he had left behind but hardly an impressive credential in Yankee Boston.

It appears that Bulger had a difficult transition with his new family, which included a stepfather and a young half brother, Brendan Kelley. Less than three years after his arrival, he and a pal were school dropouts applying to be apprentices at the Boston naval station. Rejected, they decided to run away from home, walking to Providence, Rhode Island, some fifty miles away. Newly homeless, they were picked up as vagrants and spent the night of June 23, 1899, in the Pawtucket police station. The next morning, the fifteen-year-old Bulger rethought life on the road and headed to the rail yard to hop a freight train back to Boston. He was lucky to get out alive. According to a *Boston Globe* story, he fell among moving cars and his left arm was crushed. The story states he was found in "an almost senseless condition" in the mud. His arm had to be amputated.

He returned to the Kelley home in Charlestown and was listed as a resident on Corey Street in the 1900 census. But by 1905, when he filed his naturalization papers, he was living in a boardinghouse at 22 Unity Street in the North End, a neighborhood in the final phase of drastic transformation, going from entirely Irish to mostly Italian in two decades.

Although the North End still had some Irish streets when Bulger settled there as a twenty-two-year-old, it was an Italian stronghold by then, another self-segregating reshuffle in clannish Boston. The Irish had fled the slum, and those who could do so had upgraded to South Boston, leaving behind a cholera epidemic and the sky-high infant mortality rate.

The North End was no bed of roses at the turn of the century. It was a low-rent place of jam-packed tenements and littered streets. As the Irish withdrew, there were incessant clashes between Irish and Italian gangs. In these the Irish learned that not all differences are settled with fists. Stilettos surfaced on the streets. The resentments lasted nearly a century, as Mafia capos derided Irish cops and crooks, one group as bad as the other. Whitey Bulger would become part of the ancient antipathies.

When Whitey's father, James Bulger, moved into a waterfront rooming house after the turn of the century, it coincided with a benchmark in Irish ascendancy. The North End's singular personality—John "Honey Fitz" Fitzgerald—became the first American-born Irishman of immigrant parents to become Boston mayor. Honey Fitz moved relentlessly upward, going from the common council to the state Senate to Congress and finally to the mayor's office. His career took him to Washington, D.C., the Boston suburbs, and finally to Dorchester, where he lived when he was mayor. But no matter the job, he always paid mawkish fealty to his roots, saluting the "dear old northenders" so often that they became known as "dearos."

But in 1905, Fitzgerald was long gone from the North End and the dearos were dispersed throughout South Boston, Charlestown, Dorchester, and West Roxbury. James Bulger was a young man without a country—a two-boat "Newfie" in an Italian village yet no "dearo" to the Irish, an interloper from a place so far north that icebergs are a sign of spring.

If, at the turn of the century, James J. Bulger decided to take stock of his life so far, it would have made for a bleak recapitulation: He never knew his father. His mother had left him behind in Newfoundland to be raised by in-laws. At age twelve, he became an immigrant himself, trying to connect with a new family. Then he was permanently disabled at fifteen. And here he was now, a one-armed Irishman in an alien neighborhood known for manual labor. A Dickensian life was unfolding.

3

Old Harbor

Old Harbor, in all its glory

For all the hardships in getting there, the first quarter of the twentieth century was an idyllic if meager time on the South Boston side of the railroads and Fort Point Channel. Nothing fancy. Just a good, simple life. If the place called "the town" for short tended to rhapsodize about itself, it did grow into more than just another neighborhood. There was a strong sense of being special and separate, surrounded as it was on three sides by the harbor and loaded with parks and ocean frontage—a cachet missing in other Irish camps.

The one discordant note—and a resounding one that reaffirmed the ancient estrangement from Yankee Boston—was the fury that followed the police strike of 1919, when a WASP governor, mayor, and police commissioner fired Irish cops for trying to unionize. One of the lawless insurrections took place just over the Broadway Bridge. Though order was restored, the strike reinforced the view of downtown leaders that South Boston was a truculent society within a society, stuck in survival mode far longer than necessary, clinging to enemies to define itself.

Thus the Southie paradox: congenial on the inside but rancorous at the border. The legacy of immigrant life and Boston bigotry made the South Boston Irish deeply possessive—their streets, their three-bedroom apartments, their schools, their churches, their blocks. The sense of staked-out turf extended even to the beachfront, where families always went to the same spot at the foot of I or K or M streets. Five square feet on a rocky beach and seaside chairs became family heirlooms.

But it wasn't as if Southie was conjuring bogeymen. Its paranoia began with real enemies. Even the Kennedy clan felt the hard stare of chill Yanks. Rose Kennedy, daughter of Mayor Honey Fitzgerald, wife of a successful banker on his way to being a legendary tycoon, and future mother of a president, had been shunned by Brahmin Boston. In her memoir, here's what she saw: old money was the only kind that counted and it controlled the banks, insurance companies, law firms, shipping, and mercantile enterprises in a self-perpetuating aristocracy. She wrote that the social divide in 1910 was so sharply drawn that the newspapers carried two society columns—"one about them, one about us."

The only unifying theme was mutual exclusion. The Irish, clannish to begin with, simply adopted the cloistered culture they could see up on Beacon Hill when they arrived in the mid-nineteenth century. In both neighborhoods, the premise was the medieval understanding that everyone had a proper place and stayed there.

But South Boston had its own separate history, largely unconcerned with social slights at downtown clubs. Rather, the neighborhood focused on becoming its own closed society to ward off outside intrusions. An insular mentality took deep root.

The early Irish in Southie had advantages that immigrants in the rancid North End and disheveled Charlestown lacked. The housing was better and they briefly shared common interests with Brahmins living in the big houses along City Point.

But best of all: South Boston was able to sidestep the famine deluge of fifty thousand émigrés who swamped downtown from 1845 to 1850. The Southie peninsula was still thinly populated, something of a pastoral oasis. It had a small colony of Irish who had trickled in during the 1830s, when ships from Waterford and Cork harbors first began regular runs to East Coast cities.

For the most part, the first Irish in Southie were small shop merchants with middle-class aspirations who had little use for the more recent arrivals from Cork and Galway. The *South Boston Gazette* actually joined the chorus denouncing the famine émigrés as country bumpkins and brawling drunkards. The South Boston Irish also shared the Yankee resentment of downtown officials dumping institutional buildings on what had been cow pastures.

Southie's leadership filed a protesting document known as the "Memorial of 1847," which decried the gathering of the impoverished and diseased on their stoop. It was signed by WASPs such as Cranston Howe, Samuel Perkins, and Isaac Adams. It would take a while, but the prison and hospitals and a poorhouse were all relocated. The power of protest had taken hold.

The us-versus-them outlook that remains at the core of Southie life began as a Yankee-versus-Yankee conflict over what downtown was doing to their bucolic commune. But the manifesto was a turning point for what became the ultimate Irish enclave, a place of such shrill independence as to be almost ungovernable. It was the birth of an ethos that became an article of faith to the growing number of Irish streaming into Southie—that outsiders are exploitive and downtown is not to be trusted.

Over the next decades, the steady Irish migration changed the character of a rural middle-class peninsula into a working-class mainstay. The population doubled with factory jobs and heavy industry that took over the Lower End during the Civil War. As the Yankees slowly withdrew, there was a steady flow of Irish from one end to the other, Lower End to City Point. In a quarter century, South Boston coalesced into the tight-knit Irish colony that would be known far and wide.

While Rose Kennedy fumed about separate and unequal treatment at the dawn of the twentieth century, James Bulger was struggling just to get by.

Boston employment archives show that he began a decade of work as a city employee, first as a clerk at the House of Correction on Deer Island in 1911 and later at the South Stable on Albany Street, in the horseshoe shop that serviced street cleaning and the sewer system. It appears his North End days helped him catch on with the administration of Honey Fitzgerald, who barely beat the epitome of Yankee

Boston, James Jackson Storrow, in 1910, when the Irish took City Hall in a watershed election.

Bulger kept his head down during the next election cycle, when James Michael Curley began his long if intermittent reign in 1914. It appeared Bulger didn't survive the later patronage wars when Andrew Peters, a quirky, quintessential Brahmin Republican, beat Curley in 1917 with the help of a Democratic spoiler in the race. Bulger was off the city payroll by 1919.

At the end of his public payroll days, Bulger was about halfway through a vagabond's bumpy ride in and around Boston. He would live in eight neighborhoods, six in Boston along with stays in Revere and Everett, and accumulate a dozen addresses.

After starting out in Charlestown, he lived in a series of rooming houses in the North End, then on Harrison Avenue in the South End while he worked at the stable.

In 1916, at age thirty-three, he married nineteen-year-old Ruth I. Pearce before a justice of the peace. The couple moved into 26 Melbourne Street, near Codman Square in Dorchester. But it was a short-lived union and they separated in about two years.

In 1918, Bulger moved in with his mother after Michael Kelley, her second husband and onetime neighbor from Harbour Grace in Newfoundland, had died.

His mother, twice widowed, was a rough-and-ready Newfie listed in the city directory as the janitor in the building where she and James lived, at 91 Eustis Street in Roxbury. James stayed there until 1922, and it appears he was at loose ends during this time—separated, perhaps unemployed, and approaching his forties. Records show he ran afoul of the law. Prison files for his son Whitey state the father was charged for assault with a gun in Roxbury and had been arrested on more than one occasion for being drunk.

At some point in the middle of the Roaring Twenties, James began courting a Charlestown woman, Jane "Jean" McCarthy, who was half his age. The courtship likely coincided with his divorce from Ruth Pearce in 1925, nearly a decade after they had married and well after she had remarried and moved to Chicago. Bulger claimed "abandonment" in his separation papers, an emotional blow reminiscent of being left behind in Newfoundland by his mother thirty years earlier.

McCarthy's family had moved to Everett, and Bulger showed up in city directories in Everett and Revere. Their courtship ended in a sudden elopement. On January 10, 1928, they were married in a civil ceremony at the Somerset Hotel in New York City. Their first child, Jean Marie Bulger, was born on May 15 of that year. They lived on Yeamans Street in Revere, and James listed his occupation as a clerk at a sand and gravel company, a job probably attained thanks to a connection he made during his years working for Boston's public works department.

The next year, the firstborn son, James J. Bulger Jr., destined to be Boston's foremost gangster, arrived in a Boston hospital on September 3—a month before the stock market crash of 1929. By then, the expanding family lived in Everett, next door to some of Jean's relatives on Woodlawn Street.

They moved once more to Revere before renting apartments in three-deckers in Dorchester. The Bulgers lived in three of them and added three more children, sons William and John and another daughter, Carol. (A third daughter, Sheila, was born in 1944 after they moved to South Boston.)

By the time the Bulgers got to their last Dorchester stop, they were literally on their way to Southie. They stayed two years on Crescent Avenue just across the border. Whitey was eight and old enough to be running on the street with boys headed for serious juvenile delinquency. One nearby group was the East Cottage Street Gang, which hung out on the corner of Raven and Crescent avenues. The boys, some only in seventh grade, were already into car theft, or "hot boxing," and house break-ins. They used improvised jumper cables to start cars, which they would take for jam-packed joyrides around Dorchester. They also stole tires and sold them on the black market to gas stations and taxi drivers.

Another gang operating near the Bulger's Crescent Avenue home was known as the Carsies; they too were "hot boxers" who also broke into houses and caused trouble around Columbia Station. Their main recreation was sneaking into movie theaters in South Boston and downtown.

While Whitey was never a formal member of the East Cottage Street Gang or the Carsies, one of his longtime girlfriends, Lindsey Cyr, said he told her he started stealing on the streets at a young age, in her words "out of necessity. It was to put food on the table for everyone. He said it was survival, pure and simple. They had nothing."

When the Bulgers moved to Dorchester and edged toward Southie, the city was not only in the throes of the Great Depression—it was in a housing crisis. Boston was still a city of immigrants living in dilapidated apartment buildings, especially so in Irish and Italian neighborhoods.

The census data for 1930 Boston delineated a city of renters in buildings constructed, for the most part, in the nineteenth century. With three of every four families renting, home ownership was essentially out of the question for Irish families for nearly forty years.

As of January 1934, at the height of the Depression, South Boston had the third-highest unemployment rate of any neighborhood, at 32.5 percent, well above the city-wide average of 26.1 percent. It also had the city's highest infant mortality rate.

Southie didn't really get back on its feet until after World War II, when the veterans came marching home with a broadened view of life. Just as Beacon Hill was the personification of Brahmin Boston, South Boston became the jut-jawed face of Eire, which made it more than a neighborhood. For good or ill, it symbolized all things Irish: the feisty spirit, the immigrant survivor, the aggressive Catholic rebel.

But even as it inched toward solidarity and status, its housing stock declined inexorably. It was redlined by banks that withheld home improvement loans, leading to a catch-22: Financiers saw Southie as swallowing up good money after bad, a losing proposition where the teetering homes weren't worth saving. And then they wrote off the entire neighborhood because it was blighted.

As the stalemate over housing deepened into a policy crisis in the late 1930s, the architects of the New Deal stepped tentatively into the breach, starting in South Boston.

By 1934, the Depression had stretched well beyond implacable unemployment and soup kitchens. Housing had been the neglected stepchild, even among President Franklin Roosevelt's brain trust, which focused on creating jobs. But as conditions worsened, decrepit housing couldn't be swept under the rug and so forced itself onto the national agenda. There was no ducking the overwhelming fact that one-third of all American families were living in slums. In Boston, the number was nearly half, with the hardest hit being the "in-close" neighborhoods around downtown.

As the nation faced a full-blown depression in 1933, FDR was ambivalent about getting the government into the housing business, favoring direct relief over tenement construction. While skeptical, he came around gradually as he saw the benefit of housing low-income families in a way that also boosted the lagging building industry.

Boston was one of the first cities targeted by federal housing bureaucrats. But it still took five years, from 1933 to 1938, to get the city's first project in the ground, in an area known as Old Harbor in South Boston.

Old Harbor became the first federally funded housing project in the country. It was also a bulwark for the Bulgers. Whitey lived in the homestead for four decades, with time off for bad behavior in four prisons. While he would be feared in South Boston, he was protected and even prized inside the project's connecting courtyards.

He was a rebellious nine-year-old when Old Harbor was dedicated on September 11, 1938, several weeks after its actual opening. The Bulgers were among the nine hundred founding families. The odds of landing in a project unit were the same as getting into Harvard—one in ten. A tally taken in 1940 found there were 10,000 applications made for only 1,016 units. You needed a sponsor to get in and it's possible that the father still had some City Hall connections from his days working at the Deer Island House of Correction and the South Stable. Or perhaps with someone who knew John McCormack, then a rising congressman from South Boston who had pushed hard for the project with the Roosevelt administration. McCormack would be squarely in the family's corner during Whitey's decade in federal prisons. And his attachment to Old Harbor was so strong that it was renamed in 1961 after his mother, Mary Ellen McCormack.

The grand opening at Old Harbor was a Southie holiday. Some five thousand people were at the sun-splashed dedication ceremony at Henry Sterling Square and as many others toured the facilities. With every building decked out with the American flag, residents watched from their windows and hundreds gathered on the roofs.

News photos show about 250 soldiers at attention on the edge of Columbia Park, across the street from where the U.S. flag was raised inside the project. The black cars of officialdom ringed the park. A crowd of priests, police officers, and politicians formed a crescent around the flagpole.

About seven hundred children of tenants assembled at nearby St. Monica's behind a band and marched to the grandstand. Dignitaries included Congressman McCormack, who reminisced about his boyhood in Andrew Square and crowed about his role in getting the project done. City counselor John E. Kerrigan took a bow for stopping an earlier effort to put a racetrack on the vacant land.

The project streets were designated as "ways" and each had a separate dedication. The names reflected the priorities of the time and place—military commanders, priests, and labor leaders.

In all, there were forty buildings, with a total of 1,016 units and 3,902 rooms. According to a 1940 lease agreement between the Boston Housing Authority and the federal government, the rents were $23.15 per month for three-room apartments, $26.80 for four rooms, and $30.95 for five. It's likely the Bulgers, with a new infant and four other children, needed the biggest unit. They were paying slightly more than the city's median market rate of $29.65.

And it's also likely that the Bulgers had no problem living within the annual income restrictions governing occupancy in the project, with the family average being $1,200 a year and the maximum set at $2,282.

Besides meeting the income requirement applicants had to have been in substandard housing "detrimental to health, safety and morals" for the previous six months; had to have lived in Boston for at least one year; and someone in the family had to have a job. It was explicitly not welfare housing. It was for the working poor.

Under those terms, the Bulgers' Dorchester apartment had to be discernibly substandard. And they needed the five rooms to accommodate their newest member—Whitey's youngest brother, John, was a newborn when they moved into 41 Logan Way.

But Old Harbor became the exemplar of public housing. Social compatibility became an instant hallmark. Virtually overnight, it had twelve softball teams, an eight-team bowling league, two Girl Scout and three Boy Scout troops, and numerous clubs and societies. Surrounded by the hardscrabble Lower End, it nevertheless had the lowest juvenile delinquency rate in the city.

But the new world of public housing was changing even as Old Harbor was being built. In 1937, the federal program was expanded to include slum clearance and annotated to stress anew that the units were for the working poor who needed help in getting to better housing elsewhere. But that would change.

Later, state court decisions affirmed that the housing authority had no obligation to provide housing to the dispossessed. The precedent set siege to the nearby Old Colony project—3,761 families in South Boston were displaced, only to discover one of the new hard facts of urban renewal: they couldn't afford the rents in the housing that replaced their own.

Another hard fact was that people whose houses were demolished rarely got into new units. Old Colony was the searing case in point. Only 4 percent of the evicted got an apartment on the twelve-acre site.

But in an era of radical change and scarce housing, the strapped Bulgers hit the lottery at serene Old Harbor. According to an interview with Whitey's brother Bill, the family got by even though the father worked only occasionally as a clerk at the Charlestown Navy Yard, doing the late shift on holidays. He was fifty-five when the family arrived at Old Harbor, and he never held a full-time job while living in the project. The mother worked part-time at department stores and, according to Lindsey Cyr, one of Whitey's girlfriends, had a state job after Bill got into politics.

The clan from Riverhead had landed in a clean, well-lit place near the sea that was surrounded by acres of parks and ball fields. Old Harbor had the enveloping benefit of married parents, free ice cream on the Fourth of July, and stairwells that were clubhouses, about thirty kids in each building. To this day, there's abiding fealty to hard-won community values. South Boston has consistently maintained the highest percentage of long-term residents in the city, reflecting a historic emphasis on staying put in a place that matters. But the turf loyalty was twisted as it veered toward blind allegiances. It became a protective shield for gangsters like Whitey Bulger and political camouflage for legislators like his brother Bill. The loyalty "oath" is such that criticism from within is seen as unspeakable betrayal and from outside as uninformed provocation.

William Burke, a high school classmate of Bill Bulger who grew up at Old Colony, recalled an insular upbringing in which the outer world was a mystery better left unsolved. The early days, he said, were a placid time before drugs and the government dole overran project life. In his building there were twelve families who got along in mutual respect and cohesion. But there was one false note in the lulling background music—a touch of envy about Old Harbor across the way.

Burke, who became a well-known Latin teacher at Boston College High School, reminisced that "we who lived in Old Colony always thought that those who lived in Old Harbor were better off. Isn't that something? That Old Harbor was richer, better." Decades later, he shook his head but smiled at the thought.

"Where's Jim?"

Whitey and his pals

When the Bulger family settled into their third-floor apartment at 41 Logan Way, Bill Bulger was still at a tender, preschool age where he could be steered. Whitey, older, could not. Young Bill was soon enough celebrating his First Communion, while Whitey, barely thirteen, was beyond the church's reach. He was wheedling his way out of his first arrest on a charge of larceny.

Much of Bill's boyhood involved the church—specifically, St. Monica's, located a few blocks away on Dorchester Street, in Andrew Square. St. Monica's was an old wooden building, painted white. It was not much to look at architecturally but it was always stirring—a training ground for a child's spiritual and moral development. Like any boy, Bill got into plenty of mischief and the occasional fight, but throughout he stayed connected to St. Monica's. He was an altar boy who relished the Latin chants, eagerly putting them to memory. Father Leo Dwyer, a curate at St. Monica's, emerged as a father figure of sorts. On Mondays and Tuesdays in the summer, his days off, Father Dwyer took Bill and such pals as George Pryor on day trips. "He used to spit in the palm of his hand and whichever way the wind blew, that was the direction we went off," Pryor said. The adventures included trips to the beaches in Revere, to New Hampshire, even to Provincetown. Years later, a pastor at another South Boston church said he'd come to know every member of the Bulger family, save one—the one who was nowhere to be found. Whitey.

"He missed all that," Bill said about his brother and the church life.

Whitey's training ground was instead the streets of Southie, where he could escape his father's building anger toward his shenanigans. One of Whitey's early charges in juvenile court was "wayward," which was defined under Massachusetts law as a child "between seven and seventeen years of age who habitually associates with vicious or immoral persons, or who is growing up in circumstances exposing him to lead an immoral, vicious or criminal life."

Whitey was growing up less at home and mainly in those "circumstances." On his own, fleeing the hand of a strict father who turned fifty-seven in 1940, a decade when male life expectancy was 60.8 years. His father was old and, in many ways, disengaged, so much so that it was Jean Bulger who ran things. Hers was the frequent refrain when it came to the whereabouts of the troubling eldest son. "Where's Jim?" Jean Bulger was always asking.

He was getting into trouble—or, better for him, getting out of facing any consequences for the trouble he got into. Called Jim by his family, or "Sonny" by his mother, as time went on he became known to the rest of the world as Whitey, for the reddish blond hair he kept combed back, wet with tonic in the style of the times, revealing a high forehead and a pair of piercing blue eyes. In March 1943, the thirteen-year-old Whitey was arrested for stealing. The larceny charge is the first to appear on his criminal record. Few Boston police and court files have survived about it or any of Whitey's other early brushes with the law. No record is available, for example, to explain where exactly Whitey was arrested downtown and what he was trying to steal when he was caught. Nonetheless, certain patterns and key themes emerge from the skeletal details.

In this first official tangle, Whitey's case was handled in the downtown Boston Juvenile Court—and that constituted his first break. Dating back to the mid-1930s, court officials, sociologists, and criminologists had been grappling with a spike in juvenile delinquency in Boston—and the juvenile court downtown was singled out for intense scrutiny after one study showed the recidivism rate there at an alarming 72 percent. The study triggered intense public and political debate, with angry citizens hanging the chief Boston juvenile judge in effigy while lawmakers considered abolishing the Boston Juvenile Court altogether. Progressive-minded judges and administrators implemented a new program they hoped would redirect the city's youth off the track of delinquency. It was an intensive form of probation to add to the two options that already existed—one a loosely supervised probation that had little impact, and the other a commitment to one of the state's two juvenile institutions. The new Boston program was called the "Citizenship Training Group," or CTG. Delinquent boys placed in the program were required to attend every day after school from 3:30 to 5:30 p.m. and take part in a host of activities and services. The boys came up with a derisive nickname for the new CTG program: "Crooks, Thieves, and Gangsters."

For the Boston juvenile judges, the program became an appealing middle ground, rigorous but not as severe as institutionalizing a juvenile at the Lyman School for Boys, the first reform school in the nation. Lyman had opened in the mid nineteenth century amid much fanfare and high-minded rhetoric. No public institution was more important, Governor George Briggs said at the 1846 opening, "than one which promises to take neglected, wayward, wandering, idle and vicious boys, with perverse minds and corrupted hearts, and cleanse and purify and reform them." The history of Lyman certainly included stories of boys who benefited from their commitment, but studies abound showing that in the 1940s, when a juvenile offender named Whitey Bulger was caught in the crosshairs of the law, Lyman was a harsh, militaristic reform school for about 250 to 350 boys between the ages of thirteen and fifteen, where abuse was commonplace. "Boys were kicked in the rear for minor infractions like talking," one report found. "Other physical punishments included hitting inmates with wooden paddles or straps on the soles of their bare feet." It got worse. Boys were sometimes made to scrub floors with toothbrushes, drink from toilets, or stand for hours in strange, painful positions.

By the time Whitey walked into the Boston Juvenile Court in March 1943, the court's culture had undergone this considerable change. Other courts in Boston were continuing to commit delinquent boys at a high rate, including the court in Whitey's South Boston. "The response depends entirely upon the court," a probation officer named Louis G. Maglio told one researcher. One court, he said, had no programs, so judges there "committed one of every three children." But that was no longer the case in the Boston court, which had the new CTG program of intense probation and its strict daily regimen. "The child was entitled to a first chance, perhaps a second chance," said another officer, Charles Eliot Sands.

In this context, Whitey's appearance in Boston Juvenile proved to be his lucky day. Ruling that Whitey was "delinquent"—the official term in juvenile court for guilty—the judge imposed the most severe punishment possible. He committed Whitey to the Lyman School for Boys. But then came the good news. In keeping with the new culture in the Boston court, the judge decided to give Whitey another chance, and he suspended Whitey's sentence. The news got even better. The judge did not even require Whitey to participate in the get-tough probation program every afternoon in Boston, likely because this was his first offense.

The court had cut Whitey some slack. He'd dodged the bullet that was Lyman and left court with no strings attached. Late in 1943 the case was officially "filed," a legal term meaning the arrest would not count as a prior offense. The next time he got into trouble it would be treated as if it had never happened. Meanwhile, boys in circumstances similar to Whitey Bulger—in such neighborhoods as Roxbury, Dorchester, and, yes, South Boston—were continually committed to Lyman. Four days after Christmas in nearby Chelsea, a city across Boston Harbor, a boy two years younger than Whitey, to the day, was committed to Lyman. Albert DeSalvo, born September 3, 1931, a boy who two decades later would make history as the self-proclaimed Boston Strangler, was sent off to the reform school for stealing some jewelry from a friend's mother.

But not Whitey; Lyman was not in the cards for him.

Whitey was instead set free to continue building his résumé, a track record that in most respects mirrored those of delinquent boys from all over Southie. The Southie boys, not surprisingly, squared off according to their street, street corner, or immediate neighborhood. Members ranged in age from six to sixteen. The gangs' names were often as simple and mundane as the streets where they lived—such as the Silver

Street Gang or the Mercer Street Gang. Others were more exotic. The Dripping Daggers wore sweatshirts featuring a dagger dripping in blood, while a younger offshoot of the Daggers was called the Bloody Hounds because the boys cut their arms and used the blood to initial the backs of their hands. The Forty Thieves of D Street were so named because of their self-proclaimed expertise at pilfering anywhere—from stores, cars, and trucks. The Wildcats, or Shaggers, were a gang of boys who lived in the immediate area of E Street. Their hangout was located blocks away, in an empty lot they'd taken over on Swallow Street nick-named Kelley's Island. The Shaggers were notable for their ties to the real deal—a grown-up gang. When the federal government in 1942 began wartime rationing of food and gasoline, the racketeers tapped the Shaggers to steal gas coupons and other automobile supplies to re-sell on the black market. By 1945, some members of the Shaggers were regularly stealing cars for the racketeers, delivering them to a garage where the vehicles were stripped. The boys sometimes got a hundred dollars a car.

For another gang, Steve's Variety Store on West Sixth Street be-came a hangout, and for good reason. Steve had a pinball machine and, hidden in the back room, an actual slot machine. More than that, though, Steve bought nearly everything the boys could steal—ashtrays, small vases, and knickknacks, even a case of milk they'd taken from another store nearby. Steve on occasion even placed a special request, and the boys headed off to fill the steal-order. The deal between Steve and the gang was not unique. Throughout Southie, gangster boys found their own Steves on their own corners and forged business rela-tionships with them, as well as with certain taxi drivers who moon-lighted dealing in the stolen goods.

Like Whitey, many Southie boys had their first run-in with the law when they were twelve or thirteen. But this hardly amounted to a first offense; rather, it marked the first time they were arrested. The boy-hood life of crime often began at age seven or eight, starting with shop-lifting from the counters of the five-and-ten stores along West Broadway—small articles like candy, comics, fruit, cigarettes. It moved to stealing goods from cars, trucks, and freight cars—maybe bananas from the trucks supplying the First National stores, soda from the Coca-Cola trucks making deliveries on Broadway, or watermelons from freight cars down at the Commonwealth Pier. Building on this entry-level experience, delinquent boys began executing nighttime break-ins at the local stores and warehouses. The haul might be an armful of leather jackets from the Liberty Express Company to resell on the street, or larger caches of the articles they'd previously stolen from the store counters. The Dripping Daggers developed the technique of smashing a back-door window of a five-and-ten, entering, gathering up as much candy, money, cigarettes, and other goods as each boy could carry, and then hustling back to one of the boys' cellars to split the loot and sell what they did not want.

It was a lifestyle that included hopping a ride in the summertime on the back of a truck heading south, where the boys jumped off in Quincy and headed to the quarries for a swim. Or they sneaked into the Strand, the Broadway, or any of the other theaters in Southie to watch a movie. In "chewing the rag," or talking, about their activities, Whitey and the Southie boys even had their own language, a street vernacular that to the uninitiated was practically unintelligible. *Hooking* was skipping school; *bunking out* was not going home at night and sleeping instead in an abandoned house, entryway, or a car parked in the lot at the Gillette factory; *eloping* was running away; *clipping* was stealing; *fishing* cars was breaking into cars to take flashlights, gloves, gas coupons, odd change, whatever was lying around on the seats or in the glove compartments; *fishing grounds* were areas of parked cars preferred by a particular gang of boys, such as the parking spaces along Carson Beach in Southie, or downtown around Boston Common; *junking* was stealing piping from an empty or demolished house to resell to the junkman; a *haunty* was an abandoned house that became a source for junking; going *wolving* was going out to pick up girls; to get *stinking* or *lit* was to get drunk; *rolling* a drunk or a *homo* was stealing money from either; a *hot boxer* was a boy known for stealing cars; and a *hot box* was a stolen car. Getting *swooped* or *whipped* was getting arrested.

Whitey's first arrest had occurred when he headed out beyond Old Harbor and toward the bright lights of the big city—downtown Boston. That trajectory was in lockstep with just about every delinquent boy from the neighborhood. Usually under the tutelage of an older boy, small teams crossed the Broadway Bridge, arching over Fort Port Channel that separated Southie from the rest of the city, their destination the department stores, theaters, and street life of Downtown Crossing, just east of Boston Common. The dazzling, noisy hotbed of commerce was their playground. Members of the Bloody Hounds engaged in what one boy later called "the art" of selling gardenias. Under the guise of flower salesmen, they cruised the parking lots along Washington Street and near Boston Common and "fished" the cars left unlocked. Boys headed into Filene's, Jordan Marsh, and Hovey's to steal rings, gloves, handkerchiefs, socks, fountain pens, pipes, cards, poker chips, cameras, film, boxes of chocolate—anything that was small and easy to conceal. Identification bracelets were a favorite of the soldiers and sailors who came through town, making them a top mark for the boys for their quick resale value. Boys entered Jordan Marsh, walked up to a counter, and asked the girl working there for the price of an ID bracelet hanging from a display board. The moment she turned to look at the tag, they'd grab the bracelets from the countertop displays and slip them into their pockets. When the counter girl turned back to face them, the boys shrugged at the price, said it was too expensive, and off they went. Other times they wouldn't even bother with the ruse; they would distract the salesperson, grab the goods, and run like the wind out the door. The boys shined shoes and sold newspapers, but often as a cover to sell their stolen goods to their "shine customers." By leaving on the store's price tag, the buyer would see the bargain to be had—like the fancy $15 pen and pencil set stolen from Filene's that one shoeshine boy sold for $10.

They spent their profits at the penny arcade near Essex Street, which was always bustling with kids from all over—pumping coins into slot machines in the back until the Boston police chased them away. If their luck was sour on the shoplifting front, boys begged from men in their top hats and women in their long dresses heading into a show at such film houses as the Colonial, the Wilbur, or the Tremont, where in 1943 they watched Jane Russell begin to challenge Betty Grable and Rita Hayworth as sex symbol of the wartime years in her film debut, *The Outlaw*. Before too long, Whitey and every delinquent boy who was hanging out downtown with any regularity became skilled at the best way to take in a show for free by sneaking admission. The Stuart was easy to get into from a side or rear door; the Paramount and Trans Lux were best entered through a rear fire escape; the trick at the Bijou was to gain entry through a ventilator on the top of the roof.

This was Whitey's world, and in this boy's life—be it Whitey, Bill Bulger, or any other kid from Southie, a kid who was running bad or good—it was always best to be aligned with other boys into an identifiable group, crowd, or gang. The neighborhood was carved up, by street or section, into these subsets of boys, all wary of one another, and it was these subsets that in the aggregate were part of the turf-conscious neighborhood noted for its hostility toward outsiders, a neighborhood set off not only from the rest of Boston, but from the world.

Bill and Whitey Bulger grew up to become embodiments of South Boston—so strongly identified with the neighborhood that most took it as a given that the family's ties ran deep. But the fact was they did not. Bill Bulger has acknowledged his "alien origin." And he has noted his adopted neighborhood's reflexive disdain of outsiders, writing in a memoir that "those who first opened their eyes in another part of Boston were guilty of original sin for which there was no facile absolution." But he has rarely drawn attention to the thinness of the family connection to South Boston or considered why the Bulgers never faced animosity as outsiders. He's been content, instead, to express gratitude that for "some happy reason" his family's status as interloper was "overlooked" by the folks of South Boston.

The likely reason was the fact that the Bulgers belonged to a big wave of newcomers, families from all over who came en masse to take up residence in Old Harbor. Everyone was new. In the Bulgers' entry alone, twenty-seven kids were divided among the six families living at 41 Logan Way. They were in the same boat, sharing the excitement of life in a new housing project—as well as its lows.

For example, just a little more than a year after it opened, a stretch of bone-chilling days in early 1940 created large ice floes in the waters off Carson Beach—and for the kids of Old Harbor the Monday morning of January 15 began magically. First, a predawn storm led to the cancellation of school. Then some boys discovered that a huge mass of ice had been driven ashore by the storm. Word spread, and dozens of boys headed to frolic on the ice. When the temperature rose slightly, the ice began breaking up into smaller slabs. By late morning upwards of one hundred kids from Old Harbor and other neighborhoods were dancing around on the floating ice cakes.

But the ice fantastic quickly turned tragic. The ice cakes continued breaking up into smaller slabs and, worse, the ebbing tide began taking the ice out into Dorchester Bay. Panicked boys found themselves marooned on the disintegrating slabs drifting seaward. They began screaming for help. Many lost their balance, fell into the frigid water, and splashed at the slab to keep from going under.

Police and nearby residents hastily launched rescue operations, climbing into several dories found down along the beach. The police boat, the *Michael A. Crowley*, churned its way through Boston Harbor's rough waters. The wailing police sirens were like a summons, barely outpacing the word of mouth spreading fast through the housing project. Mothers and fathers were soon running up and down the length of the beach. By nightfall, Ben Whitehouse of Old Harbor, his eyes set fiercely on the sea, paced the beach refusing to leave, even though the chances that his two sons were alive diminished with the day's light. Back home at 437 Old Colony Avenue, neighbors surrounded his wife, but she was inconsolable at the loss of eight-year-old Ralph and twelve-year-old Wallace. Just a few doors down, at 441 Old Colony, the Kendall family was overcome when told their boy, Charles, was gone. He was six.

The front-page headline in the next morning's *Boston Globe* announced, CRUMBLING CAKES CARRY 12 OUT INTO HARBOR; EIGHT SAVED, while another headline reported, THOUSANDS WATCH GRIPPING RESCUES. Three of the four boys who drowned were from Old Harbor. Of the eight rescued, five were from Old Harbor. Three were from the Bulgers' street, Logan Way, and one boy, Joe Cullinane, fifteen, was a neighbor, living in one of the six apartments in 41 Logan Way. Joe and another boy were about a half mile out when they were snatched from the water by the police boat and then rushed by ambulance to Carney Hospital.

The *Globe* reported that Old Harbor was "in deep mourning." By dawn, the police rescue operation became a recovery operation, with every one of the forty members of the department's harbor police and diving team searching for the bodies of the three boys who had slipped from ice cakes and drowned. In the days that followed, funerals were held at St. Monica's on Dorchester Street, and for weeks sadness draped the classrooms of the Andrew Square school. The parents of Old Harbor announced they wanted police to patrol the beach even in the winter and requested that lifeboats be placed along the shore permanently. It was the kind of shocking, spectacularly unexpected tragedy that brought everyone closer, revealing the family values and loyalty for which South Boston was best known. The families of the new Old Harbor housing project—the Bulgers included—forged on together, bonded by adversity and fast becoming a part of Southie, for one and all.

5

The Smile and Swagger

Whitey

The day the ice cakes cracked Bill Bulger was five years old; Whitey was ten. In time Bill became part of a crowd of Old Harbor boys called the Pirates. Compared to such gangs as the Dripping Daggers or the Junior Eagles, the Pirates were goody-goody. But it was a group nonetheless, giving Bill the grounding that came with being part of something. The Pirates held a raffle to raise money for jackets, selling chances to win a clock radio to their Old Harbor neighbors and to patrons in the surrounding bars. The jackets were black and gold, with "Pirates" written across the back and the boy's name written on a sleeve.

For Bill and many boys, Old Harbor was a place where friendships were established for a lifetime. Farther up Logan Way from the Bulgers, the Moakley family lived at number 51. The boy there, Joe, was older than Bill, but they became friends. Joe once told Bill he liked politics better than baseball, which in a boy's world was close to heresy. John Joseph "Joe" Moakley grew up to become a powerful member of Congress, serving from 1973 until 2001. Moving into Old Harbor after the Bulgers was the Connolly family—John J., a lifelong worker at the Gillette plant, and his wife, Bridget T. Kelly. Their son, John Jr., was younger than Bill and Whitey in age, but he eventually became close to both. John Connolly made his parents proud when he became an agent for the Federal Bureau of Investigation in 1968. Much older than all of them was John William McCormack. Born in Southie, he grew up in Andrew Square and was first elected to Congress in 1928. McCormack became one of the most powerful men in the country as Speaker of the House of Representatives, but he never forgot his hometown. He was always ready to help a constituent, including the Bulgers.

While Bill ran with the Pirates, Whitey took up an affiliation with the Shamrocks, also based in Old Harbor, by the time he turned thirteen, in 1942. The Shamrocks consisted of the kind of young roughnecks that gave the gang a reputation, but it wasn't as if the Shamrocks defined Whitey's identity, serving as a centerpiece in his life the way gangs did for many of the boys. His affiliation was a loose one. "He had two or three friends he hung around with," one family friend said. "Go to a show with . . . or rob off the back of a truck."

Whitey was mainly a separate entity. He was not to be tied down, at home or in the street, and his religion was not the kind found at St. Monica's. Rather, it was something he was constructing around himself. As he hustled down the staircase at 41 Logan Way and out to the streets that took him from Old Harbor and into South Boston, the street became the stage for him to create a persona in a true-life serial crime drama. Full of improvisational moments, a young Whitey Bulger began working up some star power as a standout hooligan whose prowess in the small pond of Southie contributed to the start of his legend—with the mothers, girls, other kids and gangs, and, importantly, with the authorities.

The street was where Whitey got satisfaction. Certainly more than in school, where eventually he developed an accomplished cursive writing style but where he was a chronic truant, a troublemaker, and earned lousy grades. In Dorchester he attended a parochial school; once in South Boston his parents sent him to Thomas N. Hart public school, where he was enrolled from the fifth through the eighth grades. "His scholastic record was poor," a federal probation officer wrote later in a report. "He failed in all of his subjects, receiving poor marks in Conduct and Effort." The entire school record, noted the officer, revealed that Whitey was "surly, lazy and had no interest in school work."

Certainly Whitey preferred the street to home, where he faced the glare of a disapproving father, who at times beat him. To one of his girlfriends years later Whitey described his father as a "miserable son of a bitch." By most accounts, the elder Bulger was a loner. He liked to take walks, his white hair combed straight back, a cigar in his mouth. Indoors he'd be found near the radio listening to the hometown Red Sox. He might engage in a discussion of politics, a key interest, but he mainly kept his own company. The times were the darkest of the century, darker than the Great Depression. Hitler's Germany had taken over most of Western Europe, bombed England, and set its eyes on Russia. The war became the nation's calling. Everyone who could work filled the factories, including women. Everyone who could fight enlisted in the service, including entertainers, actors, and such baseball stars as Ted Williams of the Red Sox. Everyone who was able-bodied signed up and served—which left out the elder, one-armed Bulger. He was marginalized, working when he could as a clerk, a watchman, or at some other small task passed over by the real men and women at war.

For a typical youngster Whitey Bulger's age, a key part of adolescence was watching grown-ups working from dawn to dusk, of seeing fathers and uncles going off to fight. This was not Whitey's adolescence; he saw a disabled father in the humiliating position of having to stand idly by, inadequate to meet the call. The Bulgers over the years would burnish the story of the elder Bulger's lost arm in a way that elicited sympathy, even admiration. Bill Bulger's version was that "laboring in a railroad yard, he was pinned between two freight trains." The left arm then had to be amputated. "The railroad calculated the wages due him—up to the time he had fallen, mangled, to the cinder bed—paid him and forgot him." Rather than the truth that his father was a runaway boy—just as Whitey would be someday—when he fell trying to jump aboard a freight train and his arm was crushed, the false account portrayed a boy hard at work when misfortune hit. It was cast as a ghastly accident at work that doomed a boy to a life lived less than whole. As an adult, the elder Bulger used an inelegant, awkward prosthetic arm that Bill Bulger said "he fruitlessly tried to conceal by keeping the wooden hand in a pocket."

Over the years, the elder Bulger did his own bit of fibbing, too; he concealed his true age, lying to city pollsters and census takers when the family moved to Old Harbor, telling them he was forty-three when he was in fact twelve years older, senior to any other man at 41 Logan Way by more than a decade. Even if James Bulger Sr. had been able-bodied during wartime, he was too old to serve. The elder Bulger actually turned sixty in 1943—the year of Whitey's first arrest.

So when young Whitey Bulger took to the streets of South Boston in the early 1940s, roaring out of the gate, it was if he was determined to assert his manhood and manliness in every way possible—a trait that became lifelong for Whitey.

He established his toughness, early and often. One neighborhood boy's first impression was watching Whitey in a street fight on the way to school in 1944. "He just beat the piss out of the guy," recalled Will McDonough, a family friend. "He was vicious, and he wasn't that big." The beating was both thorough and public, impressing the crowd of young onlookers who began whispering, *That's Whitey Bulger.* "He was probably fifteen then," McDonough said, "but everybody already knew he was a tough guy who always had that sort of mean streak." Whitey liked to walk up to brother Bill's young friends in Old Harbor, pull up his shirt, and order them to punch his stomach. "Whitey was in fantastic condition," one of those friends, Joe Quirk, said. "He had like a washboard-type stomach, like iron. 'You can hit me harder than that.' He'd challenge you to hit him as hard as you could."

He established his charm. While often in conflict with his father, he seduced the mothers in the neighborhood with a winning smile and an occasional helping hand. If he saw a mother with a baby carriage negotiating a set of stairs, he'd hustle over and lift the carriage to the sidewalk. If he saw a mother heading off on foot to shop, he'd stop his car and give her a lift to the stores on Broadway. "He was always willing to help," Sally Dame, one of the smitten Old Harbor mothers, said.

The manner in which he helped was at times over-the-top. One day a mother named Nancy Kelley was walking home and along came

Whitey. "Mrs. Kelley!" he yelled, pulling up in his convertible. He jumped out, gathered up her bundles, opened the car door, and put her in the backseat. Nancy Kelley lived in a building that was set back from the street in a courtyard. Whitey took off across the grassy courtyard and delivered her to her door. "He went right over the curbstone, right up to the doorstep," said Will McDonough, who was watching, incredulous.

In Old Harbor, residents were not allowed to own cars. Cars suggested an income level that might disqualify a family from living in the project. The elder Bulger did not have a car, but the ban—or his father—did not stop Whitey. He owned one, and he showed it off. "He drove fast," said Kevin Joyce, one of Bill's friends, who once took a joyride in Whitey's car down the narrow Logan Way. "I was happy to get out." When his car needed some spit and polish, he'd round up a crew of younger boys to hose it down. "He always gave them a quarter, or something," Sally Dame said. The boys loved it. "In them days, that was a lot of money."

The senior Bulger had had no father and was even abandoned by his mother for a time when he was only six. He'd grown up without a mentor to learn what it meant to be a man or a father. The elder Bulger might not impress as a provider, but the son Whitey would—and do it his way. He had the car; he had money; he had his own ways to gain access to goods and services to share with his and other families, building a following along the way. He would show the father who had let him down—betrayed him, even—how it was done.

Whitey established swagger. In the beginning the strut was exaggerated, flamboyant. He might bring around the burlesque dancer he'd met downtown at the Old Howard Theatre in Scollay Square, where sailors, soldiers, and teens like Whitey went for a good time. From the road, "Tiger Lil" sent him postcards. The boys of Old Harbor were always impressed, while his mother was not. "Our mother was horrified," Bill Bulger recalled. "Jim would get hysterical watching her reaction."

Whitey later dated the envy of many in the neighborhood— Jacqueline "Jacquie" McAuliffe. "She was stacked," Will McDonough said about the gorgeous blonde. Jacquie was two years older than Whitey—married but separated from her ironworker husband, Gerald Martin—when she began going with him. McDonough said one autumn day Whitey and Jacquie pulled up in a new blue Oldsmobile with fins. Whitey was looking snazzy in his pearl gray hat and leather jacket, and Jacquie was covered in fur. "He had the big car and the hat and jacket, and she was there on the front seat," Will said.

"You like my gal?" Whitey asked.

Will and the others could barely speak. "Our eyes were this big."

Whitey issued an order. "Jacquie, show them your coat."

Jacquie obeyed and peeled open the fur. She smiled.

The boys' jaws dropped—Jacquie was naked.

The couple laughed. "See you later, boys," and Whitey drove off.

It was as if during Whitey's formative teenage years the rules of Old Harbor did not apply and the law of the land was a nuisance. He ignored the ban against pets when he brought home an ocelot he named Lancelot. The animal lived in the bedroom he shared with his brothers—until his father, for once, put his foot down and ordered Whitey to give the growing ocelot to the zoo. To the Boston police, he was known to talk back and talk tough, defiant of their authority. His brother Bill characterized Whitey as a kid who "would not give an inch. His speech was bold. He was often beaten, sometimes savagely. For a while I thought *all* police were vicious."

The family understood that Whitey was different. "He was in a constant state of revolt," Bill Bulger acknowledged later. "He was restless as a claustrophobic in a dark closet." Or, to use another analogy, Whitey was like the ocelot confined to a cramped project bedroom. But over a lifetime Bill never went further, at least not publicly, to probe the reasons for his brother's darkening heart. Instead he and his family always acted as if in denial. They romanticized the young Whitey for his "abundance of good humor" and his "wildly creative talent for impish mischief," an example being the time he ran off with the Barnum & Bailey Circus after it had completed its run in Boston. Whitey disappeared from home for several months. But it was spun as a charming feat for which there was no consequence when he resurfaced back home. For the juvenile Whitey, going AWOL was simply standard operating procedure. "His teachers, like my mother, often discovered that Jim was suddenly missing," Bill said. Whitey may have found a way to get through grammar school, but he quit school altogether before his first year of high school.

Moreover, the family brushed off the growing list of arrests on increasingly violent charges during the 1940s as "scrapes" that, Bill Bulger said, were "small in those growing-up years." Inside the Bulger apartment, how the parents discussed the calls from police and the regular reports of Whitey's wrongdoing will never be known, but one thing was clear to all in Old Harbor: the topic of the boy's misdeeds was off-limits. "No one ever talked about Whitey's criminal ways," Kevin Joyce, Bill's boyhood pal, said. "I would always hear about his skirmishes, yet it was kind of an unwritten rule that you didn't get into that with Billy." When Whitey got in trouble, Joe Quirk said, "Bill never talked about it. I never heard Bill criticize his brother."

It was during this time that Whitey began developing a sense of being beyond the law's reach, of being smarter and sharper, of being untouchable. Looking at the numbers, he had good reason to think that way. Between the ages of thirteen and eighteen he was arrested ten times. There was that first arrest downtown for larceny, then the arrest for being a wayward juvenile in 1945. Three other arrests in South Boston in 1945 were for robbery, assault and battery, and a charge called "threats." The next year he was arrested for assault and battery again. In 1947, four Boston police officers arrested Whitey, at seventeen no longer a juvenile, in the city's South End in the early morning hours of March 18. The arrest at 1:40 a.m., on the heels of St. Patrick's Day celebrations, was for "suspicion of unarmed robberies on unknown persons." Had Whitey been caught rolling celebrants? Then that summer two other officers picked him up as a suspect in fishing, or stealing, "from autos in this division during the past month." Whitey was taken to the station house in Police District 16 and booked on the charge of

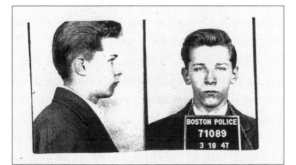

Whitey's first police mug shot

"suspicious person—larceny." The only other note in the entry in the police log recording the July 11 arrest was that Whitey "had a 3 millimeter scratch on the right side of neck."

In the end, Whitey beat all but one of the ten charges. In some cases he was found not guilty; in others he got the charges dismissed before trial. Or he was simply released after he was booked and went home, with no outcome of the case ever recorded on his criminal record. In two cases where a judge did find him guilty, Whitey appealed and got the charge dismissed at the next level. Even in the one instance where a conviction stood up, he succeeded on appeal to get the charge reduced to a minor offense. The minimal records that have survived do not provide the kind of detail to assess his astonishing success at avoiding accountability. Defying the odds the way he did raises the notion that perhaps a hidden hand was working the levers of power on his behalf—a politician, family friend, or priest. But no fingerprints of such influence have been left behind; besides, his father was a nonplayer in the affairs of government and the Bulger family had yet to establish itself as the force it would become in the future. More likely it was Whitey himself—the cunning teen who was honing skills as a hustling smart aleck able to talk his way out of trouble. Either way, the upshot of Whitey Bulger's experience between the ages of thirteen and eighteen was that there was virtually no price to pay for his transgressions.

Emerging from the confines of 41 Logan Way, young Whitey had gone looking for an outlet, for something he was good at and would make him feel good, and soon enough he found he was a pretty good criminal. He was strong, exceptionally smart, good-looking, and had a fearless swagger. His young ego got nourishment—not from home, not from an elderly father whose own emotional life as a boy had been malnourished, but from life on the street, where he soaked up the awe and admiration of other project boys and girls. Whitey Bulger could feed off all these feelings: he was someone who could take care of others, take charge and run the show. There was no limit to what he could do. No one was there—certainly not his father—to tell him otherwise. For him, it was as if the takeaway message of these early years was, Hey, I can do this, I can talk my way out of trouble, all blarney and boldness. I can do what I want. Others might get sent away—to Lyman, or to jail—but Whitey's juvenile success enabled him to think he never would.

While Whitey was stealing goods off the backs of trucks, researchers from Harvard University were fanning out across South Boston and six other of Boston's poorest neighborhoods in the early 1940s as part of a pioneering study of juvenile delinquency. The project was the brain-child of a husband-and-wife team at Harvard, Sheldon and Eleanor Glueck. Like many academics, sociologists, and thinkers of the time, they believed the vexing problem of delinquency warranted deep inquiry. "The majority of adult criminals began their antisocial careers as child delinquents," they wrote in the 1950 book *Unraveling Juvenile Delinquency,* based on their study. "Some of the more striking traits that mark delinquents are similar to the characteristic traits of Nazi, Fascist or Communist leaders." In systematic fashion, they and their staff developed data on five hundred Boston delinquents and an equal number of nondelinquents, creating what was later called "one of the most comprehensive longitudinal data bases in the history of criminological research."

They located delinquent boys for the study at the two reform schools—the Lyman School for Boys in Westborough, Massachusetts, and the Industrial School for Boys in Shirley, Massachusetts. Focusing on boys from families living in slums and tenements, they conducted home interviews and follow-ups in the underprivileged areas of South Boston, East Boston, Charlestown, Dorchester, the West End, the South End, and Roxbury. In each neighborhood, they looked to build a pool of fifty delinquent boys and fifty nondelinquents, and, once they got rolling, researchers conducted repeat interviews with the boys, their families, their teachers, neighbors, and criminal justice and social welfare workers. Each boy was interviewed by a psychiatrist and tested extensively using state-of-the-art examinations: the Wechsler-Bellevue Intelligence Scale as well as the Rorschach inkblot test, which was created in the 1920s and had become the favorite of clinical psychologists by the early 1940s.

The Gluecks were not interested in one-time offenders, only boys who were "persistently delinquent." They also sought diversity—200 boys, or 20 percent of all boys, were of Irish ancestry, 25 percent of the boys were Italian, another 25 percent were of English background, and the remaining 30 percent were a mix of Polish, German, French, Jewish, and more. When they began, the average age of the delinquent boys was fourteen years, eight months.

In all, they made up Whitey Bulger's peer group, although, of course, researchers never happened upon young Whitey since he avoided commitment to the reform schools. But researchers certainly circled Whitey, penetrating his world and the lives of boys belonging to any number of the Southie street gangs, the Swallow Street Gang, the D Street boys, and the Shaggers, to name a few. They worked with boys living right outside of Old Harbor in nearby Andrew Square, where one researcher, walking around and taking notes, jotted down the observation that this was an area where "the playgrounds are the street." He was following up on a Polish boy, a member of the Junior Eagles. The boy came from a large family in a cold-water flat in a three-decker backed up to a factory and across from an empty lot that served as "a hangout nightly for boys 14 to 17 years of age."

Quickly, too, researchers learned the juvenile record they had in hand for each boy was the tip of the iceberg. Interviewing a sixteen-year-old boy from West Sixth Street who was a member of the Little Gustin Gang, one researcher discovered the boy first began shoplifting from stores on Broadway at age six. By age seven he was picking the pockets of streetcar motormen and conductors. By age eleven, the boy disclosed, he and his pals were "rolling homos."

The Glueck researchers learned that the repertoire of many boys included preying on homosexuals who cruised the Boston theater district. In his interview with researchers on June 23, 1944, another boy from Andrew Square told about how he and his pals "delighted in the practice which he termed 'pounding them.' " The boys went downtown to the Stuart Theatre, where they "put themselves into such a position as to be approached by some of the sexual degenerates who frequented this theatre and would seem to agree with his wishes. When they were in a nearby alley, several of the gang would jump on the degenerate and they'd steal his money and beat him up. The boy said cops never cared because cops hated 'the fags' too."

It has been said that Whitey Bulger was one of the Southie boys who participated in gay-bashing—with some accounts of his early life going even further to assert he turned tricks for gay men. It certainly was not unheard-of—boys in the Glueck study admitted to turning tricks. One teenager from Bolton Street in South Boston, four years younger than Whitey, admitted that to make some money he went to the Cobb Theatre in the South End, where, his interviewer noted, "he was approached by men, and he submitted to unnatural acts with them. It consisted of playing with their genitals." No solid proof, however, has ever involved Whitey.

In time, with all the interviews and information piling up, the Gluecks pored over the data looking for commonalities. While emphasizing that "no single factor" adequately explained delinquency, they described a laundry list of traits seen far more in delinquent boys than in the nondelinquents. The delinquent juveniles were defiant to authority, resentful, hostile, and destructive. Emotionally, they were "more obviously self centered" and generally "refused to take responsibility for their behavior." Problem solving was impulsive, often involved violence, and featured "an inability or unwillingness to abide by law's restrictions." The result was an "uninhibited, untamed, unreflective child" living in the city's poorest neighborhoods in conditions providing "the theatre of action."

The Gluecks emphasized that most boys did not develop into persistent juvenile offenders. Nor did all boys who were delinquent inevitably grow up to become adult criminals. In their follow-up research, lasting throughout the 1940s and beyond, they tracked boys after their time at Lyman or Shirley or after serving in the military and getting a job—boys who, in other words, established connective tissue. The Gluecks found that many of those boys straightened out.

But that would never be Whitey's outcome. The Gluecks, in all of their interviews with Southie boys, never came across a kid like him. Had they, the Gluecks would have confronted a boy who broke the mold, a stand-alone, a virtual once-in-a-lifetime bundle of high-octane drives and antisocial impulses, of cold defiance and anger, a kid who shared many traits with the studied juvenile delinquents but not all of them. Whitey had connective tissue to family that other delinquent juveniles did not, but it would never have a stabilizing effect; instead, Whitey was in a category all his own—untamable. His edge, his fearlessness, his strut and narcissism, his need to prove himself and to assert his manhood and control over others—all combined to make him a one-off. A juvenile who did participate in the study once cut to the chase, describing crime, in its essence, as "a struggle for power. The more you say don't, the more I will." It was uncanny insight for a boy. When applied to Whitey Bulger, it could not have been truer.

Whitey Bulger and two buddies were prowling around the downtown theater district in their car on Memorial Day weekend in 1948 when they first spotted her. Mary Rae, her head down against the lightly falling rain, was hurrying along Boylston Street after taking in a late night movie. The young wife of a Marine corporal stationed in the Mediterranean, she was petite at five feet two, a pretty brunette on her way to the subway and home to Cambridge.

The car pulled up alongside her, and a voice yelled out the window offering her a ride. Mary later told police that in the rain she thought she recognized one of the men, thought she'd gotten lucky to run into him. She climbed in thinking she was accepting a ride home across the Charles River to Cambridge. But Mary Rae was wrong. Whitey, then eighteen, and his pals had other plans. Instead of heading west toward the Massachusetts Avenue bridge, they turned east. The streets at that late hour were quiet and they drove through South Boston in no time. They pulled into the parking lot of Malibu Beach in Dorchester and on the shore of the harbor the three men began crawling all over Mary Rae.

But having their way with her did not come easy. Mary turned out to be a rattlesnake. She fought them, squirming, lashing out, and screaming. She grabbed a cigarette and crushed the burning tip on one attacker's skin. Fortunately for her, Whitey and the others must have been looking for something quick and easy. The threesome decided this woman Mary Rae was not worth their trouble. They opened the door and pushed her. Mary helped by leaping from the car.

The car drove away, and as it did Mary Rae memorized the license plate. When she got ahold of the police, the plate number was one of the first things she reported. With that information broadcast over the police radio, police in South Boston spotted the Bulger car within an hour. The three were arrested.

Once again Whitey was back in the District 6 police station. He and the other two men were booked on a charge of assault with intent to rape. They were held during the Monday holiday, until the South

Boston District Court reopened for business on Tuesday morning, June 1, 1948. That's when Whitey pushed back. He pleaded not guilty. This was a case of mistaken identity, he insisted.

Judge Leo H. Leary continued the case for a week. Of all of Whitey's charges during the decade, this was the most serious. If convicted he faced the possibility of several years in prison. The heat was rising. But by this time, too, Whitey knew full well the value of money, and the next week he and his attorney cut a deal. He pleaded guilty to a reduced charge of assaulting Mary Rae, and he was ordered to pay fifty dollars. For most people, that was a stiff fine. For the eighteen-year-old Whitey Bulger, usually flush with cash from his street crimes, fifty dollars was practically spare change.

Whitey paid his way out of his worst jam yet. Just as he did two months later when more trouble arose. Capping a night of drinking, Whitey went into Jerry's Diner at 500 Old Colony Avenue and got into a ruckus. Boston police officer Bill McDermott and his partner, Eddie Griffin, arrived in their patrol car. They secured a drunken Whitey but as they were about to put him in a police wagon two of Whitey's drunken companions jumped them. With reinforcements, police squashed the melee, and all three ruffians were hauled down to the station.

This time Whitey did not fight the charge; he pleaded guilty to being drunk and paid a fine of five dollars. Two arrests in two months seemed sloppy, one involving drunkenness—a loud, public scene at the diner. He usually liked being in control, not out of it. Whitey turned nineteen on September 3, 1948, and it was as if South Boston at the end of the decade was beginning to feel claustrophobic. The closet that his brother Bill used in an analogy as unable to contain Whitey's fierce, untamable personality—maybe that closet had become South Boston itself. He'd moved away from Old Harbor—and gotten out from under his father—and was living at least part of the time in nearby Cambridge. But was that far enough away for his surging impulses?

The recruitment posters were all over, published in newspapers and magazines. Full of color, they were presented in panels, like a comic strip. One panel featured happy-looking airmen beneath the headline THIS IS THE LIFE. Another showed an airborne twin-engine bomber named after the military aviation pioneer General Billy Mitchell, along with excited copy: "You may be selected for advanced training in the *Mighty Mitchell*." Another was of a knockout blonde in a red dress fixing the medal on an airman in uniform and standing at attention. ONLY THE BEST CAN BE AVIATION CADETS, the posters announced.

The U.S. Air Force became Whitey's New Year's resolution. He certainly wasn't the first troublemaker drawn to the service—looking past its regimentation and seeing instead uniforms, travel, girls, guns, and, perhaps unconsciously, a supply of father figures. Like the circus, the service offered him a ticket out of town.

Three days into 1949, Whitey showed up at Fort Banks, the historic military base a few miles north of Boston, in Winthrop. He found his way to the Air Force's Enlistment Section, where, under the gaze of Captain Samuel J. Galzerano, he completed the two-page enlistment form: his name, date of birth, home address, and schooling—which Whitey wrote was eight years of grammar school and one year of high school. The form required an enlistee to designate a person to be notified in the event of an emergency. Whitey listed his mother, not his father. The form then asked the enlistee to designate an alternate person to be notified. Whitey still did not list his father, choosing instead a street gang pal named Mike Durand.

To the questions seeking an enlistee's criminal history, Whitey was laconic.

> *Question 32:* Have you ever been convicted of a felony, or more than once for any other offense? (If so, give details.) "No."
> *Question 33:* Have you ever been imprisoned under sentence of any court? "No."
> *Question 34:* "Are you now or have you ever been on suspended sentence, parole, probation, or are you awaiting final action on charges against you? "No."
> *Question 35:* Have you ever been arrested? (If so, give details.) "Yes," Whitey answered, but listing just one charge—Assault to rape on "6/1/48"—and noting the charge was later lowered to assault and battery.

The responses were a mix of fact and fiction—particularly to Question 35. Despite questions aimed at ferreting out any possible criminal involvement, Whitey took a less-was-better approach and revealed only the one case. To him, the slate was basically clean.

He signed the form and was administered the oath of enlistment by Captain Galzerano. And so on January 3, 1949, Whitey Bulger became a private in the U.S. Air Force. Five days later he arrived in San Antonio, Texas, for basic training in the Indoctrination Division at Lackland Air Force Base. The Harvard University team of Sheldon and Eleanor Glueck, in their exhaustive study of juvenile delinquents in Boston, determined that military service was the right tonic for many juvenile delinquents. For Whitey it proved to be a new theater of action.

6

AWOL: 1949–53

Great Falls, Montana: police mug shot

When Whitey Bulger arrived at Lackland Air Force Base on January 8, 1949, south-central Texas was experiencing an unusual stretch of bad weather. The winter had been so frigid that Lackland's commanding officer had to alter the schedule for basic military training at the base, located on the southwest side of San Antonio. Whitey was one of about five thousand new recruits. That seemed like a lot, but in fact the overall numbers at the base were in steep decline, a result of the steady fall-off in funding following World War II. In the first three months of the year, the base took in only 10,327 new personnel—the lowest number for Lackland since 1946.

During the next thirteen weeks, Whitey and the other trainees in his class underwent 520 hours of instruction. Their curriculum included physical conditioning and lessons in military tactics, customs, drills, and ceremonies. They received a basic orientation on aeronautical subjects and were even lectured on citizenship, personal hygiene, and safety. They also went to the firing range, where they learned to use .45-caliber pistols and .30-caliber carbines and undertook what was called a "familiarization firing" of the .45-caliber Thompson submachine gun. Whitey likely enjoyed that; in later years he stockpiled weapons, a collection that included a "tommy gun," as the Thompson was often called.

The cold weather was not the only unexpected element Whitey and his fellow recruits faced. By chance, the civil rights movement was manifesting itself in the military. President Harry Truman had signed an executive order the previous July requiring the military to end racial segregation, but two segregated basic training units were still operational at the end of the year and newly arriving black recruits were automatically assigned to one of them.

The new era coincided with Whitey's arrival in early 1949. He would certainly never consider himself a pioneer in race relations—always showing that he had little tolerance for blacks—but he and every recruit were assigned to a training squadron without regard to color.

The mixing of the races caused some tension. "Minor differences between Negro and White personnel and conflicting local (Jim Crow) regulations have arisen," a history of Whitey's unit noted, "but tact and diplomacy prevented their growth to a major catastrophe." There's no indication how Whitey fared during this period of integration. The unit history for the Indoctrination Division, Air Training Command, does not identify the personnel involved.

By early April Whitey had completed his basic training, and after a ten-day graduation leave, Private First Class Bulger, as he was now ranked, was on the move. From April to July he was stationed at one of the Air Force's oldest bases. Founded in 1917, Chanute Air Force Base was located about one hundred miles south of Chicago, in Rantoul, Illinois. Upon arrival, Whitey became a member of the 3346th Training Squadron and completed a basic course in aircraft and engine mechanics. For that, Whitey was awarded a Military Occupational Specialty (MOS) code of 521. In a matter of months Whitey was fast getting a taste of the country beyond Boston, moving quickly through stints in Texas and Illinois, and by early July arriving at his first real duty assignment, outside Salinas, Kansas—Smoky Hill Air Force Base.

At Smoky Hill, Whitey was immediately enrolled in an on-the-job-training program to become what the USAF called an MOS 747D, or "airplane and engine mechanic, medium bomber aircraft." It was at Smoky Hill, however, where his past life in Boston nearly tripped him up. The commanding officer of the 353rd Bomb Squadron, to which

Bulger was assigned, learned that Whitey's slate was not so clean. Whitey was brought up on a charge of "Fraudulent Enlistment" for failing to fully disclose pre-service arrests and criminal record. The matter soon landed in the lap of the unit's personnel officer.

Following an inquiry, Second Lieutenant Dale C. Smith sent a single-page report to the unit commander recommending that the Air Force keep Whitey on active duty. Whitey might well have been arrested in the past and had convictions that were not included on his enlistment application, but Smith cited an Air Force regulation stating the "general policy to retain individuals in the service who, upon enlistment, concealed a conviction not punishable by death or imprisonment for more than a year." By this measure Whitey was technically acceptable, since he had not served any jail time for trouble he got into earlier in the 1940s. Accordingly, he was cleared.

With the flap over his enlistment behind him, Whitey went on to have an Air Force career totaling three years, seven months, and four days. That term was unremarkable with regard to military service but not so in terms of the man. He was stationed for periods of between seven and twelve months at six different bases—in Illinois, Kansas, Louisiana, Texas, Montana, and Bermuda.

Whitey never saw combat. He earned no medals. He remained on the ground during his entire Air Force service—trained in engine mechanics and aircraft repair. That said, some of the units he was assigned to had played unique and significant airborne roles in World War II and after. For example, Smoky Hill's 353rd Bomb Squadron had distinguished itself during World War II in the European Theater and now, during Whitey's time, was being repurposed for the atomic age. The 353rd was transformed into a long-range aerial strike force as part of a newly formed Strategic Air Command (SAC). Whitey and his peers worked on four-engine Boeing B-29 Superfortress bombers that had been used to drop conventional bombs during World War II but by 1949 had been retrofitted to carry a single atomic bomb. In the event of another full-scale world war, the 353rd's mission would be to deliver atomic bombs to attack the Soviet heartland.

While Whitey was with the 353rd, some of its aircraft were modified in other ways. These B-29 Superfortresses were outfitted with a primitive but workable aerial refueling system first developed by the

British in the 1930s. The resulting long-range capability that would eventually be taken for granted by USAF fliers was a cutting-edge innovation in the late 1940s. These modifications enabled the 353rd's airplanes to stay aloft for lengthy periods of time, and in the fall of 1949 the squadron was strutting its stuff, sending some of its B-29s on demonstration flights of up to twelve thousand miles nonstop.

In January 1950, Whitey was sent to Texas for additional training as a mechanic at Sheppard Air Force Base, located about five miles north of Wichita Falls. The outbreak of the Korean War six months later put the Air Force and all of the U.S. military services on wartime footing. By the end of July 1950, 1,410 student-airmen were pouring into Sheppard, which specialized in training technicians. In August, the number of incoming trainees jumped by 500, to a total of 1,900 trainees. Like Whitey, most were assigned a training syllabus called Course No. 74740, "Airplane and Engine Mechanics, General," to help meet the new demands of a nation back at war.

In his first year or so, Whitey had become a working cog in the country's expanding military defense establishment. But Whitey was also restless, bristling at the military's regimentation and authority. Just as 41 Logan Way could not contain him, neither could the Air Force. His brother Bill acknowledged as much, later writing "that the Air Force apparently had more rules than planes, and he delighted in breaking or circumventing a great number of them. It appeared from his letters that he contrived a new system each week for being absent without leave, and did so with impunity."

Indeed this was so. Whitey, according to available Air Force records, first disappeared in early January 1950 while en route from the 353rd Squadron to his new station in Texas at Sheppard. Instead of making a straight line for Wichita Falls, Whitey made a zig and a zag. He was arrested in Oklahoma City on January 13. No details of the arrest have survived, but Whitey was listed as absent without leave, or AWOL, as a result. Two weeks later he was turned over to the Air Force Police at Sheppard, but there is no indication he received any punishment. It was merely a blip, and Whitey resumed his training.

Filtered through his brother Bill's eyes, Whitey the USAF mechanic was a harmless mischief-maker. "It was clear he was enjoying himself," Bill wrote about Whitey's time in the Air Force. "His conduct was not from any lack of patriotism. He was just being Jim." But the facts are otherwise and not so amenable to lighthearted conclusions. During his time in the Air Force, Whitey for the first time paid a price, albeit a small one, but a price nonetheless.

After nine months in Texas, Whitey was transferred again. In September 1950 he arrived in Montana to join the 1272nd Air Transport Wing, at Great Falls Air Force Base, in Montana. The base at Great Falls had been created in the early 1940s to support the war effort, but with a twist—its chief mission in World War II was actually to support another country. Because of its location, the base was a major jumping-off point for U.S.-built aircraft being given to the Soviets under the Lend-Lease program. In just two years, between 1943 and 1945, about six thousand airplanes were flown in stages from Great Falls to Nome, Alaska, where Russian crews took over and flew them on to Siberia. Great Falls itself had a population of only about fifty thousand people at the time, but that made it the largest city within the four-state area of Montana, Wyoming, and North and South Dakota.

When Whitey arrived, the base was already adapting itself to the same Korean War tempo that was straining Sheppard's capacity to turn out well-trained mechanics. The conditions in Montana were also the harshest that Whitey had faced—within weeks temperatures plummeted to 20 degrees below zero. But a restless Whitey found

The bars along Great Falls' south side

comfort when he left the base on the eastern edge of Great Falls and headed five miles downtown to the city's lower south side. He discovered the music and boozy crowds at the Anchor Bar, the Great Falls Cafe, the State Bar, and the Sullivan Hotel. The joints and flophouses along First Avenue South conveyed the back-home feel of Boston's own Scollay Square, and the twenty-one-year-old Whitey took to the seedy Great Falls neighborhood that was such a headache to base officials that at times they declared it off-limits to military personnel.

Whitey was socializing the night of Sunday, March 18, 1951, at the State Bar when he got into an altercation with an older woman. Police arrived and arrested him about 11 p.m. In court the next morning Whitey faced the officer's account and also that of the thirty-four-year-old woman, Grace Box, who had pressed charges. Box was quite ready to testify as a witness against him. It looked bad, and Whitey folded; he pleaded guilty to "creating a disturbance." But he wasn't done with the woman who stood up to him; during the day his case was being adjudicated, he turned the tables by filing a criminal complaint that accused Box of assaulting him. If Whitey was angling to improve his chances by muddying the record, the strategy failed. Judge David J. Ryan ordered Whitey to serve thirty days in the city jail.

The sentence was the first ever for Whitey. It appears unlikely that he did all thirty days, because twelve days later, on March 31, a court docket noted that Whitey paid a twenty-five-dollar fine "at recommendation of Major at base," implying that Whitey was released. Even so, whether he served thirty days or twelve, for the first time Whitey got a taste of what it was like to be in jail. The Great Falls city jail was old, crowded, and had basement cells that were leaky, moldy—dungeon-like. The drunk tank was a communal cell for as many as forty to fifty men where the only seating was a single wooden bench and the only way to relieve yourself was on a toilet that had no seat and flushed automatically every few minutes. In the cells where Whitey stayed, mortar between bricks was leaching; mattresses were worn, filthy, and virtually unusable; breakfast was a cold mush.

Three months later Whitey got into a second jam. On another Sunday night, June 10, 1951, a middle-aged woman and a thirteen-year-old girl came rushing into the Great Falls police station shortly after midnight. The woman told police that her two young daughters were about to go into the Anchor Bar on First Avenue South to call for a taxi when a "Mexican and a white man" in a car stopped and kidnapped her fifteen-year-old. Police began asking questions, and the thirteen-year-old girl explained that she and her older sister had previously met one of the men at the Great Falls Cafe, where she was working part-time. The mother then said she and her daughters had been in the city for only a few weeks after arriving from the tiny farming town of Hingham, in northern Montana, to look for work.

It didn't take Detective Fred Peres and another officer long to drive the six blocks from the police station to First Avenue South. They searched the bars and cafés, asking around about two men and a girl. They hurried to the Sullivan Hotel and headed into one of the flophouse's rooms. There they found Whitey in bed with the fifteen-year-old. In an adjacent room they found a drunken Mexican named Ortega. The detectives took both men down to the station. Whitey initially lied about his identity and denied he was an airman from the base.

That day's *Great Falls Leader* ran a story about the arrest on page 10, with the headline AIRMAN HELD IN RAPE CASE. The story began, "Police early this morning heard a sordid story from a 15-year-old high school freshman girl who, because she was 'afraid and did not want to get beat up,' submitted herself three times to a 21-year-old airman from the east base." It continued: "The airman, James Bulger, 21, was booked by Police Detective Fred Peres and Officer Kenny Dow at the city jail at 2:10 this morning on a charge of rape." Ortega, the story said, was charged with drunkenness.

Within a day the girl was taken to the county juvenile home. Whitey was turned over to the county for prosecution on the rape charge and held in the county jail. The matter quickly became more complicated. By mid-week, Detective Fred Peres found the woman and the thirteen-year-old "wandering in and out of bars" on First Avenue South, implying that solicitation was involved. Peres took the mother into custody on charges of contributing to the delinquency of a minor, while the thirteen-year-old was turned over to juvenile authorities. It also emerged that before the hotel bedroom arrest the fifteen-year-old and Whitey had been seen socializing together around town.

The situation was a classic he-said, she-said. To the mother, and to police at least initially, it was a kidnapping. To Whitey, it was dating. To the police, it was a rape; to Whitey, it was consensual sex, even if the girl was a minor. Whitey suddenly became the beneficiary of the various ways the coupling could be spun. The county prosecutor decided to wash his hands of the "lovers' quarrel," and the following week he ordered that Whitey be released and returned to Great Falls Air Force Base.

While Whitey was entangled in the arms of a fifteen-year-old, his family back in Boston was in a different kind of embrace. The Bulger family was on pins and needles about the fate of the husband of Whitey's sister Jean—Army Lieutenant Joseph D. Toomey. Joe Toomey was the best South Boston had to offer—a handsome and, at six feet, six inches, towering graduate of West Point. In the first six months of the Korean War he was awarded the Silver and Bronze stars for gallantry in combat and, after being wounded, a Purple Heart. But terrible news arrived just after Thanksgiving. Toomey was missing in action. Then, late in January 1951, the family received a telegram that raised their hopes. It urged caution, saying Toomey's status was not confirmed, but quoted a communist radio broadcast reporting that he and eight other captured U.S. soldiers were in good condition. But the report turned out to be a cruel hoax. Joe Toomey was dead, starved to death. "I can never forget Jean's stricken face," Bill Bulger later wrote. "In the desolation in her eyes I could see her taking sad inventory of her lost future with Joe, all the unlived years."

Whitey, meanwhile, was out of danger and back at the base. Instead of investigating his conduct further, base officials dropped the matter. That meant that twice in a matter of months Whitey had tangled with civilian police—and he'd even served his first jail sentence—but he had managed to skirt any real consequence. What could have turned out much worse instead fed the swagger. He was soon enjoying his free time back in the bars on First Avenue.

During this same period, psychiatry was pushing for a better understanding of a social deviant known as a psychopath. Leading the way was Dr. Hervey M. Cleckley, a Georgia psychiatrist. While Whitey was AWOL in Oklahoma City in January 1950, Cleckley was unveiling the second edition of his landmark study, *The Mask of Sanity*. Put simply, a psychopath *seemed* normal but was far from it. He was an empty vessel lacking empathy and morality, enabling him to function comfortably in an everyday way but unhampered by ethical and legal restraints. He knew the difference between right and wrong but that had no bearing on his choice of conduct. He was, in short, without conscience—a master deceiver who presented a mask of sanity but, in truth, was capable of committing acts that were frighteningly destructive and criminal.

It was a field continuously beset with confusion over the similarity of terms for two completely different conditions, psychopathy and psychosis. A psychotic person suffered delusions and sharp breaks with reality. The psychopath, meanwhile, was the opposite—a person in command of reality but defective in his severe emotional detachment and lack of remorse. Another part of the confusion was the different labels researchers used for the condition characterized by no conscience—*psychopathic* and *sociopathic*. The terms became used interchangeably by the layperson, but clinicians debated important and nuanced distinctions. *Sociopath* was favored by researchers who theorized the cause of the condition was external social factors and early life experiences. *Psychopathy* was used by Cleckley and his followers, who saw the disorder as a personality defect rooted in what a protégé of Cleckley called "psychological, biological and genetic factors."

With his pioneering book, Cleckley sought to chronicle and expose what he considered an overlooked social problem. Cleckley drew on data collected at the neuropsychiatric hospital in Georgia where he practiced. He wrote about patients rich and poor, criminal and law-abiding, with chapters devoted to describing the psychopath as businessman, as gentleman, as scientist, and even as psychiatrist. Cleckley made clear that the work was descriptive and that he had no explanation for the cause of psychopathy—nor could he suggest a cure.

Building on Cleckley's effort, a Canadian psychologist named Dr. Robert D. Hare, working with psychopaths in Canada's prisons, made the most profound and prominent advances. He eventually created a diagnostic tool called the Psychopathic Checklist, comprised of twenty traits, to detect psychopathy based on a subject's score. The listed symptoms included egocentric and grandiose; lack of remorse or guilt; lack of empathy; deceitful and manipulative; shallow emotions; poor behavior controls; early behavior problems; adult antisocial behavior. "It's their eyes that are the most remarkable feature," he once said. "How they drill into you."

In total, they were traits that would come to have an increasingly familiar ring when one was considering the life of James J. "Whitey" Bulger.

Following his skirmishes with police in Great Falls in the spring of 1951, Whitey managed by summer's end to trade the unforgiving weather of Montana for the tropical temperatures of Bermuda. Ordinarily, an airman in Whitey's position—deep into his third and final year of service—would have to stay put. The Air Force customarily would not go through the administrative hassle and expense to reassign an airman whose tour expired in five months. By the terms of his original contract, Whitey was due to be "separated" on January 3, 1952.

Unless he extended his enlistment. To make himself eligible to exit Montana, Whitey that summer signed on to add a fourth year to his service commitment. This paved the way for a new assignment, which came in September 1951, to Bermuda's Kindley Air Force Base. The squadron in Bermuda was equipped with eight Boeing WB-29 Superfortress bombers, and their maintenance workload was demanding. Whitey knew how to work on B-29s from his days in the 353rd Bomb Squadron at the Smoky Hill base in Kansas, and that experience made him valuable.

In Bermuda Whitey's assignment was with the 53rd Strategic Reconnaissance Squadron—better known as the Hurricane Hunters. The primary mission of the 53rd was to observe and report weather conditions in the western Atlantic and the Caribbean—and especially to identify and track major storms, which was a far more difficult undertaking in this era before the advent of weather satellites orbiting the earth. The squadron's eight WB-29s had been specially modified to conduct weather surveillance, including the ability to drop parachute-borne sensors that measured air pressure and surface water temperatures and returned the data to the aircraft by radio.

But the WB-29s also carried another set of sensors—part of a "classified mission" that Whitey and most of the squadron knew little about. Mounted on the back of each aircraft was a two-foot cube on a stubby pylon. The cube contained paper filters and a set of baffles. Its purpose was to collect dust, including the minute radioactive particles created during an atomic explosion. By analyzing the particles, the military could glean key information about a weapon's design, composition, and efficiency. The WB-29s that Whitey worked on were part of the U.S. atomic intelligence-gathering effort put in play following the detonation of the Soviet Union's first atomic bomb in late August 1949.

Whitey's arrival in Bermuda on September 8 came during the peak of the hurricane season in the Atlantic and Caribbean, and his new squadron had already been tracking one storm for four days. Whitey got there just in time to see six of the squadron's WB-29s evacuate to Florida to avoid the oncoming Storm Easy, which passed close enough to hit the base with 60-mph winds. The remaining two aircraft were tied down and protected as well as could be with walls of sandbags.

Hurricanes aside, Bermuda was a choice assignment weather-wise—where airmen could work up a tan while enjoying the beaches. But it was also a base where the workload never let up. The 53rd's WB-29s routinely flew weather missions lasting from twelve to sixteen hours. The aircraft were at least seven years old, making their mainte-nance a never-ending challenge. Half the aircraft might be unavailable at any given time due to parts shortages or mandatory inspections, or while undergoing repairs. Whitey and the fellow mechanics, armed with wrenches, labored long and hard to keep up. By March 1952, Whitey's work had won acknowledgment: he was promoted to airman second class.

Even with the accolade, Whitey's ride was persistently rocky. He was combustible, and it was only a matter of time before he would overheat. In June Whitey disappeared—AWOL for ten days. It was as if Whitey had had enough—the fourth year he'd added had gotten him out of Montana but now he wanted out altogether. According to one account, he displayed his trademark South Boston strut during the June 25, 1952, disciplinary hearing. One official, taking note that Whitey was recently promoted, suggested the advancement was unde-served.

"Well, then bust me if I don't deserve it," Whitey said.

Whitey was also informed that a finding that his conduct was dis-honorable had the potential of affecting his upcoming return to civil-ian life—airmen who received dishonorable discharges often had difficulty getting good work.

Whitey was unfazed. "I could go back to the work I used to do," he stated, "no matter what kind of discharge I get."

The official presiding at the June 25 hearing basically took Whitey at his word. He stripped Whitey of the promotion he'd earned just three months earlier; Whitey was reduced one grade to airman third class. But the presiding official did not meddle with Whitey's discharge status. It stayed categorized as "honorable," which meant he had performed credibly and never been convicted by a court-martial. The term *honorable,* however, hardly reflected the trouble he'd gotten into.

But more to the point, his discharge came six weeks after the hearing. Whitey took advantage of certain Air Force regulations allowing "early outs" for enlisted men who were approaching their date of discharge and who had no intention of reenlisting. Whitey qualified—and he was able to shave off five months. Instead of having to wait until early the next year, Whitey was on the road again in mid-August, heading home to Boston in time to celebrate his twenty-third birthday on September 3, 1952.

7

Packing Heat: 1953–56

Whitey: age twenty-three

Whitey Bulger returned to the working-class Irish enclave where he'd lived since he was nine years old, a neighborhood that was as rough-and-tumble as any in America. He'd certainly had his chances—in school early on, then in the Air Force.

But his makeup was more prone to the beast within, an anger fueled by a broken relationship that must have felt like the most fundamental of betrayals. Even as his mother had taken charge of the family's affairs she was no substitute for a boy's need for a father. There was no one to stop him, and Whitey became a strain of humankind resistant to the checks and balances, either internal or external, that guide behavior. He was smart and gifted in the art of persuasion, even as the words were lies. He was ambitious, too, and full of himself. Photographs of him in his early twenties capture the Whitey swagger, the taut arms folded across his chest, and the look—the glaring blue eyes that conveyed a cold message: Don't mess with me.

Even with the personality traits of a psychopath, Whitey could still have achieved enormous success following a conventional path that stayed inside the law. Experts Dr. Hervey Cleckley and, following him, Dr. Robert Hare treated and wrote extensively about the "psychopaths among us"—the occasional psychopathic politician or businessman or lawyer or other professional who rose to the top of his field. "Psychopaths are social predators who charm, manipulate, and ruthlessly plow their way through life, leaving a broad trail of broken hearts, shattered expectations, and empty wallets," Hare once wrote. "Completely lacking in conscience and feelings for others, they selfishly take what they want and do as they please, violating social norms and expectations without the slightest sense of guilt or regret." The behaviors might get ugly, but experts found law-abiding psychopaths. Whitey, however, would never be able to succeed at such a "normal" life to control a Fortune 500 corporation. Not with his personality's toxic mix. The impact of a crippled, distant father whom he often battled was one dark demon, but just as significant was the nourishment he found on the street, where he was somebody.

Whitey came home to South Boston and got work as a laborer. He bounced between several construction jobs, working at one point for a builder named George Callahan, but staying only a couple of months, and then working for another named Bart McDonough, earning seventy-five dollars a week. But, again, he didn't stick around.

"Since his release from the service he has made very little attempt toward obtaining legitimate employment," a federal probation officer wrote in a 1956 report about Whitey. "He spent most of his time in the local taverns where he associated with known criminals."

Whitey saw little of his younger brother Bill, who, after his freshman year at Boston College, was drafted into the Army. Bill left in September 1953 for a two-year tour of duty, stationed mostly in Texas, at Fort Bliss. And Whitey stayed away from the Bulger family homestead in Old Harbor; by 1955 he was making only rare appearances to face his father's own blue and glaring eyes. "This young man has very little to do with his parents," noted the 1956 probation report. "According to his parents, he comes home occasionally, but for the most part has been living elsewhere." He did spend time with Jacquie McAuliffe, the blond beauty, estranged from her husband, whom he had showed off to the Southie boys.

He also saw plenty of a small-time criminal well known to Boston police—Richard E. Kelly. Kelly, at thirty, was seven years older than Whitey. Teaming up after Whitey's return, the two began making their mark committing the crime Kelly specialized in—robbing trucks. The two rode around truck-delivery routes in the South End and the Back Bay stalking targets. They'd hustle up on foot to the back of the truck making a delivery and then run off with armfuls of liquor, cigars, cigarettes, or whatever else was portable and could be resold for cash to fill their pockets.

The FBI in Boston took notice. The tailgating problem had gotten to the point where the bureau had set up a task force with local police to gather intelligence about Kelly, Whitey, and any other suspects. In one report from the early 1950s, the FBI observed that Whitey "rivaled Richard Kelly as a tailgate thief." A mention of Whitey in another report summarized the reputation he'd quickly developed for "his extremely dangerous character, his remarkable agility, his reckless daring in driving vehicles, and his unstable, vicious characteristics."

It wasn't as if Whitey and Richard Kelly always managed a clean getaway. One warm early summer day they got greedy. On the morning of June 30, 1953, they targeted a truck in the South End and, when the moment was right, robbed it of several hundred dollars' worth of cigars and cigarettes. They should have gone home at that point—called it a day's work. But in the afternoon, shifting their sights to the Back Bay neighborhood, the two spotted a beer truck driving down Massachusetts Avenue. They followed the truck until it pulled up outside a store to make a delivery. Once the driver walked inside, Whitey and Kelly hopped out of their car, ran to the rear of the truck, and began opening the steel gate.

Boston police seemed to come out of nowhere. Whitey and Kelly tried to get away, rushing back to their car, but police cornered them at the intersection of Massachusetts Avenue and Boylston Street. The two had not noticed Detective Sergeant Vernon White and Detectives Danny Kerr and Joe O'Donnell following them. The officers had been assigned to investigate the tailgating problem, which the newspapers had reported was responsible for the theft of "more than $2,000 in merchandise from parked trucks in Boston during the past month." They'd gotten the call about the morning heist of cigars and cigarettes, and then picked up Whitey's scent by chance, spotting Whitey and Kelly following the beer truck in the same fashion that the earlier truck had been before it was robbed.

Police found boxes of cigars and cigarettes in Whitey's car. He and Kelly were taken to Station 16 in the Back Bay and charged as "suspicious persons, to wit: larceny of merchandise valued at over $100 from delivery trucks." Boston police took a booking photograph of Whitey wearing a fedora and staring coldly into the camera, dated March 16, 1953, that years later became the iconic photograph for Whitey in his early twenties. While they were in the lockup at the Charles Street Jail, more police arrived to charge them on warrants for an assault and battery in Roxbury, although no specifics about the incident are contained in the police log entry for the arrest. Then, in the months to come, Whitey and Kelly were arrested again on tailgating charges. Whitey, meanwhile, was stopped for speeding, arrested for driving drunk, arrested another time without Kelly for tailgating, and, in July 1955, charged with beating up a man on Shawmut Avenue in the South End.

In the two years Whitey was home, he was arrested more than a half-dozen times—some of which involved serious charges. These were the instances when he was caught, a mere sample of what police suspected Whitey was up to. But just as when he was a juvenile, and then an airman, Whitey had a knack for getting out from under his legal troubles. He talked his way out of some cases and got them dismissed. Or he benefited from a court's screwup. The Roxbury charge, for example, simply vanished. Despite an entry for his arrest in a police log, no corresponding court case was opened, and the arrest never appeared on any subsequent version of Whitey's criminal record, or rap sheet. Other times he paid small fines—such as ten dollars for driving drunk. He was actually sentenced to serve four months for the beer truck robbery, but then the sentence was suspended. Whitey never served a day. Despite multiple arrests, the system kept spitting him out.

Whitey had to be pleased. But for all his uncanny success in the cat-and-mouse game with police, tailgating had to feel dated, even stale. Tailgating was the stuff of juveniles, a crime for tough Southie boys in street gangs like the Bloody Hounds or the Forty Thieves, where the return was a few hundred dollars here, a few hundred dollars there. By 1955, Whitey had to feel a bit of been there, done that. He was turning twenty-six.

The talk of the town at the time—and the country, for that matter—when it came to crime was the biggest holdup ever, the theft of $1,219,000 from the Brink's Inc. office on Prince Street in Boston's North End. The robbery had happened five years earlier, on January 17,

1950, but it had captivated the country. The newspapers described it as being executed in the "slickest of fashions," as nothing less than "the most fabulous armed robbery in the nation's history." The investigation, its twists, turns, and frustrations, was rabidly followed ever since, and with a six-year statute of limitations ticking away, pressure was mounting in 1955 for an arrest.

The Brink's job was the headliner in a sweeping new trend that was confounding crime fighters—an uptick in the number of armed hold-ups at such cash-rich repositories as payroll offices and, especially, banks. The FBI provided the statistical proof: bank robberies in the United States had increased from 89 in 1950 to 335 during the 1954–55 fiscal year. The spike alarmed bankers and public officials alike. Conferences were held to brainstorm new safeguards. Bank employees underwent training to make mental notes of the characteristics of the holdup men, their weapons, and their getaway cars, and banks began installing grillwork on the counters, which traditionally had been open and easy to vault. Experts explained that the increase was due in part to the wave of bank branches opening in the suburbs. Robbers, they noted, found the quiet suburban branches easy to target.

Whitey was the kind of young man who would have a sense of all this—what was in the news, like the Brink's case, and its larger historical context. He might have been a school dropout, but that did not mean he lacked for intellectual curiosity. In a sense, Whitey became self-schooled during his twenties, and this important quality distinguished him from the run-of-the-mill street gangster. He was an avid reader, and his reading went beyond the daily tabloids or the monthly magazines. By his early twenties, he was already regularly devouring works of history, biography, fiction, even poetry.

Robbing banks had become all the rage, where the action was if you were Whitey, the ambitious up-and-comer seeking a bigger stage and a bigger thrill.

Two robbers came into Whitey's life in the spring of 1955, and they made all the difference. One was Richard Barchard, who was local—from Somerville—and at twenty-five a year younger than Whitey. The second was Carl G. Smith Jr., five years Whitey's senior. Smith was from Indiana, a Navy veteran and trained scuba diver. To Whitey, Smith would be the far more intriguing and, ultimately, more influential.

Barchard and Smith met while serving time in Charlestown State Prison, the oldest prison in the country. Barchard was serving sentences for two armed robberies to which he'd pleaded guilty in January 1951. He was nineteen when first he and a friend robbed a café proprietor in Saugus, Massachusetts, on December 21, 1949, and then, two days later, he and three others robbed a restaurant manager in Peabody of the ninety dollars that was in the cash register.

Carl G. Smith Jr., meanwhile, had become a local legend in legal and law enforcement circles. In the early 1950s, Smith had twice been found guilty at jury trials, one in Worcester County, where he was convicted of breaking into a building at night in West Boylston, Massachusetts, and the other in Suffolk County, where he was convicted of robbing the seventeen-hundred-dollar payroll from a restaurant called Steuben's, on Boylston Street in Boston.

Once behind bars, Smith did not sit still. He hit the books in the prison's library, training himself in jurisprudence. On his own he prepared appeals in both cases, arguing he'd been denied due process during each trial. In the Steuben's holdup, the Massachusetts Supreme Judicial Court—the state's highest court—agreed. It overturned Smith's conviction, ruling on November 26, 1951, that the trial judge had improperly excluded a portion of Smith's alibi evidence.

Having showcased his skill in mustering an appellate argument, Smith didn't stop there. When the Steuben's case went to trial a second time in May 1954, Smith was on his feet in the courtroom, delivering his own opening and closing arguments, cross-examining the government's witnesses. He was representing himself—pro se, as it's known in legal jargon. And he won. The jury acquitted him.

Smith had become the quintessential jailhouse lawyer, able to play both the legal scholar shaping a reasoned constitutional argument and then the trial attorney. Word got around. Following a prison riot at Charlestown, one of the rioters told the judge at the arraignment that he preferred Smith to any court-appointed counsel.

But Smith's legal practice remained self-centered. While mounting his own defense at the Steuben retrial in May, he continued to pursue his appeal in the second case, the break-in in West Boylston. Four months after the jury acquittal, the Supreme Judicial Court issued a ruling in this case—and, again, Smith prevailed. The high court in September 1954 threw out the guilty verdict after harshly criticizing the district attorney for not properly testing Smith's alibi. Smith quickly filed a motion to vacate his eight-to-ten-year sentence, and by year's end the court set it aside. Smith had succeeded not once, but twice; he'd erased two felony convictions and the accompanying prison sentences.

By springtime Smith was a free man. Barchard was also done serving his sentence. They hooked up, and soon Whitey was in the mix. The exact circumstances of Whitey meeting Smith are unknown; Whitey later said an ex-convict, likely Barchard, introduced them, and by May they were associated, with Smith talking eagerly into Whitey's ear about new opportunities in bank robberies. Smith was someone who would favorably impress Whitey; the man's cunning, strategic thinking, and confidence were qualities that Whitey would admire—and possessed as well. The Sunday night of May 15, Smith described a specific bank to both Whitey and a young ex-convict from Cambridge named Ron Dermody. Dermody, a thief, had married on Saturday and told authorities later he was broke and looking for a way to make money fast to finance his new marriage. The bank Smith described was a forty-minute drive south of Boston, across the state line, in Pawtucket, Rhode Island, the city where Whitey's father had lost an arm in a railyard accident in 1899.

Whitey and Dermody were in. Monday morning they drove to Pawtucket, cased out the Darlington branch of the Industrial National Bank of Providence, and rented a room at a motel owned by a Chinese man. First thing Tuesday morning, Whitey and Smith drove to a factory parking lot. They smashed open the left front vent window of a 1949 red Mercury sedan. They attached a wire from the car's battery to a point behind the ignition switch and then pressed the starter button. They drove off and got Dermody. Final touch: Smith distributed handguns to each man. But for all of Smith's leadership in setting up the job, it was Whitey who was in charge once the action rolled. When the three walked unmasked into the bank at 1:45 p.m., in what the newspapers later called a "brazen" midday robbery, Whitey led the way. He was dressed dark—a soft black hat, dark shirt, and trousers. He'd draped a dark jacket over one arm, just as his father was inclined to do on his walks around Southie. But instead of hiding a prosthetic arm, Whitey concealed a .22-caliber revolver.

"This is a holdup!" he yelled, pulling out the black gun. "Everybody down!" Smith moved quickly to the tellers' cages while Dermody, pistol in hand and wearing a hat and new sneakers, jumped onto the counter to monitor the fourteen bank employees and customers. When an assistant bank manager hesitated, Whitey glared: "Okay, junior G-man, I said lay down." Despite the armed coverage, a worker was able to set off the alarm. The three robbers turned and hurried for the door. Even though their stay was shortened, Smith grabbed $42,112 in small bills.

"They were a smooth bunch," one bank employee said afterward. "Weren't nervous at all." The police chief said the robbers appeared to be "professionals from out of town." Within minutes of the holdup, his officers and officers from neighboring towns set up roadblocks on routes leaving Pawtucket. The FBI joined the investigation. The stolen red Mercury with the smashed front vent window was found in mid-afternoon in the factory parking lot, and bank employees told police they'd gotten clear looks at the unmasked gunmen. They were confident they could identify them. The problem was, the robbers were nowhere to be found.

Whitey, Smith, and Dermody had dumped the Mercury and gone back to their room, lying low for one more day before slipping back to Boston. The heist was the first in the history of the mill town whose ironworks and textile mills had put the city on the map in the 1800s, during the Industrial Revolution. It was also a first for Whitey Bulger— but hardly his last. Whitey, years later, boasted to associates that he was involved in many holdups during his brief run as an armed robber, and that may well be the case, but records document that following the maiden voyage in Pawtucket there were two more robberies and one attempt.

Whitey and the others split the Pawtucket proceeds into shares of $14,034 (equal to $118,617 in 2012 dollars). Dermody went his own way, unaffiliated with the others, while Smith left Massachusetts with his wife to drive to Gary, Indiana, where he was from originally. By early fall 1955 Richard Barchard joined Smith to scout banks. Whitey, meanwhile, was back in South Boston. His brother Bill returned home in August after two years in the Army, but the two were like the proverbial ships that passed in the night. The future politician had his eyes, as did most Bostonians, on the city's legendary politician James Michael Curley and his last hurrah: a final, and unsuccessful, campaign for mayor. (Curley died three years later, a week shy of his eighty-fourth birthday.) In late September 1955, Whitey hit the road again. Flush with cash, he and Jacquie McAuliffe drove south to Florida. The happy couple stayed there for more than a month living the good life, spending Whitey's bounty. They registered in a series of motels as husband and wife using his true name: Mr. and Mrs. Jim and Jacquie Bulger. Then, in October, Carl Smith managed to track Whitey down.

Smith and Barchard had cased a bank in Hammond, Indiana, and they wanted Whitey's help. Whitey took Jacquie home and joined them. They showed Whitey the branch of the Mercantile National Bank, located in a small shopping center. The bank had evening hours on Thursday, and so Thursday, October 29, they set out to stage a nighttime stickup. Using a second car Smith had stolen from nearby Gary, Indiana, they rendezvoused in another shopping center, one in the Woodmar neighborhood of Hammond. They left one car there and drove the stolen car to the Mercantile branch. But as they sat outside preparing to get started, they saw a police officer pull up, climb out of his cruiser, and walk inside the bank. The vibe was all wrong.

The three reluctantly called off the holdup. They returned to the Woodmar shopping center and talked about regrouping for another try. Before splitting up, however, Whitey and Barchard both took notice of a branch bank where they were parked, the Woodmar branch of the Hoosier State Bank. A new opportunity presented itself on the heels of a setback. Whitey and Barchard agreed that the tiny branch in the sleepy neighborhood "looked like a soft touch," and filed the shared evaluation away.

Smith stayed on in Indiana, working a day job as a diver and starting a salvage company, still determined to knock off the Mercantile branch that had frustrated them. Whitey and Barchard returned to Boston. Needing money, they scouted a bank in Melrose, Massachusetts, north of Boston—the very kind of target that banking experts and crime fighters studying the spike in armed holdups had cited as most vulnerable: a suburban branch bank. This one was the Highlands branch of the Melrose Trust Company, and less than three weeks after the failure in Indiana, a pistol-toting Whitey Bulger boldly entered it at noon on November 18, 1955.

Barchard had begged off at the last minute, so standing by Whitey's side was a new man, William L. O'Brien of Dorchester, slightly older at twenty-nine and a mason by trade who was married, a father of four, and had little by way of a criminal record. O'Brien was later portrayed as a struggling father who'd gotten in over his head by getting involved with the likes of Whitey Bulger and his mates. Whitey and O'Brien each had a .45-caliber automatic pistol and were just beginning to grab cash from the drawers when the branch manager tripped the alarm. Whitey fled.

A noon train was slowly rolling through the center of town, blocking Melrose police trying to reach the bank, as Whitey and O'Brien roared off. They got away but the holdup could hardly be considered a success. The take was a measly $5,035. Chump change compared to Pawtucket, and they divided it three ways to include Barchard even though he'd been a no-show—$1,700 each. Pawtucket had been a great start for Whitey. But then came the bust-out in Indiana, and now a Melrose heist he'd barely escaped. Whitey wanted better. Within several days he and was on the road again to Hammond and its Woodmar neighborhood. Whitey also decided that for this job he would make a key stylistic change.

Whitey left Boston on the Sunday night before Thanksgiving 1955, driving the 850 miles to Hammond. He wasn't alone. By his side was Jacquie McAuliffe, later described by the FBI as his "paramour." Then there was Richard Barchard, Whitey's newest ally. Barchard brought his young wife. Like Jacquie McAuliffe, the eighteen-year-old Dorothy Barchard was a blond knockout. It was a double date, a stickup shaping up like a Bonnie and Clyde undertaking.

The couples holed up in a local motel in the small city of nearly ninety thousand residents. Wednesday, the big day, began under clear skies and unseasonably warm temperatures. Hammond, located twenty-four miles south of Chicago, was best known for the meatpacking plant a butcher from Detroit named George Hammond had founded in the latter part of the nineteenth century. Most of the locals were spending the day before Thanksgiving running errands, straightening up, and finishing plans for a holiday feast devoted to counting blessings and giving thanks.

For Whitey Bulger, however, this was a season of taking. He and Barchard dressed in matching getups. Each wore what would best be described as a hunting outfit: blue jeans, wool button-up shirts, and hunting caps with flaps that they pulled down over their ears. They tucked in their shirts and sported such a tidy look that witnesses later noted their "good grooming." Before they left, Whitey took possession of his new calling card—two blue-steel pistols.

It was just after 7 a.m. when Whitey drove to Michigan Street and to the Shell Oil Company bulk plant. He and Barchard had their pick of the parking lot. Showing his taste in cars and a preference for robbing in style, Whitey selected a red and white 1954 Oldsmobile Rocket 88 coupe, owned by a truck driver from Illinois. He and Barchard broke into the car and got it started. When they left Barchard was driving the stolen Olds. Whitey led the way over to Indianapolis Boulevard, Hammond's main commercial street, where he pulled into a tiny parking lot outside Ted's Midwest Food Mart. He left his car, hustled over to the Olds, and slid in behind the steering wheel of the shapely vehicle with its Rocket 88 engine, which was the inspiration for both a seminal rock-and-roll song and the 1950s slogan "Make a Date with a Rocket 88." Whitey and Barchard killed a little time, and then, at 10:40 a.m., Whitey drove the Olds four blocks on Indianapolis Boulevard to a shopping center between 165th and 167th streets. They'd reached their destination—the whole point of the long road trip from Boston. Whitey steered the Olds right up to the paned glass window that was the front of the Woodmar branch of the Hoosier State Bank. He jumped out and strode toward the bank's entrance, as Barchard fell in behind him.

Inside the bank, branch manager Henry C. Fehlberg was helping a customer at his desk to the left of the front entrance. Mrs. Grace Brumm, a teller, was serving a customer at the first window. Violet Pappas, the bookkeeper, was farther down the counter at another window. Peter Kayes, a third teller, was also working. In all, four employees and seven customers were inside the bank.

"Lie down!" Whitey shouted.

Everyone looked up to see two men in hunting outfits. The first one was waving two pistols. The second was hurrying toward the counter. Manager Fehlberg noticed that neither wore a mask and they both seemed so "cocky and sure" in their movements. Indeed, in the next instant, Fehlberg realized the lead gunman was marching toward him at his desk and, as he later told reporters, he found himself looking "straight into the business end of a gun." Mrs. Vernon De Vary, a housewife standing a few feet away, watched in horror as the gunman turned from the manager and stuck one gun's barrel in her chest. "Get on the floor!" Teller Brumm, watching from behind the counter, immediately did as the gunman ordered. "He only had to tell me once," she said later.

"I'll shoot the first one who moves!" Whitey yelled out.

Barchard vaulted the counter and worked his way from teller to teller, scooping up the money. Whitey stood in the middle, surveying the scene. It just did not get any better—he was in charge and at center stage; cold cash was tumbling into a bag; his girl was waiting for him. In six months he had, as one federal prosecutor would soon describe it in court, "blossomed out as a two-gun bandit."

Holding two pistols in the bank lobby was indeed a moment to savor, and it was as if Whitey had the ability to detach himself to do just that—inhale the power and glory while smack in the middle of it. Not only did he project a coolness the witnesses recalled afterward, but he uttered a line they would all remember, as if he had been composing a gangster movie starring himself. "We aren't going to hurt anyone but we have to making a living—Dillinger did."

Having delivered a line revealing his appreciation for Indiana's native son John Dillinger, Whitey covered Barchard as his partner hurriedly finished emptying the bank's cash drawers. The two then ran out the door. Racing away, Whitey veered to avoid young Hammond housewife Mrs. Verlyn Mack, bundled in an overcoat and walking unawares toward the bank. Whitey retraced the route four blocks down Indianapolis Boulevard, traded the Olds for his car, picked up their women, and headed north out of town on the freeway.

The short ride to Chicago passed quickly. Whitey and Barchard peeled out of their hunting outfits. They dumped the clothes and two pistols Whitey had carried during the robbery. Their take wasn't too bad at all—$12,612, which they split, so each got $6,306 (or $53,299 in 2012 dollars). The foursome then left Chicago for St. Louis, where it was finally the time to relax and give thanks. In the afterglow of their success the couples enjoyed a Thanksgiving Day dinner at a restaurant. They parted ways.

Whitey and Jacquie McAuliffe headed back to Florida. They slipped up when they were arrested in Miami on a vagrancy charge on

December 2. Miami police checked with Boston, learning about Whitey's reputation and even that he was a suspect in a jewelry store robbery in October. But Boston police had no warrants pending and did not yet know about his breakout into the big leagues of robbing banks. Miami police had nothing, and the couple was released within hours. For his part, Whitey's outlook at the age of twenty-six was more likely focused on the immediate rather than the long term, and the cash-rich couple spent freely. When Whitey and his girlfriend headed home to Boston for the holidays, he did so confidently. Newspaper coverage of the separate holdups reported that the authorities in each state had little to go on. By early January Boston police picked up on the return of the former tailgater, writing in an internal report that Whitey had been seen about the town "in the company of a model."

The lack of leads was not for a lack of effort. Police in Rhode Island, Massachusetts, and Indiana were working hand in hand with the FBI. In the Hammond robbery, police quickly found the getaway car four blocks from the bank in front of Ted's Midwest Market. FBI agents dusted the car, the bank's counters, and cash drawers. They sent the results to the FBI laboratory, hoping for a fingerprint identification—but none was made. In Boston, meanwhile, one FBI agent in particular emerged as a leader investigating the robberies in Pawtucket and Melrose, Massachusetts. The agent, H. Paul Rico, ambitious and brash, was homegrown, a native of the Boston suburb of Belmont and a graduate of Boston College. He'd been an agent only since 1951.

The big break occurred in Indiana—and it came from Carl G. Smith Jr. Smith couldn't leave well enough alone; on December 6, he and two ex-convicts from Tennessee robbed the bank that had stymied him, Whitey, and Richard Barchard earlier in the fall. The robbers, flush with their take of twenty-one thousand dollars, fled to Tennessee, where they spent wildly, foolishly drawing attention to themselves. Three days after the holdup they were arrested in a restaurant in McMinnville, Tennessee. Returned to Indiana, Smith was questioned by the FBI. The cagey Smith, angling for a better deal (which did not come), decided to confess. He told the FBI about Whitey and the others and their roles in the Pawtucket and Hammond holdups.

Whitey had no idea events were turning against him. Instead he learned that law enforcement had broken open the bank robbery investigation the same way everyone else did, when federal prosecutors in

Indiana announced on January 4, 1956, that a federal warrant had been issued for his arrest. The Associated Press sent the story out on the wires, and such Boston newspapers as the *Boston Herald* reported, FBI NAMES HUB MAN IN BANK HOLDUP. The story included the news that "a 13-state teletype alarm has been broadcast for Bulger, who was described as armed and dangerous." The manhunt was under way.

Whitey was now a fugitive from justice. He left Boston instantly and headed west, all the way to California, which was where Barchard had gone after they split up following the Thanksgiving Day dinner. Showing his daring, Whitey returned to Boston on January 17 to pick up Jacquie McAuliffe, and she became his road companion, with their first stop being Wilmington, Delaware.

Back in Boston, the FBI agent Paul Rico took a lead role in the Bulger manhunt. He and colleagues scoured Southie trying to pick up a scent. They pressured the street toughs for information. They knocked on the door at 41 Logan Way in Old Harbor and tried the Bulger family. But bloodlines trumped public safety. The FBI got no cooperation from Whitey's parents, and January passed without any clues to his whereabouts. "Our investigation to locate and apprehend Bulger proved unavailing," Rico's supervisor noted in a report. "Contacts with all logical sources proved unproductive. His family and associates were hostile."

Whitey's troubles deepened on February 8 when, based on Carl Smith's information, federal prosecutors in Rhode Island issued an arrest warrant for him and Ron Dermody in the Pawtucket holdup. The next day, February 9, FBI agents surrounded Dermody's home in Cambridge and arrested the twenty-four-year-old. Within weeks, Dermody confessed and also fingered Whitey.

It was every man for himself. Whitey and Jacquie traveled the country, burning through Whitey's money while staying for short spells in such locations as Reno, San Francisco, Salt Lake City, Chicago, and New Mexico. Whitey went by several aliases: Martin Kelley, Paul John Rose, Leo McLaughlin. Tapping his penchant for costumes and the masquerade, he dyed his hair black, got a pair of horn-rimmed glasses and adapted to wearing them, and to distort his facial features took to carrying a cigar in his mouth in the style of the Hollywood actor who played many leading gangster roles, Edward G. Robinson. Then, sometime in late February, the couple returned home. Whitey needed a cash refill and, as he later told one of his girlfriends, he wanted to deliver money to his mother for an operation. Besides, he later said, for all the heat from law enforcement, he actually never thought he could be captured, so full had he been of himself and his ability to outwit the law. The FBI certainly acknowledged the skill of the young, smart-aleck bank robber they were up against, noting in a report that the fugitive Whitey was "extremely dangerous, usually armed, a daring driver with feline agility." Whitey the ocelot.

Whitey scouted local banks in the early days of March. He hatched a plan to rob a branch of the Harvard Trust Company located in Porter Square in Cambridge. He enlisted a local named John R. Imperato to help him, and Whitey acquired two .45-caliber automatic handguns. The last detail was timing, and Whitey decided Monday, March 5, would be the big day.

By this time, however, Rico and the FBI were ready. Unable to count on the family, Rico had recruited a local underworld informant who, according to a later report, "could and would inform on Bulger's location." It wasn't easy. The man Rico had in mind and began wooing was initially not interested in helping; in their first conversations he gave Rico only "the usual denials and misinformation which criminal associates provide in cases of this nature." But Rico kept after him and "ultimately developed his confidence and willingness to cooperate." The identity of Rico's informant remains unknown; the name has been redacted in confidential FBI reports documenting the manhunt for Whitey. One strong possibility, however, was a young tough Whitey's age named James "Buddy" McLean. McLean was a leader of the Winter Hill Gang, based in Somerville, Massachusetts. According to FBI records, Rico had recruited McLean as one of his underworld sources by the early 1960s. If Buddy McLean was the informant Rico tapped for the manhunt, it marked not only the start of that relationship but an earlier start than known previously.

Rico's informant came through. The informant not only told Rico in early March about Whitey Bulger's return to Boston, but also said Whitey and a second man, John Imperato, were plotting a crime. The informant was not certain what Whitey had in mind, but everyone's guess was a bank holdup. Rico and his colleagues, sensing this was the break they'd been waiting for, kicked into high gear. They knew little about Imperato, but they knew where he lived. Rico and other agents spent Saturday, March 3, gathering the "necessary details concerning him, his residence, vehicle and data which would be necessary for surveilling him." On Sunday, Rico and seventeen agents huddled with the FBI agent in charge of the Boston office. Operating on the assumption Whitey was about to hold up a bank, they made plans to stake out the partner. "Assignments were made of personnel, vehicles and weapons, with arrangement to rendezvous at the office the following morning at 5:30 a.m." Keep an eye on Imperato, they decided, and Whitey would surface.

They worked all day Sunday and it wasn't until seven o'clock Sunday night that the agents dispersed and headed home to prepare for what was shaping up as a long mission the next day. But shortly after they left, Rico's informant made contact—and his information changed everything. Whitey and an underworld buddy were socializing that very night at the Reef Café in Revere.

FBI agents working on the manhunt were mustered as quickly as possible and began scrambling to get to the nightclub. The agents who lived closest to Revere, a waterfront city just north of Boston, made it there in no time—and Agent Paul Rico was among them.

Whitey Bulger walked out of the Reef Café at 8:40 p.m. and right into the hands of ten FBI agents surrounding the club. It was over just like that. Rico was one of the agents who held Bulger and handcuffed him. "The arrest was effected smoothly and without incident," noted an FBI report. "Bulger was not armed at the time but indicated in his comments to the agents that, if he had not been completely surrounded, he would have made a daring attempt to flee."

Even as he faced the hefty lineup of federal gun power Whitey managed a wisecrack—some remark to demonstrate he had attitude. But the capture was actually proof of something else—his lack of experience at age twenty-six in the big leagues of crime. Returning to Boston, where law enforcement heat was the most intense? Plotting to rob a bank in the very jurisdiction where he was most wanted? Feeling so untouchable that rather than keeping out of sight he decided to go out to a club? These were rookie moves, not those of a seasoned veteran.

Whitey's short ride as bank robber was over; he was in free fall, and the landing in the weeks to come would prove hard. He was not invincible after all, and in the game between the good guys and bad, he had not really outwitted anyone. Instead, Whitey had fallen victim to his own hubris and naïveté. He still had a lot to learn, and with his arrest on March 4, 1956, came one fundamental epiphany: the value of informants to the FBI. This was the takeaway message of his year of living dangerously, and it was a lesson that years later would be recast into an even more crucial one for him: the value of the FBI to certain informants.

8

The Informer: 1956

Whitey in custody

The night of his arrest Whitey Bulger was taken to the Boston Police Department's downtown station on Milk Street, where he was questioned briefly. The next morning, instead of robbing the Cambridge bank, Whitey was headed to federal court for his arraignment. The news of his capture spread quickly, with Boston's newspapers running photographs of him in police custody, his hair the color of black shoe polish. The FBI put out a story that agents had been hot on Whitey's trail for days and had the "Revere spot under surveillance for several nights and when two agents sighted the suspect there they called for reinforcements." The account of the arrest was not accurate, but one that accomplished two goals: it made the bureau look smart and all-knowing and shielded the fact that Paul Rico's informant was the one who had alerted them to the Reef Café, setting off the Sunday night scramble.

Maintaining the confidentiality of informants—covering for them, in other words—was paramount to the FBI. For any law enforcement agency the whole business of gathering intelligence from willing crime figures is premised on secrecy. Without it, the flow of information would cease, likely replaced by the flow of blood as the underworld closed in for the kill of a suspected informant.

The FBI valued informants as much as and probably more than any other police agency. In fact, by the mid-1950s the FBI's widespread use of informants and its trafficking in secret intelligence had drawn the attention of congressional committees seeking accountability. FBI director J. Edgar Hoover pushed back hard. In January 1956 he issued a statement in which, according to newspaper accounts, "the veteran FBI chief again made clear that the informant's cloak-and-dagger role must remain sacrosanct." Hoover fiercely defended the use of FBI informers as essential in the nation's fight against communism and crime. Confidential informants, Hoover insisted, were "invaluable in protecting national security."

FBI agent Paul Rico was one agent who certainly understood the value of informants in the context of crime fighting—as well as their value to an agent's career. The day after Whitey's arrest, Rico was one of ten agents who the top agent in Boston recommended should receive an FBI "incentive award." The boss in Boston asked FBI director Hoover to award Rico a $250 bonus. Hoover did better than that—on March 28 he wrote Rico a letter, marked "personal and confidential," to notify him that he was being promoted to the next grade in the FBI ranks, effective immediately. Hoover cited Rico's "superior accomplishments in connection with the Bank Robbery case involving James J. Bulger Jr. and others." He noted specifically that Whitey's arrest was "directly attributable" to Rico "developing a valued source of information." Then, showing privately what he stood for publicly, the FBI director hailed Rico's overall work with informants: "I am also aware of your noteworthy efforts in developing other sources of information, and you are to be commended for results in this regard." Hoover backed up the accolades with a $965 raise, increasing Rico's salary to $7,570 annually.

In court on March 5, 1956, the federal prosecutor handling Whitey's case called Whitey a flight risk and urged that bail be set high. "A vicious person, known to carry guns, and by his own admission has an intense dislike for police and law enforcement officers," Assistant U.S. Attorney Daniel H. Needham Jr. said. Needham got what he wanted. Bail was set at fifty thousand dollars, a sum neither Whitey nor his family had on hand. Under the circumstances, the best the Bulgers could do was to line up an experienced and well-connected defense attorney, Theodore A. Glynn Jr. Glynn had served as a state representative during the early 1940s and later, in 1959, was appointed to the Boston Municipal Court, eventually becoming chief justice of that court.

Whitey had to sit tight behind bars, where he had plenty of time to mull over his capture and to comprehend fully the reason for his undoing: he'd been betrayed not just once but three times by fellow criminal cohorts—first by Carl Smith, then by Ron Dermody, and finally by Rico's newly minted informant. The lessons would harden in him like cement. From this moment on he would trust few and demand supreme loyalty. Condemnation of informers reflected the cultural values of his hometown Southie. His brother Bill later addressed this cultural truism. "We loathed informers," Bill wrote later in a memoir. "Our folklore bled with the names of informers who had sold out their brethren to hangmen and worse in the lands of our ancestors."

But actions despicable in others Whitey saw differently when it came to himself. He was facing a mountain of trouble—three armed robberies in three states. It was not a case of being wayward in front of the juvenile court, or of facing an assault charge in the district court in South Boston. This was not a disciplinary board in the Air Force or the local courts in Montana. Whitey had fallen hard, and he knew it. The FBI had him—all because he was ratted out. Faced with the prospect of spending a virtual lifetime behind bars, he had to do something to try to improve his lot.

Whitey Bulger became an informer. He might tell himself he was not the first to break rank. Carl Smith held that honor, and Whitey might rationalize ratting on Smith as tit-for-tat. Indeed, there exists in the crime world a maxim that ratting on a rat does not constitute ratting. But it's a pretzel logic informants usually adopt to justify their betrayal. Criminals who refuse to talk under any circumstances, known as the truly "stand-up guys," dismiss the maxim as spin and rank hypocrisy.

Besides, FBI records reveal Whitey did more than inform on his informer Carl Smith. He admitted first that, yes, he robbed three banks and, yes, Carl Smith and Ron Dermody were with him to rob the bank in Pawtucket. The FBI report noted: "Bulger, after his apprehension, cooperated with the Bureau to the extent of admitting his participation in three bank robberies. He reduced his admissions to signed statements and named his two accomplices in the Rhode Island bank robbery." Whitey's information thus far was helpful confirmation of what the FBI already knew; indeed, Smith was in custody and, thanks to Smith, so was Dermody. But then came key information that Whitey refused to include in any signed statement, meaning he did not want to create a permanent written record. Whitey informed the FBI that Richard Barchard was with him while robbing the Indiana bank, and he also said that William L. O'Brien was his partner in the Melrose, Massachusetts, holdup. Or, as the FBI report stated: "Bulger *orally* admitted who his accomplices were in these bank robberies" (emphasis added). Finally, Whitey delivered girlfriend Jacquie McAuliffe to FBI agent Rico and his colleagues; Whitey "persuaded [her] to cooperate with the Bureau," the FBI report noted. Based on his information and "as a result of her cooperation, process was obtained for Bulger's accomplices, Richard R. Barchard, in the robbery of the Woodmar Branch of the Hoosier State Bank, Hammond, Indiana, November 23, 1955, and for William L. O'Brien, in the robbery of the Highlands Branch of the Melrose Trust Company, Melrose, Massachusetts, November 18, 1955."

Conduct considered anathema in Southie became, for Whitey, a cold calculation. No right or wrong, no moral judgment was attached; rather, informing was a strategy taken for self-preservation, which, after all, was what mattered most. And it was a secret hidden in records off-limits to the public.

The FBI picked up William L. O'Brien on May 3. They found him in Burlington, Vermont, and he was arrested at a construction site working as a bricklayer. O'Brien was returned to Boston the next day, where, like Whitey, he was held on fifty thousand dollars' bail. Ten days later, on May 14, the FBI arrested Richard Barchard in Rodeo, California. When they found Barchard he was earning $1.69 an hour working as a laborer at American Radiator and Standard Sanitary Corporation. He'd also proposed marriage to a seventeen-year-old girl he'd met in Rodeo. The marriage would have been illegal; though separated, he was still married to Dorothy Barchard. But laws against polygamy, like most laws, were apparently not going to stop Barchard.

Both men folded quickly. Barchard described how he came to admit his culpability in a handwritten statement he prepared for court several years later. He said that following his arrest in California the FBI agents asked him about "his activities, particularly with reference to his association with one James Bulger Jr. and their alleged activities at Hammond, Indiana, on or about November 23, 1955." Barchard said that initially he denied any involvement with Bulger. The agents, he wrote, "then told him that one James Bulger, who it was alleged participated in the bank robbery, had informed agents of the FBI at Boston Massachusetts that he (Barchard) had robbed the said bank with the said James Bulger." Just as troubling, wrote Barchard, he "was further told that the information Bulger had given them indicated that his wife had been involved in the instant robbery and that if he insisted on causing more trouble and expense than he had already caused, that his wife would be prosecuted for complicity in the robbery." Barchard said he was warned that if he fought the charges, federal prosecutors would seek the stiffest sentence possible. Barchard decided to end it there. He agreed to plead guilty.

Back in Boston, Whitey's case proceeded quickly following his confession. One thing he wanted in return for a guilty plea was to have the three bank robbery cases concluded together in Boston, not separately in the three jurisdictions. "After making the aforementioned admissions, Bulger indicated that he desired to plead guilty to the robberies of these banks and that he desired to plead in Boston, Massachusetts," the FBI report stated. Whitey was working every angle—a possible home court advantage, where disposing of all three at once in Boston might help shorten the length of his prison term. Whitey got his wish; on May 23 the local federal court received papers from prosecutors in Indiana saying they agreed to the proposal that the Hammond bank robbery be handled in Boston. In addition, prosecutors ultimately left Jacquie McAuliffe alone; she was never charged in connection with the Indiana holdup or for harboring a fugitive during the manhunt. In fact, her identity and role were kept out of the public eye; the closest reporters got to her was the mention in a few articles that during the manhunt, Whitey had traveled with a girlfriend.

The federal judge in Boston, George C. Sweeney, scheduled Whitey's sentencing for June 21. To assist him in considering a sentence, a federal probation officer went to work assembling a "Presentence

Report." The confidential report of more than a dozen pages—for the judge's eyes only—was based on court, school, and other records, along with interviews with Whitey's parents and Whitey himself. It included Whitey's full criminal record, going back to his first arrest as a juvenile, and contained such sections as "Narrative of Offense," which was a detailed account of the bank robberies. The report noted that Whitey now claimed he was broke, having spent his way through more than twenty-five thousand dollars in cash. "The proceeds from these hold-ups have been spent on lavish living in Florida, where he went with his girlfriend." There was another section called "General Reputation," in which the probation department reported to the judge that Whitey's reputation was "exceedingly poor," that he began breaking the law as a juvenile, and that "he has been in considerable trouble as a law violator ever since.

"During his early years he was very difficult to handle at home and in school. His companions were far from a good influence upon him. He chose to associate with known thieves and ex-convicts and has no desire to work."

In the section "Personal History," the report summarized his troubled time in school, which he quit after the ninth grade and where "he had very little interest in school work and failed practically all his subjects." The report mentioned his service in the Air Force, where he "attended school and received a high school diploma," and the fact that afterward he was not interested in finding "legitimate work" but instead resumed associating "with known criminals."

The section "Family History" was based in part on information the Bulgers provided, including the family lie that Whitey's father's age was more than a decade younger than his true age. It included as well James J. Bulger Sr.'s own past brushes with the law: "arrested for assault with a revolver in Roxbury, case dismissed. He also has previous arrests for drunkenness." Whitey's mother was described as a "housewife," brother Bill, twenty-two, "a student in his sophomore year at Boston College," sister Jean, twenty-eight, a widow working as a secretary; sister Carol, eighteen, living at home and a secretary at Carney Hospital; brother John, or "Jackie," seventeen, living at home and working at the *Boston Traveler* newspaper; sister Sheila, twelve, living at home and attending a Catholic high school. In the section "Family Situation," this point was emphasized: "It may be noted that during his formative years his father was very strict with him and on occasions beat him severely. This, however, had very little effect on him as he continued to misbehave in the community."

Whitey was described as physically fit, who denied "use of drugs, but admits drinking heavily at times." His IQ was a very solid 113, "which indicates above average intelligence." In addition, "he has always been a leader." For all Whitey's intelligence and leadership potential, however, the probation officer did not hold out much hope. Whitey Bulger, the report stated, was "a rather serious law violator to have at large in the community. He would not hesitate to use a gun." It predicted: "The prognosis for future behavior in society is poor."

Beyond those conclusions, the report included a statement that a reader might easily overlook amid the many stronger assertions. The passage, in the section "Mental Condition," stated that Whitey "knows the difference between right and wrong; his actions have been in accord with his own choosing." The comment, at first reading, seemed benign enough—certainly nowhere near as eye-catching as if the comment on his mental condition had called him a maniac or some other category of madman. But the observation actually might have been the most insightful in the entire report. It was a line that Dr. Hervey Cleckley, the leading thinker of that era about psychopaths, could have authored—essentially restating what he and other researchers of psychopathy considered to be the core characteristic of a psychopath, namely, a person without conscience, a person who knew the difference between right and wrong but who did not care one iota.

That, the report was saying in a nutshell, was Whitey.

In terms of the city's crime news that spring and summer, Whitey Bulger's first major collision with the criminal justice system was overshadowed by buildup to the sensational trial of eight men in the Brink's case—what the media were billing "the most dramatic trial of the century." In January, as the six-year statute of limitations was about to expire in the 1950 holdup, the FBI had made the bombshell announcement that it had solved the robbery by turning one of the original suspects into a cooperating witness. Joseph J. "Specks" O'Keefe had "sung," as the newspapers put it, and named the eight defendants slated to go on trial later in 1956. The spring and early summer featured the final pretrial wrangling between attorneys, and then, on August 6, amid the 1950s version of a media circus, jury selection began. "Because of the notoriety attached to the $1,219,000 holdup of Brink's Inc., in Boston's North End on Jan. 17, 1950, the eyes of the nation—indeed, the world, will be focused on the seventh floor, spacious, oak-paneled courtroom," the *Boston Globe* reported in its sprawling front-page coverage, which included photographs of the accused, the judge, and a drawing depicting the courtroom's layout. Jury selection lasted nearly a month and the trial itself spilled into early October, climaxing with the jury's unanimous guilty verdicts against all eight defendants.

Whitey did not yet have that kind of marquee power. The day of his reckoning, Thursday, June 21, turned out, coincidentally, to be St. Aloysius's feast day, a celebration held on the date of the death, at age twenty-three, of the patron saint of youth and innocence. St. Aloysius died in 1591 while caring for the sick during a plague in Rome. He was remembered for writing about entering the priesthood: "I am a piece of twisted iron; I entered religion to get twisted straight."

Whitey Bulger was brought to federal court—no St. Aloysius he—under overcast skies, with a steady drizzle and fog encircling the city by mid-afternoon. Bill Bulger, who would soon study law at Boston College Law School after earning his undergraduate degree, was seated in the courtroom listening as each side made its recommendations to Judge Sweeney. Prosecutor Daniel Needham, citing Whitey's weaponry and the multiple robberies, called Whitey a "professional bank robber" who should be sent away for twenty-five years. Whitey's lawyer, Theodore Glynn, urged the judge to impose a much shorter sentence, which would offer a ray of hope to his client for a life after prison. Glynn reminded the judge that Whitey had demonstrated "some penitence" and had cooperated since his arrest. But the guilty plea to all three robberies was all that was known publicly about the extent of Whitey's cooperation. Few in the courtroom that day, except for the judge, the lawyers, and, likely, brother Bill, knew the rest of the story—that Whitey and Jacquie McAuliffe's informing had led to the apprehension of Barchard and O'Brien.

Once he'd taken it all in, Judge Sweeney sentenced Whitey to a twenty-year term in federal prison. The newspapers dutifully covered the hearing. So. BOSTON MAN GETS 20 YEARS FOR 3 HOLDUPS, was the headline in the *Boston Globe*, atop a brief account tucked in a single column on the front page. No story questioned the sentence, not at twenty years. For the first time in his life, Whitey was going to prison. The hammer had dropped hard—a twenty-year sentence was bad.

But was it? In the context of three convictions, and compared to his fellow robbers, Whitey actually did better than could have been expected. Whitey got a ten-year sentence for the Pawtucket holdup; his partner Dermody, who, like Whitey, had confessed, was sentenced to seventeen years. Whitey got a ten-year sentence for the Indiana holdup; his partner Barchard, who also confessed, was sentenced to twenty years. Only William L. O'Brien, Whitey's partner in the Melrose holdup, got a lesser sentence. Whitey got a ten-year sentence for Melrose while O'Brien got an eight-year sentence. Prosecutor Needham had joined O'Brien's defense attorney and recommended leniency for the Dorchester bricklayer and father of four who had no prior criminal record. Judge Sweeney agreed: "It's too bad that O'Brien with his intelligence would get himself into a situation where he became a potential killer." Then there was the other informer, Carl Smith. Like Whitey, Smith got a sentence of twenty years in Indiana, in a package settlement of his crimes.

The bottom line for Whitey: he was sentenced to ten years for each robbery, but the sentence became a twenty-year term because the judge ruled that only one of the ten-year sentences was to run consecutively with the others. Meanwhile, as said, Dermody got seventeen years for his role in a single robbery; Barchard got twenty years for his role in a single robbery. On its face, Whitey's sentence was bad, but it might have been far worse if not for his "cooperation." Neither Whitey nor Bill ever discussed publicly the impact Whitey's informing had on Judge Sweeney's sentence. Whitey's informing was buried for a half century in government records. The only remark Bill Bulger ever made about his brother's day in federal court was a reference in his later memoir to Judge Sweeney being "a strict but fair man." With the benefit of the fuller context, however, Bill Bulger's observation connotes an appreciation that things could have gone much worse for his brother.

The skies were blue and clear but the air was thick and the temperatures climbed into the eighties on the day, Thursday, July 19, 1956, that twenty-six-year-old Whitey Bulger arrived at the Atlanta Penitentiary to begin his long stretch of hard time. The drive to the prison took him to the outskirts of the city, through some quiet residential neighborhoods and, finally, to the entrance of the largest of the thirty-one penal institutions operated by the Federal Bureau of Prisons.

The Atlanta Penitentiary was immense. "Stone and steel," one of Whitey's fellow prisoners wrote in the inmate magazine about first seeing the complex. "A giant among buildings. You think: it looks like a hospital. It looks like a morgue. It looks like hell, it looks like anything you want it to look like rather than what it is, a prison." The U.S. marshal led Whitey, handcuffed and in shackles, up the fifteen marble steps to a steel door, where under the gaze of a guard watching from a tower, Whitey shuffled into the prison that held about 2,600 prisoners.

Inside, Whitey was handed over to a prison guard and the marshal got a receipt certifying delivery, "exactly the same as a wholesaler of meat gets from a butcher accepting a large side of beef," an inmate wrote. Whitey got his first shakedown, with a guard going through his hair, his pockets, and his shoes. He was then led through a seemingly endless maze of secured doors, down a hallway, and up a set of stairs to the Records Office, drawing looks and stares from guards and other inmates he passed along the way.

At such a moment it did not matter that he had managed, by turning into an informant, to cut himself a break in the potential punishment for three armed bank robberies. That fact would serve only as cold comfort on the very first day of a twenty-year sentence. Prison was the end of the line, whether one year or twenty. Whitey was entering a world where he would be vulnerable in the extreme—unmoored and without the power and self-determination so central to his personality. The closest thing he had seen to what he now faced was the Air Force, and he had bucked frequently against its regimentation. Inmate articles in the prison magazine often mentioned the primal fear every new arrival felt—no convict, no matter his history, personality, or crimes, was exempt. There was simply no preparation for being caged.

Seated in the Records Office, Whitey obediently faced another round of questions, all part of being processed into the institution. His criminal records and his sentencing information were put into his "jacket." His fingerprints were taken, his hair was cut, and he was ordered to remove his clothes, which were put in a box. Then it was bend over, straighten up, and take a shower. He was given a physical: his height was five feet ten and weight was 149 pounds. Noted in his medical report were marks on the fist he led with when fighting: "several small scars on knuckles of right hand." The medical form also noted he was missing some teeth, and it concluded that Whitey was in "general good health" and ready for "regular duty."

Whitey was ordered to get dressed in a loose-fitting pair of coveralls, and a photograph was taken to insert into his jacket. The mug shot showed Whitey, his hair closely cropped, unsmiling. It seemed he was trying to project a glare. But the result looked more vacant than tough. And with the crew cut he seemed so young. In all, Whitey looked more like a shell-shocked teen than a hardened criminal.

9

"I'm No Angel, But . . ."

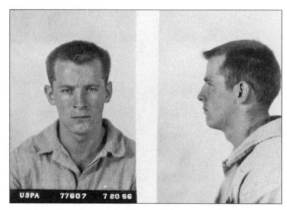

Atlanta: 1956

Whitey's arrival at the Atlanta Penitentiary marked the end to nearly four weeks in limbo that followed his June 21, 1956, sentencing in Boston. From the Suffolk County Jail, the U.S. Marshals Service had transported him to the federal detention center on West Street in New York City to await word on his prison assignment. He arrived in New York City on July 2 with only the clothes on his back, pretty much literally—a blue-striped shirt, black socks, brown shoes, and a pair of gray slacks covering his white Jockey briefs, according to an inventory taken when he was processed. Except for the $2.42 in his pocket, he had brought no personal property. No hairbrush, no toothbrush, no toothpaste, no razor or shaving cream—those items were issued to him, along with rosary beads. Whitey had paperwork to fill out that first day. One form required him to name a person to notify in the event of his death. Whitey listed his mother only. He was given a mail form to fill out listing "authorized correspondents," and he put two names down: his mother and "Miss J. McAuliffe," whom he described as "friend."

Within a few days, Whitey requested that he be allowed to add two names to the list. One was his brother Bill, of 41 Logan Way, South Boston, a student at Boston College. The second was a name that was recognizable: Rev. Robert F. Drinan, a Jesuit priest and the newly named dean of the Boston College Law School. "This is a close friend I'd like to write to," Whitey said about a man who later became the first Catholic priest to serve in Congress, elected as a Democrat in 1970. Whitey began writing to all of them, letters being a lifeline for any prisoner. Still no mention, though, of his father on the mail list.

After Whitey got word of his prison designation on July 16 and three days later arrived at the sprawling, twenty-eight-acre penitentiary compound, he did not immediately enter the general population. Every prisoner spent the first thirty days in quarantine, which one inmate at Atlanta described as "30 days of basic training for the long years ahead." Inmates called the separate area holding new inmates "the fish tank," and as one inmate said of new arrivals: "You are a fish, a little fish, and there are sharks waiting to gulp you into their stinking gullets."

The official version was less foreboding: quarantine was a chance for a new inmate to get acclimated to prison life, the daily routines, the loss of privacy—as well as the noise. In his first days, Whitey, like any inmate, became acutely aware of the clang of steel doors, the calls of bugles, and the inmate yelling that filled the halls. It seemed someone was always yelling—a constant thrum that any inmate would want to escape except for the fact there was no place to go. "You have to face it and be within it; it's all part of this," wrote an inmate who went on to infer as any psychologist would the reason for the incessant outbursts: "You hear the yelling at the checker games, the card games, all of the day room 'social activities' are permeated and generated by yelling. You think that the yelling is a cover-up for the individual feelings of being nothing but a number in a world of numbers."

Whitey was no different in this world of numbers: he became 77607.

In quarantine Whitey spent part of his time trying to straighten out the issue of just whom he could correspond with. Just as he had while in New York City, Whitey wanted to continue writing Jacquie McAuliffe, Rev. Drinan, his brother Bill, and his mother, and so the prison initiated background checks. On August 13, a Boston police detective drove to the law school in the city's Brighton neighborhood, where he met with the school's dean. Drinan, according to prison records, told the detective that he was "a friend of the Bulger family" and that he "would be pleased to correspond" with Whitey. Drinan said that the two had in fact already exchanged letters while Whitey was awaiting his prison assignment. In the years to come, Drinan was a congressman, anti–Vietnam War protester, and internationally known human rights activist, but for reasons that remain a mystery he always kept his ties to Whitey Bulger a virtual secret. Drinan never mentioned the relationship in any of his own writings, and nothing about it appears in the full-length biography written after Drinan's death in 2007. None of their correspondence was preserved in the Robert F. Drinan Papers at the Boston College Library's Congressional Archives Collection. Yet Drinan was there for Whitey during his prison years as an impressive reference, with the only known record of their connection buried in Whitey's prison files.

For her part, Jacquie McAuliffe on August 6 dutifully filled out a form the prison had sent to her confirming that she'd like to write Whitey. She wrote that she worked as a hairdresser, was twenty-nine, had met Whitey in South Boston and known him for three years, and was his "friend." She did not mention her broken marriage to ironworker Gerald Martin. Separately, the Boston Police Department on August 9 sent the prison the results of its look at Jacquie. The one-page letter noted that she had been arrested with Whitey "for vagrancy in Miami, Florida, 12–3–55." Other than that, they had little on her. "Miss McAuliffe enjoys a good reputation in her home community," and Boston police saw no reason why she should not be allowed to correspond with Whitey.

But Whitey next learned that rules for mail while in quarantine were more restrictive than detention in New York. Until he entered the general prison population, Whitey could write to only two people, and they had to be close relatives. Special permission was needed to write to anyone else, permission granted "only on the basis of special circumstances of merit." This threw Whitey, and he quickly drafted a memo to the mail officer saying that in addition to a close relative, his brother Bill, he also wanted to correspond with Jacquie. He presented his case for a rule exception, amplifying the bond between him and Jacquie to a level higher than ever before: "Jacqueline McAuliffe and I were about to be married," Whitey wrote. "She works in a hairdresser's shoppe and lives with her aunt and uncle. She was approved to visit me by the U.S. Marshals Office while I was awaiting trial in Boston. We would very much appreciate the privilege of writing each other."

Whitey was either unaware of Jacquie's marriage or, more likely, was attempting to scam officials. In the mailroom, a line was drawn crossing out Jacquie McAuliffe's name and Boston address, indicating that Whitey's request was denied and he would have to wait until his quarantine was over to hear from Jacquie again.

It all had to be unnerving—the stupefying newness of the Atlanta prison, being cut off from Jacquie, with brother Bill his only lifeline. Making matters worse was the stress of an altogether new crisis that erupted out of nowhere and was unlike anything any new inmate in quarantine typically faced.

In mid-August, FBI agents from Indiana showed up at the Atlanta prison to question Whitey. They said he was a suspect in a murder—that during the time he was in Indiana to rob a bank he had killed a man and dumped the corpse in a lake. In short order, Whitey found himself at the center of a major murder investigation, one where police in Indiana had taken boats out onto a lake not far from Hammond, dragging the waters for a body; small planes had gone on a flyover mission of a forested area looking for evidence; and FBI agents in Boston had even questioned Jacquie McAuliffe. The FBI told Whitey they'd learned about the murder from one of his former partners.

Whitey was flummoxed. He had done plenty—beat men up, assaulted women, tailgated trucks, stolen cars, and robbed banks while waving a pistol or two. But murder? Not yet. The way he saw it, he was in prison because Carl Smith had ratted on him. That was bad enough. But a bogus murder claim took betrayal to a whole new dimension. Now he was being framed, and even though he was innocent, would anyone believe him? The whole thing was enough to run Whitey's prison worries to paranoia.

The betrayer in this instance was Richard Barchard, his partner in the Hammond bank holdup. For Barchard, making the accusation that Whitey had killed a man in Indiana was part payback for Whitey ratting on him. But it was also Barchard's Hail Mary attempt to escape a bad situation in prison. Following his sentencing in San Francisco in

June 1956, Barchard was taken to Alcatraz to begin a twenty-year term. Almost immediately he got into what he later described as a "vicious fight in the prison yard." He was put in isolation, known as the hole, "with the prospect of at least a one year stay." Desperate to find a way out, he said he "concocted a wild story of murder." Making up a fictitious name for the victim, he told FBI agents about "a dramatic fight, murder and disposal of the body in a lake." He was thinking that making up a murder and tying Whitey to it would get him out of Alcatraz, into the hands of Indiana prosecutors, and, ultimately, into a prison closer to home. "I did not entertain such high hopes that [my] confessing to a serious, non-existent crime would be the road to freedom. My hope was that upon transfer to the State for trial and after a lengthy trial and exposure of the big lie, [I] might be transferred to the nearby Federal Penitentiary in Terre Haute, Indiana."

Barchard retracted the whole thing a few years later, but for Whitey Bulger in August 1956 the false accusation was the equivalent of a powerful low blow that left him staggered and struggling to stay on his feet. Once the FBI agents had left, Whitey sought counsel; he filled out a prison form on August 11 asking to meet with a staff parole officer named Mr. Boone to discuss a "personal problem." He immediately wrote his brother Bill about the FBI's visit, but the letter was intercepted. Parole officer Boone returned Whitey's letter and explained that the prison barred "discussion of criminal matters in such correspondence—that letter would only worry his family and there appears no point in getting excited about it if it is not true."

Whitey was off to a bad start. His "fiancée" was off-limits, as was Bill if the topic was the Indiana murder investigation. Haunted by this, he continued his days in quarantine, where he and a wave of other new inmates were mostly kept away from the general population. But Whitey got glimpses. Quarantined prisoners ate as a group in the giant mess hall, filled with about fifteen hundred prisoners. The experience was more nerve-racking proof of life turning upside down. "You become a specimen segregated into a section of the mess hall for 3,000 eyes to pick at and examine," one of Whitey's fellow inmates wrote about mealtime.

The staring—and stare-down—had begun. Whitey and every new inmate, according to the demands of prison culture, would need to develop a look—or mask—all his own. "You create a face that you hope will look tough and indifferent," Whitey's cohort wrote, "and you make a discovery. When you stare at one of them he drops his eyes or looks away. Now, you have a weapon with which to fight.

"The stares don't bother you any more. Now, you can eat. Now, you don't dread the trips to the mess hall. Now, you can face the crowd with your face in the crowd. You have learned one of the many lessons in the course called The Art of Doing Time."

It was surely a course in which Whitey was going to excel. One reason was a head start that gave him advanced placement. He grew up known for a cold glare that first began to solidify in the company of a distant father, who was unable to dole out love but who was quick-triggered when it came to meting out disapproval. That mistrust had deepened more recently when putative comrades turned against him, and now were trying to frame him. Through his eyes he saw a world full of betrayal, justifying a fuller hardening of any feelings of humanity.

Furthermore, there was the life decree that had become his, where any conventional semblance of right and wrong, of lawfulness and morality, was discarded in the name of survival. That was the game, on the outside and now inside prison: survival. He would make it so he could put on a number of different masks—play whatever role was necessary—to satisfy the Whitey gospel of self-preservation at any cost.

Within the prison population, then, if "the stare" was the mask necessary to survive, Whitey learned quickly. In the years to come the Whitey glare was only going to get better, more refined and scarier. It would take time because he was off to such a rocky start, and his prison stay would worsen before stabilizing, but the end result was a mask that would become his brand: a cold, dark look into the abyss.

Quarantine was also the time when prison administrators prepared an official "Classification Study" for each new inmate, a document covering the inmate's past and his hopes for time behind bars. Whitey's ran more than ten pages and, right there on the first page, officials made prominent note of the new, unsettled matter of the Indiana investigation. It was listed in the "Detainers" column, which codified in his jacket the ongoing legal interest Indiana authorities had in him. "PENDING," the typed detainer entry said, "State of Indiana for Murder." Deeper in the report, Whitey's anxiety was noted. "He appears deeply concerned," it said, "and such a warrant in all probability will affect his adjustment here."

The report also sorted out Whitey's official list of "relatives and interested persons," which would be activated once Whitey completed quarantine. His mother, brother Bill, and older sister, Jean, were listed as approved in the double capacity as "visitor" and "correspondent." For the first time on any contact list, Whitey included his father's name to the "visitors" category, joining his younger brother Jackie and sisters Carol and Sheila. From the quarantine list he carried over Rev. Robert Drinan and Jacquie McAuliffe as future correspondents.

The "Classification Study" included the fruits of several "social interviews" its preparer conducted with Whitey, which became the basis for a section titled "Inmates Version of Present Offenses." Whitey was given the floor to explain how he'd gotten into so much trouble, and he began by saying he was first introduced to Carl Smith in 1955 through an unnamed mutual acquaintance, an ex-convict. Whitey then said that he and Smith had gotten their start together by actually robbing a bank in what was not one of the holdups for which he'd been convicted. There was this other bank first—a job, he pointed out, that had been entirely Smith's idea. Whitey said he'd naïvely agreed to "drive for Smith on some deal he did not know much about." While en route he learned that the "deal" involved a bank holdup. Whitey had never done that before and he "wanted to back out but did not want them to know he was afraid." He said that "he became even more afraid when he learned he had to go into the bank." Even so, he ended up going inside and participating in the holdup. "The bank robbery was successful," he added. But that first one marked a beginning, not an end, to the story. "Afterwards he was in on three more bank robberies."

In his account of the fast and furious ride as a bank robber, the older Carl Smith had been the big problem, a real troublemaker. Whitey was basically saying he was duped into committing the first holdup— and then there was no turning back. The version, of course, contrasted sharply with reality. Instead of the documented bravado and swank that characterized his Hollywood gangster-styled robberies, Whitey's self-portrait for the "Classification Study" was that of a reluctant robber who, giving in to peer pressure, was too afraid to say no. He was saying, in effect, that none of it was really his fault; they made him do it.

The unwilling patsy reflected in the study was not the Whitey most would recognize. It was as if in the interview Whitey was already working up a new face—that of an agreeable inmate, respectful and saying the right things. Further into the interview, he brought up that he was Catholic, had attended church occasionally, and "plans to attend services here." He discussed the importance of family to him and emphasized his love of books. "Bulger said that he read a lot of historical fiction, history, biography and poetry," noted the report, and that "he expressed the desire to obtain additional educational and vocational materials to read and study."

For the Classification Committee Whitey was striking a pose the polar opposite to the one projected in the tough-guy glare. He was smart enough to understand that to accelerate the slow time that was prison, to get to parole consideration, and, hopefully, to be free again, he had to strike a note of humility and hard work. He had to manufacture a face for certain people to see, a mask that would seduce people into thinking he was the good bad guy.

The committee was impressed by Whitey's words but did not fall for them. Instead, its recommendations incorporated the do-good Whitey while never losing sight of the truer Whitey. The new inmate's interest in reading and learning was cited as a positive that should be encouraged and supported. "Recommendation: continue present reading habits," the study noted in the to-do list drawn up on August 23 for Whitey. "Inmate does have considerable ability and several work assignments were discussed, hoping that the right one would assist in his adjustment." The committee decided to assign Whitey to the prison's Education Department, "where he may work into a clerical job or learn to operate certain types of machines, depending upon his interest and abilities." The committee was also favorably impressed that "this man has close family ties and there are other persons in the community who have shown some interest in his welfare," which, though unnamed, was a clear reference to Drinan.

But this was a committee that had seen it all, and when it came to Whitey they noted that "he seems to be aggressive and present attitude is questionable." The Indiana murder investigation gave committee members pause. "This man wrote an anxious letter to his brother [Bill] about this charge but it was difficult to tell whether he was bragging or complaining about the charge." Notwithstanding that Whitey "denies his guilt," the committee's bottom line was this: Whitey was potential trouble. He should be kept under close supervision, or what was known as "close custody," on account of his "length of sentence, nature of offense, and pending case on a murder charge."

Classification completed, Whitey was moved into the general prison population. Now wearing the plain blue shirt and pants that was standard issue for every inmate, he began where every inmate did—assigned to one of Atlanta's eight-man cells. He was placed into "B" Cell House, located behind the prison's administration building. The several levels of eight-man cells were stacked in tiers. Whitey took an empty bunk in a cell holding seven other men from different parts of the country, with different personalities and serving sentences for different crimes. They had to find a way to share the enclosed rectangular space that served as a bedroom, living room, den, and bathroom—a sink on one wall with an open toilet.

Whitey and his fellow inmates spent fourteen or more hours a day together in the cell. They got out for about eight hours to work, and then another hour or so for recreation, which was called "stockade time." But most of their day was spent caged in close quarters, where they engaged in any number of possible diversions—playing cards, writing home, "bull sessions," working on "home-study" courses, listening to the radio (earphones were provided each inmate to plug into selected broadcasts piped throughout the prison), reading—and, of course, yelling. The eight-man, a fellow inmate once wrote, was "too small for privacy and too large for sanity." The way inmates saw it, the long hours confined to the eight-man cell hewed to a clocked schedule consisting of sleep, the period between meals, the few minutes before a favorite radio program, the endless simmering animosity of petty arguments, the period before mail was delivered in the evening, and the period after the mail was delivered. "The mail room can make or break a day," an inmate wrote. The one constant during and between all the segments in a weekday, wrote the inmate, was "much talk and little silence." The weekends might be different, "a chance now and then for rest and sleep during the day until some man starts ranting and raving about a program he doesn't like on the radio or someone starts arguing over a ball game or someone else starts plunking on a guitar.

"Utter chaos," the inmate wrote.

Whitey turned twenty-seven on September 3, 1956, around the time he was moved into his new cell. He wrote his letters, enrolled in a typing course, and read. The available reading material included the prison magazine that inmates published. Titled the *Atlantian,* the quarterly was a standout in the prison lit genre. Many of the nation's prisons did not even have an inmate publication, and of those that did, "Atlanta Sets the Standard," according to the *Christian Science Monitor*'s review. While there was no coverage of any illicit or disciplinary activities, the magazine included fiction and poetry, tackled such subjects as coping in prison, ran advice columns, and published photo-illustrated features about the hospital, library, the prison farm, and every possible club and activity. The sports coverage was extensive—of the segregated baseball and basketball teams, of tennis and softball—and the year Whitey entered the Atlanta Penitentiary boxing returned as an organized sport after a twenty-year ban. Readers of the magazine saw that one of Whitey's partners in the Rhode Island bank holdup was making a name for himself. Ron Dermody, who had arrived before Whitey, had a regular sports column called "The Inside Track," which featured a smiling head shot atop the page.

Flipping through the new fall issue, Whitey would have read about a couple of medical research projects under way at the prison, where inmates who volunteered earned extra good time and extra money for their commissary accounts. Two inmates wrote first-person accounts of their roles in them. In one, an inmate described taking Novocain and a muscle relaxant called Anectine as one of nine volunteer subjects. "It started in my shoulders, and it felt like a million bugs crawling over me," he wrote of his reaction to the drug doctors administered to him. "Then it dropped below my waist: when it hit my right leg I could feel the muscles in it knotting, and I thought that I was going to die." The experience was frightening, he wrote, but was part of the cutting-edge, "newest field of anesthesia" and represented once again "a doctor and a convict teaming up—for humanity."

The second article was by inmate Winfield Burdette, a staff photographer for the prison magazine who would go on to get assignments from *Life* magazine for a series examining America's prisons. Burdette was one of about twenty inmate volunteers taking lysergic acid diethylamide—LSD—once a week under the auspices of doctors from nearby Emory University who were searching "for knowledge about schizophrenia, the mental disease that fills one-quarter of the nation's hospital beds." The LSD, according to the Emory doctors, induced "near schizophrenia" in inmates who were then tested for possible cures. Burdette's article took the reader through one of his LSD trips, which included a stretch of hallucinations when "objects became distorted. Everyone took on a ghostly pallor, resembling skeletons. I seemed to have X-ray vision that could see through everyone to their bones."

The LSD Project did indeed catch Whitey's interest, and the matter was one he would return to at a later date. But the fact was that in early fall he had enough on his hands struggling to get acclimated. Between paranoia about a murder charge and the stress of the eight-man cell, he was not cutting it. While allowed two visits during the first year of incarceration, he'd had none so far. Indeed, the first visit would not happen until spring 1957, when his younger brother Jackie came. Whitey was alone. He tried to keep his head down and do the right thing. He worked his job, followed the rules, had avoided any sort of reprimand those first few weeks he'd spent in the general population, and he went to chapel on Sundays. But the eight-man was driving him nuts. No record exists identifying Whitey's cell mates at the beginning of his sentence, their backgrounds and personalities. But Whitey did not click with them. "I had hoped to adapt myself to it," Whitey wrote in a letter that fall about his conditions. But the talk and noise, the "utter chaos" that other inmates said defined life in an eight-man, was in his face now and Whitey could not take it. He was too exposed, too vulnerable and unable to control his surroundings.

"I have tried my best to read in the cell but can't do it because of the distraction," he continued in the letter, an account in which he sounded like a prison prude. "The majority of men are doing short sentences and quite a few are repeaters," he said. "Most of these men are just killing time and there is a continual idle chatter on sex, cars, money etc. To go with this is the continual game of cards, dominoes or checkers."

He had tried to cope. He told them to quiet down, but that only led to what he called "hard feelings." He considered reporting his cell mates to the guards, but ruled that option out. "If I complain it would only end up in a fight and then isolation with no reading, mail, etc." One form he did fill out was to request a move to a single cell, "and the answer was: your name has been put on a list but there will be a two or three year wait." Then he let some days pass and tried again: "I wrote again and explained and asked them to make an exception, but got no answer."

By October, after less than two months in the eight-man cell, Whitey was cracking. "I tried to put up with it and said nothing and kept holding everything in." Pressure built, and he had no outlet like he did back home, when his release was to explode. He understood that kind of response in prison would only set him back before he even got started. Then, on Wednesday, October 24, he decided he had to do something. He asked to speak to a prison parole officer. He explained to the officer about his troubles in the eight-man. "He said he was sorry but couldn't help me," Whitey wrote later. It was not the response Whitey was looking for, and he suddenly felt he could no longer contain himself. "If any one of them bother me any more I wasn't going to hold back anything," he said in a letter.

He needed desperately to get out of the eight-man, and by the end of that day he was out—but not into a new cell with fewer prisoners. Whitey checked himself into the prison's Neuro-Psychiatric Ward, where he told the treating psychiatrist that his "nerves were all shot." In his paperwork, the prison psychiatrist wrote that he was admitting the inmate onto the ward "because of strong complaints of his inability to serve a long sentence in a cell with several other men."

Whitey had been reduced to a puddle of his former self.

On his second day in the ward, Whitey put pen to paper and wrote to Rev. Drinan. "At present I'm in the Psych Ward," he said, a matter-of-fact start to a letter that quickly developed into a cry for help. "I am in a mixed up position and ask you to give me any assistance you can."

Whitey described his crisis—how the noise of the eight-man cell and its constant distractions interfered with his plans for self-improvement. "I can only help myself by an education and forming good habits and a sensible outlook on life," he said. He described the feelings of anguish and misery in the crowded cell that worsened until out of desperation he checked himself into the psych ward.

The change was hardly paradise, he continued, but it beat what he'd fled. "I dislike the present situation," he wrote, but "it's a shade better than the 8-man cell." Even so, it was already beginning to feel as if he'd traded one bad situation for another. "I'm in a single cell and kept in it 24 hours a day," he noted. "From here the Dr. is putting me in A.W.B. [a high-security cell]. It's complete isolation. This is their answer and their solution to my problem." Whitey was worried.

"I am no angel," Whitey wrote, the only concession in the 594-word, single-spaced missive that he was anything less than a model citizen, "but as you know I've got a twenty year sentence and I know if I don't help myself and put this time to good use I will have no future."

And that's when he got to his main point: Help me get out of here.

"Would you please see if I have any legal right to a Penit. transfer, any legal rights at all."

The problem for Whitey was that Drinan never saw a letter that read like the ode of a good bad guy. It never left the prison. Not only that, but Whitey was brought before the Special Interview Board, which informed him that his letter had been "disapproved for delivery" because its contents were not social. He was issued a written warning: "Inmate was cautioned as to the effects of a violation of the mailing regulations on his privileges."

The letter was then placed into Whitey's jacket, where it stayed for more than half a century.

10

Acid Head: 1957

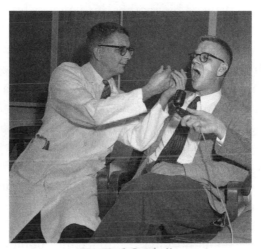

Dr. Carl C. Pfeiffer

Whitey's epistolary plea to Rev. Drinan in October 1956 may have gone undelivered, but when Whitey was released from the psych ward he did get one thing he wanted—a move to a different cell. He underwent a couple of days of "treatment" (not specified in his prison file) while on the ward, to which he had a "favorable response." He met with an associate warden and told him, "I can't make it in the quarters I'm in now. I have to be by myself. These guys in the cell get on my nerves." The warden's ruling was then noted: "Given a cell change."

Even so, Whitey came out fighting from the psych ward. He was standing in the bath line on Saturday morning, January 12, 1957, when another inmate needled him. Whitey went after him, no more Mr. Nice Guy. The fight was so fierce that three guards were required to pull the two apart. Both men were immediately taken to the Segregation Unit. Two days later Whitey told a three-person disciplinary panel, which included an assistant warden, that the other inmate had "made some remarks toward him." The panel's one-page report did not specify what was said, but for Whitey they were fighting words. Taunted, Whitey "grabbed him" and fists flew. For the infraction, Whitey was sent back for eight more days of "punitive segregation." In addition, his privileges were restricted for a month and he lost ten days of "statutory good time" in the ongoing calculation of a prison term's length. Whitey paid a stiff price for a few punches and would have to learn to dampen his rage.

He tried settling down a bit. He wrote to his family regularly; his main correspondents were his mother, his younger brother Bill, and Jacquie McAuliffe. For his first Christmas in December 1956, and for the next several, Bill Bulger sent him books. Whitey's reading interests grew, ranging from history to the classics, including a biography of Al Smith, the former governor of New York and the first Catholic to run for president, Evelyn Waugh's *Brideshead Revisited,* and Boris Pasternak's *Dr. Zhivago.* He wrote to Bill that he "had a dormant desire for literature that was shocked into awareness with the start of imprisonment." Later, he told his brother in a letter that W. Somerset Maugham had become his favorite author. As with any inmate, reading passed the time and provided a distraction from all the roiling emotions that came with being locked up. In one letter, for example, Whitey had shared that talking about Boston left him feeling "homesick."

In his memoir Bill Bulger wrote only briefly—not even a page—about Whitey's nine years in prison, and his main point was admiration for his brother's toughness. Bill wrote that Whitey "was no more docile in prison than out." He said when he asked Whitey whether other prisoners caused any trouble for him, Whitey replied, "Nothing I couldn't handle." He also said Whitey had little use for the guards, once telling Bill, "You have to score very high on the stupidity test to be a guard in this place." The morsels created the persona of Whitey as a man in full control and they gave no hint of Whitey's vulnerability and struggles.

Bill Bulger's scant coverage also left out a major fact: his brother had a benefit most inmates did not—powerful allies—and by early 1957 there was evidence of a second ally to add to the law school dean. The Bulger family had engaged the interest of their congressman and South Boston neighbor—John W. McCormack, the House Democratic majority leader. That the Bulgers could turn to such a powerful national figure for "constituent services" gave new meaning to the luck of the Irish, and they weren't about to eschew the connection with the Southie-born politician, now sixty-five years old and known in Washington as "the Leader." Beginning in March 1957, Bill Bulger regularly turned to McCormack for help. Even though much of the nation's business was on McCormack's mind—he and other Democratic leaders were busy finding their footing with Republican president Dwight Eisenhower after Ike's landslide victory in the fall—he nonetheless looked after Whitey. It was what McCormack was admired for—responding to the worries of his neighbors, especially when a savvy, motivated constituent like Bill Bulger was the one lobbying him. For the Bulgers, McCormack's first favor was a simple one: McCormack alerted the Bureau of Prisons director—the top official of the nation's federal prison system—that Whitey's youngest brother, John, or "Jackie," was planning to visit Whitey.

The director, James V. Bennett, certainly took it seriously; he, in turn, immediately sent a telegram to the prison warden: "We understand from Congressman McCormack's office that John Bulger of Boston will be in Atlanta next Tuesday and will contact you regarding a visit with his brother James J. Bulger Jr." Routine visits from relatives hardly required the intervention of national power brokers. But more than a courtesy heads-up was likely in play. The McCormack contact served as a message to the prison bureau's hierarchy, from the top down: one of the most powerful political figures in the country had a personal interest in a particular inmate serving a twenty-year term in Atlanta.

Jackie Bulger's visit on March 5 was Whitey's first from a family member in the nearly seven months he'd been at Atlanta, and the welcome contact was soon followed by visits from other family friends and relatives. In April, Mr. and Mrs. Thomas J. Clifford, neighbors in the Old Harbor housing project who lived on O'Callaghan Way, were traveling to Kentucky to visit a daughter, a nun, and to Ohio to see their son, a seminarian. "We have been close friends of the Bulger family for many years and have known James Bulger since he was an infant," they wrote to the warden. The couple was granted permission to see Whitey, and they visited him in early May 1957.

Bill Bulger wrote the warden on June 13 asking for advice about a first visit he was planning. Explaining he would be able to travel from Boston to Atlanta only once a year, "I would appreciate any information or advice you might offer that would enable me to make the most of my stay there." For example, he asked that if he showed up at the end of July, could he draw on Whitey's unused visits from June and July as a way to double the time he spent with his brother? Whitey, he wrote, "has had only two visits since his term began." But Bill Bulger's creative proposal got him nowhere. He was notified that he could see his brother in July. No mention was made about extra visiting hours; instead, the note Bill Bulger got in reply read: "Enclosed is a copy of our Visiting Regulations for your use and information."

Whitey, meanwhile, alternated between his tough-guy, good-guy personas. He was never able to get out from under the strict classification requiring "close custody," but he made positive strides establishing a rapport with a prison chaplain, Father John J. O'Shea. The two would meet and talk, and they hit it off. Eventually O'Shea got to meet one of Whitey's sisters as well as brother Bill, and the family impressed him. O'Shea wrote a letter to prison officials that became a part of Whitey's prison file—a character reference of sorts—in which he noted that Whitey "still has close ties with the family and is especially close to his brother Bill. I have hoped that his high regard for the family would some day bring him back to a sound, wholesome life." The priest made it clear he was not under any illusions. "I am not laboring under any false impression that he was St. Aloysius or an altar boy type on the outside because I know he was a tough little nut in the free world." But the priest had become a supporter full of hope. Whitey "does have some good points," O'Shea wrote. "I feel confident that with God's help he can straighten up."

Whitey seemed able to move out from under the cloud of suspicion that had haunted his entry into the prison the previous August—the Indiana murder probe. While the investigation continued to be noted in his prison paperwork, it had fizzled into inactivity. No more unwanted visits from the FBI or Indiana investigators. It would take a few more years before Whitey's worry ended entirely, when Richard Barchard finally admitted the murder was a hoax, but the fact that he was no longer facing questions was a relief for Whitey in the spring of 1957.

Springtime also marked the start of a long good-bye to the woman he'd declared he was planning to marry but for his arrest. Whitey and Jacquie McAuliffe wrote to each other that first year, but she never visited him. In March one letter arrived with a cover note written by her aunt. It notified prison officials that Jacquie was unable to send a letter herself. "Dear sir," the aunt began, "I am writing this enclosed letter to James J. Bulger for a dear friend of his Jacqueline McAuliffe. She is quite ill in the hospital and unable to do it herself. I am her aunt with whom she lives and she asked me to write and tell him how she is progressing." Jacquie's illness went unspecified, and she did recover, but in the months to come the letters became more infrequent and, eventually, her name was dropped from Whitey's approved list of correspondents. While she faded from Whitey's life, Jacquie McAuliffe was his first significant girlfriend and companion and in many respects became a prototype for his future significant others: beautiful, usually blond, travel-sturdy, and, most important, loyal and obedient. Jacquie remained in the Boston area in the years to come, employed for twenty-five years at the Massachusetts Department of Revenue. She never divorced Gerald Martin, though, and she died suddenly at Cape Cod Hospital on December 11, 2010. She was eighty-three years old.

True to his word in letters to Drinan and others, Whitey in 1957 began in earnest a program of self-improvement. He completed a typing course he started in September, enrolled in five correspondence courses, and was borrowing books and magazines from the library, as well as subscribing to the national Catholic weekly magazine *America*. While he was not a "joiner" or team player—he never played on any of the prison sports teams or became a member of the various prison clubs or activity groups—Whitey was a regular spectator at sporting contests.

In early July 1957 his job was shifted to the prison hospital, where he worked as a physiotherapy technician, meaning he assisted patients needing physical therapy. He liked the job, stuck with it for a couple of years, and drew positive reviews from officials. "He demonstrates cooperative work habits and a cheerful personality," an annual progress report noted. "His efficiency is good, he is an energetic worker and quick to learn. He has earned a Meritorious Award."

It was the new job that gave Whitey an up-close look at the LSD Project, now nearly two years old, held on Tuesdays and Thursdays in the basement of the prison hospital. Word about the project had already spread publicly beyond the walls of the prison. The *Atlanta Journal-Constitution* had run a feature story about the experiments under the headline DRUG-FED PRISONERS AID STUDY, along with a photograph showing one of the doctors interviewing an inmate volunteer. The article began: "Sixteen prisoners at the Atlanta Penitentiary are helping medical researchers study mental diseases by voluntarily taking a potent drug that induces symptoms of schizophrenia." The newspaper interviewed the lead doctor, Carl C. Pfeiffer of Emory University, and quoted from a colorful account of one inmate's LSD trip. The newspaper did not identify the inmate, but Whitey and other prisoners easily could have recognized him as Winfield Burdette. The newspaper, without credit, had lifted the description of an LSD trip that Burdette had written for the *Atlantian,* the inmate publication. In other press coverage, a national magazine called *Man's Magazine,* in an issue that included such articles as "Ted Williams—Heel or Hero" and "Virgins: Would You Marry One?," ran a cover story titled "I Went Insane for Science!" The author was a doctor writing anonymously about his experimental LSD trip, and the article included mention of Pfeiffer's work in Atlanta.

Whitey met with Pfeiffer and Pfeiffer's associates just a few weeks after he started working in the hospital in July. He underwent a screening process overseen by Laurence L. Bryan, the prison psychologist who had admitted Whitey to the psych ward the previous October. Inmates called him "the nut doctor." Dr. Bryan interviewed Whitey and administered "psychometric tests," which included a Rorschach test, designed to confirm a volunteer was "normal." Doctors involved in the LSD Project, when writing or talking about the inmates, meant "normal" in quotation marks, because none of them was that. The lead doctor was quoted saying inmate volunteers had all scored high in tests "for psychopathic tendencies." They were not normal, he said. "They were psychopaths."

The point of the psychological screening, then, was to ensure the inmate was stable and could withstand the project's regimen of LSD and other drugs. "Except for character disorders, no psychiatric abnormalities were present in these subjects," the doctor wrote in a journal article about the prison's LSD experiments.

Finally, to make it all seem legal and ethical, Whitey sat down on August 6, 1957, with one of Dr. Pfeiffer's associates and signed on the dotted line. It was a document of disclosure, explaining the benefits and risks, that Dr. Pfeiffer had created specifically for the LSD Project, and the one-page form bearing the signature of "James J. Bulger" carried a heading in capital letters: "CONTRACT BETWEEN DEPARTMENT OF PHARMACOLOGY, EMORY UNIVERSITY SCHOOL OF MEDICINE AND HUMAN VOLUNTEERS AT U.S. PENITENTIARY, ATLANTA, GEORGIA."

One morning two months later, after eating a light breakfast in the dining hall, Whitey was taken by a guard to the hospital, a building located on the west side of the prison compound, behind the B Cell House, where he'd been kept initially in the eight-man cell. With a prison population of more than 2,600, the size of many small towns across America, the hospital was fully operational. It had seventy-five beds and four full-time doctors assisted by eleven medical technicians. Prisoners staffed other positions, from clerk to head operating nurse. In any given year, 250 major and 750 minor surgical procedures were performed.

Whitey walked through the main floor and down into the basement to Ward F, or the Neuro-Psychiatric Ward, where a large room, secured with a steel door and steel bars, was set aside for the LSD Project. Whitey was a member of the Tuesday group of eight inmate volunteers checking in for a twenty-four-hour stay. He walked into the plain, sterile room with its eight beds and joined the others. By now Whitey knew the drill—he'd been part of the LSD Project for more than a month. He sat on the bed. The doctors always encouraged subjects to remain in bed for the duration. By 8:30 a.m., or about two hours after breakfast, Whitey took the LSD dosage prepared for him, drinking it in a glass of quinine-flavored liquid. The drug was odorless and colorless. Then he waited. Would this be what the doctors called a "trivial dose," meaning 25 micrograms, or something stronger? In his first month he'd been given increasingly stronger doses of the psychedelic drug so that he could, as one doctor wrote, "become fully familiar with the effects of the drug both qualitatively and quantitatively. The first dosage was 25 micrograms, the second 50, then 75, and finally 100. Whitey would know in about an hour the strength of the dose after the symptoms began to manifest, when the LSD began working on his brain and causing havoc in the interaction between his nerve cells and the neurotransmitter serotonin. In the human body it is the serotonin system that acts as a kind of control tower for behavior, perceptions, and moods.

The first sign Whitey was on his way was a sensation that the lights were alternately dimming and brightening, as if someone were playing with the power supply. In fact, the lights were constant but his pupils were dilating, changing in diameter and affecting his light perception. To help him pin down the power of the trip, Dr. Pfeiffer or an associate would soon come by to ask a series of twenty-eight questions. Certain questions addressed symptoms evident from taking a low dose. (Does the light bother you? Do you feel fatigued?) Others addressed symptoms seen only with higher dosages. (Are things moving around you? Do you feel as if in a dream?) Whitey would know the dose was on the stronger side if, when he closed his eyes, he saw an array of geometric patterns accompanied by a kaleidoscope of colors.

Letting go could not have come easily. Whitey Bulger had always felt most secure when in control. But prison had changed all that; he'd lost nearly every measure of control—the eight-man cell being one ever-present reminder. Hallucinating on LSD meant losing even more. "For someone who has a tremendous need for security through control, this could lead to a tremendous sense of anxiety," Dr. John H. Halpern, a psychiatrist at McLean Hospital in Massachusetts, commented later about the combustible mix of Whitey Bulger and LSD.

It was October 8, 1957, when Whitey began this particular round of the drug. The date was exactly one week after America began sending B-52 bombers loaded with nuclear weapons airborne around the clock in case of a Soviet attack. And it was only four days after the Soviet Union shocked America with its successful launch of the Sputnik satellite. The focus of the world was on the Cold War and Russia's ride into space—while Whitey was lying on a bed in Ward F bracing himself for a different kind of trip, featuring tangerine trees and marmalade skies.

The project's lead doctor, Carl C. Pfeiffer, had forged a clinical research partnership with the Atlanta Penitentiary after he had joined the faculty at Emory in 1954 at age forty-six, as chair of the medical school's pharmacology department. He came to Emory from the University of Illinois in Chicago, where he had also served as chair of that university's pharmacology department. Illinois was where he first began experimenting with LSD, which doctors at several other universities, including Harvard, had also begun using in their research into schizophrenia.

Pfeiffer was a champion of LSD. He gave interviews about the LSD clinical study, was quoted regularly in the mainstream media in stories about LSD work, and coauthored a number of medical journal articles. He made no secret of his own use of the drug. He first took LSD in 1949 while still at Illinois, and then went on to trip sixteen more times for what he described as "scientific purposes." The LSD, he discovered, "was a profound brain stimulant, and most brain stimulants will produce some degree of abnormal psychotic behavior." While at Emory he literally became the face of LSD research. He agreed to trip on camera for a local Atlanta television station that was working on a piece about the prison's LSD Project. The camera rolled as an associate injected a dose of LSD into his mouth as he sat in a chair in a TV studio. The camera captured the crew-cut Pfeiffer, wearing a tie, white shirt, and jacket, falling under the effects of the hallucinogenic. He took a Rorschach inkblot test and grew animated and laughed hysterically during it. The segment was aired in November 1955 on the station's *Newsroom* show.

Pfeiffer displayed an almost playful attitude about the drug. When he approached the prison about starting a clinical study using inmates, the psychologist Bryan wanted to try LSD so he could describe a trip to prisoners. Pfeiffer said fine, but he had Bryan come to one of his classes at Emory to take 25 micrograms of the drug. Pfeiffer, Bryan recalled, "had me sit up in front of a class of sophomore medical students after he sprayed some LSD in my mouth." Bryan was on display as he began to hallucinate and the room began to move. "One student asked why I kept staring at the palms of my hand," Bryan said, "and I said, 'I'm doing it because I enjoy looking at the beautiful colors.' "

Another time Pfeiffer seemed flip in the way he wrote about LSD in the preface to a research paper that had the otherwise solemn title "Psychometric Agents: Neurophysiologic Effects." Wrote Pfeiffer: "Any scientist who can spare 8 hours from his busy life and who has a good friend to act as his keeper can enjoy the fascinating revelations of temporary insanity." He went on to herald the growing public interest in LSD as a veritable boon for their research. "Medical students, journalists, and television announcers clamor for the chance to be 'lysergized' in order to tell their friends and to sell to the world the stories of their trips to the brink of insanity," Pfeiffer said. "This 'brinkmanship,' this ubiquitous interest in insanity, may eventually prove to be a help in relieving the ever-growing burden of our present predominantly custodial care of the mentally ill."

But Pfeiffer also had a secret—a big secret he told no one at the Atlanta Penitentiary, nor Bryan or any other prison doctor. And certainly not Whitey or any of the inmate volunteers. The secret was the Central Intelligence Agency, and its hidden hand in his LSD work. Pfeiffer, who had top-security clearance from the government, had been a CIA partner going back to his days in Illinois in the 1940s.

Whitey was training as an aviation mechanic in the Midwest in 1949 when LSD had quietly made its debut in the United States in his native Boston. The city was home to some of the nation's leading mental health researchers and practitioners, working out of the Boston Psychopathic Hospital, which was affiliated with Harvard Medical School. The doctors had hosted a talk in 1949 by an internationally known Viennese doctor named Otto Kauders, who sang the praises of a new drug named d-lysergic acid diethylamide, or LSD, which a Swiss scientist had discovered by accident a few years earlier. Kauders had told his audience that LSD had the potential to blow open the doors in the scientific study of the human mind and mental illness. The Harvard doctors soon arranged to obtain LSD from a Swiss pharmaceutical company and began devising a clinical testing program.

The doctors at Harvard were not the only ones intrigued. Soon enough LSD caught the attention of the federal agency whose mission was the nation's security. The possibility of employing LSD as a weapon in the spy game fit right into the CIA's developing interest in drugs and in all possible ways to defeat the enemy by taking over their minds. The 1950s saw the launch of an espionage free-for-all, driven by the Cold War and atomic fear. The worry was that the Soviet Union, the People's Republic of China, and other communist-bloc countries were way ahead in chemical and biological weaponry. "It is awfully hard in this day and age to reproduce how frightening all of this was to us at the time," a CIA official testified decades later about conditions in 1950. "But we were literally terrified."

It was in 1949, when LSD first appeared in the United States, that Carl Pfeiffer had received a visitor in Chicago named Sidney Gottlieb. Gottlieb was head of the chemical division in the CIA's Office of Scientific Research, which, in lay terms, meant he was the maestro of the CIA's chemical warfare initiatives. The CIA had little interest in Pfeiffer's or any other researcher's medical goal of finding a cure for schizophrenia; it was interested in LSD as a covert spy weapon for use in the Cold War. "There were reports that two kilograms of LSD had been purchased by the Russians," Pfeiffer recalled later, "and so there was interest then in whether or not this could be a drug to cause hallucinations in whole populations of the earth."

The CIA worried that the Soviet Union was developing the capability to pollute the nation's water supply with LSD, triggering mass hallucinatory chaos, Pfeiffer said. The CIA's initial strategic interest, then, was a defensive one—to find an antidote in the event the Soviets employed LSD as a chemical weapon against the United States. In that way, the interest of the doctor and the CIA in finding an antidote to LSD was overlapping, although their motivations for doing so were not.

It did not take long, however, for the CIA to become offensive-minded. In early April 1953, CIA director Allen Dulles approved, at Gottlieb's urging, an expansion of the covert program to develop biological and chemical weapons. Its code name was MK-ULTRA, and the relatively new and still obscure LSD drug occupied center stage. Gottlieb and his tight, classified group of colleagues were enthralled by LSD's potency. "The most fascinating thing about it was that such minute quantities had such a terrific effect," one of Gottlieb's associates told the journalist John Marks in an interview for his 1979 book, *The Search for the "Manchurian Candidate": The CIA and Mind Control.* Gottlieb's group pondered a myriad of possible uses: Could LSD, for example, be used as a truth serum against a Soviet spy? Wrote Marks: "The MKULTRA team had literally hundreds of questions about LSD's physiological, psychological, chemical and social effects. Did it have any antidotes? What happened if it were combined with other drugs? Did it affect everyone the same way? What was the effect of doubling the dose? And so on."

Gottlieb, in a memorandum he wrote on June 9, 1953, or two months after Dulles gave him the green light, described his high hopes for LSD: "Emphasis will be placed in this coming year on translating the basic [LSD] data to date into operationally pertinent material along the following lines: a) disturbance of memory; b) discrediting by aberrant behavior; c) alteration of sex patterns; d) eliciting of information; e) suggestibility; f) creation of dependence." Gottlieb said he wanted to compile an LSD "operational field manual" for agents to use.

Just as the world was witness to a nuclear weapons race and a space race, a new chemical weapons race was covertly under way, driven by the CIA.

And Dr. Pfeiffer climbed on board. The CIA funded his work in Illinois and continued funding it after Pfeiffer moved to Emory and set up shop at the Atlanta Penitentiary. Pfeiffer got between $40,000 and $50,000 annually for "Subproject 47," as it was code-named, and money was laundered through a front—the Geschickter Fund for Medical Research—so that it appeared he was receiving backing from a philanthropic foundation.

Each year Pfeiffer submitted a budget request to Gottlieb listing his financial needs—the salaries for doctors, technicians, equipment, and so forth—including a line-item request for two thousand dollars to cover stipends paid to Whitey and other inmates, at three dollars a trip. His project wasn't the only one the CIA was secretly backing. LSD research was under way in New York City at Mount Sinai Hospital and Columbia University as well as in Boston at the Boston Psychopathic Hospital. In the other clinical studies, students rather than prisoners were the subjects. The public face remained the humanitarian goal of finding a cure for schizophrenia by testing drugs on tripping subjects, while the covert face was the CIA's spy game.

In his annual budget requests, Pfeiffer often made it clear that some of the drugs he planned to test in the coming fiscal year had nothing to do with schizophrenia research but involved "materials of pharmacological interest" to the CIA. One budget form noted he had "30 chemicals awaiting testing in man."

The CIA chemicals that Pfeiffer tested on Whitey and the others have never been identified. While Pfeiffer coauthored medical journal articles identifying drugs he used in the schizophrenia research, he never specified the CIA "materials." By the time the intelligence agency's covert role exploded into public view in the 1970s, the CIA had destroyed most of its MK-ULTRA files. Pfeiffer destroyed his files in 1971, including records naming the prisoners who had participated. This meant Whitey and others would never know the full menu of chemicals they took during the LSD Project. But Pfeiffer, defending his work, always insisted LSD did no harm. During an unsuccessful federal lawsuit that several of Whitey's fellow inmates brought against the CIA in the early 1980s, Pfeiffer offered himself up as Exhibit A to prove his point. "I am a living witness that seventeen doses can be taken of LSD and still have normal mentality at age 72," Pfeiffer said in a June 26, 1980, deposition. In another interview, Pfeiffer asserted LSD caused no long-term damage. "There is no cumulative effect," he said. "Only tolerance is produced." To illustrate the latter, he took four of his seventeen doses of LSD in four days. "I did take LSD daily," he said. "You become tolerant to the effects of LSD when given daily."

Later research, however, raised flags. LSD has been known to cause flashbacks in the short term, a condition that was given the name Hallucinogen Persisting Perception Disorder, or HPPD, a phenomenon listed in psychiatry's *Diagnostic and Statistical Manual of Mental Disorders*. In one 2002 review of previous studies of LSD flashbacks, researchers concluded that HPPD was a "genuine but uncommon disorder, sometimes persisting for months or years after hallucinogen use and causing substantial morbidity." The researchers made a key distinction between LSD used in the lab versus the LSD that, beginning in the 1960s, was sold on the street and mixed with other materials. Flashbacks, they said, were "reported most commonly after illicit LSD use, but less commonly with LSD administered in research." Concern also arose that LSD caused genetic damage, but no studies have shown that conclusively as a long-term consequence. "From our own work and from a review of the literature, we believe that pure LSD ingested in moderate doses does not damage chromosomes in vivo, does not cause detectable genetic damage, and is not a teratogen or carcinogen in man," a key study said.

Most telling, however, is that for all the LSD experiments—in prisons, hospitals, and on college campuses—the research never yielded anything of value either for the treatment of schizophrenia or for the CIA's espionage initiatives. The bottom line: LSD has never been shown to have a medicinal effect against any disease—and thus there is no known therapeutic dose. To the contrary, there is enough evidence that LSD is harmful—certainly in the short run, less so in the long run— that it is illegal, a Schedule I substance under the Controlled Substances Act.

Pfeiffer, in the face of later controversy, was undeterred and always proud of his LSD work with Whitey and other prisoners in Atlanta. He maintained this posture even when two of Whitey's fellow LSD takers had "adverse reactions" and were removed from the project. "They bugged out," another inmate said of their psychotic breakdowns. One of the men, a Canadian, "went berserk; he went nuts," the inmate said. The two were taken to the psych ward, where Bryan monitored them. But after a few weeks, and with no change in their psychotic state, Bryan had them transferred to the federal prison hospital for the mentally ill in Springfield, Missouri. "I never heard any more about them," Bryan said. "It's quite possible they recovered and were sent to some other institution." Pfeiffer, Bryan, and other doctors were never able to recall their names, and their identities were officially lost with the destruction of records.

But Whitey never forgot. "The men were named Jennings and Benoit," he wrote in the early 1990s, describing the LSD experiments. Whitey said that the two men "went insane" and were "shipped to Springfield, Mo., and placed in a wing for the criminally insane." He wrote that he and his mates never got any feedback from the doctors on their fate, but eventually "one man from Atlanta prison said he was there in Springfield doing some electrical work, saw Benoit who was a friend of his in Atlanta and said he was in a catatonic state and couldn't effect any response." The doctors, Whitey wrote, also never explained what had happened to cause the men's breakdowns.

The way Pfeiffer and his colleagues saw it, however, LSD stoked a preexisting psychiatric vulnerability in the two men that had escaped detection during the screening process. In fact, the ability of the drug to animate a preexisting trait or condition was one of the discoveries he and other researchers had made in LSD experiments at the prison and elsewhere. In Boston, for example, doctors noticed that a subject's basic personality structure affected his reaction to LSD and that "more than anything else, LSD tended to intensify the subject's existing characteristics—often to extremes." Pfeiffer had noticed this in his own use of LSD—that the nature of the trip was affected by personality. Being an upbeat person, he said, "In me, I'm more apt to get euphoric." The one instance he noticed feeling otherwise was when he took LSD for the TV station in Atlanta. "I got quite paranoid and the cameras and all that was a factor," he said. CIA agents who tried LSD as part of the agency's own internal experiments also observed the connection, with one agent telling author John Marks that he and CIA cohorts who were basically stable personality types "tended to enjoy themselves on LSD."

But, the agent said, the LSD trip was altogether different and darker for certain of their colleagues. "The stereotypical CIA operative (particularly the extreme counterintelligence types who mistrust everyone and everything) usually had negative reactions," the agent explained. "The drug simply exaggerated his paranoia."

So as far as Pfeiffer was concerned, the "weak psycho personalities" of the two inmates led to their breakdowns when they ingested LSD. That outcome was a rarity, he insisted, while pointing to the math—that they were two inmates out of the estimated seventy-five participants during the LSD Project's five years. "That is a rather good record, to have perhaps only two that might have had psychiatric difficulties." Overall, Pfeiffer said, the project had successfully employed LSD to explore mental illness and its effects on humans. Ever proud, he said that a number of the inmates would tell him that taking LSD was a "very pleasurable experience" and one even wrote him a note saying he thought LSD "was the best invention since sliced bread."

Whitey Bulger's personality was certainly closer to that of a wary, mistrustful counterintelligence operative than to the sunny, assured Dr. Carl Pfeiffer—making Whitey theoretically more prone to a lousy LSD trip. Whitey nonetheless dutifully reported Tuesday after Tuesday for a new round of the psychedelic drug—five Tuesdays that October 1957, and four more Tuesdays that November, according to his prison files. His prison records, particularly his annual progress reports, do not indicate he had trouble participating in the LSD Project. The reports always mentioned that Whitey was in overall excellent health. He wrote to his brother Bill that he was excited to be participating in the experiments, that they were going well, and that he was earning "good time" off for volunteering. Whitey spent both Christmas Eve 1957 and New Year's Eve in the psych ward tripping on LSD.

But years later Whitey told a very different story in several handwritten pages describing the LSD Project. "We were in the room for 24 nightmarish hours," he wrote in the early 1990s. "Given LSD in varying doses—sometimes light, sometimes massive," it "would plunge me into the depths of insanity." He recounted one hallucination where he "looked down and saw a cockroach—he exploded into the size of an elephant and I shrunk to the size of an ant. Fear had me screaming and climbing the wall." In another hallucination, he turned to look at a nearby inmate and watched "the flesh on his face melt and fall off revealing his skull; flesh melt from his hands turning into bare bones; blood spew out of the light bulbs." The room turned into a long black tunnel, and he "could hear voices talking about you (Paranoia), feeling the doctor was the enemy as he would come with syringe for a blood sample." Then there was the recovery; he'd feel depressed after a six-hour trip, with "suicidal thoughts and nightmares and interrupted sleep."

Whitey recalled how the weekly hallucinations left him "emotionally drained and exhausted—and felt life was not worth the effort." He said he went to Dr. Pfeiffer and told him about his struggles—his suffering—and that he "couldn't take it any more and had to quit." But Pfeiffer, he said, would have none of it.

In fact, as far as Pfeiffer was concerned Whitey possessed the very traits he was looking for during the screening. "I would say the ideal subject would be one of high intelligence, high IQ," Pfeiffer said during the later court case. Next came "reliability in their prison work habits, so that they had done a responsible job in the prison hospital." Pfeiffer, without mentioning him by name, was describing Whitey Bulger. Noted Pfeiffer: "The stability of the individual, the psychopath with whom we dealt at that time probably was the opposite of the schizophrenic, in that the schizophrenic is unstable in his personality. These individuals were quite stable."

Whitey, in his later writings, said that after telling Pfeiffer he needed to stop, the doctor "begged me to stay on—that I was one of his best and most conscientious subjects," and so, Whitey wrote, he continued taking LSD.

11

Ringleader

Alcatraz: 1959

Whitey stayed with the LSD Project into the next year, 1958, with the Tuesday visit to Ward F becoming a kind of anchor to his weekly prison routine. Benefits were felt immediately: he got back good time he'd lost for fighting in the shower. In restoring the ten days, the warden wrote Whitey had had "no further misconduct reports and he is doing good work as a hospital attendant and also participating in a Medical Research Project." In sum, the warden said, "He is serving a long sentence and restoration should encourage him to keep up his present good adjustment."

Whitey wrote an upbeat letter home, full of New Year's resolve to buckle down and make the most of prison, where there were "no late hours, whiskey, women or fast cars" to distract him. The summer brought welcome visits from his brothers, with House Majority Leader McCormack once again paving the way for brother Jackie to visit Whitey in early July 1958. Later in July, brother Bill wrote to the warden about his upcoming "annual" summer visit, his second to see

Whitey. Because he could visit only once a year, due to the distance and "heavy expense," and because of his work and school commitments, Bill was hoping to visit Whitey on back-to-back days—a Thursday and Friday in August. He therefore asked the warden for an exception to the "customary 7-day intermission period between the visits." Bill Bulger, a future attorney, deferentially argued that the prison rules on visits allowed for such an exception "under special circumstances." He hoped the warden would "consider my situation as worthy for the privilege which I am seeking." Finally, he noted he'd chosen a time that would not disrupt his brother's routine. "I would like to add, also, that my request is for a Thurs. and Friday because these days do not conflict with certain L.S.D. experiments which he is now undergoing."

Prison officials in early August rejected Bill's proposal due to "limitations on our visiting space," but they left open the possibility he'd get his way once he arrived, depending on the logistical factors. Every indication is that Bill's second visit later in August went off without a hitch, and it may even have had a thawing effect on Whitey when it came to the icy distance between the eldest son and their father. The next month—after Whitey turned twenty-nine on September 3—Whitey requested that his father be added to his mailing list. The senior Bulger, who would be turning seventy-five years old the coming November, had never been on Whitey's approved list of correspondents. "My father is physically ill and despondent," Whitey wrote on the Inmate Request Form he submitted on September 25. He asked that a South Boston priest be removed from his mailing list to make room for his father: "Mr. James J. Bulger, 41 Logan Way, So. Boston."

But by early November, something was up with Whitey. He'd been with the LSD Project for fifteen consecutive months, reporting nearly every week for the glass of clear liquid with its unknown dosage of LSD, tripping up to fifty times, according to his records, and becoming a bona fide acid head. Suddenly Whitey was bounced from the program. Little explanation was given in his file, except for this: "Dropped on Nov. 10, 1958 due to being persistently noisy and boisterous to a rather extreme degree."

Getting thrown out of the LSD Project was the first sign. The run of uneventful months, the routine he'd established after his rough beginning in prison in the eight-man cell, the string of positive reports he'd gotten—it was over. A new year arrived, and 1959 began in crisis for Whitey: he was put into the Maximum Security Unit after guards foiled a prison breakout.

Three other inmates from B Cell House, using a hacksaw blade, had sawed their way out of the hospital where Whitey worked and taken off on foot to the nearby Dining Room building. Guards saw them, closed in, and captured the men on the roof of the dining hall. The three inmates immediately began talking, saying Whitey had been part of the plot. "The blade that had been used in the hospital," a later report said, "was found in a cell at precisely a place designated by an inmate informant and this inmate stated that Bulger had supplied the blade to those people." Whitey was pulled from his cell and placed in segregation pending an investigation headed by an associate warden named W. H. York.

York wasted no time. He filed a memorandum on January 6, 1958, to the warden in which he made clear his low regard for Whitey. His investigation, he wrote, "discloses this man furnished a hacksaw blade to three men in 'B' Cellhouse for an escape attempt." Perhaps worse, York's intelligence on Whitey cited him as a ringleader. "Almost every time information is received about some escape plot, Bulger's name heads the list." To emphasize the negative, the associate warden even resurrected the bogus Indiana murder investigation. "When he was received at this institution the state of Indiana had a pending murder charge against him." York at least included the pertinent fact that after more than two years no "detainer," or murder charge, had ever been brought against Whitey.

But even with that caveat, York's memo—three paragraphs long—put a different face on Whitey than the one reflected in his file for much of the previous year. In short order, the good Whitey was undone, and the next day the warden added his own thoughts at the bottom of York's memo, forecasting more trouble for Whitey: "I have reviewed this case thoroughly and am familiar with this man's record and activities," Warden F. T. Wilkinson wrote. "We should prepare recommendation for Alcatraz," he said.

Meanwhile, from his cell in segregation, a frantic Whitey wrote his brother Bill several letters, one dated January 7, a second dated two days later. But two weeks passed before Bill received them in South Boston. Bill was alarmed. The same day he received the second letter, on January 22, he decided to write the warden to find out what had happened to Whitey and to get an explanation for the holdup in his brother's mail. But before writing he consulted with a judge in South Boston who was both a personal friend and a former top aide to John McCormack in Congress—and then, as if to add weight to the letter he drafted, Bill name-dropped the judge's name to the warden. "I am writing at the suggestion of Judge Joseph Feeney of Boston who has said that my letter of inquiry will be answered."

Bill told the warden that his brother Whitey "has written several letters to me from the isolation unit there where he has been held in solitary confinement for two weeks. No reason has been offered to him for the curtailment of his privileges and his mail has been subjected to unusual delay." He went on to report that Whitey had told him no one at the prison had even spoken to him in ten days, and that "except for two trips to the shower" Whitey had been confined to his cell.

The whole turn of events left Bill flummoxed. "He swears he has done no wrong," wrote Bill, "and from the general tenor of his letters and his somewhat cheerful attitude I had been led to believe that he was doing quite well prior to this further restriction to his freedom." Bill asked for an explanation for the confinement. "If the reason is one that you can divulge I would be most grateful," he said. "He seems to have been getting along well and this disruption of routine can do no good."

Bill ended his entreaty by asking a favor of the warden. He wanted to hear back quickly but he also wanted to keep Whitey's troubles hidden from his parents. He therefore set up a system where the warden could address letters to him in care of a family friend in Old Harbor— the Gills at 100 O'Callaghan Way. "I cannot receive the letter at my home address (that which is on my brother's mailing list) without causing great anxiety for my parents," he wrote in closing to the warden.

But Bill Bulger was not about to sit still waiting for a reply. He tugged at the levers of power he had access to, which to his good fortune amounted to nuclear political power: he asked Majority Leader McCormack to intervene. McCormack, in turn, immediately contacted Bureau of Prisons director James V. Bennett for a full briefing. Bennett, in turn, fired off a teletype to Warden Wilkinson in Atlanta. Whitey was in trouble, and Bill was responding like a firefighter to a five-alarm inferno.

In fact, in the weeks that followed, Bill Bulger's relentless work on his brother's behalf constituted the most concrete evidence to date of the powerful bond between the two. The public appearance of Bill, age twenty-two, at Whitey's sentencing on June 21, 1956, in federal court had revealed brotherly support, and Bill's early prison correspondence clearly established him as the point person for the family. But it was Bill's reaction in early 1959 to Whitey's newest calamity that threw the spotlight on the fierce loyalty—deep and abiding—that Bill would shift into overdrive to do all that he could to try to improve Whitey's station.

Interveners on Whitey's behalf had always been suspected. Dating back to his juvenile delinquency in the 1940s, Whitey's uncanny ability to avoid any real consequence for his crimes suggested that more than luck was on his side—and that perhaps a helping hand had been in play. Not Bill, of course; he was a young boy then. It would have been an older family member or family friend. But, if true, that help always stayed hidden, with no fingerprints in the records that have survived.

Whitey's prison crisis was different.

The record, beginning here, established Bill as Whitey's advocate in chief. Not all siblings are automatically close—especially when they are four years apart in age. But Bill and Whitey were as one. And early 1959 was unequivocal proof, still a time when Bill and the rest of the Bulger family could rally in the sincere hope that brother Whitey, not yet thirty years old, would serve his time in federal prison and come out a different person, a person who had plenty of time to live a long, decent, good life that would make them all proud.

Beginning here, and in his subsequent writings and comments, Bill hit on themes, or talking points, to explain or excuse Whitey's crimes and wrongdoing—a refrain undoubtedly built on faith that the wayward Whitey would eventually find his way. Young Whitey had fallen under the spell of older criminals who steered him wrong—that was one. Another was that despite his crimes, Whitey was not really so bad. This could be expressed variously—Whitey as the good bad guy; or that he may be no angel, or no St. Aloysius, but he was full of goodness. Finally, no matter what he did, Whitey was certainly not as evil as the police or, eventually, the media portrayed him—and, as Bill's political career soared, the addendum to this point was that grossly unfair depictions of Whitey were the dirty work of Bill's enemies in both politics and the press looking to undo him through Whitey.

There was certainly a kernel of truth to the good bad guy notion. For one thing, Whitey was a master at flattery who drew others in. It was found in Whitey's letters to Rev. Drinan, in his relationship with Father O'Shea, in his dealings with prison officials—the earnest, polite inmate who also showed a touch of wit. More important, Bill experienced Whitey as a good brother—loyal to him, the family, and others in their neighborhood. He mainly saw his brother's mask of sanity.

Bill Bulger's advocacy was as hard as rock, a position from which he would never deviate. Even in the decades to come, as Whitey not only stayed bad but became a monstrous underworld crime boss, Bill stayed true. Whitey's eventual criminal conduct certainly made it clear that he had not done his part, that perhaps he no longer deserved such devotion. But Bill Bulger never seemed to consider breaking the ties that bound them. Instead, the supportive notes he understandably struck in 1959—genuine and full of hope—would later collide with a reality that stripped them bare, leaving the defense of Whitey sounding hollow, even cynical.

The associate warden, W. H. York, rather than the warden, promptly replied to Bill Bulger's urgent letter of January 22, and the update about Whitey was mailed on January 27 to the Gills of Old Harbor, as Bill had requested. The letter's tone was formal and informational; the associate warden first wanted to "correct one error" in Bill's communication. Whitey, he wrote, was not in solitary confinement; rather, he was in the Maximum Security Unit, a routine placement once an inmate was suspected of an escape attempt. Moreover, Whitey was in fine condition, "receiving regular meals and is visited by a member of the Medical Staff twice each day." York also noted that, in addition to the mailing address, he'd done the Bulgers another favor by letting the brothers correspond at all. "Ordinarily when a man is confined in the Maximum Security Unit he would only be permitted to write to his father, mother, or wife. However, in the case of your brother, I made an exception and permitted him to continue corresponding with you."

York mostly urged Bill to rest assured that justice would be done in the internal probe of the breakout attempt. "All facets of the conspiracy are being investigated." York said he expected that investigation to be concluded shortly. "If it is determined that your brother is not one of the ringleaders, he will undoubtedly be released from this unit and returned to regular quarters in the institution."

Upon receipt, Bill Bulger had no way of knowing the disingenuousness of York's comments. York—and the warden for that matter—had already concluded that Whitey was guilty as a ringleader in the escape plot. In fact, by the time of York's letter the warden had already initiated the prison's administrative process, through its Classification Committee, to get Whitey transferred.

But events showed that Bill Bulger was the one who actually had the upper hand—and Majority Leader McCormack was his trump card. Because the very next day, January 28, the warden unexpectedly received the teletype from his boss in Washington, D.C., Prison Director Bennett, asking for immediate information about Whitey that he could relay back to the inquiring McCormack.

Warden Wilkinson folded on the spot. He replied to Bennett via airmail the very same day. The letter began forcefully enough; Wilkinson stated flat out he thought Whitey Bulger was trouble. "There have been persistent reports that Bulger was among one of several groups who had planned to escape." He further told the director he had no doubt that Whitey "had a major part in the abortive escape attempt." But for all the strong rhetoric, the warden clearly sensed the winds of power. He informed his boss that he had decided to cut Whitey loose. "We have now released him from the Segregation Unit and he is back in the population," the warden wrote. "He is now on equal status of all other men in the population."

It was game over—the tandem of Bill and Whitey had won.

The rest was playing out the string. Hearing from the warden, Director Bennett in Washington, D.C., was able to quickly get back to McCormack. "My dear Congressman McCormack," began the deferential one-page letter. "In compliance with your personal request I have looked into the matter about which Mr. William Bulger of Boston wrote you." Bennett first did away with the bad news: "I regret that I have to report that he has had some difficulty at Atlanta." Whitey, he explained, had been put in maximum security on the suspicion of being part of an escape attempt. But the rest was good news: "James has been returned to the general population, and at present he seems to be getting along quite satisfactorily." All was well that ended well. "We are hopeful that his problems have been resolved," the director concluded. "The two brothers should have no difficulty in corresponding, and the parents should receives James' letters as regularly as he wishes to write."

There remained one last snag back at the prison—the warden's Classification Committee. It had gone ahead and reviewed Whitey's status, his role in the foiled breakout, and the evidence that Whitey's name was always in the mix whenever they got intelligence on an escape attempt. The inquiry was done, with action suggested: "The Classification Committee recommends that subject be transferred to U.S. Penitentiary, Alcatraz Island."

Except this, too, was quickly undone by the powers that be in Washington. Bennett's office soon notified the warden that he was rejecting the Classification Committee's action. "For the present we are not approving a transfer." The letter noted two inmates in the escape plot had already been transferred, making Whitey's removal "not as urgent." There was also a feeling in the Washington headquarters that in Whitey's case "you might be able to continue to work with him." And the director expressed hope Whitey would be wiser for the intervention that had reversed the prison committee's ruling: "That with the others transferred he [Bulger] will see the advantages of making a good adjustment."

Even after the break his brother had engineered, Whitey stayed on a downslide. With the clock ticking on his time in Atlanta, he no longer seemed in the adjusting mood. For one thing, his job in the hospital was taken away from him, and while he received decent reports at his new job in the printing office in the prison industries building, he resumed hanging out with inmates the guards considered hard-core troublemakers. The group was known for its restless, breakout sensibility. It was a crowd that included another bank robber who had been transferred to the Atlanta Penitentiary one month after Whitey's arrival in August 1956. Frank Lee Morris, three years older and with an IQ twenty points higher than Whitey's IQ of 113, seemed to have been on the run since birth. Morris grew up in Virginia in various foster homes and juvenile institutions that could not hold him and from which he ran away continuously. He began serving hard time in the 1940s in Louisiana and then in Florida for a series of burglaries and bank holdups, and during the next decade distinguished himself for escaping custody eleven times. In the future he would distinguish himself further, as the leader behind the sensational and history-making escape from Alcatraz Island on June 11, 1962.

During the previous three years at Atlanta, Morris, described in his records as an "unstable sociopath," had gotten into fights, and, like Whitey, was put into Administrative Segregation. In February, as Whitey and his brother fended off his transfer following the hacksaw incident, guards found lock picks among Morris's belongings in his cell. This led to a stint in isolation, and after he was returned to the general population in the spring of 1959, guards noticed he immediately became "re-affiliated with his old cronies," a group, the warden wrote, "whose plans to escape from this institution have been frustrated for one reason or another."

Guards had their eyes trained on the likes of Whitey, Frank Lee Morris, and others associated generally with this group, and as far as the warden was concerned Whitey was turning "more sullen, resistive and defiant by the day."

But any downturn in how he was regarded did not get in the way of Whitey returning to Pfeiffer's LSD Project; he signed a new contract on July 9, 1959, to resume taking acid. This second enlistment did not work out, however, and quickly took a scary turn. Seven days after signing up, and now a member of the Thursday group, Whitey suffered an overdose of some kind. He asked for an "emergency pass" the next morning to see psychologist Bryan in the psych ward. Bryan ordered bed rest. In his outpatient notes, Bryan wrote that Whitey "was so badly shaken by medication given him on the LSD Research Project yesterday that he had to be idled today."

Whitey, in his own account of the LSD Project, said Pfeiffer was the one who had "requested I take a dose larger than regularly given—very powerful. I agreed—this dose produced a horrible experience and I completely went over the edge." It was in this later account, written after the CIA's covert role was revealed, that Whitey angrily denounced Pfeiffer for hiding the CIA's involvement and for exploiting him and other inmates in the testing of a myriad of unknown drugs. "Carl Pfeiffer—he betrayed his oath, betrayed us," Whitey wrote in his five-page, single-spaced LSD screed. "We were recruited by lies and deception," he continued. "Encouraged to volunteer to be human guinea pigs in a noble humanitarian cause."

In addition to the cover-up about the CIA and the nondisclosure of the host of chemicals that were tested on the men, there was indeed this fundamental issue of voluntariness—whether a prisoner could ever freely volunteer for anything.

In the mid-1970s, no less than the director of research at the Federal Bureau of Prisons spoke out in criticism of the Pfeiffer-led project in Atlanta. "There is no such thing as volunteerism with a prisoner," Howard Kitchner told a newspaper reporter. "They aren't free agents." To him, Pfeiffer was mistaken in using inmates in his LSD Project. "The prison population has been exploited long enough."

Whitey recovered from his bad trip on July 16, even went back for more, but a few weeks later his prison status unraveled altogether when he was implicated in a breakout plot for the second time in nine months. Whitey did not see it coming or realize that officials were on to him. In late August, Congressman McCormack helped arrange an exception to visiting rules so that Whitey's brother-in-law could visit him. McCormack had sent the warden a last-minute telegram on Friday, August 21, saying that Marine Corps Lieutenant Robert D. McCarthy, his sister Carol's future husband, was traveling to Georgia that Monday and wanted to swing by. McCormack got his wish; first thing Monday morning the warden sent a memo down to the "front corridor" in which he said, "Permission is hereby granted for special visit not to exceed 2 hours duration when and if Lt. McCarthy comes to the institution."

But within twenty-four hours of that favor, Whitey was in segregation, as McCarthy headed back to Boston to break the news to Bill Bulger. Bill pulled out all the stops in the weeks to come—writing letters, calling the prison, even traveling to Washington, D.C.—to lobby on Whitey's behalf. The campaign began with a letter to the warden on September 1—two days before Whitey's thirtieth birthday. "I have just learned of the events which took place since Lieutenant McCarthy's visit to my brother, James Bulger, last week," he began. Bill was incredulous that Whitey was in trouble again, and he challenged the warden's position. "Despite the supposed tangible evidence," he wrote, "I am convinced that my brother has been doing all possible to make himself eligible for parole." He said he planned to call Father John O'Shea to get his take on the situation and was considering a trip to Atlanta. "I do try to be objective in the matter in spite of my strong emotional involvement. Few things are as important to me as his eventual return to a decent life."

On the heels of his letter Bill Bulger got on the telephone, but the warden did not take his call; instead an associate warden briefed Bill on Whitey's involvement in a thwarted breakout conspiracy. The warden afterward sent Bill a reply noting that Whitey "has been identified with some rather serious irregularities during the past few months." Seeming upbeat and hopeful, the warden encouraged Bill and the rest of the Bulger family to keep writing Whitey "letters of a cheerful type."

The patronizing tone did little to calm Bill Bulger. He and Whitey were indeed writing each other furiously about the latest crisis, but the warden then went and intercepted at least one of Bill's letters, explaining to Bill that his letter "concerns institutional affairs and happenings and is not a social letter in the true sense." The very day, September 17, that Bill received his rejected letter he angrily called the prison. He only got through to a "count clerk" on the nighttime shift, but he nonetheless launched into a tirade that he was getting the runaround and not being dealt with honestly. "Mr. Bulger seemed very perturbed," the clerk wrote in his memo to the warden's office. "He was advised to contact you tomorrow."

Bill Bulger and the warden were now in a full-scale quarrel about Whitey. Bill Bulger accused the prison of improperly holding up the brothers' mail and the warden responded that Bill was the one who was playing fast with the rules. "I don't lie," Bill retorted in response to the warden's claim. He insisted that it was important for him to raise the interruptions in their correspondence in his letter to Whitey. "When I complain to Jim about the irregularity of his mail arrivals," he continued, "I do so mainly in order that he may see the reason for my delays in answering him. At both instances of such irregularities I thought it extremely important for his morale that he not be led to believe that we were simply ignoring his plea for help."

But Bill Bulger apparently protested too much. The prison administration resurrected the matter of Whitey's transfer on the same day—September 29—that the warden received Bill's argumentative letter. In a new memo, Associate Warden W. H. York summarized the latest intelligence obtained from their inmate informants about Whitey: "Bulger is again confined in Administrative Segregation in connection with information received that he and Devaney 79217-A and possibly one or two others were again plotting an escape from the institution." York's advice: enough was enough. "It appears that Bulger will continue to become involved in escape plots. Therefore, I wish to renew my recommendation that he be considered for transfer to Alcatraz at this time."

Not surprisingly, the warden agreed, and two weeks later he made a formal request to Bureau of Prisons director James V. Bennett in Washington. The warden mentioned Whitey had already been given a second chance earlier in the year, but that despite "our patient efforts to counsel Bulger toward constructive program participation," he had blown it. The Atlanta prison was no longer suitable for him. "We do not believe we can return him to the population here without inviting further serious trouble." Five days later, on October 21, the transfer was approved.

Whitey wasn't alone—he wasn't the only inmate bounced from Atlanta that autumn for needing stricter oversight. It was as if the prison administration in Atlanta was cleaning house of the loose group identified as being preoccupied with breaking out—the most notable in this string of transferees being future legend Frank Lee Morris. On Sunday night, September 20, while Whitey was already stuck in segregation, Morris was caught running from a window in B Cell House after the window's bars had been spread with a "bar spreader" and the glass was smashed. Morris then joined Whitey in Administrative Segregation, and soon enough, Frank Lee Morris was on his way out of Atlanta, too, arriving at the U.S. penitentiary at Alcatraz early the next year.

Within days of Whitey's October 21 transfer order, U.S. marshals came and accompanied him on a bus ride to a holding facility in Washington, D.C., pending transportation to California. No amount of political intervention could derail the transfer this time—although that did not stop Bill Bulger from attempting, in effect, a Hail Mary pass. Now a first-year law student at Boston College School of Law, Bill persuaded a Boston attorney to write prisons director Bennett asking that he halt the transfer. Bill then made his own way to Washington, D.C., and on November 12, without an appointment, showed up at the Bureau of Prisons headquarters. Even though Whitey was already in a holding facility, Bill asked to see Director Bennett so he could argue his case in person that Whitey's order be rescinded. He did not get the audience he sought, however, and had to settle for a meeting with a member of Bennett's staff.

In a letter to Bill's Boston attorney the next day, Director Bennett explained that the decision to transfer Whitey was made "only after a very lengthy review and serious consideration." Whitey's failures in Atlanta, wrote the director, "left us no alternative." Said Bennett: "Rest assured that the Staff at Alcatraz will assist Mr. Bulger in every possible way and will bring him to my attention periodically for review and determination when he should return to one of our other institutions."

The same day Bennett wrote those words, November 13, 1959, Whitey Bulger, accompanied by federal marshals, boarded a TWA Boeing 707 jet at Baltimore's Friendship International Airport. In every way he was heading in the wrong direction, away from family as well as up the inmate classification ladder to the Bureau of Prisons' super-maximum-security facility. The whole prison system was structured on a classic carrot-and-stick philosophy, with a range of prisons of graduated security levels. The carrot, or incentive, for a prisoner to stay out of trouble was the prospect of a transfer to a less restrictive prison. But for the troublemakers and escape risks there was the ultimate sanction—a transfer to "the Rock." Following his five-hour flight, Whitey landed in San Francisco and was transported on the prison launch *Warden Johnston* across San Francisco Bay. In leg irons, he shuffled into the white prison atop the rocky island often enshrouded in a thick, soupy fog. He'd been done in once again by informants. Carl Smith had led to his capture for robbing banks. Now inmate informants had buried him in prison, sending him farther from home and family and across a continent to the country's most notorious prison, where he would continue to grow more guarded and more hateful toward betrayers.

Whitey was certainly on the move—done now with Atlanta and done with the prison's LSD Project, during which he had tripped on acid more than fifty times. But Whitey wasn't the only one moving on. The project's guru, Dr. Carl C. Pfeiffer, left Emory University early the next year to head north for new duties as chief of a lab in Princeton,

New Jersey. Pfeiffer continued conducting his LSD experiments there—and freely admitted a preference for his new subjects over prison inmates like Whitey Bulger. He even emphasized the "improved quality" of the civilian volunteers in Princeton in an annual budget request to the CIA, "a better group for this kind of research," he wrote, "since they may be closer to the normal population."

12

The Rock: 1959–62

Alcatraz

The morning of Saturday, September 3, 1960, marked Whitey's thirty-first birthday, and it was the day Whitey decided to stay put. The floor guard, standing right outside his cell in C Block, ordered him to get up and make his way to his job as a "bin man" in the clothing room. But Whitey stayed in bed, ignoring the guard's words, as he looked past him and had a view of the tall windows and ceiling skylights, which someone else once said made that side of the prison resemble a vast aviary. The oversized windows provided plenty of natural light, as well as a tantalizing reminder of a life beyond.

The guard again told Whitey to move. But Whitey did not budge. The reason was not his birthday—as if he were simply indulging himself and deciding to spend the day in the cozy confines of his cell. The reason was the "lay-in" strike that had taken prison administrators by surprise. The guards, mystified about its origins, were pressing certain inmates for an explanation while trying to cope with a protest in which a majority of inmates were taking part.

Whitey wasn't sure why he was on strike, either. There was talk that an angry cadre of litigious-minded inmates was behind it, convinced that the warden's office was improperly getting in the way of habeas corpus petitions they wanted to file in federal court in San Francisco. But no one seemed to know for sure, because there was also talk that the instigators were inmates fed up with the declining quality of the food after the arrival of a new chief cook.

Whitey did not know what to make of any of it. He actually liked the food, and his weight was on the climb from about 150 pounds. In fact, given his makeup, the Rock—the prison that for many inmates was the hardest of hard time and to the public was an otherworldly house of horrors—was not such a bad place. "Things have changed—for the best if anything," he wrote to Father O'Shea after his arrival ten months earlier. "I have never felt more at ease in prison than I do now," he continued. "I have a pleasant job in the clothing room and a single cell."

Alcatraz, the notorious prison that held the country's most dangerous criminals—including, in years past, Al Capone, George "Machine Gun" Kelly, Robert "Birdman" Stroud, and Alvin "Creepy" Karpis—was like a village compared to Atlanta with its several thousand inmates. Indeed there were no eight-man cells—and no four-man or two-man cells for that matter. Every one of the less than three hundred inmates there had a single cell, and with it far more personal privacy than Whitey had ever known while behind bars.

With the guard standing there ordering him to get up, Whitey could see his personal belongings exactly where he'd placed them in his five-foot by nine-foot cell—the shaving mug, toothbrush, and dental powder, the tin cup, nail clipper, and mirror. His prison-issued socks, trousers, and shirts—neatly folded—were kept where he wanted them. He could scan the titles of books he'd arranged on a shelf, the books *Ireland* and *World Literature Made Simple,* along with *Webster's New Collegiate Dictionary,* the *New Oxford Book of English Verse,* and a three-ring binder with his own writings. The guards, of course, could rummage through his cell whenever, but no inmate was ever going to mess with his things. Whitey had reclaimed a modicum of control over his space, an expression of will so important to him.

The guard finally walked away, and Whitey remained inside on his steel cot. The inmate strike continued that day and into the next, and the day after that. Whitey's prison records note that the next week he still refused to leave his cell for work, and then again the following Monday. Meanwhile, the strike began to weaken. One by one inmates quit it, and began falling back into line and attending to their prison jobs. The inmates believed to be the instigators were thrown into isolation. Some managed to get hold of bits of razor blades and, in a perverse brand of protest, sliced their heel tendons. This only complicated the whole affair, with the warden losing patience.

By Wednesday, September 14, every inmate had returned to work except for eight holdouts—and Whitey Bulger was one of the stubborn eight. Except for the ringleaders, no punitive action was taken against the striking inmates who had trickled back to work. But with only eight holdouts left, patience was exhausted. That Wednesday morning a guard once again ordered Whitey to work. He once again refused. He later said he wasn't sure why he held on, except to say that a couple of his friends on the block had been placed in isolation and he felt an obligation to back them up. Part of it also might have been that he'd always bucked against being told what to do, and the strike seemed a way, however foolish, to tap into that. Whatever the reason, the guard returned in the afternoon and ordered him one last time to get moving. Whitey refused—and that was it. No more waiting out the final few strikers. Whitey was now really in trouble, brought up on official misconduct charges.

When Whitey had first arrived at the Rock ten months earlier, on November 13, 1959, the hardest part of the transfer was the gaping canyon of space between him and his family. His siblings and parents did not have the financial wherewithal to travel across country to see him. Whitey's first visitor would not come until June 1961—nineteen months later—a career Navy officer named Edward E. Hesse, who was a few years older than Whitey and a boyhood neighbor from Old Harbor. Whitey had to make do with writing letters, mostly to Bill and his mother, and occasionally to Rev. Drinan and Father O'Shea. "My mother hoped I was being sent closer to home," he wrote Father O'Shea. "She feels I'm in a terrible place." Whitey worked hard at lifting his mother's spirits, and, as he did with the priest, he shared surprisingly positive feelings about the prison that was reputedly the toughest in the country. "The food is excellent," he wrote home, "carefully prepared, and the diet is well balanced. After years, eating has become a pleasure again and I look forward to every meal."

In one letter to Father O'Shea he said he'd made headway with his upbeat message to the family. "My brothers and sisters have accepted my description of things and in time my mother will. We intend to make the best of things and hope that one day I'll be transferred closer to home." The letter, though, was mainly a chance for Whitey to express his gratitude to the priest, as Whitey assessed "the end of the Atlanta chapter." He wrote the father, "I was always on edge down there and never did thank you." He even closed on a self-mocking note about a "chapter" that was hardly joking fodder but was full of turmoil, fights, LSD, and the crack-up at the start. "I hope that some day our paths will cross again, not in prison though, and we can both laugh talking about that shook up Bostonian."

For Whitey each day began at six o'clock with a rise-and-shine horn blasting through the three cell blocks set in rows—A, B, and C. Whitey's cell was on the outside of C Block, consisting of three-tiers with twenty-eight cells on each level, all facing the prison wall with the tall windows. Whitey's cell was on the second tier, and he was fortunate to have another veteran from Atlanta occupy a cell farther down the tier—Richard B. Sunday. Whitey had met Sunday, convicted of rape while in the Army, when they both worked in the hospital at Atlanta, and they discovered a mutual interest in weight lifting. The friendship would continue and grow at the Rock.

Long before Whitey arrived, names had been given to the waxed corridors running between the cell blocks. Whitey lived on Park Avenue, while the corridor that ran between C and B blocks had a name quite familiar to him—Broadway. Just like the Broadway in his South Boston hometown, the prison version was a main drag where cells looked across at one another like studio apartments on a busy street. The prison was segregated—separate meals, separate showers—and Broadway provided a solution of sorts for housing. The cells on the inside of C Block facing Broadway were for newly arrived white inmates, while cells on the inside of B Block were for black convicts. The arrangement meant white prisoners never had to live for long near their black counterparts, only during their introductory quarantine. But blacks always faced whites, albeit a revolving roster, meaning the policy certainly wasn't one of separate but equal.

Following the wake-up blast, Whitey had twenty minutes to dress, wash using the cold-water sink, and make his bed before the guards took the first of twelve official head counts. He then filed out with the other inmates for breakfast in the dining hall, located through the back of the cell block, then returned to his cell until he was "rung out" to his assigned job in the clothing room. Filing into the dining room or later into the yard, he might pass through a metal detector, nicknamed the "Snitch Box," with an electronic eye that blinked if metal was detected. Prison-issued belts had wooden buckles so as not to activate it.

Lunch was followed by "sick call," with more head counts spaced throughout the day, and then Whitey was rung out again for work in the afternoon, as well as some recreation time outdoors in the yard. Dinner in prison was early—5:30 p.m.—and after that and yet another head count, Whitey was sealed in for the night. Cell doors clanged shut in unison, usually fifteen at a time, by a guard at a manual control box at the end of the block. Whitey had the next thirteen hours alone, to sleep, read books borrowed from the library, write letters, or plug his head-phones into the radio outlet located in each cell. "We get some classical and semi-classical music, better radio programs in this part of the U.S.," he wrote enthusiastically in one letter. The true end of the day came abruptly at 9:30 p.m., when lights turned off automatically and the cells went black, when a quiet settled in and inmates might hear the drafts of cold air moving through the cavernous cell blocks or, if fog filled San Francisco Bay, the foghorns located at each end of the island.

This was the basic structure of each day, one day like another, the sum of which was prison time. In prison, *Time* with a capital *T* was the core currency of an economy built around time transactions. Time could be added to an inmate's sentence, or taken away. It was central to the Golden Rule an associate warden once explained to a new arrival: "Good behavior begets good time, and good time means a shortened term." Words Whitey Bulger needed to learn to live by.

After settling in, Whitey also noticed that Frank Morris was transferred to Alcatraz in early 1960 and, after quarantine, assigned to a cell on the far side of B Block. Eventually two other Atlanta alumni—the Georgia-born brothers Clarence and John Anglin—were put in side-by-side cells a few down from Morris's. Like Whitey and Morris, the Anglins were moved to the Rock as high risks for escape, and it wouldn't be long be-fore Frank Morris, the Anglin brothers, and a fourth man would get to work on a plan that Morris had come up with.

Whitey also learned that he'd missed Carl G. Smith Jr., who had been at Alcatraz until his transfer the year before. Crossing paths again with Smith might have proved interesting, to say the least—a meeting between Whitey, scorched by betrayal, and Smith, the slobbering informant who had told on everyone. It turned out that after his arrest Smith had unabashedly pleaded with authorities for a break in exchange for dirt on Whitey and the others. But no break came. One prosecutor's report at his 1956 sentencing referred to Smith as a "menace to society, and a mental case" who was undeserving of any significant slack—and so he got twenty-five years. During his few years in prison the medical staff had diagnosed Smith as a "vicious psychopath" who outwardly displayed a "big shot complex" but was really "a coward at heart." And over time Smith began exhibiting "pronounced paranoid trends." He insisted that an associate warden at Alcatraz was trying to kill him, that his food was poisoned, and that it was his "duty" to get the warden before the warden got him. This landed him in the hospital's psych ward, where he continued to be "violent, hostile and obscene." Eventually the "Sanity Board" at Alcatraz decided he was a paranoid schizophrenic who posed a hazard to hospital personnel. In 1958 he was moved to the federal prison system's medical center in Springfield, Missouri.

Whitey may have missed Carl Smith but he was reacquainted with the other strange bank-robbing bedfellow from 1956; Richard Barchard had been sent directly to Alcatraz in 1956 following his guilty plea in the Indiana holdup. Barchard actually reunited with Smith at Alcatraz, but their reunion ended badly. One afternoon in late 1956 the two of them, at Smith's behest, strode across the yard lugging baseball bats. They attacked an inmate, inflicting "severe wounds on head, trunk and extremities," according to a report. When questioned about the "brutal attack," Smith said he was not trying to kill the victim, only "cripple him on the legs and body." For the assault, both men spent nearly a year in isolation in the Hole.

Whitey soon learned from Barchard that it had been Smith's idea for Barchard to concoct the story of a murder committed after the Indiana holdup, where the corpse was dumped in a lake, a story that implicated Whitey. Barchard explained he meant no harm, and his only angle was to have the phony confession bring an end to his stay in the Hole. The glare came back into Whitey's eyes as he made clear the extent of the grief Barchard had caused at the start of his term in Atlanta—the FBI visits in prison, the questioning of Jacquie McAuliffe, the official "detainer" hanging over his head, and the possibility he might actually be charged with murder.

Their back-and-forth culminated in a Barchard mea culpa—a four-page, handwritten, single-spaced letter he submitted to Alcatraz officials to "straighten out the record." Barchard began, "This is an honest attempt on my part to right a wrong." He said that when he and Whitey Bulger met again at Alcatraz, Whitey got "very upset." Whitey, he wrote, "explained his being questioned by the F.B.I., how his girlfriend had been questioned, how much anxiety it had caused his family, how he felt that this charge being recorded on his file may have influenced anyone in reaching decisions regarding his future, how it affected his hopes for eventual parole because he was a first offender." The letter made clear Whitey had drilled into Barchard and given him plenty to think about. "In retrospect I can see the seriousness of it and the immaturity of myself." Ending with an apology, Barchard said that his letter was written "in good faith and under no coercion in any form, but rather a sincere effort on my part to right a wrong, and clear James Bulger."

In his first ten months at Alcatraz, Whitey performed his job to acceptable reviews from the guards, and he stayed out of trouble. He continued a nearly daily regimen of weight lifting he'd begun in Atlanta, at first using a set of homemade weights the inmates had on hand and later, new weights the prison ordered. "I get to the Yard almost every day and work out," he wrote in one letter, adding the weights were "a great outlet for excess energy and many of the guys put them to use."

His workout partner in the yard was Richard Sunday. The two lifted together regularly, one spotting for the other. In fact, they managed to be around each other during day periods when inmates were not confined to their cells. Not only did they live a few cells apart on the same tier; they worked together in the clothing room and later the laundry. During mealtime, when inmates were released from their cells one by one to walk single-file into the dining hall, Whitey would often step outside his cell and hang back, let a few other inmates pass him, and then step in line ahead of Sunday. This way they could sit together.

Sunday, a year younger than Whitey, was a private first class in the U.S. Army when he was convicted in 1951 by a general court-martial in the rape of a Korean woman. In prison, Sunday was practically maniacal about pumping iron—as a way to stay fit and to take out his deep frustration that he had gotten a bum rap. "I didn't pump iron for show, but for the physical value," Sunday said later. "It took a lot of pressure off you and you could feel better and really healthy doing it."

In many ways, Whitey made a smart choice in Sunday, whose strength and fighting skills, when called upon, were legendary in prison. "I was probably the toughest young guy on The Rock," Sunday said, a declaration that was not a boast but simple fact. Sunday was the same height as Whitey—an ordinary five foot ten—but he was all muscle: seventeen-inch biceps, a fifty-four-inch chest, and a thirty-one-inch waist. In one altercation, he struck his opponent three times and that was it, fight over—plus his opponent's face had to be rebuilt. Another fight, "I was holding the guy's eyeball in my hand, ready to pull it out and throw it out of the Yard. But then I let it go." Sunday said he got no pleasure from violence, but this was the Rock and "sometimes you had to be really rotten." Whitey and Sunday had come to trust each other—the fact one spotted for the other while lifting hundreds of pounds of weight proved that. They had each other's backs and, for Whitey, Sunday was a human shield. "If any one wanted to mess with Jimmy, they'd have to get through me," Sunday said. "That's the way it was—I thought that much of the guy."

In prison society, Whitey apparently circulated more easily than his friend. "I didn't hang out with some of the crooks that Jimmy did," Sunday said, "because I really had nothing in common with them." But even if Whitey seemed to fraternize more with "the crooks," he never became identified with any one inmate clique. In that way, too, Whitey and Sunday made for a good match—each felt alien from the typical convict at the Rock. Whitey felt superior and smarter. He found most convicts crude and off-putting, and he likely thought he was not bad in the depraved way violent murderers and rapists were. For Sunday's part, he had no prior criminal record, and he saw himself as a patriotic soldier who had been railroaded.

The two also had another interest in common—reading and writing—that likely separated them from much of the prison population. Sunday wrote poetry all the time. His "Ballad of Billy the Kid" was one of Whitey's favorites, he said, and years later Whitey still carried a copy of the poem with him. The poem, in rhyme, began with a young seventeen-year-old Billy the Kid, light-haired, walking into "the Golden Saloon" with a look in his eyes that drew everyone's attention.

> He was just a boy, of maybe seventeen,
> But his steel blue eyes, flashed real mean.
> And not till every man there had felt his gaze,
> Did his eyes lose some of their blaze.

"You can maybe see why Jimmy would like it," Sunday said.

The other notable inmate Whitey befriended was Clarence V. Carnes, a Native American from Oklahoma known as the "Choctaw Kid." Carnes was only eighteen when he was transferred to Alcatraz in 1945—the youngest inmate ever to enter the Rock. Carnes, two years older than Whitey, was going nowhere—serving a life sentence for murder and kidnapping and another ninety-nine years for participating in a prison escape in 1946 that turned into a violent uprising and resulted in the deaths of three inmates and two guards. It became known as "the Battle of Alcatraz." But Whitey wasn't alone in counting Carnes a friend. Carnes, mythic by this time, was easygoing and easy to know. "Clarence was a friend with anybody," Sunday said. And Whitey's relationship with Carnes was not social. They did not usually hang out together during recreation time in the yard; Whitey was usually busy lifting weights and, Sunday said, "Clarence wasn't with us doing that." The connection was books—Carnes worked in the prison library. He was the inmate who rolled the cart down the tier delivering books inmates had requested. That was how inmates borrowed books from the library; they didn't go there, Carnes delivered them, and Whitey, the avid reader, always appreciated and would never forget the way Carnes got it right and brought him the books he'd asked for. "The thing they had in common was books," Sunday said. "Jim was a big reader, so he and Carnes hit it off."

The one major hardship Whitey apparently suffered was a private hell he described three decades later. "I realized I still had LSD problems—visual hallucinations and audio hallucinations," he wrote in papers police discovered during a search of his condominium in early 1995. The claim did not square with the medical examinations contained in his prison records, which always said "general health good" and "subject has no particular complaints." The only indications that Whitey might have unrevealed health issues were a doctor's comments that he was "at times apprehensive in regard to his physical condition" and "inmate has fear of needles." Also, there was the episode four months into his stay when he sought out a doctor because of his heart. The doctor's notes from that March 31, 1960, checkup said: "Apprehension re heart—states 'heart pain' at times. Weightlifter. Probably muscle strain. Heart sounds normal. Lungs clear. Reassured." The notes suggest hypochondria more than anything else, but years later Whitey insisted the reason for the clean record was his fear of reprisals if he talked about flashbacks and hallucinations. "I never mentioned it to the officials or doctor—at that point I feared they may permanently commit me to a mental institution." There was no explanation for why he would fear a reprisal; he just said that was the way it was. In his view, at Alcatraz and forever after he was a victim, "still affected by LSD."

Whitey also apparently never explored these LSD fears in letters to his younger brother Bill. Instead Whitey's letters were sprinkled with pep talk. "Keep studying," he wrote in one. "Don't worry about writing so often," he reassured Bill in another. When he received a new photograph of his brother, Whitey wrote back complimenting Bill that he looked "nifty" in his new suit—like something "out of Esquire." The Bulger family was celebrating a milestone when Bill was elected in 1960 to his first public office as a state representative from South Boston, and on that occasion Whitey wrote that he was so proud of Bill and thought Bill had chosen well to go into politics, as it "pays a good salary" and provides "a pension."

Whitey signed these letters "Jim," or "Big Brother," or sometimes even "Whitey." He might as well have signed them "Dad." Maybe that was the point—at times Whitey seemed to be acting like a father figure. Whitey had not experienced a father in a nurturing sense—psychologically, even physically—with the elderly and incapacitated Bulger always a remote presence. In his prison letters, it was as if Whitey did not want his younger brother to also go without, and so he included lines that were the kind of thing a parent would write. To Bill the law student, Whitey would advise, "Stick with the books."

The letters were filled, too, with news about the many books he was reading and the weights he and Richard Sunday were lifting. "I have never felt better physically," he wrote. In a notebook he dutifully kept track of his regimen of bench presses, lateral raises, and bicep curls. Overall, and compared to Atlanta, Whitey's first year at the Rock unfolded uneventfully. Things really seemed to be going okay—okay, that is, until the day he decided he wouldn't get out of bed.

Not only was Whitey brought up on charges of "refusal to work" and "participating in a strike," he was also linked to a group suspected of plotting against inmate scabs who worked during the strike. Guards picked up talk from their "inmate sources" that two members of the reprisal team were planning to jump a targeted inmate in the yard while, according to a report, the "other two were to do the job. Knifing. Plans went astray and nothing happened."

Whitey denied any role in the planned attack. Right away, though, he expressed regret about the strike. To the panel of five prison officials at a "Good Time Forfeiture Hearing," he said he had been "foolish and blind" for having gone along with it. He was not "in sympathy" with the strike, but had "felt bad about the guys in the hole I worked with." Said Whitey, "I made a mistake."

The panel was unforgiving. It lowered the boom—unanimously recommending that he forfeit two hundred days of good time, a harsh blow in the context of prison, where time was infused with value outsiders might find hard to grasp. No freedom could come to Whitey—no parole when eligible—until those two hundred days were restored. In addition, his job in the clothing room was taken away, and he was relegated to "sweeper" on C Block, a lowly position that did not qualify for earning good time. He'd messed up big on the balance sheet where time was added and subtracted, coming out on the wrong side of the ledger.

The penalty also came with a lecture from a veteran officer on the panel, delivered with laserlike clarity. "Remember one thing," this officer told Whitey. "Your sentence is yours alone. Anytime you fool around with a thing like this you are fooling with your own time." The straight talk captured the most basic premise for inmate conduct—be selfish—and it must have made a world of sense to Whitey Bulger, playing into the self-centeredness, self-importance, and narcissism so central to his personality, and which such experts as Dr. Hervey Cleckley had cited as traits of the psychopath. How foolish he'd been to go on strike, and how obvious the truth—*his* time, that's what mattered. *His* survival. *Him*—that was what this was about, ultimately. It was as if Whitey finally got it, with the strike a turning point, because beginning in the fall of 1960 he launched a makeover. He began displaying a new kind of criminal maturity and discipline in which, in a sustained way, he showed them—the guards and prison authorities—only what they needed to see. The teenage charm with the smile he used with the mothers in Old Harbor and later the flashes of the good bad guy he managed in the Atlanta Penitentiary—that was a dress rehearsal for the performance to come.

From that point on at the Rock, Whitey behaved. He pitched in without waiting to be asked (or ordered). "He was very helpful," one guard said, "in moving the new beds into the cells" on his block. His hard work with weights sculpted his physique, so that it was as hard and flattened as the shirts pressed and folded tightly in the prison laundry. By year's end, he requested and secured a job in the laundry "in order that I may eventually earn some good time." To everyone he projected earnestness, complaining in that almost prudish way he had about the crude, vulgar, and bad manners of other inmates. "He didn't use profanity, and he didn't like others swearing," Richard Sunday said. In the laundry room, he and Sunday worked side by side as "feeders" who fed clean linens into the mangle to be pressed. Whitey befriended the laundry room foreman, a guard named A. G. Bloomquist, and "Bloomie" became his strongest supporter. Whitey became such a get-along, go-along inmate that another guard praised his overall cooperative spirit and admirable ability to get "along with both colored and white inmates."

Whitey seemed born-again and nearly evangelical. He talked about his love of God and country, about his brother Bill's political accomplishments, and about his shame at being the family's "black sheep." Sunday said that while talking admiringly about Bill Bulger's election to the Massachusetts House of Representatives, Whitey commented, "I've got to go straight now, Sunday." When seating arrangements in the dining hall were changed radically—so that smaller tables replaced the long rectangular ones—Whitey offered his two cents, telling a guard he was "pleased with the new four-man tables as it enables him to avoid listening to unsavory characters." He kept up an appearance of religiosity, but in fact rarely attended Sunday services. When asked why, however, he had the right answer: "He says too many inmates scoff, sneer and criticize the clergy after the service is over and he does not want to risk getting into trouble by expressing objection to their remarks." He was suddenly the altar boy he'd never been, a bona fide St. Aloysius.

The inmate "Progress Reports" filed later in 1960 and for the next two years reflected the huge gains in his "institutional adjustment." The first report following the strike commented that Whitey was "quiet and cooperative" and commended him for his "improved attitude." His review the next year on October 16, 1961, observed that Whitey, acting like some sort of morality watchdog, struggled "to avoid serious conflict with other inmates; he resents bitterly any disparaging remarks made by others about religion, Country and womanhood."

Most were sold on this new persona, but one guard assigned to Whitey's C Block seemed to be wondering whether Whitey's new face was genuine or a hustle. "He smiles a lot," the guard said, "as though he has some sort of joke to himself." *Some sort of joke to himself.* The guard seemed onto something: Was the smile—or was it a smirk—evidence that Whitey's swagger was back?

By the fall of 1962, Frank Lee Morris and his partners on B Block were well under way with a wild plan for escape that Morris had devised. They were secretly hoarding soap and paper in order to make life-sized decoy heads, and they were using stolen spoons to methodically chip away holes behind vents in each of their cells. Eventually the holes would be large enough to crawl through. The crew, without question, was breaking out the hard way. Whitey, meanwhile, was well under way with his own exit plan, one that would take him out the front door.

Whitey had something Morris and the others did not—"friends" in power. While he was doing his part on the inside, his brother Bill kept up the campaign on the outside. The goal was not his release; Whitey was not eligible yet for parole. But when that moment came, when Whitey was parole eligible beginning in 1963, there was no way he wanted to be at the Rock. Only two prisoners had ever been released into the free world directly from Alcatraz. The goal, then, was to get Whitey off the Rock and into a prison back east, closer to home. In Bill's steady correspondence with the prison system's top official, Director James V. Bennett, he was now the "Honorable William M. Bulger, House of Representatives, The Commonwealth of Massachusetts," so that Bennett's replies began with the salutation "My dear Representative Bulger." Bill also expanded the circle of supporters to include George F. McGrath, the commissioner of the Massachusetts Department of Corrections, who wrote Bennett in the summer of 1961—as one corrections chief to another—urging a transfer for Whitey. That letter was soon followed by a telephone call from the most long-standing supporter, House Majority Leader John McCormack. McCormack's power, already substantial, was about to get another boost. Within months he would become Speaker of the U.S. House of Representatives, the nation's third most powerful office, replacing Sam Rayburn of Texas, the longest-serving Speaker in history, who died of pancreatic cancer in November. McCormack reminded Bennett of his personal interest in Whitey and inquired about a transfer.

Immediately after their telephone chat, the Bureau of Prisons director on October 10 ordered the warden at Alcatraz to initiate a "special review" of Whitey's situation. But winning a requested transfer was not easy, even when the inmate had such a distinguished lineup of supporters. The Classification Committee's report of October 19, 1961, certainly documented Whitey's great strides, but the committee said even though he had adjusted "more satisfactorily, the fact cannot be overlooked he was actively engaged in a sit-down strike." Plus, there was no way around the "two hundred days statutory good time outstanding." The bottom line: the committee did "not feel disposed to recommend transfer at this time."

The decision simply meant a redoubling of everyone's efforts. In a typewritten note back to McCormack on November 9, Bennett said he'd made his personal interest in Whitey crystal clear and had advised the warden to bring Whitey's "case to my attention in the not distant future for consideration of his transfer East." Bennett even met with Whitey in December during a trip to the prison. Then, with the director looking over its shoulder, the prison's Classification Committee in February 1962 once again took up Whitey.

During its deliberations, the committee now had before it laundry foreman A. G. Bloomquist's handwritten, two-page praise of Whitey's work ethic "sorting and shaking out items to be mangled, folding and pressing shirts and loading and unloading laundry on and off motor trucks. He has been doing these jobs well and consistently." "Bloomie" also cited Whitey's "physical prowess with weights," poetry writing, and voracious reading. "He has an urgent desire to be well thought of in all things," the laundry foreman wrote. "His hopes are that he can go to school on his release and that he can some day redeem himself."

The committee also had in hand a report from the officer in charge of Whitey's cell block, whose review was restrained but positive nonetheless. John Herring picked up on Whitey's fixation with order, commenting that he kept "a slightly better than average cell," had a "very neat and well groomed appearance," and spent most of his time in the yard lifting weights. Herring said that "although some of his friends are known trouble makers Bulger seems to have a mind of his own and does not follow this group." In closing, Herring referred to Whitey's meeting with the chief of the prison system, saying that since his "interview with Bennett, when he last visited this institution, his conduct has been excellent."

The committee also met with Whitey, and he poured it on, making the case that he was ready for change, while also name-dropping along the way. He sought a transfer east, he said, to be closer to home so that he could "receive visits from family and from Rev. Drinan, Dean of Boston College Law School." He said he and Drinan had corresponded for six years and that Drinan had taken an "interest in his future plans." Plus, the larger prisons back east had bigger libraries and more extensive educational programs than at Alcatraz, and he wanted to take advantage of those resources. He also made certain to apologize again for the "sit-down strike" and promised never to be "suckered into anything as stupid in the future." Finally, Whitey stressed the importance of going to a "lesser custody" prison in anticipation of his eligibility for parole in just one more year, so, the committee reported, "he could demonstrate by his adjustment that he is deserving of favorable parole consideration."

The committee, four months after ruling that Whitey was not ready to leave the Rock, suddenly switched course and decided in early March 1962 that he was good to go. "This very friendly individual, with an ebullient personality, appeared eager to create a favorable impression at the time of the interview," the committee wrote in a report that soon landed on Director Bennett's desk in Washington, D.C. The committee's first action was to restore one hundred of the two hundred days of statutory good time he'd lost as punishment for striking—meaning Whitey was halfway out of the hole he'd dug. The committee then confronted the nettlesome fact that endorsing the transfer of Whitey meant that he would be leaving the Rock after only twenty-eight months, a comparatively short stay in comparison with all inmates at the maximum-security prison. The average stay was eight years.

The committee therefore came up with a two-step plan that would get it behind the wave of support to move Whitey out. "Since he has now been at this institution approximately 28 months the Committee further recommends that he be given a trial at Leavenworth with the idea that this would eventually earn a transfer to Lewisburg." The outcome was clear: Leavenworth was viewed as a pit stop for Whitey on the way to Lewisburg Penitentiary, which, by reputation, was an easier place to do time—as well as about a six-hour drive from Boston.

Three months later, under the cover of night on June 11, 1962, Frank Morris and John and Clarence Anglin scurried down to the eastern side of Alcatraz Island after they'd crawled through holes in their cells, navigated their way onto the cell block roof, and climbed down to the ground. They inflated the raft they'd made by gluing raincoats together, climbed aboard, and paddled away. The three men disappeared into San Francisco Bay, triggering a massive manhunt and a legend about "the Escape from Alcatraz." The three were never found.

One month after that, on July 24, 1962, following all the paperwork to process a transfer, including Director Bennett's official approval that Whitey was "suitable for test at a lesser custody institution," Bulger stood in his cell on C Block for the last time. He packed up his books and personal papers and was taken through the various checkpoints and then out the prison's main entrance. Down on the dock, in the company of marshals, he boarded the launch *Warden Johnson* for a ride across the bay under clear skies, the first leg of his trip to Leavenworth.

13

The End of Time

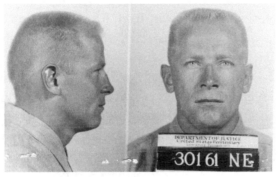

Lewisburg: 1963

When Whitey Bulger walked into the visiting room at the Leaven-worth Federal Penitentiary in Kansas on Thursday morning, July 18, 1963, he found Will McDonough already there waiting for him. McDonough was seated near the open windows that looked out onto the flat green acres surrounding the country's largest prison. Other in-mates were also seated in the small room with their visitors.

McDonough, six years younger than Whitey, had grown up in the Old Colony housing project, across the rotary from Whitey's Old Har-bor. He was one of many boys in the neighborhood who, back in the 1940s and early 1950s, were swept up in the thrall of the strutting street tough on the make. McDonough had witnessed firsthand Whitey's quick-trigger brutality the day Whitey pounded the daylights out of a schoolmate one morning on the way to school. Later he witnessed Whitey's way with women, the day Whitey drove up to a group of boys in his convertible, decked out in his slick leather jacket and brimmed hat, with the blond Jacquie McAuliffe snuggling next to him in a mink coat, naked underneath. Over the years Will McDonough's ties to the

Bulger family had only deepened; he had served as the campaign manager on Bill Bulger's successful run for state representative in 1960.

McDonough, now twenty-eight years old, was in the area because of his work covering the Boston Red Sox as a sportswriter for the *Boston Globe*. The Sox were in Kansas City, Missouri, to play three games against the hometown Athletics, and this gave McDonough a chance between games to come calling—and to serve, in effect, as a family ambassador, someone trusted to check on Whitey and then report back.

The visit marked the second time in two days McDonough had driven the fifteen miles northwest from Kansas City to Leavenworth. The day had dawned hot and was only getting hotter, climbing into the mid-nineties. His back-to-back visits replicated ones he'd made on May 4 and May 5 during an earlier Sox road trip to Kansas City. Each visit required an end run around prison rules restricting visits to family members, and that's where House Speaker John McCormack came in handy once again. Arriving ahead of McDonough was a memorandum from Bureau of Prisons director Bennett to the prison's warden: "I understand from Speaker McCormack's office that Mr. William McDonough of Boston, a close friend of the family of James Bulger, will be in your section of the country." Bennett made clear he saw no problem making an exception. "I have told them that the visit would be approved and suggested that Mr. McDonough call you as soon as he arrives in Leavenworth to make the necessary arrangements."

Whitey and Will McDonough sat together and exchanged greetings. The visits from the young sportswriter were welcome for a number of reasons, not the least of which was the chance to sit near the windows that lined the visiting room. The forty-foot walls that enclosed the prison's more than twenty-eight acres blocked any glimpse of the countryside, but the visiting room at least was situated with a view outside, and McDonough caught Whitey looking out the window.

"You know," Whitey finally said, "I haven't seen a tree in years."

McDonough also caught Whitey looking at something else—the woman seated at a nearby table with another inmate. Then it dawned on him: Whitey hadn't been in the same room with a woman in years, an open room with tables and chairs rather than one where panels of glass separated the visitor from the inmate.

"You think she's good-looking?" Whitey asked.

McDonough studied the woman. "She's okay," he said.

"Do they all wear their hair like that now?"

Whitey was talking about the woman's bouffant hairdo—a style that by the summer of 1963 had been made famous by Jackie Kennedy.

"Yeah," McDonough said, "they wear it like that now."

Since his arrival at Leavenworth twelve months earlier in July 1962 Whitey had played it perfectly. He was an old hand now at being processed into a new institution, sitting through an interview and undergoing a physical and mental examination. His weight now topped out at 176 pounds, the most he'd ever weighed, a thick hardness that showed in a new mug shot. The look hardly resembled the one of a frightened new inmate in his first mug shot in Atlanta in 1956. He dutifully filled out a health questionnaire, answering fifty-seven questions, mentioning that his only health concern was his back, which he'd strained lifting weights in Alcatraz, and for which he requested a bed board. Despite twenty-one questions aimed at determining drug use, Whitey said he'd never tried any of ten listed drugs—from marijuana to heroin. He made no mention of his LSD trips.

He soon won positive reviews for making a seamless adjustment to the new facility. He was assigned to work on a sanitation detail in the B Cell House, and he was given the charge of exterminating four-legged nuisances from his living area—the rats. Whitey got ratings of "very good" as a rodent and pest controller whose duty was to set the poisonous bait for rats and to spray insecticide in the cell house.

Whitey also squared away his approved list of correspondents and visitors, and given the relatively shorter distance from South Boston, his brother Jackie was able to bring his frail father to see him in February 1963 for two consecutive afternoon visits. There was no longer any sign of the beautiful Jacquie McAuliffe in his life.

No record exists indicating how Whitey and his father got along during the visit. Likely they discussed topics deemed safe—family news, for example, such as brother Bill's impressive juggling of his reelection to the state House of Representatives in 1962, his finishing law school and taking the state bar examination around the same time, and the birth of his two sons following his marriage to the former Mary Foley in 1960. The boys were aptly named—Bill and Jim. Whitey would know that his parents were well settled by now into their new home in Old Harbor at 252 O'Callaghan Way. The two-story brick row house was an upgrade from the third-floor unit at 41 Logan Way—larger and located at the far end of a row of attached homes built sideways from the street. No more climbing the thirty-three cement steps from the common entry of Logan Way to reach their apartment. The front door was now an easy step up from a courtyard. Between the location and the separate entrance, the Bulgers had far more privacy now.

Whitey and his father may have discussed other news from Old Harbor, such as the accomplishments of Johnny Connolly, whose family had lived at 250 O'Callaghan Way until moving out of the project to another South Boston neighborhood. Connolly, six years younger than Bill and eleven years younger than Whitey, often tagged along after Bill as a boy and had, in effect, continued following in Bill's footsteps by gaining admission to Boston College. In 1963, John Connolly had settled on a major—marketing—and was on track to graduate in two years. Whitey might not recall much about Johnny, given the age difference, but the opposite was the case for Connolly. John Connolly would never forget that when he was eight years old, in 1948, he and two pals ran into the teenage Whitey at a corner store. Whitey, already a neighborhood legend, bought a round of ice cream cones for the boys. John Connolly years later would describe the awe and wonder of the special Whitey encounter as equal to meeting Red Sox slugger Ted Williams.

Beyond the family, there was plenty of other news from the home front. Lawmakers in the spring of 1963 were heatedly preoccupied with Governor Endicott Peabody's quixotic bid to abolish the state's death penalty while, on a lighter note, the Boston Police Department decided to paint its fleet of patrol wagons blue and gray because Boston kids were mistaking the white wagons as ice cream trucks. The new colors would match the cruisers and be more in line with a look of authority.

The Boston crime world, meanwhile, was likely not something for the father and son to mention, although Whitey was monitoring from afar the various turns in Boston gangland politics. His incarceration certainly carried this one unintended consequence—it kept him out of harm's way, perhaps even saved his life during one of the most violent stretches in Boston's underworld. And he also wasn't alone in monitoring the city's underworld chaos. In the Boston FBI office, the young agent Paul Rico kept busy navigating the mob turmoil, looking to recruit informants. Rico had already shown a knack for that in the 1956 arrest of Whitey, and since then informant work had become one of the bureau's highest priorities. FBI director J. Edgar Hoover, as part of a major policy initiative to take on organized crime in the nation's cities, created the Top Echelon Informant Program. To fight organized crime, "it is mandatory that the development of quality criminal informants be emphasized," Hoover wrote in a 1961 internal memorandum announcing the program. The new program was unprecedented in its scope. Hoover wanted agents to sign up high-level criminals to provide high-level underworld intelligence—not for a single FBI case but in an ongoing way as part of a long-term special relationship. Hoover also demanded that his new program be kept strictly confidential—its very existence unknown to the public as well as to most federal and state law enforcement agencies. FBI agent Rico was assigned in 1963 to work full-time on the "TE program" for Boston. He'd already made headway with Buddy McLean of the Winter Hill Gang, and he was on the prowl for more, pitching the idea that with the FBI you've got a friend. The FBI's new program and the Boston underworld—it was all in the future of Whitey writ large.

During Will McDonough's summer visit to Leavenworth that July 18, Whitey and the sportswriter picked up from the day before. McDonough sat back and listened to Whitey speak entertainingly about a wide range of topics—his in-depth analysis of competing World War II generals and their respective strategies, for example. Whitey had read books about U.S. military leaders, read others about the Nazis. "He would study the same battle from everybody's perspective," McDonough said. "He had all these cross sections of views on the thing." Whitey was looking at how leaders lead. "It was like a game with him."

Or Whitey regaled McDonough with stories about Alcatraz—and he didn't strut out the evangelically coated version of himself he used with prison officials. Whitey bragged to McDonough about the unrest he and others caused, "stories," McDonough said, "about how they started the riots." Whitey told the sportswriter that at an agreed-upon time he and other inmates stuffed paper and magazines into the toilet bowls in their respective cells, lit the paper until it was flaming, and then flushed in unison. "They would blow the toilet up," McDonough said, "and all the water would come cascading down the side—that's the way they used to protest."

Whitey talked excitedly to McDonough about Frank Morris and Morris's escape from Alcatraz with the two Anglin brothers just a few months before his transfer off the Rock. He boasted he knew the escapees personally in Alcatraz and, before that, in Atlanta, and that he was confident the men had survived the waters of San Francisco Bay. "I know the guys made it," he told McDonough.

Whitey looped back to the bank robberies that had landed him in prison, describing each one in dramatic detail. McDonough noted Whitey conveyed no real sense of remorse or wrongdoing. The only time he seemed to get worked up was talking about how everything ended. That was the eye-opener—he'd actually been caught when he was used to outrunning his pursuers and eluding any real consequences for his crimes. "He figured he would never get caught," McDonough said. Whitey turned darker revisiting the cause of his capture. "He was upset because a guy stooled on him," McDonough said. That's what everything boiled down to—not that he'd done wrong, but that he'd gotten caught, and he'd gotten caught because he was ratted out. Just as he could deconstruct a World War II battle, Whitey had had plenty of time in federal prison to retrace his own missteps.

But instead of wallowing in anger, McDonough saw, Whitey had a businesslike attitude. He showed no bitterness, McDonough said. "He just wanted to get out of there." Whitey could not bear it otherwise. Said McDonough: "He used to say, 'If I ever got sentenced to life, I would kill myself.' " But Whitey was not a lifer, and it had been in Alcatraz, of all places, where he'd turned a corner in terms of his prison game plan. "He did everything to avoid trouble," McDonough said. "He walked around it, wide around it, and he did everything he could to do it the right way."

It was a do-right Whitey that McDonough certainly wasn't accustomed to seeing. But McDonough understood—the mask was Whitey's strategy. It was a war game of sorts; he could beat the enemy—the prison administrators—by maintaining discipline and denying them any more of his time through misconduct or a lack of discipline. "Keep your nose clean," McDonough said, summarizing Whitey's approach. "He had to do it."

This was a revelation for McDonough, and led him to see, when later taking measure of Bulger's mystique, that Whitey had a great many masks. "People all knew him, but nobody knows him. I don't think his family knows him. We had glimpses of him, we have images of him, we want to think we own a piece of him, because he is a legend."

Following the two-hour visit the morning of July 18, Will McDonough returned to Kansas City, where that night the Red Sox won the final game of the three-game series against the Athletics. Young Carl Yastrzemski hit his tenth home run of the season for the Sox to start the ninth inning and secure a 10–6 victory. The Sox were returning to Kansas City in September for another series, but Whitey would not be around by then for any more visits from the sportswriter. He'd won a transfer to the prison in Lewisburg, Pennsylvania—the outcome of his first try for parole earlier in the year.

He'd become parole eligible in February, and brother Bill got right to work adding to his lobbying list the federal agency deciding Whitey's fate: the U.S. Board of Parole. The day after Christmas 1962, Bill Bulger wrote parole board executives in Washington, D.C., about Whitey's application, and he followed that with a telephone call.

While the Bulgers remained hopeful Whitey might win release in his first crack at parole, the reality was otherwise. Whitey was still in debt—owing one hundred days in forfeited good time from the strike in Alcatraz. Clearing that up was crucial. Whitey "would not be considered to be in a parolable status until all forfeited good time is restored," a parole official explained to Bill Bulger in a reply letter.

It came as no surprise, then, that Whitey was denied parole at the February 7, 1963, hearing. But Leavenworth's Classification Committee was also reviewing Whitey's status, and that's where he got the good news. The committee recommended restoration of the one hundred days, which meant Whitey's slate was clear going forward. It then approved the transfer. "The Committee feels that a transfer should be recommended at this time to place him near relatives, release residence and for his excellent adjustment here."

The best possible outcome was the one Whitey managed to get. The processing of final approvals would take until midsummer, but Whitey knew he was on the move when he spent several hours in the visiting room with Will McDonough. There was good feeling in the air—in that room and elsewhere. Bill Bulger and House Speaker John McCormack soon exchanged notes. "I felt that you would enjoy hearing the good news," Bill wrote on August 7. "The Bulger family is extremely pleased that Jim's request has been granted." The family was upbeat, he added, about Whitey's chances for parole next time around, in early 1964. "We feel heartened," Bill said.

"I'm so glad," McCormack wrote back. Moreover, he was gratified his interventions seemed to have paid off. "I am glad I was able to make my contribution in the way that I did and that the transfer has been approved."

Whitey's arrival on September 3, 1963, at the Lewisburg Federal Penitentiary in central Pennsylvania coincided with his thirty-fourth birthday. He got off to a great start in the remaining months of the year, impressing his new overseers with, as one guard wrote, his "quiet approach to authority." He was first assigned to a cell in the A-2 Cell Block, but then requested a move to A-1, saying, "I know a few of the fellows that live on that tier and understand it's always very, very quiet." The guard who worked the night shift in A-2 wrote a memo saying he had no objection to the move, noting that A-2 "with the influx of a younger element is quite active," while Whitey "has proved to be one of the more stable, quiet men." Whitey, he said, "would probably be better off in A-1."

Whitey was assigned to work as a clerk in the Sanitation Department, where the supervising guard was quickly taken with Whitey's managerial skills in keeping track of the cleaning supplies and maintaining the janitorial equipment. The position gave Whitey the chance to pursue his growing expertise in exterminating rats. He won praise for "fogging the dining room—on off time in the evenings," and for demonstrating a "particular skill—knowledge of pest control." He enrolled in courses in bookkeeping and accounting, joined a "literary forum," and kept up with his weight lifting. He was not one for team sports and stayed away from them.

The fall also saw the beginning of a stream of visits from family. Brother Bill and sister Jean accompanied their mother and father on two afternoon visits on December 3 and 4. The ailing elder Bulger had turned eighty the week before. The atmosphere at the family gathering was surely far from festive—not for the big chill between father and son but because the entire nation, even the world, had been plunged into profound grief when President Kennedy was assassinated in Dallas eleven days before.

More family visits followed early in the new year. Brother Jackie Bulger drove down with his father in mid-January. The prison's visiting records, spare as they are, suggest all was not warm between Whitey and his father. The first visit on January 16 was over after twenty-five minutes. The next morning Whitey's father did not even show up. Instead Whitey visited with his brother Jackie for two and a half hours, after which Jackie gathered up his father and headed back to Boston.

Possible family friction aside, Whitey was riding high overall. His second shot at parole was in the offing. With good reason he was expecting his time had come. He'd stayed on task and, as he had in Leavenworth, had continued his gospel of goodness. "Expresses a concern for his family, anxious to make a new start," a work supervisor wrote. "He is plainly a man who is serving his own time and doesn't want to be bothered by anyone," noted his progress report of February 14, 1964. He'd done his part, his brother had done his—all signs were favorable.

But the parole board rejected Whitey's bid. In the memo the warden received from Washington on March 11, no explanation was given. The parole board, it simply said, "does not find sufficient justification for change in the parole status, at least at this time."

Whitey was not given news of the setback right away—a delay resulting from a second, simultaneous blow that, like a parole ruling, was extremely personal. Whitey's father died suddenly on March 11 in Boston at St. Elizabeth's Hospital. Bill Bulger called the prison the next afternoon. He spoke to the Catholic chaplain, Rev. Andrew P. Marinak, at 5 p.m., and the priest in turn immediately located Whitey to break the news. "Inmate needed no medication," the priest wrote in his notes. Whitey, the priest added, wanted to call his mother. "A phone call seems to be all that is required here, preferably in the morning."

Before Whitey made the call the next morning the priest came by bearing the other punch of bad news—the denial of his parole bid. Whitey was shocked. "Had set hopes too high," the priest wrote in his notes following their meeting, "and from what he says, due to staff members from the Bureau [of Prisons] level down giving him too much encouragement, so apparently came to depend on it." Whitey collected himself and discussed with the priest his father's death and his call to his mother. He wanted to go to Boston to attend the funeral, but understood, realistically, that it was not possible "due to the time factor." He was clearly angry about not being paroled, but decided not to get into it with his mother on the phone.

"Discussed with subject—attitude excellent," the priest noted. "Will make phone calls as above—disappointed about parole denial but won't tell mother now. I repeat—excellent attitude despite some bitterness."

Beyond the priest's comments it would be hard to gauge Whitey's emotions at the news of his father's death, except to call them complicated. In a letter written to his brother Bill while their father's health was declining, Whitey stated the obvious—that "he never hit it off with their father." But Whitey also included he regretted "all the heart ache I caused him." Later, Whitey's girlfriend Lindsey Cyr said there was no love lost between Whitey and his father. "If he felt bad when the father died," she said, "it would be to the extent it made his mother unhappy." Cyr said that during her relationship with Whitey the subject of his father was taboo. She said he was emphatic, telling her, "I don't talk about him. He's dead and that's a good thing."

Following his talk with the priest, Whitey called home just before lunch—at 11:40 a.m. on Friday, March 13. The priest monitored the call and first spoke briefly to the newly widowed Jean Bulger. Whitey then talked to his mother for about five minutes. Whitey then spoke to his sister. Then he hung up.

The next morning James J. Bulger Sr. was buried at St. Joseph's Cemetery in West Roxbury, Massachusetts.

Whitey immediately wrote the U.S. Parole Board asking it to reconsider, but it would not. Everything—all that hard work, the buildup to being set free—was suddenly in jeopardy. And on the morning of April 7 Whitey suffered a lapse in the Gandhi-like pose of nonviolence he'd mastered. In the shower he exploded and pummeled an inmate who was cursing one of his friends about a cigarette debt. The guard found the victim with "a bruise on his chin and his back was scraped as if from a fall." Whitey had little to say to the guards investigating the incident, except that he became "angry at some of the language" the inmate used against his friend.

Initially Whitey's burst of violence did not seem to present much trouble for him. He received a warning and a reprimand. By month's end, however, things seemed to spiral out of control. The prison's Classification Committee recommended that he be moved back up the ladder in the prison system's hierarchy to a more secure facility—to the new super-max prison in Marion, Illinois. Marion had replaced Alcatraz to hold the most dangerous prisoners, opening in 1963 after Alcatraz closed permanently.

But Whitey apparently had too much momentum going for a single fight to trip him up. The warden rejected the recommendation, and in early May the committee rescinded its action. Whitey's next "progress report" in May, as well as a May 27 letter from the warden to his bosses in Washington, glossed over the fight. There was a hint some guards doubted that Whitey's do-good posturing was genuine. Wrote the warden: "He is reported as one of the group of serious potential escape risks who has been seen observing the reconstruction project at the rear gate to see if any security weakness could be found." But these were blips. Overall future assessments were positive; they did not even cite the aborted transfer. It was as if it never happened, and the warden said Whitey's "adjustment at this institution is good and he is trying very hard to make a good record in order to be granted parole." Plus, he said, Whitey showed maturity in "the way he handled himself when he received notice of his parole denial and notice of his father's death on the same day." Furthermore, the reports cited his political connections. "It is also noted his family have a very close relationship with the Speaker of the House."

Whitey was back on track, ready to stay the course as the do-good inmate. Do-good and say the right thing again and again in repetition, just like a weight lifter pumping iron. His brother Jackie came to see him in April, and returned in June. His sister Carol and her husband came in late June, and the next month his mother, accompanied by family friends, made the trip. In September Whitey wrote up an "inmate request" seeking a move to an "honor block." His curling, cursive writing style had grown fancier and carefully crafted from when he first entered prison in 1956. "The reasons for the requests are, I like fresh air," he wrote. "And of primary importance to me is that perhaps if I lived in an honor block in good standing coupled with a good work and conduct record somehow it may help to influence future decisions of the parole review board."

Whitey wanted a window—one step closer to the outside and part of the windup for his next parole hearing, for which everyone was pulling out all the stops. Bill Bulger traveled to Lewisburg for a visit on September 10, and he began coordinating with House Speaker John McCormack. In December McCormack started the offensive, sending a single-spaced letter to the chairman of the U.S. Board of Parole that, in depth and detail, resembled the kind of statement he might make on behalf of a major piece of legislation he cared deeply and personally about. McCormack was at full throttle in articulating his feelings about the Bulgers. "The Bulger family in Boston are very close and dear and valued friends of mine and a very fine family—an outstanding family, and one of the members, Representative William Bulger, is a distinguished member of the Massachusetts House of Representatives, having just been reelected to his third term. I have a very high regard for Representative Bulger and for his entire family."

McCormack reminded the chairman that "in the past two years I have called in connection with the possible parole" of Whitey. The House Speaker then addressed what would become of Whitey upon his release: Whitey would live at home in Old Harbor with his mother and his nineteen-year-old sister; in addition, his brother Bill, "who is also a very able attorney, is in a position to give considerable help to him and, if paroled, to help him view the future and live as a law abiding citizen."

The same day of the December 15 letter, McCormack dashed off a note to Bill Bulger in which he enclosed a copy of what he'd written to parole board chairman Richard A. Chappell. Reading it, Bill Bulger must have been pleased; it would be hard to imagine topping the show of support for Whitey that the nation's powerful Speaker of the House had expressed. The federal government was historically anathema to anyone from South Boston—it was an outside force that had no business intruding on the neighborhood. But Whitey was experiencing an upside to federal intervention, made possible when that power was channeled through the hands of someone else from the neighborhood.

Chairman Chappell was out of town when McCormack wrote to him, but his office did not wait for the chairman to return to get back to the House Speaker. One of the other board members immediately replied in the chairman's stead, saying the letter had been made a part of Whitey's file "so that your comments will be available to the Members of the Board at the time a decision is made in his case." Once again, McCormack turned around and sent a copy of the letter to Bill Bulger in Boston.

The hearing was set for Tuesday, February 2, 1965. For McCormack, the month of January was a nonstop affair. He played a key role during the inauguration of President Lyndon Baines Johnson, giving the oath of office to Vice President Hubert H. Humphrey in the cold sunlight on Capitol Plaza on Wednesday, January 20. He was also a key figure in the president's legislative ambitions for the Great Society.

But Bill Bulger wanted no surprises like the year before and was determined not to leave anything to chance this time around. He stayed on the Speaker as the days drew closer. "Representative William Bulger called as a reminder regarding his brother," said a telephone message for McCormack taken by an aide in January. "He wanted to know if the Speaker would place a call on his brother's behalf prior to February 1, to Richard A. Chappell, Chairman—Board of Parole. Tel. No. 187–2872."

McCormack got the message and made the call on January 27. "I have just talked personally with Chairman Shappell [sic] in re your brother," he wrote in a telegram to Bill Bulger. "Urging favorable consideration by him and his associates. He told me he would look into the matter and report back later." The Speaker did not stop with the chairman; he called other board members, and the next day informed Bill Bulger of his additional lobbying efforts. "Supplementing my telegram of January 27, will say that I have today talked with James Carr, who is a member of the Board of Parole, conveying to him my interest in your brother."

Five days later the parole board convened. McCormack had spoken personally to several members, his fingerprints were on Whitey's file in the form of his strong recommendation, and Whitey's positive progress reports were all in hand. The "Notice of Action of Parole Board" made out for that day recorded the big news: "Reopened and granted, effective March 1, 1965." The chairman, keeping his word, called McCormack afterward to tell him personally about Whitey's parole. McCormack then reached Bill Bulger in Boston and broke the news. "Good luck, good news," McCormack scribbled in his notes about the telephone call.

That night John McCormack headed to the White House to attend a black-tie dinner as one of the president's three guests of honor, along with the vice president and Chief Justice Earl Warren. President Johnson was hosting the elegant affair to court congressional leaders for his programs before the new Congress. The Bulgers, meanwhile, relished their victory, and three days later, on February 5, Bill Bulger drove down to see Whitey. They talked all afternoon. They'd done it.

The next several weeks were taken up with preparations for Whitey's release, with officials putting the finishing touches on his so-called parole plan. The core areas of concern in any parolee's plan were place of residence, work, and mentoring. In a February 23 letter, a federal probation officer in Boston reported that Whitey would live at home. In terms of employment, the union official who in previous drafts of the plan had promised Whitey work had been replaced. "Mr. Mel Berman, owner of Farnsworth Press Company in Boston, is willing to employ the subject at a salary of $1.50 an hour." Rev. Robert Drinan, who in every previous draft had been listed as Whitey's parole adviser, was suddenly no more. "We will dispense with the parole advisor at this time," the probation letter said. No explanation was given, whether all along Drinan's name had been window dressing to make Whitey's plan look more impressive, or whether Drinan's ever-expanding interests meant he no longer had the time. Except for Whitey's prison files, no record of any further contact between Drinan and Whitey Bulger exists.

Come March 1, Whitey's mug shot was taken—the last from his prison period. He was thirty-five years old now and thicker in build than when he entered prison. His hair was clipped short, and the intense glare of earlier mug shots was replaced by a calm look. He'd been away for just shy of nine years. He walked out of prison a free man that morning at 10:32, according to his release authorization form, a clear, chilly day. He had $64.27 in his pocket.

Whitey Bulger was heading home, and he owed a ton of gratitude to his brother Bill, the loyal younger brother who had done so much to win his release. They'd always been close, but after the past nine years the brothers' bond only deepened—and it would always remain deep, a mutual loyalty tested but never broken. No doubt Bill Bulger and the rest of the family wanted only the best for their ex-convict. Surely Whitey did, too—though his idea of what was in his best interest turned out to be wholly different from what others had in mind.

14

Chandler's Summit

Douglas

Whitey

Lindsey Cyr was living a quiet life in a small urban village until Whitey Bulger stopped by for coffee one morning.

She worked the early shift as a waitress in a restaurant across the street from the law office where she was secretary. She was spunky but recuperating from an abusive relationship with an ex-marine who got physical with her and depleted her bank account.

Then everything changed. Whitey, a year out of prison, was working the jackhammer on a construction job at a bank up the street and showed up for a late breakfast of tea, toast, and eggs over. And he liked what he saw.

At twenty-one, Cyr had an eighteen-inch waist and a quick smile. Whitey flirted with her and she liked his rugged looks and confident way. After a few visits, he asked her out but she demurred, saying she was taking a break from dating, mending from her time with an abusive boyfriend. Whitey persisted and she relented.

Once in a while, she worked a third job as a runway model at Bonwit Teller, an old-line upscale clothier where she wore Chanel apparel for Back Bay audiences. But her day-to-day life was one city block in North Quincy. She played catch-me with Whitey for a couple of weeks, but succumbed to his final pitch in the spring of 1966. "I've got an idea," he said one morning. "How about you come to a cookout at my brother Billy's this Sunday? It won't be a date. It'll be family and daylight and no alcohol. My mother will be there." She went and made a lasting connection with Whitey's mother, Jean.

Prosaic as it was, it was a breakout moment for Whitey, an instinctive stab at normalcy after a decade in prison. Cyr wasn't Southie and she worked in a law office. He took her home to Mother. To Billy's for a cookout. To a courting dinner at the Parker House downtown.

It was a clean slate with a glimmer of hope for family life. Again, Cyr was outside the flow of Southie. She was plucky, but a question soon arose. Could she lure Whitey away from all he knew, the hijacking, the bank robberies, and now the loan-sharking?

The long shot took a fitful course, with Whitey never fully committing, trying to have it both ways for a couple of years, moving between the two discrete worlds of Southie and Quincy almost as a spy, leaning more and more toward the money and the streets. As life choices went, husband never had much of a chance against crime boss.

After some courting dates, the terms—and turf—changed with an ultimatum. "I'm not going to stay celibate," he told her with a sly smile. "You know where you can find me—at Triple O's." Cyr recalled that he gave her the telephone number and the address. "I took it and thought 'OK.' " Their next social event was dinner and then back to her Quincy apartment to relax.

She said there was power in Whitey's mere presence, a cocky bearing and a sure-footed awareness. "The thing I remember is that he knew everything that was going on. He'd know what was going on at my law office. How'd he know that? He knew what was going in general. I could never figure that out. It was a little spooky at times. He was just so alert and ready for anything."

Cyr said Whitey was on the straight and narrow long enough to show up at a Bonwit Teller fashion show, and the incongruity was not lost on her. "I spotted him right away, sitting in a leather jacket at one of the small cocktail tables in a room full of women. It was funny."

But within months he fell back in line with his destiny; in late 1966 he enrolled in the Killeen brothers' gang at the Transit Café in Southie and the bookmaking/loan-sharking life. Cyr said it wasn't hard to figure out. "He stopped construction work but always had money," she said. But they never talked about it.

They were together most of the time for some busy years. Cyr got pregnant right away and they had a son, Douglas, in May 1967. Whitey, elusive as ever, more or less lived with her, staying in her apartment two or three nights a week and visiting most weekends. But his address remained Old Harbor at his mother's unit.

Whitey doted on Douglas but chafed against the domestic life. Cyr remembered a big night for them in November 1967 when they got a babysitter for their first "date" since Douglas had been born. "Jimmy was after me to get his life back. Get a babysitter. Do something. It was fine by me. I hadn't been in an evening dress in a year." So they went to the Parker House for dinner and then to Triple O's, the South Boston barroom she came to dislike.

The saving grace for her was time with Whitey's best friend, the congenial Billy O'Sullivan, who had six kids and a sense of humor. A former marine, he wore his toughness with a smile. Sitting on a barstool, Cyr spent most of the night talking with "Billy O" while Whitey, standing beside her but with his back turned, did business in low conversation with a stream of supplicants. Around eleven o'clock, she reminded Whitey they had to get the babysitter home by midnight, but he said no way. He said they'd pay her extra to stay longer. She said they'd never get her back again. To Billy O, Whitey said, "Can you believe I'm turning into a pumpkin?" Billy O: "Never get between a mother and her babysitter."

Whitey sighed and said to Cyr, "Okay, let's go."

When they got to their car on West Broadway, across the street from the bar, she said she heard pinging sounds from the granite buildings behind them. "My God," she said. "Someone's shooting at us." Whitey pulled her down behind the car and returned fire as the attackers fled from across the street. She sat there in stunned amazement in the sudden silence. He looked at her and said, "Relax. I said I'd get you home by midnight."

Whitey Bulger was back in town.

At the beginning of the decade, when Whitey was reading World War II history in Alcatraz, the Boston underworld map was cut in stone along ethnic lines. The Mafia roosted in the furtive North End on the edge of the financial district and the rest of the wiseguys called it "in town."

The other gangs were ensconced in neighborhood outposts. The Irish had three branches. The cluster around the Charlestown wharves was run by the McLaughlin brothers, who were loan sharks to longshoremen before moving "up" to be contract killers for the Mafia. Next door in Somerville was the Buddy McLean Gang, who were teamsters that dominated Local 25 and specialized in hijacking trucks. Big jobs. They morphed into the more muscular and enduring Winter Hill Gang, named for its neighborhood.

And Southie, as always, stood truculently alone. Its bookmaking and loan-sharking were run by the bruising Killeen brothers, whose "office" was the Transit Café. By the time Whitey was nearing parole, the Killeens were jamming with the hijacking Mullen Gang over territory and treasure. They were scoffed at by the Mafia for their pointless squabbles, such as when one of the Killeen brothers bit the nose off Mickey Dwyer.

The next separate territory was Mafia-controlled East Boston, which came to be dominated by Joseph "Baron" Barboza, a Portuguese-American who was the go-to hit man, until he turned crazy violent, killing for no reason. East Boston stayed a Mafiosi outpost even after becoming a mostly Hispanic neighborhood.

Last, there was the Roxbury/South End faction run by the entrepreneurial Bennett brothers, who were loan sharks and bookmakers. They preyed on marginal minorities and were in and out of a score of businesses, staying just long enough to milk them and then torch them for insurance money. Their foremost apprentice was a dangerous hustler named Stevie Flemmi, who years later would turn on them all.

The Mafia boss, Gennaro "Jerry" Angiulo, grew up in the North End. When he mustered out of the Navy after World War II he became a shrewd moneymaker in the rackets. He talked tough but left enforcement mayhem to underlings, relying on his five brothers and the fearsome South End loan shark Ilario Zannino.

Angiulo became underboss by sensing that the way to the capo di capos' heart was cold cash. He'd brought a bag of it to New England crime boss Raymond L. S. Patriarca in the 1950s and the partnership flourished. Angiulo came to detest the only other Boston gangsters who had clout with Patriarca—Edward "Wimpy" Bennett, the energetic leader of the profitable Bennett enterprises, and Barboza, the haywire enforcer who always got his man. They had to make an appointment but they were the only non-Mafiosi welcome on Federal Hill in Providence, Rhode Island, where Patriarca was based.

Shortly before Whitey was transferred from Alcatraz to Leavenworth, the Boston underworld was convulsed by an incident at a Labor Day beach party in 1961. Georgie McLaughlin, the youngest of the three crime brothers, got to drinking all day and capped the party by spitting beer in the face of a moll not interested in his proposition. Two McLean gangsters took exception and beat him senseless, then dumped him, barely alive, on a hospital lawn north of Boston.

Georgie was dragged in to the emergency room and survived. His brothers filed a strong protest but Buddy McLean refused reparations and a five-year war ensued, claiming forty victims, one of them beheaded. Its wanton persistence moved it from tabloid back pages to a four-page spread in *Life* magazine.

The decapitated body was found in South Boston in the trunk of a stolen car. The body of another gangster bobbed to the surface in Boston Harbor near Logan Airport, strangled with the "Chinese torture knot," used to hog-tie victims so that they choke to death as they try to free their hands and legs. Yet another victim was a name familiar to Whitey—Ron Dermody. He was Whitey's accomplice in the 1955 Rhode Island bank robbery and also did time in the Atlanta Penitentiary. Paroled, Dermody tried to make a name for himself in the war by shooting Buddy McLean, but he failed. Instead McLean got him, shooting him three times in the head in September 1964.

The gangland upheaval forced nearly everyone to choose sides and constantly look over their shoulders. For years Southie and the Mafia kept their distance as best they could. At first Angiulo was happy to let the Irish gangs decimate one another and scoop up their now-unmoored "independent" bookies into his network. But the body count got so bad and brought so much heat that Patriarca demanded a cease-fire, and that meant killing Punchy McLaughlin, the last brother standing. The hit made Stevie Flemmi's reputation.

As the war finally wound down, Angiulo thought he was in the catbird seat, but he didn't see Whitey Bulger gathering himself a mile away.

In 1965, resourceful Will McDonough helped Whitey get his first job after being paroled. Working from a galaxy of contacts in his Rolodex, McDonough landed Whitey a slot at a nonunion printing company.

McDonough said he set up the job because he knew that Bill Bulger, as a new member of the state House of Representatives, would have trouble putting his ex-convict brother on a public payroll. At least right away. So Whitey reentered civilian life as a printer at $1.50 an hour before moving on to higher-paying construction work.

But after two years of keeping his nose clean, Whitey took the inevitable patronage post, arranged by Bill in 1967, when the timing was right. It was a "check-in" job of night janitor at the Suffolk County courthouse. Whitey showed up in late afternoon for a couple of hours, poked around private offices at will, and then went to his real job in the South Boston rackets. When he didn't need the custodial job to pacify his parole officer, he stopped going completely. But he stayed on the books for years.

Whitey was more subdued than he'd been in his mustang years at Old Harbor, and McDonough didn't see him as often. But he always looked forward to meeting with Whitey three or four times a year just for his smarts and the conversation. "He's a hell of a guy," McDonough said. "It's just if you are on the wrong side . . ."

Citizen Whitey lay low for several years as he juggled the sub-rosa world in Southie with taking care of his mother in Old Harbor and trying out a tenuous domestic life with Cyr in a new apartment in Weymouth.

But there were still flashes of the old Whitey when he roared through Southie streets or along expressways like a crazed race car driver. Some trips left Cyr breathless. Even at that, he was ticketed only twice—a five-dollar fine for running a light in 1967 and ten dollars for speeding in 1968. He seemed restrained enough for cameos on election day for brother Bill—as long as no opponents got in the act. That always went badly. When Billy was in a big race to move up to the state Senate in 1970, Whitey was the one who brought umbrellas to the project women who were working the polls on a rainy day. It was a rare sighting of Whitey, but neighbor Sally Dame remembered it as a "family affair," with the whole clan out in force. Whitey never lost his soft spot for Old Harbor mothers.

But flitting from one world to another was not just a necessary expedient for Whitey—it was his elixir. He always enjoyed the challenge of keeping several balls in the air, the duplicity of a double life, of having things both ways with no one the wiser.

But his sly hand was unexpectedly forced when Cyr became pregnant in the fall of 1966. Whitey was a less than ecstatic new father. He told Cyr it was a complicating problem for him and urged an abortion. She said she didn't believe in it and was prepared to raise the baby on her own. He said his work in South Boston precluded fatherhood, that it would make him vulnerable. She said that's your world, not mine. He grimaced and said, "I need to think about this, how to handle this. It could be dangerous for all of us." Cyr told him, "You'll figure it out."

By this time, Cyr recalled, Whitey had told her some of his history, about being on the run from the FBI for robbing banks and then going to prison for nine years. He had told her his concerns about being in the LSD Program at the Atlanta Penitentiary, that it may have affected his genetic makeup and increased the chance of having an unhealthy child. Cyr replied, "Well, I'll be healthy for both of us."

So the baby came in the spring of 1967 and Cyr learned to accommo-date Whitey's past and livelihood.

The closest they ever came to a brass tacks talk about their future tumbled out of an interlude they had in San Francisco in 1968. Douglas was about a year old when Cyr took him with her on a visit to a girl-friend in California. She decided to stay longer but couldn't reach Whitey to let him know and left a message with his mother instead. Two days later, control freak Whitey showed up unannounced at the apartment, irate that she didn't clear the vacation extension with him.

She talked him down from high dudgeon and, the next day, they went on a walking tour. Along the waterfront, they came across a tour boat for Alcatraz, which had been closed for about five years and was in limbo before being revived as a national park. There was no tour guide as such but Whitey knew his way around, having spent two and a half years there as an inmate. She said he was excited by the idea of the impromptu tour. "Let's take the baby out to see where Daddy used to live," he said wryly. She said she was a little spooked by the eerie empty place but, on their own, they made their way to Whitey's old cell. She said he was transfixed inside it and had tears in his eyes. "Never in my life did I think I'd be here in this place with my son in my arms."

In a way, she said, he was proud of having been in Alcatraz—about having survived it. "I never thought I would get out," he told her. "Billy kept telling me he was working on it. But at the time it seemed like a death sentence."

After the visit, they talked about his two worlds. Cyr said, "When we were first together and Douglas was a baby, he was still looking for his place. To find where he fit in. In a way, I know this sounds funny, for a career path."

He also spoke matter-of-factly about the inexorable pull of his old life. "I don't have any choice," he told her. "What am I going to do? Nine-to-five? And things need to be straightened out in Southie. Somerville or the North End can take it all away. And it's ours."

Whitey's territorial imperative evolved into his first murder in the dog-eat-dog proving ground of South Boston. It was genuine warfare, kill or be killed, and Whitey was eager to establish himself and stabilize the Southie underworld. It wasn't just earning his spurs. He was after primacy.

But he was too eager to get going. It may have been a case of rookie nerves but the hit was a screwup, a case of mistaken identity that Whitey later downplayed as the minor price of gang warfare. Southie stuff happens. But it was a bad miscalculation that made things worse. The muffed murder made the Mullens out for blood.

In November 1969, Whitey was after Mullen leader Paulie McGonagle, an assassination that would have tilted the intermittent conflict in the Killeens' favor. With Billy O'Sullivan at the wheel, they pulled side by side with another car, Whitey opening fire and shooting the other driver in the head. The man behind the wheel was a McGonagle, but the wrong one—Paulie's younger brother Donald, who wasn't even a gang member.

Instead of a knockout punch, the botched job made the notion of peace preposterous and the Killeens against it. A year and a half later, the heightened tensions in Southie spilled over in one of the worst nights in Whitey Bulger's life. It happened in March 1971, when Billy O'Sullivan teetered home around midnight to find three Mullen gang members lying in wait.

O'Sullivan might have been good for bonhomie on a barstool, but he was still a hard-drinking loan shark who could go for his gun as quick as his smile could disappear. A month earlier, he and Whitey had a violent altercation with Mullen gang member Buddy Roache, who gave them an ultimatum in a lounge on West Broadway. Roache said if they stuck with their boss, Donald Killeen, they would all be killed. The threat led to more threats and Roache went for his gun. But O'Sullivan got to his first, with a shot that severed Roache's spine, paralyzing him for life. Retribution was thick in the air. Whitey became extra vigilant but Billy blithely underestimated how bad it was to be that outnumbered.

O'Sullivan was whistling past the graveyard when he sauntered to his front stoop late at night, feeling no pain. The men suddenly appeared around him and O'Sullivan made a run for it. He dodged two bullets but tripped on a manhole cover a short distance up Savin Hill Avenue. Witnesses told police that the trio circled around him and, as he struggled to get up, one of them shot him in the head three times.

An hour later, Cyr took the call, jumping on the phone quickly so it wouldn't wake Douglas. A voice said, "Tell Whitey not to go home. Billy O. has been hit. Don't go home." Cyr said Whitey turned pale and she got weepy and a little hysterical. He had tears in his eyes but said, "Calm down. I need to think." After an hour or so, Whitey got more information on the phone and turned coldly furious when he found out O'Sullivan had been shot in front of his house. "Jimmy suffered with that," Cyr said. "He cried over Billy. Jimmy was just so furious about it for a long time. How it was done was unforgivable to him."

It turned out that Tommy King, the main muscle of the Mullen Gang, was the triggerman.

But Cyr never knew any of that. She said when things grew tense, Whitey withdrew, telling her only that there was trouble. He'd signal "stop" with his hand to the voluble Cyr.

"That was all I ever got," she said. "Trouble. I never knew the names or the circumstances."

Among the things she didn't know in 1971 was that Whitey Bulger was a marked man.

Dennis Condon saw it all unfolding and rubbed his hands. In the FBI ballpark, Whitey's dilemma was a fat pitch.

Condon, an agent who worked Organized Crime for decades, saw a beleaguered gangster in the middle of a turf war as a golden opportunity. The upheaval was fertile ground for informants. And the veteran agent was well versed in the gamesmanship of reeling in a wiseguy in trouble.

Condon waited about six weeks after the O'Sullivan murder for things to settle down, then made his first overture to Whitey on May 13, 1971. The theme was "you've got a pal in a dark hour" as a grim-faced Whitey related the lineup of Mullen members arrayed against him. The first FBI file noted two related items—"his life may be in jeopardy" and "he could be a very valuable source of information relative to the organized criminal activities in South Boston."

The second meeting, about three weeks later, produced a three-page memorandum that elaborated on Whitey's quandary. It covered his history with O'Sullivan, an active loan shark who had aligned himself with Roxbury stalwart Stevie Flemmi and the Bennett brothers, who ran Roxbury rackets during the 1960s gang war. After the armistice, Billy O'Sullivan had signed on with Donald Killeen and Whitey as the best game in Southie. But then the conflict with the Mullen Gang was inflamed when O'Sullivan paralyzed Buddy Roache.

Whitey recapped options for settling the trouble in Southie. He and Killeen mulled having a Mafia leader impose peace but discarded that idea because the "organization" would demand too much in return. They also thought about asking Howie Winter, boss of the Winter Hill Gang, to mediate. But they decided against that because Howie was friends with a couple of Mullens. The bottom line was dire: Whitey would be murdered if things weren't resolved.

But after two more perfunctory meetings, Whitey's initial FBI file was "closed." The Condon memoranda in July and August noted Whitey's "inhibitions" about providing more information and said that hope was fading that he'd sign on. The September entry was to the point: "Contacts with captioned individual have been unproductive."

Reading between the lines, it appears the transactions were too one-sided for Whitey. He was giving and not getting, never his favorite arrangement. It wasn't that he had any compunction about ratting out the length of West and East Broadway, which bisected Southie. He'd do that in a minute. But it quickly became pointless for him to offer repetitive reports from his stalemated battlefront.

And perhaps the personal dynamics weren't working. Condon was no Paul Rico, who developed most of the informants in the 1960s with a hard-stare flippancy that appealed to wiseguys. While only five years older than Whitey, Condon was austerely patriarchal, gray, even gnarled. Maybe too much like Whitey's father. Condon was strictly by-the-numbers and Whitey needed more conversation than that.

Someday maybe. But not now. Whitey needed to think, to regroup.

It's as if Billy O'Sullivan's ghost led Whitey out of the wilderness.

Billy had always told Whitey that if he got in a jam, he knew a guy who knew a guy. Nine months after Whitey called it off with the FBI, he made his move. His ace in the hole was a favor O'Sullivan had done for Johnny Martorano in 1966.

The good turn for a bad guy started the day O'Sullivan opened an after-hours joint in Roxbury and asked Martorano, a hulking up-and-comer who loved the high life, to stop by for a drink.

But the club opened and closed the same night.

Things went haywire almost the minute a soused ex-boxer from Southie, Tony Veranis, rolled in around 3 a.m. There was recent bad blood involving Martorano's brother Jimmy, a loan shark who had tried to collect a debt from Veranis a week earlier in a Southie bar. Jimmy had the bad judgment to take up an overdue debt on enemy turf and was badly beaten. Veranis began rubbing it in with Johnny. They exchanged *fuck-yous* and went for their guns, with Johnny shooting down on the smaller Veranis. Forty people poured out of the club and Martorano hauled off the body, leaving it to O'Sullivan to clean up the blood and gore. A spotless crime scene before police got involved was a big-time favor owed and both men knew it. Whitey used it to seek mediation with the Mullens.

He looked up Martorano at Duffy's Tavern, in the dilapidated area of the South End on the bad edge of Back Bay. Martorano owned the fifteen-stool bar with his brother Jimmy and they were in the process of transferring its liquor license next door to a much larger restaurant they'd recently acquired. The brothers bought it with new partners—

the big guns of the Winter Hill Gang. They would call it Chandler's and it became the wiseguys' watering hole of choice for years.

Martorano was a fierce street warrior and compulsive gambler who worked in the shadow of Howie Winter, the towering survivor of the Irish gang war of the 1960s. An ex-marine, Winter connected with the Mullens and was happy to fence their wares from hijacked trucks. Johnny's muscle and sports betting expertise got him to Winter Hill as a fast-rising apprentice.

In the spring of 1972, Whitey arrived at Martorano's bar in a business suit and introduced himself politely as Jimmy. Martorano had met him once before but didn't recognize him right away. He beckoned Whitey to pull up a stool. Whitey told him that Billy O'Sullivan said to look him up if he had a problem. Could Martorano set up a meeting with Howie? Johnny said "done."

The Chandler's summit was scheduled for the next night in a studded room with a bare ceiling in the building next door.

It would be Whitey's finest hour, the boldest of strokes to consolidate South Boston under his control at a time when he was surrounded and in a corner.

The sit-down took place late at night, with Howie at the head of the table and four Mullens—Paul McGonagle, Pat Nee, Jimmy Mantville, and Tommy King—on one side and a solitary Whitey on the other. The meeting lasted into the wee hours but Whitey's pitch was simplicity itself: I'll help with Donald Killeen and redistribute the town's gambling money but I have to be boss and the war has to end. The wedge Whitey used was steady gambling income to replace the sporadic paydays from truck hijacking and armed robbery.

Howie nodded gravely, saying that he had been through a much worse war and stressing the diminishing returns for everyone.

Martorano said that even with the high stakes, Whitey was unfazed. Coolest guy in the room. "If he was feeling anything, he didn't show it," Martorano recalled. "And he was definitely an underdog at the time. No question, he was going to lose that thing. He was outnumbered."

On May 13, 1972, Donald Killeen was in his suburban house at a backyard birthday party for his four-year-old son when he received an urgent call to get back to the city. After he got in his car in the driveway, several men ran at him from the nearby woods. One jammed a machine gun into the front seat and sprayed Killeen as he fumbled to get his .38 from the glove compartment.

The execution led to a wary truce with the Mullens. But, with money spread around, Southie was taking shape as Bulgertown.

By the summer, Whitey had another audacious proposition for Winter Hill. At the second Chandler's summit, he proposed that the gang restructure itself into a two-tiered operation, with five partners splitting up new revenue from a cash cow just lying there for the taking. They would extort bookies unallied with the Mafia, extracting monthly "rents" for the right to do business. The partners would also force corralled bookies into the more lucrative world of betting on NFL games.

His sales pitch: We'll have our cake and eat it, too. Everyone keeps their existing rackets and liegemen but the five partners can whack up the rents. Whitey would still control gambling and loan-sharking in South Boston. Johnny would retain his betting network in Roxbury, Howie his hammerlock on Somerville's horse race book. And the tandem of Joe McDonald and Jimmy Sims, both of Somerville, would continue with truck hijacking and holdups. To each his own.

The brazen kicker was the partnership shares: one sixth to each except for Bulger, who would get one-third. His rationale for the lion's share was that he had to spread it around with the Mullens, which he said reduced his personal take to 5 percent. It raised eyebrows but the alternative was one-sixth of nothing.

The great bookie shakedown of 1972 was under way.

Lindsey Cyr had started out with Whitey in a Weymouth apartment they quickly outgrew. Over his objections, she bought her parents' summer cottage, overlooking a marsh in North Weymouth, for $19,900. Whitey was there and not there. She commuted to her job in Boston as a legal secretary and the cottage gradually became a home as it was winterized. She said Whitey never fully committed to the cottage but liked it better when things got fixed up inside and out. He paid for most of it.

She said Douglas had Whitey's bearing. "He had the same look of determination. He was so serious and alert." She said he walked at nine months and talked at a year. Douglas had his third birthday at the renovated cottage. One of the party photos shows the other kids blowing horns and him frowning at the head of the table as if he's running a board meeting. "Jimmy was like that," she said. "All business."

Three years later, after Whitey had subjugated Southie and was a full-fledged partner at Winter Hill, managing a portfolio of his own making, Douglas became deathly sick.

Lindsey didn't think much of it at first. Douglas had just recovered from chicken pox and been on aspirin every four hours for days, which turned out to be the worst thing to have done. He suddenly became listless and ran a high fever. She didn't know it but he was already in a lethal stage of Reye's syndrome, which is exacerbated by aspirin and generally accompanies a viral infection like chicken pox. His brain was swollen by the time he reached South Shore Hospital, where he slipped into a coma. Cyr talked to Whitey and they agreed to have him rushed to Massachusetts General Hospital in Boston. But it was too late. He died over a weekend in October 1973, sick on Friday and gone on Monday.

Lindsey said the death was shattering to Whitey, who couldn't get over the fact that he wasn't able to save his son, no matter the level of medical care. "He was terribly saddened and frustrated that he couldn't fix it," she said. "He just couldn't get over how fast it happened and how he couldn't do anything about it."

Douglas and his mother, Lindsey Cyr

She said they went through an agonizing weekend at Mass. General as things went from bad to worse. She told doctors that if it was hopeless, then no heroics, that she didn't want Douglas to suffer needlessly. "But Jimmy rejected that. He just wanted to get him home no matter what. He said, 'We'll just bring him home and you'll stop work to take care of him and I'll pay for everything.' "

By eight-thirty Monday night, they confronted the inevitable when doctors couldn't stop the bleeding. Cyr told the medical staff that "if this is going to be all life-support machines, I'll pull the plug myself. Jimmy said, 'I can shoot people but I could never do that.' It was clearly coming but when the doctor told us, it was so devastating. What was so hurtful is Douglas had been so healthy and we had been so vigilant.

"We went to a room there to be alone and we just hugged each other and cried. It was really awful. Jimmy said, 'I'll never hurt like this again.' "

From the hospital, they went to Jean Bulger's unit in Old Harbor, where Whitey's mother broke down sobbing. "Jimmy hated that," Cyr said. "It was very painful and he cut the visit short."

Then they went to her mother's home, where things got even more emotional. "My mother was a difficult woman, always, always, and she began carrying on," said Cyr. When she keened about where the burial money would come from, "Jimmy picked her up and then put her down and said, 'Money is my problem and none of your business.' "

At the funeral home, she said Whitey took three thousand dollars in cash from one pocket and five hundred from another and thrust it at the undertaker. "Use the best one," he told him when asking for a casket.

Blood money for his son's funeral. It's as if the power of money was his only ally against fate's wrenching turn. Douglas had indeed made him vulnerable. Home life left him cold. Construction work was for suckers. His only comfort zone was his dark place. After Douglas, there was simply nothing for him in the legitimate world.

In the aftermath, Whitey followed classic psychopathic propensities, further stifling feelings, turning more disciplined, and controlling in a compulsive way. Emotions were liabilities. As he had for Billy O'Sullivan, he cared deeply for his son and was dealt a shattering blow. Never again. No more children. No more risk of pain. No more commitment to others. He had only himself in an underworld of expendable people, which reduced informing and killing to simple self-interest. No-brainers. Cyr soon symbolized vulnerability. Unruly Mullens were dead men walking. The ruthless pursuit of money became a secular religion that precluded lasting loyalty or real friendship.

Cyr said after the funeral, Whitey told her she was going straight to an apartment at Harbor Towers in Boston to live and they were never going back to Weymouth. He told her he couldn't bear being at the cottage with its ghosts.

"Jimmy's approach to bad events was to never deal with them again. It's like he wanted to kill the memories. I think he would have burned the cottage if he could have." But Cyr wouldn't budge on relocating to Boston. "Jimmy, the cottage is my home, my base," she told him. "I want to hold on to the good we had there."

Whitey's solution was to rent an apartment in Weymouth off Route 3A so Cyr could keep her cottage and they could still be together nearby. When he felt like it. Cyr recalled that Whitey "could seem very reasonable when he was trying to get you to do what he wanted. He said to me, 'You could really fix this place up. It'll be just what you want. Here's some money.' I said, 'Oh, sure.' "

She sighed at the memory. "But it was a tryst place for us. Pure and simple. I came to hate it. I wanted a home and I felt like we were doing something wrong there." He'd call and they'd meet and have sex, sometimes all night. He'd come in and cover his mouth; she'd start to say something and then he'd cover her mouth, shaking his head to indicate no talking. Then he'd walk straight to the bedroom. Still, his hold on her was such that she went there "whenever he called."

After Douglas died, Cyr said, Whitey changed and so did their relationship. He went from being somewhat remote to coldly silent most of the time. She said he had lost his fleeting sense of fun after Billy O'Sullivan was murdered. But after Douglas succumbed, there weren't even caustic asides. He never laughed and there was nothing for them to talk about.

They stayed on autopilot for years, leading intersecting but separate lives. He stopped by the cottage occasionally on weekends. She commuted to Boston and turned to raising money to promote awareness about Reye's syndrome into an avocation.

Finally, after about three years, she forced the issue of their ships passing in the night. "Where are we going?" she asked. "Do you want to be here?" He said, "If I didn't want to be here I wouldn't be here." Then he closed the door. "I don't want to talk about it."

"It was tough getting through to him," she lamented. "He could function on several levels all at once. You could almost see it going on. I wrote him a letter and sent it to his mother's house. It was something like 'You're just not there and everything is so cold.' Then Jean called me. He had left the letter on his dresser and she read it. She said Billy had his family and Jimmy needed one, too. 'You're good for him. He'll be safe with you.' But it was over."

Among the things Cyr didn't know was that by then Whitey was juggling two other striking blond girlfriends from Southie, waitress Teresa Stanley and career-minded Catherine Greig. Being with one woman was too tied-down for him. So he added two more while adhering to none.

And Jean Bulger couldn't make that safe for anybody, either.

15

Go and Talk

Whitey and Stevie Flemmi

They came together at the same dank fortress in 1974, a cinder-block garage with several bays, battered cars, and a cold heart. Marshall Motors in Somerville was a front for insurance fraud and much more. It harbored the hard-eyed killers of the Winter Hill Gang, all scarred survivors of the Irish gangland warfare of the 1960s, and the only crew in town who could stand up to the Mafia.

The boss was Howie Winter, who had led the hunt for the McLaughlins of Charlestown a decade earlier. Its main enforcer was stone-cold killer Johnny Martorano, who was feared even by the Mafia.

But its rising stars were Whitey Bulger and Stevie Flemmi, who had something the others lacked. They were cagey planners who were always one step ahead in a gang that sometimes couldn't shoot straight. Both had been hunted men and survived after being surrounded.

Whitey had surmounted an existential threat in South Boston when it looked like it was over for him before it began—that he would be on the losing side in a turf battle.

Flemmi was a "new-old" member of Winter Hill who had worked with Howie in the Irish war when Stevie was so hunted there was an assassination car out there cruising just for him alone.

But even with hostilities over, there were still scores to settle. Stevie went too far in 1969 and was part of a failed attempt to blow up a lawyer despised by the both the FBI and the Mafia. The car bomb took a leg off the unfortunate barrister and sent jagged shards into the legitimate world. Flemmi fled indictments and hid out in Montreal for five years. But now he was back after a key witness conveniently changed his mind; Flemmi was good to go with Winter Hill.

Flemmi and Whitey had known each other casually in the 1960s, bumping into each other once in a while at a Roxbury after-hours joint. But they never talked business and their distinct crime orbits never intersected. Neither friend nor foe but with some wary respect.

A decade later, they drew together at Marshall Motors, into what approaches friendship in the here-today, gone-tomorrow underworld.

Both had strong partners before and knew what worked. And what didn't. Flemmi had been allied with his deeply disturbed younger brother, Jimmy the Bear, and then more reliably with boyhood friend "Cadillac Frank" Salemme, though Salemme could be reckless in his blind pursuit of becoming a made Mafia man. Stevie needed a careful partner.

Whitey also had the good and bad of partners—first with the compatible but carefree Billy O'Sullivan and then the headstrong Donald Killeen. Whitey wanted "careful" as a credo.

So they shared traits and outlook. Both had wiseguy élan and were image-conscious. They were workout fanatics, with Whitey chiseled and Stevie darkly handsome. Both could be deceptively charming. And both were being silently tracked by FBI talent scouts Paul Rico and Dennis Condon.

Whitey proved his mettle with Winter Hill in 1973 in the long hunt for an elusive bookie whose independence had offended Jerry Angiulo.

The pursuit of "Indian Al" Notarangeli was like something out of Al Capone's Chicago, with wrong men shot dead and a machine-gun attack on a busy downtown street. The yearlong campaign was Whitey's graduate school in homicide and he took to search-and-destroy missions with bloodlust. It was his calling.

Angiulo had handed out the assassination assignment to Winter Hill with the promise of more work if the job got done.

Five associates of Indian Al were killed before Winter Hill finally got their man in 1974. Through it all, Martorano was the triggerman and Whitey drove the "crash" car. Whitey's job was to cause a distracting accident if the hit car had problems clearing the scene. After a year of near misses, Indian Al sued for peace. He jumped in a car with his white flag and was immediately shot in the head. With the body transferred to the trunk, Whitey dumped the car in Charlestown. The solution to Indian Al brought a fifty-thousand-dollar bonus from Angiulo and a chary alliance between the Mafia and Winter Hill.

For his part, Johnny Martorano was glad to have Whitey in the crew. "I mean he had been a bank robber," he said. "Man's man on the street. Took care of himself. He looked and acted like an SS colonel. Someone once said he was like Richard Widmark—the actor in that movie where the guy smiles and then throws the old lady down the stairs. That's Whitey Bulger."

But Whitey connected quickly with Flemmi, a perfect match for the time and place. Stevie saw the possibilities right away and moved quickly to bond with Whitey. Shortly after he got back from Montreal, he threw a homecoming party for himself around the backyard pool at his suburban house. He told his common-law wife, Marion Hussey, to get a party dress and play hostess to forty gangsters. Those included his new friend from the garage, Whitey Bulger.

Although Whitey was first among equals, Stevie had a bigger résumé when they started out together at the garage. Flemmi had emerged from the 1960s bloodbath as the preeminent hit man of the era, involved in a half-dozen murders, but also a grifter who had learned to bob and weave with law enforcement. It was part of his survival kit.

Whitey and Flemmi started their work together in 1974 with an easy job—terrorizing a Jewish bookie who was late with his monthly rent into doing business within Winter Hill's expanding jurisdiction. It was the easiest work in the underworld and Whitey relished being the menacing face-to-face part of it. Ax in hand, he threatened the tardy bookmaker with dismemberment and the man collapsed of fright.

They capped their first full year with Winter Hill with a deadly paragon. Whitey set up a hit on his home turf so he could show his stuff as a triggerman. Eddie Connors, who owned a pub in Savin Hill, was talking loosely about a murder he'd helped arrange for Winter Hill, and Howie Winter was worried that Connors would turn informer about an armored car robbery done by the gang. The bar owner was up against the underworld's fatal four words—He Won't Stand Up.

Connors got word that Howie wanted a number where he could be reached and the one he gave was traced to a phone booth at a Dorchester intersection in front of a gas station. When Connors picked up the phone there, it was a call for the dead. Whitey and Flemmi, armed like commandos, were on foot behind the station. Their blitzkrieg attack was over in minutes. They raced at Connors from the shadows, with Whitey opening fire with a sawed-off shotgun in one hand and emptying a .38-caliber revolver with the other. Flemmi finished the job with seven shots from a carbine at ten feet. Martorano was the driver this time and raced in to pick them up but he took off too fast for Whitey's sense of a safe getaway. He yelled at Johnny to pull over and took the wheel himself, driving toward town at a slower pace. Whitey Bulger was in the driver's seat for good.

One day toward the end of 1974, Whitey sidled up to Flemmi at the garage and asked a question that would leave law enforcement torn asunder for a generation. It was hardly an idle query. Whitey may have played dumb but he knew the score. He was aware Stevie had had help from the FBI in surviving the Irish gang war a decade earlier. And Flemmi knew he knew. More than that, Whitey had had his own successful gambit with Agent Paul Rico when he'd been arrested for bank robbery in 1956 and rolled on his accomplices.

Indeed, their casual conversation had been scripted by Rico, who saw the pair as an FBI dream team, with Flemmi providing intelligence about the Mafia and Whitey about Winter Hill. Rico convinced two district attorneys to drop charges against Flemmi and then summoned him with a warning: Come or I may not help later.

So each man stood on his stage mark at the garage. What should I do, Whitey wondered nonchalantly, if an agent wants a sit-down?

"Go and talk," Stevie said.

Whitey had still been in Alcatraz when the teletype in the Boston office of the FBI danced a single sentence that changed everything. The 1961 directive from J. Edgar Hoover was to the point: "Infiltrate organized crime groups in the same degree that we have been able to penetrate the Communist Party and other subversive organizations."

The pressing priority landed on the desks of seasoned agents

Condon and Rico. They were given the "ticket" on Jerry Angiulo, with orders to make a Mafia case—and fast.

Rico specialized in tracking Irish mobsters and Condon bank robbers. The Mafia imperative changed old tactics into a new religion—informants at any price.

With the Irish war under way, Rico handicapped the field and picked Winter Hill as the winner. Two wiseguys stuck out in the bedlam, each serving vastly different purposes: Stevie Flemmi and Joseph Barboza.

For the agents, Flemmi was a long-term asset, a survivor who was brutal on the street but wily as he moved around the criminal landscape. Barboza was a different proposition. They had to use him fast, before he got killed, since he was a beast who had run his course, used as a killer by the Mafia and then thrown away. But a potent malcontent nonetheless.

Flemmi was the first of three sons of Italian immigrants, Giovanni and Mary Flemmi. He grew up in the Orchard Park housing project in Roxbury. Mean streets. His father was a bricklayer and street vendor and money was tight.

First arrested for "carnal abuse" at age fourteen, Flemmi compiled an extensive juvenile rap sheet before serving time in a detention center. The solution for wayward teens in those years was military service. At age seventeen, Flemmi was assigned to the 187th Airborne Division in Korea and saw heavy combat duty right away. In his first action, his unit encountered a Chinese platoon. Flemmi got his "rifleman" nickname that night by killing five enemy soldiers in rapid succession. After two tours from 1951 to 1955, he returned home a hardened combat paratrooper who had distinguished himself as a marksman.

After mustering out, he teamed up with a boyhood friend, Frank Salemme, and became a skilled player in the Roxbury rackets. He was an entrepreneur of sorts around Dudley Square, owning a series of bars, bookstores, garages, and real estate offices that never made much money but were only way stations anyway for the real businesses of gambling and loan-sharking. It was wide open in those days, with police on the take and business done casually at the counter.

Paul Rico recruited Flemmi as a comer who just might survive the Irish war. And so began Flemmi's career as a prolific killer and double agent. He was nimble enough to serve two masters who detested each other—Paul Rico and Jerry Angiulo.

Flemmi started out with the McLaughlins because they did so much Roxbury business, but he quickly turned on Charlestown, again to serve both masters. Rico was against the McLaughlins because they were useless as informants and because they spread derisive rumors that he was gay. Stevie's other inducement to change horses was that Angiulo liked the Winter Hill Gang as the least crazy of the mad Irish.

But Flemmi's deal with Rico in the early 1960s set the informant equation for decades: a blind eye on crimes in exchange for Mafia intelligence.

Rico had no compass or compunction as the journey began. In a matter of months, he was directly complicit in murders and later in sending innocent Mafiosi to jail, eagerly trading justice for a three-hundred-dollar bonus and commendation from J. Edgar Hoover.

From his perspective, Flemmi saw how lawless the bureau had become and how its allegiance to a top informant carried carte blanche benefits. Indeed, a license to kill.

By his own account, Flemmi murdered ten men, most famously one of the McLaughlin brothers. Flemmi used a road map provided by the FBI.

The murder of Edward "Punchy" McLaughlin in 1965 took some doing and was ranked equally high by Winter Hill and the FBI. Punchy had survived withering cross fire on a suburban road, a paramilitary ambush that involved Stevie shooting a rifle from a treetop. Two months later, Flemmi, in disguise, shot McLaughlin six times in the chest with a long-barrel .38 at a West Roxbury bus stop. His onetime colleague, Johnny Martorano, said the Punchy murder got very high praise in their world: "That was big. Everyone knew how hard that was."

While killing Punchy put Stevie on the underworld map in bold and, for practical purposes, ended the war, his real coup was manipulating Barboza. Turning him into a witness made Flemmi a Top Echelon informer for nearly thirty years.

Short-legged and slope-eyed, Joe Barboza was a brutish brawler who roared out of the New Bedford, Massachusetts, waterfront to become such an accomplished killer that he thought he would be the first non-Italian to be inducted into the Mafia. But the Angiulos came to see him as a mad slasher, out of control. They began plotting against him.

By 1967, Barboza was in jail after being arrested by Boston police who found illegal guns that rival mobsters had planted in his car. Then two friends collecting bail money for him were slaughtered in a Mafia bar. Rico knew Barboza was ripe for revenge and sent Flemmi at him in the Walpole state penitentiary to stoke his fury. Stevie knew him as a close friend of his younger brother and Johnny Martorano.

Flemmi always could reason with Joe. But this was a high-wire act, a Le Carré exercise in double dealing. The FBI was concocting a dubious murder case against Mafia leaders and needed Barboza as a facts-be-damned witness to implicate them. Flemmi's dual job was to keep Barboza on the FBI team yet also make Jerry Angiulo think he was doing just the opposite—convincing Barboza not to testify. It was a paradigm of duplicity.

With Flemmi egging Barboza on, Barboza's testimony in the 1968 Teddy Deegan murder case got the FBI what it had so blindly pursued—Mafia henchmen doing life sentences.

But the orchestrated testimony turned the case facts inside out. Barboza had indeed murdered Deegan, but that's where the semblance of truth ended and suborned perjury began. Barboza knew the murder details cold but, working from a script prepared by Rico and Condon, he counted himself out and innocent men in.

The evidence evolved in a perverse loop. Stevie took bogus information from the FBI agents to Barboza, who parroted it back to his other frequent prison visitors—Rico and Condon. In turn, the agents handed it off to a malleable state prosecutor.

In a pitch-black tale, Barboza got away with murder and the FBI trampled justice. While it stayed under wraps for decades, the railroading of four innocent men by Barboza is a debased trial that stands alone. His false testimony convicted two men who died in prison and two who served more than thirty years.

In a two-hundred-page decision that awarded survivors and estates $101.7 million in damages and measured the perfidy in a dozen ways, U.S. District Court Judge Nancy Gertner boiled it down to one sentence. Barboza lied and the FBI not only knew but arranged it.

For his testimony, Barboza received early parole on the weapons charge and became the first-ever criminal placed in the Witness Protection Program. He relocated to California but stayed incorrigible, getting convicted there of second-degree murder in 1970. After being paroled, he moved to San Francisco, where he met his inevitable fate in 1975. He left his apartment at midday and was getting into his car when shotgun blasts from a passing white van killed him instantly. The high-noon hit man, J. R. Russo of East Boston, became revered in the Boston underworld for making it look so easy.

The Barboza decade was a shattering precedent, the evil genie out of the bottle. It became the cancerous prototype for an informant system that gave a maniacal killer the upper hand with the country's top law enforcement agency. License to kill. Reduced sentences. Early release. The Barboza entitlements were not lost on Stevie Flemmi.

Around the time that Barboza was killed, Paul Rico retired after working five years in the Miami office to live the good life on the seashore. Whitey Bulger consolidated power in Southie. And the Winter Hill Gang began to fall apart.

Whitey may have come to terms with the Mullens in the aftermath of Billy O'Sullivan's murder, but he never forgot. Top on his grudge list was Paul McGonagle. Whitey had tried to kill him five years earlier and saw his chance to settle up with Paulie in the fall of 1974.

Whitey played on dissatisfaction with McGonagle by other Mullens and brought them aboard on a fast-moving plan that he knew would lure in his victim. Using real bills as samples but presenting them as counterfeit, Whitey told McGonagle that he would cut him in on money made from working the bogus bills into South Boston commerce. With three other Mullens, Whitey met Paulie at the O Street Club and walked him to a car parked in front. He and McGonagle got in the backseat with a suitcase supposedly jammed with phony money. Whitey opened the suitcase, pulled out a gun, and shot Paulie dead. Paulie's old partners, Pat Nee and Tommy King, were reduced to digging the boss's grave in the sand of Tenean Beach in Dorchester, near the expressway.

The Mullens were now the "Bulger group."

Whitey had more to do but it amounted to mopping up. And his hegemony in Southie coincided with the bad tidings about Winter Hill.

In 1976, Johnny Martorano was charged with running an extensive bookie ring on Boston's South Shore, up against the potent evidence of Massachusetts State Police wiretaps. It wasn't hard time but he was going to jail.

And that was nothing compared to the morass that charter members Joe McDonald and Jimmy Sims got themselves into with a heist and a clumsy murder. They would be on the run from 1976 until their capture in 1982.

The case started in 1971 when they stole one million dollars' worth of rare stamps from a Back Bay firm. The FBI got involved and tracked down some of the stamps to a California art dealer, Raymond Lundgren, who then helped in the recovery and agreed to testify against McDonald and Sims. But in 1976, Lundgren, with his wife by his side, answered his door to see McDonald wearing a handkerchief bandana across his face. Lundgren was shot dead in broad daylight. It was so brazen that Sims vowed he wouldn't do any more slipshod, impromptu jobs with Joe Mac again. They both went into hiding in Florida, but in separate locations.

And that left Howie Winter. Despite all kinds of warnings, he got tilted by his own pinball machine scam. He decided he would put his muscle behind installing machines all over Somerville. It was small-potatoes stuff in his hometown of Somerville but it was also a do-it-or-else extortion—a felony and not some gaming misdemeanor with a three-month sentence.

Right from the start, there was no talking him out of it. Howie had a friend at City Hall who could make things wide open by greasing the Board of Aldermen. After a 9-to-2 vote in favor, the machines proliferated. But Howie had leaned on several mom-and-pop venues run by seniors who didn't know his reputation and thought they should be able to choose their own wares. They told the truth to investigators. Howie was a goner against the geezers. In early 1978, he got a sixteen- to twenty-year sentence and would have to do a minimum of six.

What Whitey and Flemmi saw was this: Winter ignored advice to back off when word got back to the garage that an investigation was under way. Instead he kept going and seemed preoccupied about getting himself a hair transplant. They now had a new perspective on the boss—that he was a dope.

In less than two years, the Winter Hill Gang was moribund, with two leaders who weren't even from Somerville. It consisted of Whitey and Stevie and the mechanic and some minor-league enforcers. Time to get a new garage closer to home and to break in Rico's successor, a young agent who looked like a perfect fit.

John Connolly.

Instead of gnarled, John Connolly was youthful. Gregarious rather than aloof. And Southie, not Charlestown. Better still, he was Old Harbor Southie, growing up there when Whitey became a legend. He not only knew some of the same people; he was a protégé of Bill Bulger, chasing after him as a kid to St. Monica events and later working on his political campaigns. Bill pushed him toward books in a sports-mad town and then urged him toward Boston College.

Connolly had a few early encounters with Whitey, one at Old Harbor when Whitey stopped an older boy from pummeling Connolly during a baseball game, and the other when Connolly was a senior at Boston College in 1965 and Whitey was working there on a construction job after he was paroled. So they knew each other.

After Connolly graduated, he spent a desultory few years teaching high school in Boston and starting law school at night when Boston detective and family friend Eddie Walsh suggested he try the FBI. His application also got a huge boost from the Bulger family patron, U.S. House Speaker John McCormack, who had a relationship with J. Edgar Hoover and could put his priceless imprimatur on a constituent's candidacy.

Connolly clicked in early interviews with Dennis Condon, who was a friend of Walsh and could see Connolly's street-savvy potential for landing informants, perhaps sensing strengths he lacked. Connolly was hired in 1968 and did tours in Baltimore, San Francisco, and New York City. Throughout, Condon was his anchor and adviser, urging him homeward.

In 1972, while Connolly was in New York, Condon tipped him off that Boston fugitive "Cadillac Frank" Salemme was posing as a jewelry salesman in Manhattan. Along with Flemmi, Salemme had fled Boston indictments in the attempted murder of a mobster's lawyer. Connolly's collar of Salemme on Third Avenue was a coup and his ticket home.

He would get to his home turf in record time for a novice in the FBI but there was a last-minute glitch. Hitting a home run in New York was not quite enough, so Connolly had to get creative. He sought a hardship transfer because of his father's deteriorating health. The FBI transfer document claimed Connolly's father, "Galway" John, had never fully recovered emotionally from his wife's 1965 death and had been "diagnosed as having terminal cirrhosis of the liver and other serious medical problems." The transfer was approved in February 1973.

But "Galway" John Connolly was hardly at death's door. Far from it. He died more than ten years later, on November 21, 1983.

The hardship embellishment was just the beginning of Connolly's deceptions.

16

My Own G-man

FBI agent John Connolly

Whitey Bulger was in the driver's seat when he turned into a parking lot near Carson Beach in South Boston at the end of a warm autumn day in 1975. In the backseat of the "boiler"—a car stolen for the occasion—sat Howie Winter and Johnny Martorano. Stevie Flemmi pulled up in a second car. Whitey looked around the lot to see if the man they were meeting had arrived, because once they hooked up with Tommy King the gang could then get on with the business that was at hand. Whitey Bulger hated Tommy King.

Most of Boston on this date, November 5, 1975, was either celebrating or cursing the results of a bitter, hard-fought mayoral race the previous day. Mayor Kevin H. White had defeated state senator Joseph F. Timilty to win a third term. But Whitey Bulger was preoccupied with Tommy King, not mayoral politics. Big, tough Tommy King—the longshoreman from Southie whom Whitey had once battled in a bar fight. Whitey prided himself on not making mistakes, but taking on Tommy King was plainly that. Tommy King—a key enforcer in the Mullen Gang, an enemy to Whitey in the South Boston gang war. After Whitey had outmaneuvered them all at the Chandler's summit, they were supposed to be one—Whitey, Tommy King, and everyone else blended into the Winter Hill Gang. But how could Whitey consolidate his power in Southie with holdovers like Tommy King lurking about? Plus there was this: Tommy King was the shooter who had killed Whitey's friend Billy O'Sullivan on Whitey's front lawn four years earlier. Maybe that was the worst.

Whitey never forgot any of it. But it had taken him time to convince Howie Winter and the others that fellow gang member Tommy King had become hazardous. He'd lobbied several which ways. Tommy King, Whitey told them, had talked vulgarly to a young girl in the neighborhood. The girl's father took exception and went to see Whitey for counsel. So Tommy King went after the father for whining to Whitey. The whole thing, Whitey argued, made him, Whitey, look bad. Then Whitey pushed a story that Tommy King had gone off and threatened to murder a Boston police detective. How reckless was that? Whitey argued. Imagine the law enforcement tsunami that would come the gang's way if King killed a cop! That was the clincher. Tommy King was out of control, the others finally concurred.

The plan Whitey had devised had plenty of moving parts, but when King slid into the front seat next to him everything was in place. Whitey had told King they needed his help killing an underworld associate who had too big a mouth. Whitey's story was partly true; the gang did have a killing in mind. But the plan was a sleight of hand or, more accurately, a sleight of hits to lure King to meet him and the others. Stevie Flemmi later called Whitey's plan "a ruse hit."

It worked. Tommy King climbed in next to Whitey in the front seat of the car, thinking he was joining the others for an act of gang mop-up. Whitey could see that as he settled in, King had come ready for work; he was wearing a bulletproof vest. Whitey then could see Stevie Flemmi, on cue, get out of his car and walk toward him carrying a small package. Whitey took the package and removed four handguns—one for himself, one for Howie Winter, one for Johnny Martorano, and one for Tommy King. Whitey was careful to make sure the weapon he handed King was the one preselected just for him, the gun with no real firepower, only blanks. Whitey had also brought along some walkie-talkies, and he handed those out, too. It all looked so by-the-numbers.

Whitey drove out of the parking lot. He saw that Stevie had started his car and pulled out of the lot behind him. Whitey headed around Columbia Road in the direction of the Old Harbor housing project.

But before the car even reached the rotary at Preble Circle, Johnny Martorano quickly shifted forward and put his pistol to the back of Tommy King's head.

Tommy King pitched forward into a heap. He was dead, and the car's interior on his side was spattered with blood and brain matter. Whitey hated messes, but by using a stolen "boiler" the mess was someone else's, not his. With Stevie Flemmi following, Whitey headed south through side streets, his destination a marshy area along the Neponset River near the bridge that connected Boston to the city of Quincy. The ride, ordinarily about fifteen minutes, was delayed briefly when Martorano asked Whitey to pull up to a pay phone so that he could check on the results of a horse race. Arriving at the shore of the neglected urban waterway, they met two men waiting next to a freshly dug hole in the sand. The gang dragged King's corpse from the car and dumped it into the grave, the second in an area that, as other graves were added, became known as the Bulger burial ground.

Whitey stayed behind to oversee the interment while Stevie Flemmi left, taking Howie Winter and Johnny Martorano. Only later did Stevie learn that Whitey was not finished, that he had another move in mind, a twist to the evening's drama he had concocted without the others' counsel. Whitey and the two graveyard workers headed back into Southie looking for Francis X. "Buddy" Leonard. Leonard, thirty-five, grew up in Whitey's Old Harbor neighborhood, but ties that might bind at one time had a way of unraveling. Whitey and his associates disliked the loose, heavy-drinking Leonard, but worse, he was Tommy King's friend.

Whitey jumped Leonard coming out of a bar, pushed him into a car, and shot him in the head. He then abandoned the car with the corpse in a conspicuous spot, on Pilsudski Way in the Old Colony housing project, where it was noticed right away. Just what Whitey wanted, because Buddy Leonard was a pawn in his strategy to cover up the murder of Tommy King. Baffled police told reporters afterward that Leonard's murder had "gangland overtones" but they had no leads. Whitey, meanwhile, pretended as if he had it all figured out; he spread a story that Tommy King had fled Boston after killing Buddy Leonard during a beef.

Stevie Flemmi was impressed. Whitey had crafted a final touch that pointed the finger of culpability in another direction. Pin the

Leonard hit on Tommy King, and King was now nowhere to be found. That was the added value of Whitey's plan to make Tommy King disappear. In fact, a quarter century passed before King's decomposed body was recovered and, until then, the murders of King and Leonard were officially listed on the books at the Boston Police Department as "unsolved." Only Whitey, Stevie, Johnny Martorano, Howie Winter, and a few others knew the real story. Whitey acted playful at times about their deadly secret. He and John Martorano were once driving across the Neponset River when, out of the blue, Whitey pointed to the marshy burial area and said, "Say hi to Tommy King."

But unknown to the others in the Winter Hill Gang, the murders of Tommy King and Buddy Leonard carried historic significance for Whitey Bulger. Sure, they featured the same brutal efficiency of the bullet-riddled killing of Eddie Connors in the telephone booth the previous spring. And with Whitey at the helm, the two murders also featured his ever-maturing leadership skills—a maestro who could orchestrate two executions in perfect harmony. But those elements were not what made the homicides on November 5, 1975, significant to Whitey's career.

Whitey was now killing while on FBI time, a newly minted Top Echelon informant.

John Connolly had wanted Whitey badly. It didn't matter that the very idea of recruiting Whitey Bulger was in violation of FBI regulations. Whitey was still on "supervised release status," and the FBI's *Manual of Instructions*, section 108, paragraph D-12, barred a paroled convict still under supervision from acting as an informer. Only when the period of supervision ended could a convict "be considered for development," and Whitey's supervised status did not expire until June 20, 1976.

And it didn't matter that, while FBI regulations discouraged embracing killers as informants, the Boston FBI already had a stockpile of evidence that Whitey had established himself as an underworld monster, a gangster who drew on a deep reservoir of ferocity and even seemed to enjoy spreading his terror. "Whitey is a vicious individual," one 1975 FBI report said. "Bulger's crew would whack a guy out even for small amounts of money if they are delinquent." Another informant told an agent in September 1975 that of all the Winter Hill gangsters,

Whitey Bulger was "by far the most vicious of all these individuals and is feared by many people because of his ability to kill anyone without even thinking twice." This intelligence was soon followed by another report describing Whitey "as a vicious animal who will not take 'no' for an answer."

Connolly simply countered the intelligence by casting Whitey as mainly running gambling rackets, with a bit of loan-sharking thrown in. Besides, in Boston the FBI's regulations were made to be broken. Agents Paul Rico and Dennis Condon had seen to that, in the tempo they'd set throughout the 1960s. The FBI had grown obsessed with taking down the Mafia, at virtually any cost, even if it meant striking secret deals with killers, and in Boston, where the FBI office maintained more than 250 criminal informants, John Connolly was looking to position Whitey Bulger as the informant of all informants—the Boston office's number one asset, who, in the FBI's war against the Mafia, would also require its total protection.

Like Rico and Condon before him, Connolly was not about to let rules or any other obstacles get in his way. He'd learned what having Whitey would mean for his FBI career. During his brief stint in New York, he had received a couple of terrific reviews for his work as a "diligent agent," earning marks of either outstanding or excellent for "personal appearance," "attitude," "resourcefulness, ingenuity and initiative." His outgoing review, however, had noted that while in New York he had developed "0 potential informants," and a supervisor added this comment: "The value and importance of the Informant Program has been stressed to Connolly and he is aware of it." Coming home to Boston, Connolly was indeed aware. "If you did develop a TE [Top Echelon informant] it was the greatest thing in the office, that was the ultimate, that was the pinnacle in the FBI," he said later. Connolly was going to prove what he hadn't in New York City, that he was somebody, and he was going to exploit a home-court advantage to finish what others had tried—bringing the gangster Whitey Bulger of all people, the tough guy with the reputation as the ultimate stand-up guy who loathed betrayers, into the FBI fold as an informant, as a betrayer himself.

In a series of meetings throughout 1974, which included at least one get-together that also involved Stevie Flemmi and Dennis Condon at a coffee shop in the close suburb of Newton, Connolly drew from the playbook his predecessors had developed. Paul Rico and Condon had always coached that the best approach to a "target" was to stress a vulnerability so that, as Rico said, when the target got "jammed up they might start to be productive informants." Condon had tried that in his failed bid to recruit Whitey, when he stressed the perils of the Southie neighborhood gang war.

It hadn't worked, and Whitey not only survived the war but prospered. It was Connolly's turn now, and he aimed higher. Whitey Bulger was the fast-rising star in the underworld constellation, and Connolly's pitch stressed a threat to Whitey's survival that loomed larger than a rival neighborhood faction. It was a threat more formidable than anything Whitey had ever faced before, a real and present danger now that Whitey's underworld ambitions had grown to where he aspired to be not just a local presence but also a regional and perhaps even a national one. John Connolly pitched the Mafia—that Boston Mafia underboss Gennaro "Jerry" Angiulo and his five brothers stationed in the city's North End neighborhood were out to get Whitey. Jerry Angiulo was a profane bully but a half-pint, the prototypical Little Caesar whose outfit nonetheless controlled most of the rackets in Boston and the North Shore, while Whitey's Winter Hill Gang had piecemeal spots in such neighborhoods as Southie, Roxbury, and the South End. Connolly told Whitey that the Mafia had a slew of its own "sources" at the local level of law enforcement, and that Whitey therefore needed a friend at a higher level. The FBI would be an ideal match. The Mafia was on the radar of both the FBI and Whitey, and just as the slogan advised, the enemy of my enemy is my friend.

The deal made sense strategically—Whitey aligning with the FBI was a smart business move. But it also made sense on personal grounds. Connolly brought something to the table that no other agent could—Southie, the Old Harbor project, and a close relationship with brother Bill Bulger. Connolly adored Bill Bulger. His wife said that after they'd moved back to Boston in 1973 her husband John "frequently socialized" with Bill Bulger at a private club and also in Bulger's home. Marianne Connolly observed that Bill Bulger had had a "significant influence" on her husband, that without Bulger's support he might never have gone to college.

The three intertwined lives were pivotal in Connolly's talks with Whitey. "Think about using your friends in law enforcement," Connolly told Whitey.

Connolly's timing was perfect. Whitey had already lived half a lifetime—he was in his mid-forties—most of it spent beyond the reach of the law, beginning as a juvenile and continuing during his service in the Air Force, the tailgating that followed, and then the bank hold-ups. There were plenty of lessons learned along the way, but none as powerful as the one from getting busted after thinking he would never get caught. His fall—and the nine years in federal prison for bank robbery—were the result of betrayal. That was the lesson, especially as he matured and continued working his way up the power rungs of the underworld. He would never countenance anything less than complete loyalty, and he responded with violent decisiveness to any hint of be-trayal.

But more than that, he'd come to realize the value of actually being what was fatal for others—a betrayer. He'd had a taste of informing in 1956 after his arrest, but more important than that single event was what he'd seen recently in Stevie Flemmi—the eye-opening benefits Flemmi had received as a favored FBI informant, where from lawless agents he got as much as, if not more than, he gave. Whitey's readiness, then, was a confluence of these factors—Flemmi's history, Connolly's corrupted FBI—as well as the fact he'd already had his own positive experience with federal power. Having House Speaker John McCor-mack and other federal officials watching out for him while in federal prison had given him an edge no other prisoner had enjoyed. If it worked out, having Connolly's FBI watching out for him would pro-vide an edge few others could enjoy in the underworld. And just as in prison, when the federal assistance flowed through a son of Southie, the helping hand that Whitey stood poised to accept belonged to an-other son of Southie. Based on the federal aid he'd gotten, Whitey might even have acquired a sense of entitlement to its benefits.

There were other parallels. Brother Bill had served as the enabler while Whitey was in prison, continually lobbying Congressman McCormack on Whitey's behalf. With the FBI, Bill Bulger was also a presence, seeming to hover over everything. He was a mentor to John Connolly, and Whitey's Winter Hill Gang certainly believed that the link with Bill Bulger was the very reason John Connolly had reached out to Whitey.

Whitey himself encouraged this notion. Following Connolly's

overture in 1974 Whitey had to come up with something to tell his Winter Hill partners about why he was meeting with an FBI agent. Except for Stevie Flemmi, there was no way he could tell the whole story that he was negotiating to serve as an FBI informant. Suicidal, plain and simple. Instead Whitey told the others that Bill Bulger had gotten the ball rolling. "He informed us that his brother, who was Billy Bulger, came to him and said that John Connolly wanted to meet with him," Johnny Martorano said.

Martorano and the others easily envisioned the upside—a new "source" inside law enforcement that had standing they didn't usually see: the FBI. They all had corrupt sources at the local level. Stevie Flemmi had contacts with a number of Boston cops dating back to his days in Roxbury. Johnny Martorano for years had paid a corrupt state police trooper named Richard Schneiderhan for information. The trooper seemed hopelessly enamored with helping out the gang; the gangsters were not about to question why, and Martorano eventually shared the trooper with Flemmi. "It's the only way you're going to survive," Flemmi once said. "If you can develop sources, you're gonna get protection. If you can't you're not gonna be able to survive."

And the gang was not surprised when Whitey mentioned the link between John Connolly and his brother Bill. They already knew Connolly and Bill Bulger were friends. "They're all South Boston people," Flemmi noted. To the others, then, Whitey was simply coming across as the ever-loyal member of the gang looking out for their greater good. He was promoting an opportunity to line up a source to trump all others—a source at the highest level of law enforcement. It was a no-brainer. "Be a good listener," Martorano advised. "See what he has to say."

When Whitey next reported back, he invoked his brother's name once more, this time to explain Connolly's motivation for wanting to help the gang. Whitey told them that Connolly had brought up the subject of his brother Bill during their meeting. Connolly had said he owed Bill a debt of gratitude "for helping him go to college and stay on the straight and narrow," and that after his transfer to the Boston FBI office he'd asked Bill what he could do to show his appreciation. Connolly reportedly said Bill Bulger had replied, "You could help my brother stay out of trouble."

Bill Bulger would later deny under oath ever asking Connolly to protect Whitey. "Whatever was done by Connolly would not have been done at my urging," he testified during congressional hearings in 2003. But the idea that Bill Bulger might ask someone to look out for his brother hardly seemed out of the question given the history of instances where Bill stepped up as Whitey's advocate. The critical factor, if he said those words, was what kind of "help" he had in mind. Was it dark and nefarious? Or was it the kind of innocent remark a well-intentioned brother might make to any law enforcement figure when asking him to keep an eye on a sibling?

But what Bill Bulger said—or whether he said anything—was not the point. The point was that *Whitey said* Bill had said those things— first, that Bill had matched him up with John Connolly and, second, that Connolly's allegiance to Bill was the reason the agent had offered to be Whitey's "source." That was the point. Whitey was willing to put his brother's good name in play and at risk. Whitey used his brother Bill— used him to sell the Connolly alliance to the gang.

The gang, of course, would know only the half of it—that going forward Whitey had "John Connolly as a source," as Flemmi later said. The rest—that Whitey was Connolly's informant—was closely held. Whitey might insist that Connolly call him a "strategist" or "consul- tant" and never an informer, "rat," or "snitch" (and Connolly catered to him in this regard, insisting that others in the FBI refer to him this way). But that was just wordplay. Whitey, a ripened psychopath deter- mined and disciplined to succeed above all else, had twisted every- thing. He insisted on supreme loyalty from those who served him and inflated himself as the model stand-up gangster—exploiting a core South Boston value of fidelity to do so—all the while working secretly as an FBI informant. Plus he had used his own brother to sell the deal to his cohorts. The rationale was business, of course, but that business was himself, Whitey Bulger, with everything, every person, and every principle in play as a means to that end. Jerry Angiulo could have all the corrupt cops he wanted. "If they want to play checkers we'll play chess," Whitey had told Connolly.

Whitey's secret FBI designation became BS-1544-TE.

BS stood for Boston.

1544 was his identification number for the FBI's informant filing system.

TE stood for Top Echelon.

The arrangement was sealed when BS-1544-TE was officially "opened" by the FBI on September 18, 1975—and around that time Whitey and Connolly met to finalize the terms in the agent's decoy car, a beat-up Plymouth, under a harvest moon along Wollaston Beach. The bright Boston skyline was in the distance, the Red Sox were on a World Series run, and the city was in turmoil over court-ordered busing to achieve school desegregation. Having just turned forty-six, Whitey looked across the harbor at Boston and was eyeing a stage far grander than anything he'd ever considered. It was the city itself—as a kind of sovereign right—and in his quest for underworld supremacy the Federal Bureau of Investigation would prove to be the critical asset.

John Connolly got what he wanted out of the bargain, too—and fast. One week after Whitey was opened officially, the special agent in charge at the Boston FBI office submitted the paperwork recommending Connolly for an incentive award. Connolly, wrote Richard Bates on September 25, 1975, "has displayed a real talent and skill for gaining the confidence and cooperation of his sources." FBI director Clarence Kelley, Hoover's successor, notified Connolly of his $150 award in a personal letter October 21. "It is indeed a pleasure for me to commend you in view of your excellent services in connection with the development of several sources," Kelley said. The next year Connolly won a promotion to "Grade GS-13," which included a modest increase to the annual salary of $19,693 he had been earning as an agent "Grade GS-12." For years to come the accolades praising Connolly's star power continued virtually nonstop.

Connolly also opened a paper trail showcasing his new Top Echelon informant, filing confidential "209 reports" containing underworld intelligence Whitey gave him. Whitey seemed to have plenty to say, about Howie Winter and the workings of his own Winter Hill Gang—proof right off that Whitey had no qualms about sharing information about his own associates. The early entries also reveal that Whitey immediately viewed the FBI's secret files as a bank of intelligence into which he could strategically deposit fiction benefiting himself. One notable example was what Whitey had to say about the murders of Tommy King and Buddy Leonard. Whitey met with Connolly four days after killing them, and Connolly typed up what he learned from his prized informant: "On 11/10/75 source advised that BUDDY LEONARD'S death was the result of a violent argument between himself and TOMMY KING. Source stated that to his knowledge, the murder was not a sanctioned 'hit' but rather grew out of some 'bad blood' between the two."

The FBI's target was the Mafia, however, and that's the kind of information Connolly's supervisors were looking for most intently from the agent's reports. Connolly's 209's on Whitey therefore contained chunks of information about the Angiulos. But they did not tell the full story, which was that Whitey was unwelcome in the North End and, as a result, had little of the firsthand information the bureau most coveted.

"They didn't particularly like him because he was kind of a violent guy," Stevie Flemmi said later. The Mafia did not trust Whitey, and the feeling was mutual. That's where Stevie Flemmi came in. He had access to the "Dog House," the nickname for the Mafia office at 98 Prince Street in the North End. "I can hang around with those people," Flemmi said. "I knew them. He couldn't."

Flemmi was vital to Whitey. He had what Whitey needed, and Flemmi understood what was in play between Whitey and the FBI agent. Flemmi was the old pro at the FBI game, even if he had not officially been an FBI informer since he'd fled Boston in 1969—and would not be one again for another four years, when Connolly reopened him as a Top Echelon informant on September 12, 1980. Until then, and especially during Whitey's start-up as Connolly's new key acquisition, the three began laundering Flemmi's intelligence through Whitey, so that in the FBI files Connolly could portray Whitey Bulger as worth his weight in gold.

"I was giving him Mafia information," Flemmi said, and "he was passing it on to the FBI, John Connolly." Before too long the three simply began meeting together so that Connolly could get Flemmi's Mafia intelligence directly. They'd meet at Whitey's mother's house in Old Harbor, at Connolly's South Boston home, at other agents' homes, or at one of their four beach locations—Castle Island in South Boston, Tenean Beach and Malibu Beach in Dorchester, or Wollaston Beach in Quincy. In all, over the years, there were "over a hundred meetings," Flemmi said, "if you want to include telephone calls and beach meetings. It's quite a few." Connolly frequently credited Whitey with Stevie Flemmi's information; he was cooking the FBI's books.

The FBI had its rules and regulations regarding the management of underworld informants, codified in what was known as section 137 of the *Manual of Investigative Operations and Guidelines,* or MIOG, and in a separate *Manual of Rules and Regulations.* While guidelines stressed that criminal informants were indispensable to the FBI's work, one point emphasized throughout was that the balance of power must always favor the agent. "Special care must be taken to carefully evaluate and closely supervise their use to ensure that individual rights are not infringed and that the government itself does not become a violator of the law." The agents were supposed to regularly conduct "suitability reviews" evaluating the informant's "emotional stability, controllability, reliability, truthfulness and conformance to instructions." Most of all, as one federal judge later noted, the agents "were instructed to direct the activities of the informants as much as possible, and to make every effort to control the informant's activities."

But this was not the case with Whitey Bulger. Connolly was like a drug addict who was ready to break just about every rule in the book to maintain his fix. In addition to padding Whitey's 209 informant files, Connolly quickly stepped in to redirect investigations away from Whitey. In one case of extortion that autumn, Whitey and his associates were going around demanding that local bars and restaurants replace vending machines from Melo-Tone Vending Company, a firm based in Somerville, with machines from a company they owned through a front. To show they meant business, a Melo-Tone salesman was summoned to the gang's Marshall Motors office, where Whitey, gripping a hatchet, "threatened to bury an axe in his head if he caused any more trouble," according to one FBI report. But once Connolly got involved late in 1975, not only was Whitey's name no longer mentioned in any further internal FBI reports on the matter, but the investigation and a court case fizzled. In another instance that fall, Flemmi was about to collect on a "shylock loan" from the owner of a dry-cleaning business in Quincy when Whitey headed him off. Connolly had told Whitey that the owner was "wired up." Flemmi, in later testimony, said he made sure to personally thank Connolly for the tip.

Whitey was able to show the gang that his new deal with Connolly as his "source" was paying off—the FBI agent had saved them all from being indicted—and he decided a token of appreciation was in order.

He, Martorano, and Flemmi picked out a two-carat diamond from their stash of stolen precious jewels and took it to a jeweler, who set the stone in a gold ring. Connolly presented the ring to his wife. But Whitey knew its actual significance was greater than a gesture of gratitude; Connolly was now on the take, and the ring was a symbol of their unholy marriage.

In a way, Connolly was only doing what others before him had done. Paul Rico had bent and broken the law to protect Flemmi throughout their days together. But it was different then; Rico always seemed in charge. His personality was that large, and, though lawless, he always projected a sense that Flemmi was working for him, not the other way around. Flemmi later said that Rico had never accepted anything from him or any member of the gang—be it a ring, any other "gift," or cash. With Whitey, the dynamic was different. From the start, Connolly seemed no match for Whitey, the master of the chessboard.

Connolly himself once addressed the central issue of control. The FBI featured him in an instructional video used to coach agents on handling informants. In it, Connolly noted that a struggle for power characterized every informant relationship, where if the agent did not assert control the informant would. Prophetically, Connolly said, "if they're ruling you you're wastin' your time and the Bureau's time and you could put yourself and the Bureau in a very melancholy situation." In 1975, when he was padding the files and tipping Whitey to extortion cases, John Connolly began what became a "melancholy situation" of historic proportion for law enforcement. It was going to get much worse very quickly.

Richard J. Castucci, or "Richie," was a player in Boston's underworld, a gambler and nightclub owner in Revere, his hometown just north of Boston. In the early 1970s he owned the Beach Ball Lounge and later was co-owner of the Squire Lounge. Except for a scar on the left side of his mouth, his appearance was unintimidating, on the short side at five feet, six inches tall, weighing about 160 pounds, with black hair and hazel-colored eyes. In every way, he was ideal for the Boston FBI to recruit as an informant—no reputation for violence but plenty of access, to both the Mafia and the Winter Hill Gang. Castucci, according to a 1970 FBI report, was "very friendly with many well-known hoodlums in the Boston-Revere area. He is an avid gambler and race horse owner."

Another FBI report noted that the nightclub owner paid the Winter Hill Gang "through Bulger a tribute each and every week."

Castucci began cooperating with the FBI in 1970 and was soon designated a Top Echelon informant—BS-1236-TE. Castucci, like plenty of wiseguys before and after, was expecting he'd cover his flank by secretly snitching for the FBI, and for six years it worked. But everything changed during the fall of 1976, or one year after Connolly had forged his alliance with Whitey. On September 30, 1976, Castucci gave his FBI handler, an agent named Thomas J. Daly, what ordinarily would have been a gem of a tip—information on the whereabouts of the two hotly sought Winter Hill gangsters, Jimmy Sims and Joe McDonald. The two had been fugitives ever since their indictment in the stolen stamp case, after which McDonald killed the art dealer cooperating against them. In April McDonald had been named to the FBI's "Ten Most Wanted" list, and by September Castucci had learned the two gangsters were hiding out in New York City in an apartment. "He has heard from an excellent source that Top Ten Fugitive JOE MCDONALD and possibly Fugitive JIMMY SIMS are definitely living in Manhattan," agent Daly wrote in his 209 report. Continued Daly: "The Hill are taking care of both SIMS and MCDONALD at this time and the informant is attempting to get the exact location of the apartment from the source."

Castucci delivered. By early December the FBI informant was able to give agent Daly the specific location of the hideout—a townhouse apartment at 14 Christopher Street in the West Village that Johnny Martorano had found for the fugitives and prepaid fourteen thousand dollars for a year's rent. The FBI agent, in his internal 209 reports, stressed repeatedly that Castucci's information was "extremely singular in nature and should not be discussed or disseminated outside the FBI."

The cautionary note did not matter. John Connolly had learned Daly's informer was providing intelligence that was way too close for comfort—and he was not about to be censored from discussing or disseminating it. Connolly in December told Whitey about Castucci, and Whitey quickly convened Flemmi and the others. "He said that he got a call from John Connolly that the FBI had information that Joe McDonald and Jimmy Sims were using the apartment up in New York," Flemmi said. Added Martorano: "Whitey Bulger come in and told us that Richie Castucci went to the FBI and told them McDonald was in New York."

The first thing Whitey and the others did was to notify McDonald and Sims to clear out of the apartment. The next thing they decided was to bring Castucci in. Martorano contacted the nightclub owner in the days following Christmas. "I told him to come by and pick up some money," Martorano said. They made an appointment for the afternoon of Wednesday, December 29, 1976.

Castucci left his home along the coastline in Revere that day about mid-morning. He first headed into town to his barbershop for a haircut. The skies were gray, and a light snow was falling. Then he swung by the credit union to make a payment on a loan in his daughter's name. Following lunch, he climbed into the front seat of his new 1976 Cadillac DeVille four-door hardtop and headed south to the Marshall Motors garage in Somerville.

When he arrived, Castucci was thinking he was going to settle up with Martorano for more than one hundred thousand dollars in gambling accounts they were all involved in through a bookmaker in New York City named Jack. "I gave him a bag of money, and I told him to go down the street to the apartment we had and count it, and see what was in there," Martorano said. "I sent him down with Whitey."

Castucci, escorted by Whitey and also Stevie Flemmi, headed out into the snow. Castucci carried the bundle of money for the short walk to the apartment, about fifty yards away from the garage's 14 Marshall Street address. The apartment belonged to Howie Winter and his girlfriend. Inside, Castucci sat down and began counting the pile of bills. Whitey and Flemmi hovered nearby. Then Martorano walked into the room carrying a .38-caliber handgun. He moved quickly and pointed the gun at the left side of Castucci's head. "I shot him," Martorano said.

Whitey took command of waste disposal. One associate was sent out to a nearby Kmart store and returned with a blue nylon, child-sized sleeping bag. Using a piece of packing rope, Whitey and Flemmi tied Castucci's hands and feet behind his back. They stuffed the body into the sleeping bag, and then carried the bag to the trunk of Castucci's new Cadillac. They climbed into the Cadillac and drove Castucci home to Revere. They abandoned the car on Lantern Road in front of an apartment building near a shopping center, less than four miles from his beachfront house on Revere Beach Boulevard. The body was found the next day at 12:30 p.m. After the funeral a few days later, Whitey and Flemmi told Castucci's co-owner of the Squire Lounge that he had new partners. Whitey was taking over Castucci's 42 percent interest.

It was a win-win: the rat was dead, a new business interest in hand.

Normally the murder of an FBI informant was a major crisis. Had the informer's ties to the FBI been compromised? Was that the reason he was killed? But against the working partnership of Whitey and Connolly's FBI, normalcy went out the window. "It does not appear that the FBI launched its own investigation into the murder of Castucci, despite the fact that he was an important FBI informant and provided information on fugitives," a federal judge later observed.

The Boston FBI certainly had plenty of reason to suspect Whitey Bulger. Within weeks other agents in the Boston office began hearing from informants that Whitey and his gang were responsible. "RICHIE CASTUCCI was killed by members of the HOWARD WINTERS gang, specifically WHITEY BULGER AND STEVIE FLEMMI," one informer told his FBI handler on January 13, 1977. Later, another agent heard from another informant that "the Winter Hill crew" killed Castucci.

But the FBI allowed Connolly to rule the day. Following the murder, Connolly briefed Whitey and Flemmi on the talk going around. "He told us we were suspects," Flemmi said. The three came up with a plan that drew on Whitey's penchant for the redirect—pointing blame elsewhere—and Connolly went to work deflecting attention. When the Boston Organized Crime Strike Force held its weekly intelligence meeting on January 3, less than a week after the murder, Connolly told the task force of Boston's leading local and federal crime fighters that, based on his expert analysis, Whitey and Flemmi didn't do it.

"FBI—John Connolly: Doesn't think WINTER people did the CASTUCCI hit—not their M.O.," said meeting notes. Connolly offered an alternative, one he and Whitey had devised. "John (Connolly) believes it may have been a rip-off by an independent." Connolly continued at future meetings to challenge the nagging thought that Whitey might be involved. "The Winter group has been credited by some sources with the CASTUCCI murder," said notes from an April meeting. "Connolly believes this is speculation."

Within the FBI, Connolly faced an additional challenge—to quash the idea that Castucci might have been executed because he was an FBI informant. His supervisor on the Boston FBI Organized Crime Squad, Jim Scanlon, helped him out in early January when he sent a teletype about Castucci to FBI headquarters: "In the recent past subject has won a considerable amount of money from local bookmakers and it is the feeling that this was the reason for his demise," Scanlon wrote. "Bureau is assured that subject's demise had nothing to with his relationship with the FBI."

Of course the "subject's demise" had everything to do with the FBI. Castucci had made the fatal mistake of informing on Whitey's world, and, from the gang's perspective, Connolly's response was spot-on. Flemmi certainly was not surprised the agent tipped them off. He had assumed the moment they began meeting with Connolly the previous year that he was "one of the gang." Indeed, for Whitey, just as the mop-up killing of Tommy King in 1975 was historically significant as being his first murder on FBI time, Castucci's killing at the end of the nation's bicentennial year marked another historical milestone. Castucci was the first murder resulting from a Connolly tip—a killing, no less, of an FBI informant who was cooperating against them. "Castucci was the first [informant]," a federal judge later ruled, "killed by, or at the behest of, Bulger and Flemmi after the disclosure of his identity to them by Connolly."

Castucci was the "gateway killing." No turning back now. Whitey and Connolly had crossed the dark divide, hand in hand. The padding of the 209 files, the heads-up on extortion probes, accepting the ring—those illicit pleasures were a great start. They allowed Whitey to see a corrupted agent complicit in wrongdoing, at something close to the worst. But now Connolly had gone the distance—violating every FBI rule in the book, exposing an informer and conspiring, in effect, in murder. Connolly had proved that he was on board completely and at any cost—just what Whitey needed going forward to feel safe, trusting, and, most of all, in control. He owned Connolly forever more. Whitey had his own G-man.

17

Wild West Broadway

In its charred aftermath, it's hard to imagine that school desegregation snuck up on Southie. But indeed it did.

It had been dismissed out of hand in the beginning. Busing blacks into the preeminent Irish bastion to desegregate schools? Never happen. Who would even propose something that explosive? Who had the political firewall to withstand what it would unleash?

And if it ever became a real prospect, the battle-tested town would simply do what it always did—shout it down without letup. The way it had routed urban renewal a decade earlier. And it always could depend on how the Boston School Committee genuflected before its ballot box. The whole thing was preposterous.

But enter Judge W. Arthur Garrity, a focused man impervious to street noise.

A former U.S. attorney with strong Kennedy connections, Garrity had been a federal judge for ten years, a job he seemed destined for by intellect and disposition. But the appearance of a quiet ascetic with refined manners and excessive politeness cloaked a man of steel. Once he made up his mind, the matter was considered closed. Forthwith and period. Raucous protests notwithstanding.

It took a while for Southie to realize it had met its match.

It began on a sultry day in 1974 with the suddenness of a summer storm. A case suffused with precedents that supported busing to remedy segregation had quietly worked its way through the federal courthouse. On a June morning, less than three months before schools reopened, the court sprang a cataclysm on a sleepy town.

Garrity ruled that decades of intentional discrimination against blacks by the Boston School Committee now required that schools be racially balanced and resources equally shared. The findings, taken from committee minutes, were irrefutable. But the remedy of large-scale busing turned Boston upside down for nearly a decade. It achieved neither balanced schools nor better education. In fact, the opposite happened.

The Achilles' heel of the ruling was the most radical provision— that black students from Roxbury High be sent to South Boston and vice versa. The idea was to slay the "never" dragon dead on Telegraph Hill in South Boston. Within weeks, the unthinkable was under way.

Whitey Bulger's rise in Southie did not just result from doing in Donald Killeen and then troublesome Mullens one by one. Or from becoming a Top Echelon informant for John Connolly. Or from falling heir to Winter Hill's jackpot after Howie Winter went to jail and handed off a gambling network that rivaled the Mafia's.

His home turf was in historic turmoil that worked to his benefit. Among the legion of unforeseen consequences of Garrity's radical solution was that it proved good for Whitey Bulger's business. A town at loose ends was a crime haven.

Indeed, the peak year for serious crime for the last half century was 1975. This was the first full year of busing in South Boston. And it was the year that class warfare became the bitter backdrop to a vicious election between Mayor Kevin White and his downtown liberal supporters and Dorchester marine Joseph Timilty.

It almost got lost in the white noise of the election, but a crime surge was in full fury across the city and especially in South Boston. According to Boston Police Department data for 1960 to 2011, the "part 1" category of murder, rape, robbery, aggravated assault, house breaks, and car thefts doubled from the prior decade and nearly tripled in South Boston.

The major-crime category reached its zenith in the first year of busing at 80,530 incidents across the city and 3,975 in Southie, according to the data. The property crimes were at a record level and the homicides were the second-highest ever at 119. The lawless era was exacerbated by a reduction in arrests, decreasing by 11 percent in the city as a whole and by a jarring two-thirds in South Boston.

Whitey's kind of town. It was the perfect raging storm: busing madness through the decade, a sustained crime wave, and Whitey.

Forced busing in Southie became the twentieth-century counterpart to the Irish Potato famine, leaving similar scars on the Irish psyche from events swirling far out of their control. You couldn't get your arms around it, let alone kick its ass.

For independent Southie to lose oversight over its schools was to discover anew that it wasn't really in charge of its fate. Once again, meddlesome outsiders were deciding matters that profoundly affected South Boston's children and they couldn't stop it. The Yankee oligarchy had been replaced by a federal judge.

After months of agitation, anti-busers grappled with the realization that no amount of bloody street fighting was going to change a line of the nonnegotiable edict. It led to what was once unimaginable—defections to the suburbs by 20 percent of the population. They were the vanguard of white flight that changed Irish neighborhoods in a fundamental way.

But bad news was good news for Whitey.

The deeper Southie went into a rabbit hole of despair and defiance, the better it was for Whitey's business. The more it hated outsiders, the better it was inside Triple O's. It meant the town was down to the hard core who would rally around any Irish flag during its wild-west resistance, even one firmly planted in the underworld. And the mounting futility of the cause led to more drinking, which begat more barroom gambling and, inevitably, loan-sharking.

Even the disciplined Whitey almost gave in to the urge to strike back in the first disorienting days when black students arrived at South Boston High in September 1974. After the ugly opening week, rumors rocked a weekend crisis meeting at a City Hall that was struggling with managing a protest march set for Monday. Police told Mayor Kevin White that Whitey's Mullen Gang might be arming teenagers with handguns and if police tried to interfere with the march, the wiseguys were prepared to shoot it out.

"We can't screw around," White said. "We gotta call the feds." An aide with law enforcement connections called FBI director Clarence Kelley, once White's top pick for Boston police commissioner. Kelley ordered agents to knock on Mullen doors. Leaving no stone unturned, a panicky White called House Majority Leader Thomas "Tip" O'Neill of Cambridge to alert President Gerald Ford that federal troops might be required if resisters starting shooting at police.

But Whitey backed down on Monday. Mullens stayed home in an FBI-canvassed Southie. The march was angry but without gunplay.

Yet Whitey was so in control of subterranean Southie and so well known for brutal retaliation that he worried Kevin White for the duration.

While White had repeatedly stressed he was against busing, he knew that stipulating they were all stuck with the law of the land cut no slack in lawless Southie. So the mayor fretted about Whitey Bulger with his staff in half-serious asides about assassination and mused about it once when he thought the mikes were off at the end of a television interview.

Still on the air, the mayor reminisced about the night in 1975 during his tough reelection fight when he thought he spotted Whitey as White exited the Boston Athletic Club in South Boston. White got spooked and thought Whitey was going to shoot him as he got into his car. "Whitey takes me out, and they win all the marbles," the mayor told host Christopher Lydon.

The "marbles" were Kevin White's opulent City Hall office being occupied by Louise Day Hicks, a former congresswoman and two-time mayoral candidate. She was still the preeminent if fading Southie stalwart in the busing wars and in line to be president of the City Council, a position that made her the designated successor if there was a sudden vacancy in the mayor's office.

It's unclear how big a threat Whitey ever was to White. His possible assassination joined other rumors that Whitey was going to firebomb Judge Garrity's bungalow in reclusive Wellesley and retaliate against Senator Edward Kennedy, a steadfast proponent of busing, with an arson attack on the landmarked family homestead in Brookline and birthplace of President John Kennedy.

It's likely that Whitey was content to have people fear the worst and let that make his point.

Mayor White was in the line of fire the longest but he was also prone to hasty extrapolations and to melodrama. Whitey Bulger became another one of his vivid metaphors for busing—the black hole of politics where there are no winners and everyone disappears into oblivion.

The fact is that the first busing crisis of gangsters arming kids with pistols was never a real prospect. Whitey was too smart for pitched street warfare. He also saw the boomerang in having federal agents in numbers working Southie streets. He regrouped. It was clear Southie was ready for a lengthy siege and police would be in a defensive crouch for years. He could work with that.

After the first exhilarating month of sound and fury, when the worm turned and the power of what Southie was up against came more clearly into focus—the inflexible judge, the state police helicopters, the Boston tactical patrol force in battle gear—the tenor shifted. The clamorous crowd thinned into the never-say-die brigade. They couldn't win so the fight became the thing. It devolved into sheer lawlessness. Dodge City. Wild West Broadway.

In this combustible atmosphere, Whitey Bulger may have backed off from street violence but he hardly retreated. Like most hard-liners in Southie, he brimmed with disdain for the *Boston Globe,* based two miles from South Boston High. The newspaper was also implacable about busing, but on the other side. On the street, its editorials supporting the court order symbolized the unshared burden of Southie's struggle.

The daily violence at South Boston soon spilled over to the *Globe,* which had major highways at its front and back. Night riders put bullet holes in windows on both sides, most symbolically in the large glass façade in front of its presses. Police put sharpshooters on the paper's roof.

No one was ever arrested for the shootings but Whitey confided to his onetime Winter Hill associate Johnny Martorano that he was the one who fired at the *Globe.* With ironic inadvertence, he may have helped the paper win a Pulitzer Prize for public service.

Bill Bulger, who had moved up the state Senate leadership ladder, also boiled over about busing toward the end of the fraught first year, when tempers were frayed to the nub and the middle ground had dissolved. One morning after police had arrested demonstrators outside of a school, Bulger arrived and denounced the police for over-reacting.

The diminutive Bulger confronted the strapping police commis-sioner, Robert diGrazia, and railed against "Gestapo" tactics and spun on his heel to march away. A weary diGrazia yelled after him that none of the protests would be necessary if politicians had had the "balls" to deal with desegregation when it first became an issue.

Infuriated, Bulger raced back toward the police commissioner and jumped off the ground to get in his face: "Go fuck yourself." Bill Bulger, the scholar who loved to quote the classics, put a guttural coda on a lawless year.

The second year of busing produced the closest mayoral election since James Michael Curley left the scene, with Kevin White barely holding on. Schools opened as a replay of the first year, with slightly less inten-sity because some of the futility had sunk in. White eked out a victory over Timilty and promptly turned his back on the endless contretemps of Boston schools, a political loser that his well-heeled voters stopped caring about. By decade's end, one-third of the white families with children had left town, and the ones who had stayed soon abandoned the "balanced" schools as well. South Boston High became known as the "federal school." A system that began 60 percent white in 1974 was down to 11 percent within a decade.

In the run-up to the 1975 race, Ray Flynn, an up-and-coming state representative who was simpatico with blue-collar Southie, began to test the waters for a mayoral run down the road by saying he might be a candidate that year. Bill Bulger didn't like getting outmaneuvered in his home base. Although he didn't poll well across the city, he too made coy references to running in 1975. Flynn and some of his supporters called it for what it was—a political ploy to head off Flynn. But Whitey was aggrieved.

One of Flynn's early liegemen, Brian Wallace, said he got a call at home from Whitey. "I'll pick you up in five minutes."

With trepidation, Wallace got in the car parked out front. Whitey didn't say a word and took a slow drive around Southie's periphery, let-ting the menace build inside the car, leaving Wallace soaked with sweat and darty-eyed. About a mile from Wallace's house, Whitey pulled to the curb and looked directly at Wallace: "You've been running down my brother. I won't have that. Now get out." Wallace stumbled home.

In the wake of incessant busing strife, life lost a step for working families in blue-collar neighborhoods. The strife put the schools in a downward spiral and white flight pushed up the poverty index. It wasn't a complicated equation—middle-class white families with school-age children left town and were partially replaced by low-income immigrants from the Caribbean and Asia.

By 1980, Boston was in bad shape, hardly the world-class city that's extolled today. The Brookings Institution gave Boston the lowest ranking of 154 cities measured for urban travails. When Mayor White took office for his final term in 1980, his city ranked below Detroit, Newark, and Oakland in the misery index of unemployment, violent crime, and poverty.

But in South Boston, the lost decade was the coming-of-age for Whitey Bulger, who could now stand his ground with the Mafia and operate with murderous impunity on his home turf with the FBI secretly in his corner.

He was one of the few winners in the busing maelstrom, emerging with the mystique of a "good bad guy," if not quite Robin Hood. He killed a couple of Mullens and extorted bookies and you didn't want to owe him money. But outside the unhappy circle, nobody much cared. Southie always loved rogues. Whitey hadn't strangled any women yet and the bloom was still on the black rose.

The pitched battle over the schools may have become a lost cause, but that didn't change anybody's mind, with positions hardening into dogma on both sides of the line.

When the dust settled, if Southie wasn't quite the raw-boned Selma of 1963, it was openly hostile to blacks. Hometown historian Thomas O'Connor summed up the town's perspective: "It was certainly true that most people in South Boston didn't like blacks. People didn't know them, didn't understand them, and weren't comfortable with them."

While everyone thought the summer of 1975 would be a respite from racial rancor, one of the ugliest incidents came out of the blue on a lazy day in late July. Six black men, who were Bible salesmen from South Carolina visiting Roxbury, decided to cool off at Carson Beach, on the outskirts of South Boston. They were quickly surrounded by whites who drove them off the beach and put one of them in the hospital. Blacks said it was a racist attack; whites said it was a wanton provocation.

It simmered for two weeks and then erupted again with a confrontational caravan of three hundred cars with blacks asserting their right to go to a South Boston beach. There were nearly as many police on the Carson Beach scene as protesters—eight hundred cops, two Coast Guard boats offshore, and a state police helicopter circling overhead. After much saber-rattling by whites and blacks, the trouble dispersed.

The first-year fireworks had propelled a Mullen gang associate into prominence as the main spokesman against busing at the South Boston Information Center. A good friend of Whitey's, James Kelly was a hard-drinking sheet metal worker who carried a gun and had a criminal record. Yet he turned his busing bully pulpit into a long career on the Boston City Council.

While he set the record straight on declining student enrollment and accelerated white flight, Kelly's pronouncement on Carson Beach was Southie in the raw. "We've always welcomed good colored people to South Boston but we will not tolerate radical blacks or Communists. Good colored people are welcome in South Boston. Black militants are not."

But Kelly was more than a fiery advocate and Whitey Bulger's friend. He was an employee of Bulger Inc. Tucked away in law enforcement's debriefing of Stevie Flemmi years later, which itemized bribes paid to Boston cops, a state trooper, and FBI agents, as well as donations to antibusing politicians, was this: Kelly got a hundred dollars a week from Whitey during the busing era until 1983, when he was elected to the City Council.

Whitey had his hand in all phases of Southie life, including a secret subsidy for the public face of the antibusing movement. He had an acerbic press spokesman of his very own.

Kelly died of cancer at age sixty-six, in 2007. Thirty-three years after busing became an issue, it dominated his funeral service. To thunderous applause, Bill Bulger eulogized him as a valiant crusader in the cause. "Jim, you were heroic, you were steadfast, and you were right."

18

Whitey Rules

JAMES J. BULGER, JR. "WHITEY"

The first time Whitey Bulger learned about the covert role the CIA had played in the LSD Project—and that he and hundreds of inmates, students, and civilians had taken drugs the spy agency had wanted tested—was in the mid-1970s. That's when the *New York Times* began publishing articles about the general outlines of the mind-control experiments Dr. Carl C. Pfeiffer and others had conducted at prisons, colleges, and hospitals. The reports about the program with the code name MK-ULTRA prompted a congressional inquiry.

In the summer of 1977 the new CIA director, Stansfield Turner, was summoned to testify before the joint Select Committee on Intelligence and the Subcommittee on Health and Scientific Research. Turner arrived on Capitol Hill under overcast skies on a muggy

Wednesday, August 3, 1977, to face questioning that began with a senator from Whitey Bulger's home state of Massachusetts. Edward M. Kennedy, forty-five, chairman of the health subcommittee, seemed to be speaking for Whitey, other LSD volunteers, and, for that matter, all Americans.

"What we are basically talking about is an activity which took place in the country that involved the perversion and the corruption of many of our outstanding research centers," he said. "Much of it was done with American citizens who were completely unknowing in terms of taking various drugs, and there are perhaps any number of Americans who are walking around today on the east coast or west coast who were given drugs, with all the kinds of physical and psychological damage."

The director of the CIA offered a mea culpa that was quoted around the world in the next day's news coverage. "Senator Kennedy," he said, "it is totally abhorrent to me to think of using a human being as a guinea pig and in any way jeopardizing his life and his health, no matter how great the cause."

The hearing on Capitol Hill was held about nine months after Richie Castucci's murder in Somerville, and while Whitey Bulger was preoccupied with that killing's aftermath he took it all in—that he was one of the CIA's human guinea pigs. He would never know all the drugs he'd taken and would always wonder whether they caused his nightmares and sleeping difficulties.

But, as with everything, Whitey also took it in strategically—as a piece of intelligence that might someday prove to have value. He sometimes talked to his brother Bill in the years to come about the LSD Project, especially about the betrayal of Whitey himself by Dr. Pfeiffer. He also talked to some FBI agents, including a supervisor named John Morris, who became John Connolly's boss on the Organized Crime Squad. Morris soon joined Whitey's circle of corrupted agents, and Whitey vented a bit with him about the CIA, the LSD, and the scandalous use of people like him as guinea pigs. One time he told Morris that he was even considering suing the government. Indeed, a handful of former inmates did just that in 1981, although the lawsuit they filed in federal court in Atlanta never gained much traction and eventually was dismissed.

But Whitey also had another, bigger idea for being a victim of the

CIA mind-control testing. If ever he got indicted, he told Morris, he would use LSD as a defense for his crimes. The LSD made me do it, he would say—that would be the strategy.

Whitey Bulger, of course, was not planning on getting indicted anytime soon, especially as one decade was ending and he enjoyed further evidence that his special status with the FBI translated into invincibility.

During 1978 a new threat had crystallized in the form of a federal indictment against the Winter Hill Gang for fixing horse races. For most of the decade the gang was teamed up with a barrel-shaped hustler named Anthony "Fat Tony" Ciulla. Ciulla bribed jockeys, trainers, and racetrack officials so that certain horses were held back and did not finish in the money. "For example," Martorano said, "like, if there was seven horses racing, Tony Ciulla would be paying the three best horses not to be in the money. So, then, the other four would be the only ones there." The gang would then bundle bets involving the four horses— win, place, and show.

The scheme was both lucrative and proof that the gang's reach extended far beyond an urban street corner. They fixed races at Suffolk Downs in East Boston and at tracks in New Hampshire, New York, New Jersey, Rhode Island, and Pennsylvania. Howie Winter and Johnny Martorano worked most closely with Tony Ciulla in the day-to-day planning and coordination of the gang's bets with bookmakers, while Whitey and Stevie Flemmi stepped in as enforcers if a bookie balked or a jockey dared to act up. "If there was a problem," Flemmi said, "we would actually contribute to the physical aspect of it." The winnings were mainly divided six ways, between Winter, Martorano, Whitey, Flemmi, Ciulla, and another key member of the Winter Hill Gang, Billy Barnowski.

But eventually Ciulla tripped up in New Jersey, and that meant trouble for the gang. He began cooperating with investigators, and by late 1978 the legal storm had moved up the coast to Boston, where federal prosecutors were putting together an indictment that would feature Fat Tony as the star witness. Whitey kept track of the indictment's progress through John Connolly, and by year's end it became clear that Whitey and Flemmi were targeted. The solution?

"Connolly's gonna try to get us out of it," Flemmi recalled.

Connolly went to work, enlisting his new supervisor John Morris, and together they met with Jeremiah T. O'Sullivan, the arrogant but tough Mafia-hating federal prosecutor who was in charge of the race-fixing case. The two FBI agents disclosed that Whitey and Flemmi were their informants and vital to the greater goal of taking down underboss Gennaro Angiulo. The move worked; the final draft of the race-fixing indictment left out Whitey and Flemmi.

The coast was clear, but "with a stipulation," Flemmi said. "We had to give our word we wouldn't kill Tony Ciulla." Martorano certainly wanted to. "I would like to have found Ciulla," he said. "I'd have shot him." But that was out of the question. It was one thing to kill Castucci, a secret FBI informant few would notice missing, and quite another to murder a gangster publicly identified as a government trial witness. Killing Ciulla would be bad business, and for once Whitey kept his word.

When the fifty-plus page indictment was filed on February 2, 1979, and Whitey and Flemmi were not among the twenty-one men charged, the prosecutorial pass that Whitey's G-man had engineered was another pivotal moment for Whitey. The case triggered a major reshuffling of the deck, not unlike the realignment that occurred earlier in the decade. That time, to resolve the Southie gang war, Whitey had emerged from Chandler's summit atop a newly imagined South Boston branch of the Winter Hill Gang. This time, as part of a shake-up caused by the race-fixing case, Whitey came out ahead again—atop the Winter Hill Gang itself.

Of the principals, Howie Winter, already off-site, was now certain to stay out of the picture; the state prison sentence he was serving for extortion would roll into a ten-year federal sentence once he was convicted at the race-fixing trial during the summer. Joe McDonald and Jimmy Sims were still fugitives (although they might have been behind bars had the FBI not compromised Castucci's tip about their apartment in New York City). Then there was Johnny Martorano, who was packing up and getting ready to go on the lam ahead of the federal indictment.

In preparation, Martorano, Whitey, Flemmi, and a few other gang members gathered at a restaurant. Martorano was actually content to learn that, with the FBI's help, Whitey and Flemmi were able to dodge the indictment. "I figured I was going to get indicted anyway," he said. Better to have two key men left standing than a complete sweep. Over dinner, then, the gangsters reviewed the changing landscape, with Whitey and Flemmi taking possession of the gambling accounts and other financial records that Martorano kept. "We accepted the books," Flemmi said. "He gave me all the figures and what we had, what Winter Hill obligations there were." One debt in particular nagged at Whitey—the $250,000 loan from the Mafia's Jerry Angiulo to finance the gang's loan-sharking and sports betting operations. Chief among his first actions was revising that debt load; Whitey knocked off $50,000 and informed Angiulo. The imperious Mafia underboss, accustomed to absolute fealty, was thrown, but he chose to carp to his underlings about deadbeat Irish treachery rather than start any gangland blood-letting. Whitey won the stare-down, a sign not only of his long-standing animus toward the Mafia but also his growing confidence.

Whitey, Flemmi, and Martorano also worked out other logistics, such as how to get money to Martorano and how to regularly stay in touch. For that they chose their associate George Kaufman, a bookie who lived just outside Boston. Kaufman acted as the liaison—whenever Martorano wanted to talk to Whitey or Flemmi he contacted Kaufman to set up a telephone call, and vice versa. Then, with business squared away, Martorano was gone, bound for Florida in the company of his girlfriend Patty.

The hit man Martorano figured he'd be back in "six, seven months." To help him stay ahead of police while away, Whitey's agent John Connolly once again came in handy. Not only did Connolly several times alert Whitey when the authorities had zeroed in on Martorano's where-abouts, giving Martorano time to get away, but the agent also presented Whitey with an ingenious idea. "John Connolly suggested we keep him out there," Flemmi said. "Keep him out there as a source of security."

With the gang's leadership stripped down in 1979 to Whitey and Flemmi, others in the underworld, particularly the Mafia, might falsely perceive weakness and vulnerability. But with Martorano on the lam, anyone considering a move on Whitey and Flemmi would have to consider a master killer seeking revenge. Flemmi knew the Mafia was "very concerned" about Martorano. "Johnny was a formi-dable person," he said. Having someone of Martorano's stature lurking about out there would protect them. "He's a bogeyman against the Mafia," Flemmi said.

Whitey and Flemmi liked Connolly's idea, and together they conspired so that Johnny Martorano's tenure as a fugitive from justice remained open-ended—meaning a departure Martorano had thought might last only six months extended for years, into the 1990s. Eventually, too, a second purpose materialized. As Whitey spread his rackets beyond state lines problems arose where certain people got in the way of his progress. It was to be expected in an underworld economy. But thanks to Connolly, Whitey had Martorano perfectly positioned in the wings to execute business solutions, solutions that were not pretty but that the hit man excelled at.

For some attending the gang's last supper on the eve of the race-fixing indictment, the gathering had been a chance to bemoan the havoc Tony Ciulla and federal prosecutors had wrought against Winter Hill. For Whitey Bulger, though, it was a chance to celebrate an ever-opening road to power, to toast privately, no doubt, that so much was breaking his way. Over at the FBI, John Connolly was working out better than he could have expected. The corrupted agent was showing real promise, going beyond the usual tip-offs that aid a gang's welfare to propose innovative ideas that strengthened the enterprise—the bogeyman role for the fugitive Martorano being a prime example. By 1979, Connolly had even brought into the fold John Morris, the agent who took over as supervisor of "C-3," the Organized Crime Squad, in late 1977.

Morris, slightly younger than Connolly, was thin-lipped, ordinary-looking, and small in stature. He became enamored of Connolly soon after they met, with the local Boston agent possessing "a lot of qualities that I didn't have." Said Morris, "He was mentally tough. He's physically tough. He was from Boston; he knew the streets. He's charismatic." Morris soon considered Connolly "my best friend."

By the summer of 1979 Morris was one of the boys, hosting the first of a series of illicit dinners at his home in the Boston suburb of Lexington, where agents and gangsters broke bread, drank wine, and eventually exchanged gifts. Morris saw right away how Connolly bent and broke the law to protect Whitey but also how Connolly enjoyed adulation inside the FBI as a star informant-handler. Morris jumped in to ride his tailwind. Whitey and Flemmi soon had nicknames for their FBI counterparts. Connolly became Zip, Elvis, or Neighbor. Morris was Vino.

In all, a black mass had settled into the Organized Crime Squad—a toxicity inherited from older agents Rico and Condon but which Connolly and Morris embraced and spread. The foulness did not go unnoticed by some agents newly transferred to the Boston office during this period. James C. Crawford arrived from Chicago in 1977 and was assigned the "Top Ten" fugitive case of Winter Hill enforcer Joe McDonald. Crawford's new supervisor warned him about the C-3 squad's "smoke and mirrors" games and not to expect help from Connolly or Morris's men. But Crawford forged on. There was an agent in Boston he'd worked with in Detroit, an agent now friendly with Connolly in Boston. Crawford went to this agent and asked how to tap into the intelligence Connolly had on McDonald. The agent told him point-blank, "You're not," and said he should forget about it. Crawford was stymied by a Boston FBI way of life called the "C-3 mentality."

And when Connolly brought new agents around to meet his premier informant, Whitey generally won them over with his trademark charade, the mix of charm and deference he'd perfected during his prison years. In one instance he buttered up a new special agent in charge, or "SAC" as they were called, soon after the agent arrived to take over the Boston office. Lawrence Sarhatt had gotten an earful from other police agencies, particularly the Massachusetts State Police, about Whitey, and the new SAC had concerns about the FBI's ties to a gangster whose reputation was so monstrous. Connolly and John Morris then arranged a meeting—lasting four hours—during which Whitey delivered a lecture about their wonderful life together and their shared mission against the Mafia. Ranging far and wide, Whitey talked about his disgust for drug dealers (even though, at that moment, he was expanding into drug trafficking) and emphasized his commitment to the bureau. To drive home his patriotic zeal he described a state police official who had "made very disparaging and derogatory statements about the professionalism of FBI personnel," according to a report Sarhatt wrote later. Whitey would not stand for such FBI trash talk. "He took great umbrage inasmuch as his association with the FBI has been nothing but the most professional in every respect," the Sarhatt report said.

Whitey might well have been writing a letter to Rev. Drinan from the psych ward in Atlanta twenty-five years earlier, or talking up the guards on his cell block in Alcatraz or parole officials in Lewisburg. He was, as always, the good bad guy, and his latest performance was no different. Combined with Connolly's and Morris's internal FBI politicking, the trio successfully circumvented Sarhatt's concerns.

Whitey certainly understood full well that he had FBI agents Connolly and Morris on a string, and he continued applying the right touch to keep them there for years to come. In 1980 Connolly's first marriage was falling apart, and Whitey helped the untethered agent buy a house on Thomas Park, an oval-shaped street atop Dorchester Heights overlooking the harbor. Whitey got the seller, a bookmaker named Bobby Ford, to give Connolly a break on the price, and he then arranged for Connolly to outfit the new home with appliances bought from an associate at cost. In addition, Whitey decided around this time to establish a special account from which to occasionally make cash gifts, especially at Christmastime, to Connolly, Morris, and other agents, as graft widened. Whitey called it the "Ex-Fund," for "expense fund," with an eventual balance of between $250,000 and $300,000.

Whitey tapped into the fund to take Connolly on breaks from their hectic city life. During one trip the two bachelors managed to dodge the Blizzard of '78, which dumped a record 27.1 inches of snow on Boston and paralyzed the region. They were off in Mexico, although they suffered their own minor mishap. Whitey, always the driver, got into a car accident. Connolly hit his head on the windshield and when they got back Flemmi noticed Connolly was nursing a bruised eye. Returning another time from Acapulco, Whitey had some fun posing as a G-man at the airport. It was Connolly's idea to bypass the long lines—Connolly flashed his FBI badge, identified Whitey as another Boston agent named Jim Cullen, and then insisted to airline officials that they be allowed to board the next plane to Boston. The two were quickly escorted onto the jet, past the ordinary people.

Closer to home, they drove south from Boston on occasion to Cape Cod, where Whitey took the FBI agent to visit Provincetown on the Cape's outermost tip. "P-town" had become one of Whitey's favorite getaway spots. Once a quiet fishing village, it had transformed during the late 1960s and 1970s into "a hedonistic cabaret of artists, celebrities, gays, lesbians and outsiders," as one magazine writer wrote. The resort was only a couple hours' drive from Boston but was an interplanetary voyage of sorts, far unlike Whitey's customary surroundings.

The club scene—featuring drag queens and discos—made Provincetown one of the most popular vacation spots in the country for gay men and lesbians—and, in his own way, for Whitey. He favored one inn in particular in the center of town, the Crown and Anchor. It had a pool, two restaurants, and three bars. One, the Ms. Room, was a lesbian bar; another, the Vault, featured S&M. The Crown annually held a drag queen contest that drew huge crowds, gay and straight.

Whitey stayed at the Crown and befriended its owner, Staniford Sorrentino. The two, about the same age, couldn't have been more different. Sorrentino was gay and garish, obese and giggly, a pill popper and cocaine snorter. One magazine described Sorrentino as a "decadent, roly-poly Nero." When the club owner later faced tax evasion charges he insisted he never knew the real-life Whitey. "I know him as Jimmy Bulger and I enjoy his company," he said. Instead of a killer with a glare, Sorrentino said his Whitey was a "sensitive, intelligent, intuitive person."

Whitey's stays in Provincetown have been the basis for speculation he was gay. How else to explain why the toughest of gangsters—Boston's powerful ruler of men and women alike, fit and macho—frequented a gay retreat and associated with the likes of Sorrentino? Indeed, some writers have cited Whitey's fondness for Provincetown as proof positive he was bisexual. To be sure, the idea that Whitey Bulger might have acted out homoerotic fantasies would not be unthinkable for someone as sexually potent as he. But no firsthand, on-the-record evidence has surfaced to corroborate the claim. Flemmi, Martorano, and others in his inner circle have all said they never saw Whitey as homosexual.

And Whitey certainly wasn't in the closet about his Provincetown connection. He took Connolly there, and his girlfriends. Putting sexuality aside, then, P-town arguably offered Whitey something else—an extreme escape. The gay scene was insular, intensely secretive, and private. No one would bother him, and he could have a "gay" time, in its old and possibly new meaning, surrounded by people who were not the type to judge the behavior of others. Provincetown might have had nothing to do with sex. Even a crime boss like Whitey Bulger could have had a fundamental need to get away from the severe, dehumanizing daily business that was his life: the robbing, extorting, cheating, lying, the violence and the killing. Provincetown represented a total change of scene for him, where he could relax and not need to be on guard about what was going on around him. It was radical R&R.

In addition to all the comings and goings, of new faces and old, and the underworld shifting, the end of the 1970s also marked a personal milestone. While Whitey was finding his stride, poised to take full command in the decade to come, he was hitting the half-century mark. In 1979 he turned fifty, and no one was clearer-eyed than Whitey himself about how far he'd come. The self-assessment was captured in a 1979 report Connolly prepared after one of their meetings, during which Whitey egotistically told his handler a piece of intelligence that was self-promoting but that he knew to be true: "James Bulger runs the Irish Mafia."

From here on it was the Bulger Gang. (Not the Bulger-Flemmi Gang, but the Bulger Gang.) The era of Winter Hill was over. The fallen and jailed boss Howie Winter had even asked Whitey and Flemmi to clear out of Marshall Motors. "Howie asked us to leave Somerville, leave the garage," Flemmi said. Whitey was free to consolidate back home in Southie. He had associates scouting for a new garage downtown in the shadow of Boston Garden, but that did not preempt using several Southie locations for different purposes. There was Triple O's on West Broadway near the bridge connecting Southie to Boston's financial district. Whitey liked the ambience of a second-floor room upstairs—its grit and darkness—for shakedowns. The gang's bookmaking operations were based out of a club in the neighborhood's City Point section. Some called it the Mullens Club because years earlier it was headquarters to the gang that was a rival of Whitey's; others called it simply the O Street Club because of its location at the corner of O and Third streets. "It was basically a place where we associated," an underling said. "Different members of our organization went down there, had loan-sharking, gambling business and stuff." Within several years, Whitey also extorted a liquor store from a South Boston couple and took over a variety store, both on the rotary at the Old Harbor housing project. Whitey and Flemmi used them to oversee their rackets, but the stores also gave the appearance of a legitimate source of income.

Whitey and Flemmi also continued to build up their arsenal of weapons: machine guns, with and without silencers; sawed-off shotguns; pistols with silencers; high-powered rifles; assault rifles; hand grenades. "A large assortment of firearms," Flemmi said about firepower that could outfit a small army. They kept weapons in several "hides," or hiding places, usually behind wall panels. One was in the basement of associate George Kaufman's home in Brookline; other hides were in the South Boston homes of some of the gang's relatives and parents.

Whitey went so far as to oversee the creation of a gang "hit-mobile," which he christened with the code name "the tow truck." Whitey spotted a late-model blue Chevrolet and ordered an associate to buy the car from its elderly owners. Whitey then had the engine souped up so it could perform at up to 200 mph. He devised add-ons that were right out of a James Bond movie—an oil slick option and a way to create a smoke screen. Space was created in the interior panels to stock pistols, an assault rifle, and a machine gun.

In the comfort of Southie virtually everything was within reach—the offices, the guns, the manpower. Whitey was thriving in ways he never had before, on the very same streets where the beast within had been first nourished as a juvenile in the late 1930s, when he discovered his knack for criminality. Over the years it had all been so circular and reinforcing in the hometown, and now he was shaping a criminal enterprise in his own image: lean, brutal, disciplined, and carnivorous. His operational strategy going forward could be likened to a closely held corporation; he and Flemmi stood at the center of a small and trustworthy inner circle overseeing an expanding lineup of bookmakers, loan sharks, extortionists, and drug dealers. Like any good manager, Whitey was quick to recognize a good business concept and run with it. He took the practice of charging "rent," which had worked so well with the bookmakers, and adapted it to the drug trade, which he moved into after taking a shine to a smart and successful dealer in Southie named Billy Shea. Like Whitey, Billy Shea had served hard time—in Shea's case at the state's toughest prison, in the town of Walpole. Whitey liked the way Shea carried himself, suspicious to the point of paranoia about people he did not know. Whitey soon worked out a deal with Shea where together they rounded up drug dealers in Southie, put them under Shea's direct management, and ordered them to pay rent.

"He organized all the drug dealers in South Boston," Flemmi said, and then set each dealer's drug tax based "on the amount of drugs that they were selling."

From this launch in 1981 Whitey's drug profits grew rapidly; in addition to the regular payments from local dealers he began to extort payoffs from some of the biggest wholesalers in the Northeast—dealers like Frank Lepere, Mickey Caruana, and Joe Murray, who moved loads of marijuana and cocaine through Boston. Whitey, learning about major shipments, would confront them with his readiness to kill. "We would get them in the right spot," one associate recalled, "and let them know that if they don't pay us they're not walking out of here." Whitey, said the associate, had a favorite line for the traffickers: "You can always make money, but you only have one life. So what's it gonna be?" The cuts ranged from $25,000 into the millions of dollars, with one score totaling $5 million.

Whitey raked it in, a millionaire several times over. And as far as the underworld went, there was a neat efficiency to his governance. He did not bother with the street-level, day-to-day grunt work but instead set policy. When conflict arose, he certainly did not hesitate to intervene with his legendary hands-on brutality. But mostly Whitey remained insulated as a presiding head of state reaping the benefits of underworld tithes.

The fast-paced expansion did not go unnoticed. Whitey detected an uptick in attention from law enforcement. But, ever since 1975, Whitey held that trump card. Boston police, state police, federal drug agents—they all might have a heightened interest in him, but John Connolly's FBI did not. The FBI had his back—a claim few crime bosses anywhere could make. Moreover, Connolly was the best image-maker he could possibly ask for. The agent padded the FBI's secret informant files with lies, at once inflating Whitey's value as an informant and minimizing his criminal activities. For example, at the same time Whitey's drug-dealing subsidiary was growing exponentially, Connolly wrote that Whitey hated drugs and kept them out of his neighborhood. Connolly spun the myth of an antidrug Whitey, an idea that on the streets of Southie every dealer, addict, and wiseguy knew was a sick joke.

Getting his house in order at the turn of the decade, Whitey asserted control not only over the streets but over his women as well. Lindsey

Cyr had faded steadily to black, their relationship irretrievable after the death of their son, but when Whitey's mother, a heavy smoker, became seriously ill, Cyr stepped back into Whitey's life. She found him in Triple O's. "You didn't think it was important to tell me your mother has cancer?" she said. Whitey looked at her and replied, "I don't say that word." Then, on New Year's Day 1980, the widow Jean V. (McCarthy) Bulger, age seventy-three, died at Massachusetts General Hospital of kidney cancer, or hypernephroma, which had spread to her brain and lungs. Lindsey Cyr said she wanted to help, but trying to patch things up with Whitey was useless. "If he turned cold when Douglas died, he was a block of ice after his mother was gone," she said.

Whitey had turned instead to his other two women for solace—Teresa Stanley and Catherine Greig—both fitting his preference for women who were young, blond, and from Southie. Of the two, Teresa was more securely anchored in place. Whitey had started up with her in the late 1960s while he was still with Cyr. Stanley had four kids and was single. Whitey eventually bought her a house on Silver Street and began providing her with money to run her household. She cooked dinner regularly for Whitey at five-thirty and Whitey got to play a cameo family role, telling her how to keep her life in order, acting strict but caring with the kids—as if he knew how to be a father, in contrast to his own father. Stanley later described Whitey as possessive and controlling, volatile and aloof, more drill instructor than companion. But she knew her place—the quintessential woman who stood by her man asking no questions—and Whitey stayed with her for that reason.

Catherine Greig was different. By the late 1970s, with Cyr receding, Whitey became deeply involved with Greig. Greig had gorgeous good looks like Teresa Stanley. She was voted best-looking girl her senior year at South Boston High School in 1969. She also had assets Stanley lacked—bookish, smart, well spoken, and focused, all appealing to a man who considered himself the epitome of all those qualities. Whitey and Greig began dating in 1975, when Greig was twenty-four and coming off a broken marriage. Her husband was Bobby McGonagle—of the old Mullen Gang's McGonagles, two of whom, Donald and Paul, Whitey had killed. But neither Greig nor Whitey was inhibited in any way by this complicated past—indeed Greig, angry about a cheating husband, possibly had payback in mind when she first started up with Whitey. From his perspective, Whitey not only enjoyed the pretty young blonde's shapely figure but also took note of the condition of her heart—wounded. It was the kind of disadvantaged position he looked for in someone whenever he was mulling a move. The FBI did it that way, too—targeting as a possible informant a criminal who was in a jam and vulnerable. Courting a hurting Greig as a love interest, Whitey showered her with gifts—furs, gold, a Cartier watch on her birthday. It made her feel good. "She was completely and totally enthralled with him," one of her coworkers said.

But there was a sticking point for Whitey—Greig was career-minded, a fact that was coming to a head. Greig had earned an associate's degree in dental hygiene in 1972 from the Forsyth School for Dental Hygienists in Boston and had then become a dental instructor. She'd enrolled in classes at Northeastern University, where, in 1978, she earned a bachelor's degree in health science with honors. Back at Forsyth she was working as the clinic coordinator for second-year students. Whitey was not impressed by her accomplishments. Greig knew it; she told some of her friends at work that Whitey wanted her to quit so she could dedicate herself to him.

Whitey wanted stay-at-home molls, along the lines of Stanley. He tried to curb Greig's ambition and make her increasingly dependent on him. The gifts were part of it; isolating her from colleagues and friends at Forsyth, and even her from her family, was a bigger part. It would take time, however, and he wasn't quite there by decade's end. But this was how Whitey took control of her life, so that eventually Catherine Greig orbited exclusively around him. Neither could know it in 1980 but the relationship, over the long term, would prove Whitey's most important.

To his women and minions Whitey Bulger was in charge, a didact always barking orders and giving instruction, and at this juncture another relationship began that would also turn out to have long-term ramifications. Kevin Weeks entered Whitey's world, a new pupil of sorts who moved quickly into coveted status as Whitey's confidant. He came to the work qualified. His older brothers were amateur boxers, "so, naturally I went into fighting," he said, "sparring with my brothers," and eventually he fought three times professionally. Weeks graduated from South Boston High in 1974 and the next year, the peak years of busing, he roamed the halls as a school aide. He joked that his true job title was "bouncer," explaining that he mainly "broke up a lot of fights." In addition to working security at the school, Weeks was a bouncer at an upscale bar in Back Bay called Flicks, began freelancing as a bookmaker, and then impressed Whitey as a bouncer at Triple O's.

"When I was working down at Triple O's," he said, "I'd take a ride with Mr. Bulger around town." Whitey had noticed that Weeks had a useful skill set, and it was as if the rides were a tryout. "I'd get into fights for him," Weeks said. "He used me for muscle. He had other people, too. But he used me." It didn't hurt, either, that Weeks had a gun permit and carried a handgun legally. In all, Whitey liked the package: Weeks had a swagger about him but was not quick-triggered or out of control. With Whitey, Weeks was respectful, deferential, and deeply loyal; he was known later to say he'd watch harm come to his mother before turning against Whitey Bulger and cooperating with the police against him. Weeks was an astute listener, too, and Whitey, as their relationship grew, realized he liked having a younger man around to absorb his monologues on all manner of topics. Whitey was at ease with Weeks and brought him under his wing to the point where he grew closer to the boss than perhaps even Flemmi, whose name would always end in *i*.

By 1979 and 1980 young Weeks was getting full daily doses of the gangster boss. Most of all he learned that Whitey demanded supreme loyalty and despised informers. "Jim Bulger," Weeks said later, "always said you never rat on your friends, you never rat on your enemies. If we have a problem you take it to the street and figure it out that way. You never involve law enforcement." Weeks also saw that Whitey loved to read, was a health and fitness fanatic, a stickler for common courtesy, and germophobic to a degree rivaling Howard Hughes. When someone in his company sneezed and did not cover his mouth, Whitey threw a fit. Weeks saw that Whitey enjoyed a night out with drinks and good food but was not loud the way some of the other guys partied. In terms of business, he heard the Crime 101 lecture from Whitey on the twenty-four-hour rule, of not acting impulsively but taking a day to consider every possible angle before reaching a decision.

"We had a few rules," Weeks said. They assumed the police had them under surveillance, that a car, telephone, or room was bugged. "That's why we'd get out of the car and walk around." Whitey liked Castle Island in South Boston, where walking along the harbor causeway put them out of the reach of electronic surveillance and gave them an open view of possible stalkers. Whitey also introduced Weeks to his FBI agent pal John Connolly. But Weeks, of course, only got half the story—not the part about Whitey being a Top Echelon informant. Weeks found Connolly friendly enough, and he even got a good deal from the agent when he bought a 1978 green Thunderbird from him. Weeks sometimes drove Whitey and Flemmi to meet with Connolly.

But one episode in particular seemed to jump off the page during the days when their relationship was deepening into a full-time commitment. In late 1979, the apprentice Weeks experienced Whitey in full Monty—as martinet, manipulator, murderer, and macabre humorist.

It was the matter of Louis Litif. Whitey had never much liked Litif—a flashy dresser, abrasive and full of himself. Whitey liked the bookmaker less once Litif began considering himself a big-time drug dealer, and Whitey's tolerance neared a breaking point when Litif decided he was a killer, too. Litif had shot an associate during an argument, and then killed the lone witness. In September 1979 Litif had been arrested, charged with murder, and released on bail. (Litif had also been an FBI informant for several years, but the bureau "closed" him once he was charged with murder.)

In February 1980 Whitey summoned Litif to Triple O's. Weeks was present, and he saw that his boss was in no mood for small talk, that his voice was flat, the corner of his mouth curled, and the clear blue eyes glaring—the signs, Weeks was learning, that Whitey was "dead serious." Whitey berated Litif about his antics, his running around like he was some kind of murderous stud. "You're a bookmaker; you're not a killer." He warned Litif: "People are going to look at you differently."

"As long as I have you as a friend, I don't have a problem," Litif said.

Litif didn't seem to get it.

Whitey's final words: "We're not friends anymore."

Then came the tipping point. Litif, following the meeting and desperate to find a way out of the murder case, went to the authorities. He offered to cooperate against Whitey. FBI agent Connolly, becoming aware of the ploy, alerted Whitey immediately. On April 13, 1980, Whitey summoned Litif back to Triple O's; a few hours later Litif was taken out the back door in a body bag.

Weeks was not present for the killing but he soon picked up a hint that Whitey had found a final solution to the Louis Litif matter. Weeks and his fiancée were making arrangements for their upcoming nuptials later in April and he asked Whitey where to seat the obnoxious Litif. Whitey, ever the wedding planner, told Weeks not to worry. "He probably won't show up," Whitey predicted.

Next Weeks got a taste of Whitey's gallows humor. The corpse of the wedding no-show was discovered in a car trunk in the South End of Boston. Whitey commented to Weeks that the clotheshound Litif had worn green underwear the day he died. Whitey then noted the body had been stuffed into a matching green garbage bag. Whitey thought it was funny—the green touches.

"Louie was color-coordinated," he joked.

Then, with the body's discovery, the gruesome details emerged. Whitey had used an ice pick, stabbing Litif thirty-eight times. "The puncture wounds perforated Litif's liver," a federal judge wrote later, "a wound thought to cause exquisite agony." In case that hadn't done the trick, Litif was shot in the back of the head.

Kevin Weeks came to realize that from start to finish, the Litif case covered the gamut of Whitey at work, completed with the requisite savagery. Let the word go forth: Whitey rules.

19

Categorical Bill and the Tulsa Trilogy

Clockwise from top left: Bill Bulger, Roger Wheeler, Brian Halloran, and John Callahan

George Kaufman knew the perfect skid-row spot.

When the pared-down Winter Hill Gang was evicted from Marshall Motors, the mechanic relocated the garage to Lancaster Street, in the West End near the old Boston Garden. The alley was a remnant of an expired immigrant neighborhood.

But the site couldn't have been better. It was a few blocks from Jerry Angiulo's office in the North End and a couple of miles from Southie. In the mornings, there were clanging, banging auto repairs but in the early afternoons the garage fell silent for the real business, when Whitey showed up for work.

By the spring of 1980, consigliere Ilario "Larry" Zannino was swinging by the garage regularly in his blue Lincoln Continental along with capo Danny Angiulo. Mafia associate Phil Waggenheim and soldier Nicky Giso were patrons. Whitey even had a Mafia hanger-on of his very own—beefy cokehead Nick Femia was a sometimes driver. But Zannino's comings and goings were *Godfather*-like events, grand entrances that had mechanics scurrying aside and Whitey getting kissed on both cheeks. Winter Hill and the Mafia were congregating for a common purpose on middle ground.

It was the perfect below-the-radar setup—until state trooper Rick Fraelick checked out a tip about a stolen car ring on Lancaster Street and his jaw dropped at the parade of underworld heavyweights.

The next day, Fraelick and his boss, Robert Long, did surveillance from up the street and understood immediately what they had—a real-time criminal conspiracy at the highest level. They rented a fetid room above a gay bar across the street from the garage and did weeks of due-diligence camera surveillance. They were in over their heads but knew this much: they needed audio to go with the visuals to get a killer case against the top tier of Boston's underworld.

They had never done anything other than get wiretaps on bookie telephones. This case required a dead-of-night break-in and bugs planted throughout the garage. They were so strapped for equipment and expertise that they bought microphones at RadioShack.

The Lancaster Street bugging became a comedy of errors—without a laugh in it.

But it wasn't just the bumbling troopers trying two times to get bugs in place and then having the only one that worked be drowned out by pager calls from the nearby Massachusetts General Hospital.

The day after the bugs were installed, it was clear right away something was wrong. From their flophouse perch across the street, the troopers saw the daily patterns change instantly. Whitey no longer used his office; he talked with Stevie only in a car inside the garage; they scanned the flophouse with suspicion.

Whitey knew. But how?

In the acrimonious aftermath, the feds said the troopers were amateurs who blew it and were looking for a scapegoat. The long-suspicious staties shot back with vehemence and said it out loud—the FBI protected an informant in a case that could have brought the house down.

Both were right.

Years later, Flemmi told investigators that Whitey and he practically needed a secretary to keep track of the dime droppers on the hapless state cops above the gay bar.

But the primary source upended the state police. First word of the taps came from state police trooper Detective Richard Schneiderhan, who had been on the take from Winter Hill for nearly a decade.

He had become friendly with Johnny Martorano in the late 1960s at Enrico's Restaurant in downtown Boston. In 1972, Schneiderhan had some health problems and Martorano began paying him a thousand dollars a month, at first to help out in a rough patch, and then as a regular stipend in exchange for information.

Six years later, when Martorano went on the lam to Florida, he handed off Schneiderhan to Flemmi. The crook's code name was "Sarge" and the cop's was "Eric." Schneiderhan's intelligence had been mostly giving Winter Hill a heads-up on gambling wiretaps or pending raids on bookie joints. But he was ideally suited for intelligence on Lancaster Street—his specialty was wiretaps and he talked regularly with state troopers Fraelick and Long.

On the eve of the late-night entry by the troopers into the garage, Schneiderhan called "Sarge" to set up an urgent meeting at a small out-of-the-way Braintree mall, where they had met before. Flemmi came away from the fast conversation thinking the garage phones were tapped, though it turned out that the troopers bugged wall outlets and a sofa.

Flemmi and Whitey huddled immediately and decided to double-check Schneiderhan's information with FBI handler Connolly. The chain reaction sizzled through the federal building with fast confirmation from prosecutor Jeremiah O'Sullivan, who knew of the state police operation. Then the FBI Organized Crime Squad's boss, John Morris, warned Whitey. According to Flemmi, even the Mafia got into the act. Jerry Angiulo had regular electronic sweeps of his office done by a freelance technician who had Boston and state police contacts and passed along the scuttlebutt.

Flemmi wasn't sure but he thought they gave Schneiderhan a bonus for being first in line with the tip-off.

Schneiderhan was in it for the long haul, a mole for twenty years. According to Flemmi's figures, the trooper's take, including bonuses for tip-offs protecting Whitey's seafaring pot smugglers, exceeded a quarter-million dollars. Although Schneiderhan lived modestly in a cookie-cutter neighborhood in Holbrook, a blue-collar town south of Boston, Flemmi noted that he put two sons through private school. And that he hid his Winter Hill bribe money from his wife by putting it in a shed behind his unassuming house.

Part of the bitter Lancaster Street legacy was punitive legislation in 1981 that would have forced the retirement of the state police commander who had targeted Whitey Bulger.

The legislation was stealth itself. There were no fingerprints since no sponsor was required for a short amendment that was slipped into the state budget in a late-night session. It required that officers fifty years or older make a choice—take a reduction in pay or in rank or retire. While five high-ranking officers were in the category, the real target was Detective Long's boss, Lieutenant Colonel John O'Donovan.

The bill originated in the Massachusetts House of Representatives in June 1981, where it was quietly approved and whisked to the Senate Ways and Means Committee, which was under Bill Bulger's thumb since he had become state Senate president in 1978. Two weeks later, the amendment was incorporated into the chamber's version of the state budget at the behest of Senators Chester Atkins and Anna Buckley, two of Bulger's biggest supporters. Later the same day, Bulger himself formally moved the package along toward enactment. On June 20, the Senate approved the amendment along with others but no vote was recorded. It was sent to the governor's office for final approval.

O'Donovan was on the verge of being forced out of office by an anonymous act of the legislature. But state police advocates convinced Governor Edward King that the amendment was retaliatory, and he vetoed it along with other amendments.

The crisis passed but law enforcement remained convinced that Whitey's cherubic brother was behind the vindictive measure.

It took two decades and an avalanche of publicity about FBI misdeeds in Boston and about Whitey Bulger, but in 2003 Congress finally held hearings that included whether Bill Bulger used his political power to protect his older brother.

Bill did his best to deflect the inquiry and succeeded in getting immunity from prosecution in exchange for truthful testimony, but he failed to get the hearing closed to the public.

The 2003 hearing was spearheaded by bull-in-the-china-shop Dan Burton, the combative ranking Republican from Indiana, who challenged Bill Bulger's coy circumlocutions before the House Committee on Government Reform. Burton was affronted by the FBI's rampant misconduct, calling what happened in Boston "the greatest failure in the history of federal law enforcement."

While the committee considered several possible transgressions by Bill Bulger, either his own or on Whitey's behalf, it spent much of its time on something that Bill had always stoutly denied—that he'd had a hand in the reprisal legislation in 1981.

Burton bore in after a series of dim recollections and word parsings by Bulger about Lancaster Street and the budget amendment. There were a lot of "I don't think so" answers.

Exasperated, Burton put the question to Bulger: Can you categorically say you did not talk to anyone about the amendment forcing the retirement of state police leaders?

But Bulger equivocated again. "My preference is to say that I categorically cannot recall ever talking with anyone but I think it is hazardous over 20 years . . . to suggest that is absolutely so."

Burton: "But this affected people that were after your brother."

Drawn to battle, Bulger turned assertive: "The amendment? Never. I never asked anyone to do any such thing."

The final exchange was overseen by Republican congressman Thomas Davis of Virginia, who chaired the committee. He sought to resolve the lengthy interrogation and to ease into a recess. To Burton, Davis said in so many words, Haven't you got what you're after?

Davis to Burton: "He [Bulger] said that categorically, right?"

From the witness table, Bulger chimed in again with the categorical "Never, no."

Stevie Flemmi later told quite a different story. He said Billy put the amendment in play because Whitey asked him to.

In his debriefings with law enforcement—in which the penalty for lying would have been a death-penalty murder trial in Florida or Oklahoma—Flemmi recalled Whitey strategizing on what to do about the relentless state police. After the Lancaster Street bugging and constant surveillance, Whitey had had a bellyful of Lieutenant Colonel O'Donovan's men.

Flemmi said the "pressure" was getting in Whitey's way and that he told Stevie he was going to talk to his brother Bill "about the situation." Whitey speculated to Flemmi that if O'Donovan was forced to retire, the pressure would likely decrease. Whitey later reported to Stevie that legislation was filed but that the state police fought it off.

Although Bill Bulger testified that he was unfamiliar with the Winter Hill Gang and was vague about Whitey's cooperation with the FBI, Flemmi disagreed dismissively, telling investigators it was "absurd" for Bulger to argue he was in the dark. He said Bill walked in on a meeting at Flemmi's mother's house, which was yards away from his own in South Boston, when Stevie and Whitey were sitting at a table with FBI agent John Connolly and supervisor James Ring. Flemmi described Bill's visit as a cameo appearance for the FBI's benefit. He said Bill "nodded in his direction upon entering the residence, talked briefly to Mary Flemmi, and then left quickly."

In Flemmi's 2003 debriefing, which occurred a few months after Bill Bulger's televised testimony, Stevie offered his personal reaction to the excerpts he saw, which included Bulger's categorical "nevers" about playing any role in the legislation. Bill Bulger, he said, "was not forthright when answering questions."

Testimony given under oath. With immunity. Unless Bill Bulger lied.

The bugging of Lancaster Street meant the "Bulger group" had to evacuate the notorious garage. In a final move, it came full circle to a liquor store on a rotary near Old Harbor that had been wrested from a South Boston couple.

With the state police in retreat and the FBI targeting the Angiulos, Whitey's enterprises entered their most profitable period with bookie and drug dealer tribute pouring in each month.

But prosperity has its price. Whitey was given pause by a dangerous proposition out of Florida that would expand his purview into legitimate business. The deal would pay him ten thousand dollars a week in "protection" money skimmed from a gambling cash cow known as World Jai Alai, which operated in Florida and Connecticut. But the easy money turned deadly with the prospect of murdering the

FBI agent Paul Rico

firm's uncooperative owner, who also ran a high-tech conglomerate in Oklahoma.

The jai alai venture for Whitey was the brainchild of John Callahan, a wiseguy wannabe from Boston who was in the banking world by day and at Chandler's at night, a drinking buddy of Johnny Martorano and Winter Hill leg-breaker Brian Halloran.

In the mid-1970s, Callahan gained the controlling interest in World Jai Alai, a business for the lightning-quick racquetball-style game that has courts called frontons. World Jai Alai had frontons and betting windows in Hartford and Miami. In 1976, after Paul Rico had retired from the FBI in Miami, his underworld connections put him together with Callahan and he became head of security for the gambling business. But Rico's "respectability" veneer didn't save Callahan from being forced off the license when Connecticut State Police found out about his Winter Hill associates.

Callahan saw a way back in when he found a new buyer and an irresistible financing package from one of his clients, the First National Bank of Boston. He put Roger Wheeler from Tulsa together with a $50 million loan and got the bank to insist on two provisions—that Rico be retained for security and a former accounting partner of Callahan serve as president.

Wheeler had built an eclectic empire that specialized in electronics and computers through its flagship company, Telex. His Oklahoma companies earned $8.1 million a year on revenues of $86.5 million. But he had been in the market for something with the higher profit margins of the gambling industry, first looking at a Virginia racetrack and then a Las Vegas casino. Then along came jai alai in 1978 and the promise of $6 million a year in gross profits.

But Wheeler was no waif and when the profits weren't as advertised, he suspected he was being skimmed for $1 million a year. He brought in an outside accounting firm, which put Callahan and Rico at risk.

The Miami difficulties complicated what had been a simple matter for Whitey—getting a half million a year to be a "protection" buffer against Mafia encroachment on the betting business. Callahan needed to be back in charge.

But in late 1980, Wheeler rejected a $60 million package and remained intent on catching underlings who were stealing from him.

Callahan and Rico feared embezzlement indictments and became co-conspirators in murder. Whitey lusted after the ten grand a week, but he wasn't sure it was worth killing a "civilian." He told Flemmi to talk to Rico, his FBI handler from the 1960s, about the necessity and reward of murdering a well-known businessman.

Rico pushed back hard: Wheeler had to go and Martorano was the man for the job. Rico said the skimming arrangement for Winter Hill would continue after the company was wrested from Wheeler's bereft widow. Rico won out.

Johnny Martorano had been bumping along nicely in southern Florida and had resumed his friendship with Callahan, who was in the Sunshine State frequently on business. Martorano briefly resisted killing Wheeler as a dangerous intrusion into the legitimate world. But then Whitey, converted by big money and Rico's imprimatur, made it an order.

Whitey put a machine gun with a silencer and a .38-caliber long-barrel handgun in a duffel bag and sent it by a TrailWays Express bus to Tulsa, where it would be picked up by Martorano. Roger Wheeler, high-flying executive and father of five, was in the crosshairs.

On a bright Saturday afternoon in Tulsa, a pair of killers waited for a half hour in a stolen 1981 Ford for Wheeler to finish his weekly round of golf at the Southern Hills Country Club. They parked well back from Wheeler's Lincoln.

Wearing a fake beard and clear, gold-rim glasses, Martorano spotted a well-dressed man walking briskly in the lot and fell in behind him. Martorano carried the .38-caliber revolver in a paper bag. If the man walked by the Lincoln, Martorano would turn back. But if he got in the car, he was a dead man. Having just shot an 88, good for his handicap, Wheeler had a bounce in his step when he stopped at his car. He had just settled in behind the driver's seat when Martorano suddenly pulled open the door. Wheeler leaned away while still looking directly at Martorano, who shot him once between the eyes.

The first detective on the scene was Mike Huff, a disarming good old boy but a homicide rookie who would work on the Wheeler murder for the next two decades. The career case left him haunted by what it meant for the family and the community. Law enforcement in Oklahoma and Connecticut quickly learned that Winter Hill was probably involved, but they were thwarted at every turn by an uncooperative FBI.

Martorano could never quite figure out the reason for the Wheeler murder. He thought the rationale was that Wheeler's widow would be amenable to a sales deal the husband had rejected, dropping the audit and taking the money. But the byzantine Rico never tried to renew talks once the embezzlement threat disappeared with Wheeler's demise. Johnny eventually concluded that had been the point.

The next teetering domino was Brian Halloran. He sealed his fate with the late-night murder of another gangster in September 1981. Coked up and unraveling, he shot a drug dealer across the table in a Chinese restaurant and woke up the next morning as a wanted man without a friend. His tight spot was claustrophobic—he faced murder charges and had lethal knowledge that Whitey Bulger was behind the Wheeler murder.

Time to trade up. Out on bail, Halloran began talking to the FBI in hopes of getting a break on his murder charge. He refused a lie detector test but agreed to wear a wire. The FBI got special authorization for a recorded meeting with Callahan but Connolly found out and it never happened. Then there was another fateful misstep when his contact agent, Leo Brunnick, checked with the Organized Crime Squad chief John Morris about Halloran's credibility. Morris ran Halloran down and then told John Connolly about the alarming turn of events. Connolly warned Whitey that Halloran was talking about Wheeler. The death knell tolled.

A week before it was too late, several FBI agents became aware from a North End snitch that Whitey was going to hit Halloran. They went to higher-ups and pleaded with them to put Halloran in the Witness Protection Program. A supervisor went to O'Sullivan but he said no, that Halloran was a drunk who wasn't worth the trouble. One protesting agent, Matthew Cronin, nearly vomited at what happened next.

By the spring of 1982, Halloran was hiding out on Cape Cod when he got a call that a family member living in South Boston wanted to see him. He made his way to Southie, a danger zone he had been avoiding. By mid-afternoon on a May day, he was in the Topside Lounge in the Pier Restaurant and bumped into a former neighbor, Michael Donahue, who agreed to give Halloran a lift to a family member's home. At four-thirty Halloran called the FBI, a desperate last-ditch call to Brunnick seeking admission to the protection program, hoping for another chance to make good. But Brunnick had his orders and cut him loose, warning him that it was "crazy" for him to be in Boston and he should go back to the Cape and figure something out.

Halloran said, "Rome wasn't built in a day, you know," and slammed down the pay phone. He had a few consolation drinks to mull over his predicament.

About the same time that Halloran hung up on Brunnick, Whitey Bulger got word that Halloran was seen in a bar on Northern Avenue, on the outskirts of South Boston. Whitey scrambled to find Flemmi, who was out of town, but settled for Patrick Nee, a former Mullen gang member who had once been a bitter enemy. Whitey put on a disguise consisting of a long wig and floppy mustache and fired up the "tow truck," which was stashed in a K Street garage. By six o'clock, when Donahue pulled his blue Subaru in front of the bar to pick up Halloran, Whitey was in place.

After Halloran jumped into the passenger-side seat, the souped-up green Chevy roared up beside the Subaru and opened fire. Donahue's car drifted slowly away from the restaurant to a dead stop. Halloran staggered free of the car and fell on the street. Whitey did a U-turn and, while driving, sprayed the prostrate Halloran with bullets before disappearing back into his Southie sanctuary. Donahue, the ultimate innocent victim, was killed for giving a neighbor a ride home.

By the summer of 1982, Tulsa detective Huff knew he couldn't trust the Boston office of the FBI and that John Callahan was the key to the

Wheeler case. Huff learned the accountant had played fast and loose with Winter Hill and held a Swiss bank account. He and colleagues from the Connecticut State Police wanted him before a grand jury.

But John Connolly, the Boston agent Huff saw as a poseur who thought he was in his own movie, found out about their plan. For the second time that year, Connolly set a murder in motion by warning Whitey of danger.

And for the second time, Whitey went to his assassin of choice, Johnny Martorano. If the complication with Wheeler was the risk inherent in slashing into the legitimate world, Callahan was even more difficult. He was Martorano's good friend, first in Boston and then in South Florida. Martorano resisted and was summoned to a face-to-face meeting at a hotel at LaGuardia Airport in New York. Whitey made his case about the peril posed by John Callahan to all of them.

In an hourlong meeting, Whitey started with a misleading gambit, presenting the Halloran massacre as something done to protect Martorano, and that now it was time for Johnny to return the favor. Although Martorano protested, he also understood the jail-for-life consequences if Callahan folded. He heaved his shoulders and reluctantly agreed to do the deed.

Martorano arranged to pick up Callahan one evening after Callahan flew into Fort Lauderdale on a business trip. He took Callahan's briefcase and walked him to a rented van in a far corner of the airport's parking lot. Callahan settled into the passenger seat while Martorano put the briefcase in the back and reached under the seat for the revolver planted there. He immediately shot Callahan twice in the back of the head. He and an accomplice, the seasoned Winter Hill associate Joe McDonald, transferred the body to the trunk of a car Callahan used in Florida and then drove it to the Miami airport garage. It was discovered the same day. Whitey later complained about the clumsy disposal but considered the problem solved.

Hardly. The Tulsa trilogy of murders, one leading to the other with deep involvement of the FBI, was a drastic miscalculation. Whitey's license to kill was for molls and Mullens who disappeared. Debra Davis and Tommy King. But there was a reckless prominence to the Tulsa sequence, a psychopath misreading his prerogatives. Roger Wheeler was a high-profile CEO shot between the eyes at a country club. Brian Halloran was mowed down on a busy street at rush hour on the edge of downtown. Callahan was a businessman stuffed in a trunk. Whitey's power-tripping was out of control and would bring them all down.

Mike Huff was in hot pursuit of Callahan in late July 1982, but when he flew into Miami, he had already lost the witness chase to Johnny Martorano. Even as Huff pulled his carry-on out of the overhead bin, Callahan was already jammed in a trunk in the same airport.

After all the murders and all the recriminations, there was a grand conclave in the FBI's Washington headquarters in the fall of 1982, overseen by the Organized Crime section chief Sean McWeeney. Given the blowback from state and local investigators who were convinced Rico was being protected by the Miami office and Whitey by the Boston office, follow-up meetings were held.

FBI supervisors sympathized with locals but then asked for proof of bureau cover-ups. And they repeatedly reported none was forthcoming. The last paragraph in McWeeney's long summary memo to his boss seems to have been the real reason for the FBI's high-level interest—negative publicity was heading its way on the sequential murders. The Miami office had advised McWeeney that ABC News was running a story on the World Jai Alai troubles that evening.

After things died down, Rico left the foundering jai alai world and lived in the gated community of Miami Shores without incident for nearly two decades. But his retirement of golf and bridge was jarred off its seaside mooring when he was summoned before Congress in 2001 to answer questions raised by dislodged FBI documents about frame-ups in the 1965 Deegan murder trial. Congress wanted to know what Rico knew about the suborned perjury that convicted innocent men and, finally, if he even cared. Rico was clear-eyed and laconic in his answers, never more than when he responded to a query about whether he had any remorse. He answered the question with one of his own: "What did you expect, tears?"

But the obdurate agent couldn't so easily sidestep Johnny Martorano, who he had insisted must murder Wheeler. Martorano had been arrested as a fugitive in Florida and began cooperating as a government witness when he realized that Whitey and Flemmi had been informants for decades. His punchy rationale was it was okay to rat on rats. He pled guilty to nineteen murders in exchange for future testimony against Whitey and his FBI allies. Martorano served only twelve years in prison. As a series of cases unfolded, Rico was ensnared in the Wheeler murder conspiracy.

It took nearly twenty-three years to get there, but Huff was part of a gaggle of cops at Rico's condo on October 9, 2003. The Tulsa cop had been stymied by Connolly in Boston and snubbed by Rico in Miami. But he persevered to put the cuffs on the agent wearing a cashmere World Jai Alai cardigan sweater. Told he was being taken to the infamous Dade County/Miami jail, Rico soiled himself.

Rico was assaulted in the Miami prison and had to be hospitalized. His health rapidly deteriorated and he lost fifty pounds. But he was nonetheless transferred to Tulsa to stand trial in January. Shortly after his arrival on January 8, 2004, he became gravely ill. In less than a week, he was transferred to the prison hospital, where he died suddenly on January 16, at age seventy-eight.

Larry Wheeler, one of the tycoon's sons, kept abreast of Rico's short stay in the Tulsa prison and recorded the stark death scene in later correspondence with federal prosecutors in Boston. He wrote that Rico "died at a midnight shift change, attending physicians were not notified; the room was swept clean and medical charts destroyed. Rico's body also was rushed out of the hospital and sent to a local funeral home within four hours of his death." It had to be retrieved for an autopsy, which found he'd died of internal bleeding.

It was as if the master manipulator behind the Bulger-Flemmi partnership, the steely-eyed, dapper H. Paul Rico, had never happened, dispatched in a bare-bones Winter Hill burial with no tears.

20

Gravediggers

Deborah Hussey

Stevie Flemmi, Kevin Weeks, and associate Pat Nee met just before sunrise in front of the house owned by Nee's brother. The address was 799 East Third Street in South Boston, about a block down from where Whitey's brother Bill lived with his family at 828 East Third. It was a simple single-family structure built in the late 1800s, overshadowed by the surrounding triple-deckers and apartment houses, and came with a driveway, which was unusual for the compact neighborhood.

Carrying shovels and picks, the three headed inside and down into the cellar with the low ceiling and dirt floor. They had bought painting masks to protect their faces and one of the men carried the vinyl body bags Flemmi had gotten from a friend who owned a funeral home. The threesome was assigned the dirty work, while Whitey planned to stand by and monitor their progress, ready to arrive later in the day in the wood-paneled station wagon he called "the hearse."

It was Halloween weekend, 1985.

City kids were dressing up in costumes of Darth Vader, Care Bear, and Cyndi Lauper, filling their bags and plastic pumpkins with treats. City and state transportation officials were brainstorming a solution for the ghastly stretch of elevated highway running through the heart of the city, devising what turned into the most expensive public works project ever, Boston's Big Dig.

Whitey Bulger, meanwhile, was settling on a plan he hoped would put to rest permanently this totally unexpected crisis involving three buried bodies—choosing Halloween to assemble his men before dawn's first light to carry out a private works project he and the gang could easily have dubbed Whitey's Little Dig.

The men set up in the area that Flemmi and Weeks best remembered was the place to start. It didn't take long before they hit bones and flesh. Digging farther into the shallow grave they saw a body partly mummified. They dug around some more, pushing the dirt and rubble aside to get to a point where they could lift the remains—and that's when they were all taken aback.

The corpse's rotting head fell away from the rest of the body.

Burying the bodies in the cellar had been Whitey's big idea—each corpse the answer to a particular challenge to his supremacy as his power steadily grew in the early 1980s. He could never have imagined unearthing them; he wouldn't have chosen the site in the first place if he had. Perhaps that was an oversight on the leader's part, a failure to foresee life's possibilities, but Whitey was not about to admit to any shortcoming. Instead, when Pat Nee broke the news earlier in the summer that his brother had decided to put the burial house on the market, Whitey had angrily chastised Nee for not being able to control his sibling. The new predicament, in other words, was not Whitey's fault but Pat Nee's.

The headache was certainly unwelcome, arising at a time—mid-1985—when Whitey's rule was peaking, and things had settled down, relatively speaking, following a long, hard stretch of conflict. Due largely to his cunning, Whitey had emerged at the top of the heap, though much blood had flowed to keep the gains coming: Louis Litif, Roger Wheeler, Brian Halloran, Michael Donahue (collateral damage), and John Callahan. The FBI side, meanwhile, was working amazingly well for him, with John Connolly and John Morris rising to every challenge to protect Whitey's flank from other police agencies.

Moreover, the two corrupted FBI protectors had essentially credited the FBI's successful bugging of Angiulo's office at 98 Prince Street in 1981 to Whitey. In a last-minute sleight of hand, Connolly and Morris had persuaded prosecutors to slip Whitey and Flemmi onto a list of confidential informants used in their application to persuade a judge to approve electronic surveillance.

"Connolly came to me and asked if I was aware that Bulger and Flemmi were not used in the affidavit," Morris later admitted, "and I agreed to have them added."

The bugging operation that followed therefore served as a twofer: it led to a racketeering conviction against Angiulo that effectively cleared the way for Whitey to assume control of Boston's underworld, and it allowed Connolly to claim that his informant Whitey had made it all possible. The claim wasn't close to the truth—the bugging application was all ready to go without Whitey—but it sure sounded good whenever Connolly needed to defend Whitey.

The early 1980s had also seen Whitey's financial well-being take off, fueled by his entry into drugs and imposition of a tax on major traffickers like Joe Murray and Mickey Caruana. The cocaine-crazed, high-flying 1980s were proving hugely lucrative. In this regard, Whitey-as-businessman neatly fit the times. Down in Washington, President Ronald Reagan's economic policy was decidedly probusiness, its goal to either eliminate or "under-enforce" government regulation of the economy to enable entrepreneurs to more freely pursue their self-interests. Mainstream economists dubbed it "Reaganomics," and it was a decade that became known for its renewed fixation on personal wealth, where the fittest survived and prospered. Whitey Bulger, entrepreneur in the underworld economy, was fully in synch—a free market advocate who was benefiting hugely from federal (FBI) regulation that was woefully "under-enforced." Indeed, Whitey was making history with "Bulgernomics." No crime boss during the twentieth century had ever rivaled his accomplishment—the breadth of his power combined with his unique harnessing of the FBI.

The news, then, in mid-1985 that Nee's brother was going to sell the burial house was an abrupt irritant in the greater scheme of Whitey's world. Once his anger was vented, though, Whitey attacked the problem as he did any other—by thinking several moves ahead to avoid getting cornered. The game he played was self-preservation, at any cost. It's what made him tick—a drive to elude arrest that, combined with his psychopathy, had made him a monster who could strangle young women, shoot people's brains out, and tear apart a city without blinking.

Whitey talked through the options with Flemmi. At first he wondered whether they should simply buy the house from Nee's brother, but then he tabled that idea, in part because it was overpriced. He considered having his men pour a cement floor in the rear basement room where the bodies were buried, but that meant digging a deeper cellar because the ceiling was so low. Flemmi all along had been pushing for moving the bodies, and in the end, Whitey came around and decided that was indeed the way to go.

In the weeks leading up to Halloween, Whitey and Weeks had driven around to scope out a new grave site. Whitey settled on a location in Dorchester in the vicinity of the final resting places for three earlier victims—Paulie McGonagle at Tenean Beach, and Tommy King and Debbie Davis near the Neponset River. The new location was down Hallet Street across from the popular Florian Hall, which unions and families rented to hold "times." The spot Whitey chose was at the far end of an empty lot beneath the roaring Southeast Expressway. He liked the fact that trees and shrubs would provide cover while they worked on the graves. Plus, from the site, they could see anyone coming their way. Whitey then ordered Weeks to buy ten duffel bags made of a heavy canvas. Flemmi said he'd get military trench shovels.

The day before the exhumation at 799 East Third Street the three had met at Hallet Street dressed in black and wearing gloves. The first thing Flemmi did was build a makeshift blind so that while they dug one of them could keep an eye on Hallet Street. Weeks ended up doing most of the digging, with help from Flemmi, while Whitey kept watch. They filled the duffel bags with dirt and then dropped the bags into the empty group grave. The idea was to have the hole dug and the dirt all ready to rebury the remains. They covered the bags with a dirt topping.

Everything seemed set. But ever the strategist, Whitey took out a twenty-dollar bill and tucked it under a rock he put on top of the hole. He told the others if the money was gone when they returned the next day it meant someone had been there—and then Whitey would have to come up with a new dumping ground.

In the cellar the head they'd struck was that of Arthur "Bucky" Barrett—the late safecracker, bank robber, and jewel thief. Barrett was the first of the three cellar dwellers at 799 East Third Street—buried for some thirty months, ever since the summer of 1983.

At the time Whitey had had Bucky Barrett on his radar for a while, ever since Barrett and a crew robbed $1.5 million from a Medford, Massachusetts, bank on Memorial Day weekend 1980. Whitey didn't cotton to the idea that Barrett thought he could pull a job like that without paying a tax. Moreover, he and Flemmi claimed that some of the money on deposit belonged to the former Winter Hill Gang, just as Mafia underboss Jerry Angiulo was claiming Mafia money was also kept in the Medford bank. Once Whitey learned that Barrett had paid $250,000 to the Mafia to appease the underboss, he became further incensed.

But Whitey went ballistic in the spring of 1983 when he learned that Barrett and Joe Murray had thought they could haul their drugs tax-free through Whitey's backyard. It didn't matter that federal drug agents and the FBI had seized a huge load of marijuana hidden in a warehouse on D Street. Barrett owed him. Whitey and Flemmi talked; it was then, according to Flemmi, that Whitey "decided he wanted to extort him." Whitey concocted a plan based on Barrett's fondness for jewelry.

"We sent the word to him we had some diamonds that we wanted to sell," Flemmi said.

They arranged to meet, and one morning in early August 1983 Barrett casually walked into the house at 799 East Third Street. But everything changed once he stepped inside.

"Whitey put a gun to him," Flemmi said, before shoving Barrett into the kitchen and forcefully sitting him down. Flemmi was there, along with Kevin Weeks. Using chains, they tied Barrett to the chair. Then Whitey roared, relentlessly interrogating Barrett before zeroing in on his ultimatum: he wanted his money, and he wanted it now.

Whitey demanded a complete rundown of the bank heist and an accounting of Barrett's assets. Barrett confirmed he'd paid Angiulo, and he then told Whitey about two stashes of cash he could put his hands on quickly. He said about $60,000 was hidden in his home under the washing machine, while another $10,000 was at Little Rascals, a bar in Boston that he co-owned.

Whitey was making headway; Barrett offered no resistance. He handed the telephone to the chained Barrett, and Barrett called home and told his wife to take the kids and go do something. Barrett gave Whitey the combination to the house alarm. Whitey and Flemmi took off, leaving Weeks to babysit, and they returned with the pile of cash Barrett had described.

Whitey handed Barrett the phone again, and Barrett called the bar and told a partner someone was going to swing by to pick up his stash. This time Whitey and Flemmi stayed behind while Weeks went to the bar to retrieve the $10,000 in cash. Whitey even had Barrett call Joe Murray in a bid to get Murray to make a drug tribute; Murray refused.

Barrett, terrorized, had been chained to the chair for hours. Whitey continued interrogating him, pressing him specifically about the "law enforcement contacts" the safecracker maintained. Barrett denied vehemently that he was anyone's informant, but Whitey was suspicious—firmly believing at this point that everybody was a rat, that talking was part of everybody's game.

The original plan was to extort Barrett for as much as they could and instill the fear of Whitey in him—at least that was what Whitey had explained to the others. But now Whitey had second thoughts—or revealed thoughts he'd had all along but kept secret until now. Pulling Flemmi aside, Whitey said they could not set Bucky Barrett free, that Barrett was apt to go whining to the Mafia, that Barrett was trouble and if they let him go he would simply cause them continued grief.

It wasn't as if Flemmi had any kind of veto power, not after Whitey made up his mind. Instead Flemmi watched a singularly focused Whitey return to the kitchen, release Barrett, and point him toward the nearby cellar door. Flemmi stepped ahead and went down the staircase first. Barrett followed.

Whitey stood at the top of the stairs. He put on his eyeglasses and flipped off the safety on the gun equipped with a silencer. Then he aimed the weapon at Barrett's head, blasting him point-blank.

Barrett's body tumbled forward past Flemmi. Flemmi couldn't believe Whitey had shot him like that.

"I was in the line of fire," Flemmi later said. "The bullet could have went through him and hit me."

Barrett lay dead on the cellar floor in pooling blood. Flemmi saw a bullet hole in the back of Barrett's head but could not find an exit wound, meaning he hadn't been at risk after all. No one saw any reason to find a resting place different from where they were—a cellar belonging to Pat Nee's brother was a safe house. So Flemmi dragged the body to a back area of the basement. Whitey, Flemmi, and Weeks knew the drill. They stripped the body. Weeks and Flemmi began digging a hole in the earthen floor, and then Flemmi, wielding a pair of pliers, extracted Barrett's teeth, one by one.

Whitey controlled the money—all in a day's work. He told the others he was holding back some of the proceeds to put in the "Ex-Fund," the account for FBI "gifts," and would split the rest. Flemmi made a telephone call to have a bag of lime delivered to the house. They hung around until the lime arrived, which they spread underneath and on top of Barrett's body. They covered the corpse with dirt. They were almost done but for one last thing: Flemmi crushed the teeth using a hammer he found. Then he flushed the fragments down the toilet.

In the dank cellar, the more Flemmi, Weeks, and Nee dug around and turned up body parts the worse the stench became. The men breathed heavily, and even though they had the painting masks covering their noses, Weeks wasn't sure how much more of the odor he could take.

They were working with shovels and pickaxes, and soon enough ran into more macabre pay dirt. John L. McIntyre's corpse, the second to be buried in the 799 East Third Street cellar, had been rotting for eleven months.

The young McIntyre had been a fisherman who built and fixed boats. He'd also moved drugs for trafficker Joe Murray. His fatal entry into Whitey's world happened when he served as a crew member aboard a fishing trawler stocked with guns and ammunition destined for the Irish Republican Army in September 1984. The boat was named the *Valhalla,* and the mission to arm the IRA was a joint venture between drug trafficker Murray, Pat Nee, Whitey, Kevin Weeks, Flemmi, and other IRA sympathizers.

Whitey and Weeks served as lookouts the night the weapons were unloaded from six vans and carried onto the fishing trawler docked in Gloucester, the famous fishing community north of Boston. They used binoculars, walkie-talkies, and scanners to stay in touch with the workers, including McIntyre, during the loading operation, which took several hours to complete. The *Valhalla* departed on September 14. It traversed the Atlantic Ocean before reaching the coast of Ireland, where in early October it met the *Marita Ann* and transferred its cache of weapons. The sea-battered *Valhalla* then limped back to Boston. But any thoughts of mission accomplished were crushed when word spread that Irish authorities had seized the *Marita Ann* before it reached port.

While Joe Murray, Nee, Whitey, and others debated what had gone wrong, U.S. Customs officials found the *Valhalla* docked in Boston and went searching for its captain, a seaman named Robert Anderson, and the deckhand, John McIntyre. By early October, police in Quincy had McIntyre in a holding cell after the thirty-two-year-old was arrested for attempting to break into his estranged wife's apartment. Caught in the crosshairs of the law, McIntyre began talking, and he was released on the condition he become a cooperating informant. Federal prosecutors began a grand jury investigation and various law enforcement agencies were jumping all over him—besides the customs agents, federal drug enforcement agents wanted a piece of him, as did the Boston office of the FBI. In short order, McIntyre disclosed details about the arms shipment, about his work for drug trafficker Murray, and about an upcoming drug shipment into Boston. With McIntyre's tip, the authorities were ready to pounce when Joe Murray's *Ramsland* entered Boston Harbor on November 14. Federal and local police seized the ship and discovered thirty tons of marijuana.

When word filtered back through the underworld about the bust, no one was more angry than Whitey—he, Flemmi, and Weeks were due three million dollars from Murray as payment for using Whitey's waterfront to move drugs. Murray, convinced an informant had betrayed them, began going around telling everyone he wanted blood. But he was flailing about, hot with suspicion yet lacking anything firm to go on. No one had the edge Whitey had when it came to investigating a leak.

Whitey obtained from John Connolly the exact sort of secret FBI information he'd come to expect. Connolly told him a crew member from the *Valhalla* was ratting on everyone. The informant red alert marked Connolly's fourth since the agent began serving Whitey, with the earlier tip-offs enabling Whitey to act quickly. Richie Castucci, Brian Halloran, John Callahan—all dead.

This one was a bit trickier. Connolly was unable to deliver a name on a silver platter the way he had with Castucci, Halloran, and Callahan. The agent did not know the informant's identity for certain; the best he could do was to narrow the leak to the two men found on the *Valhalla* in Boston—either John McIntyre or Captain Robert Anderson. Whitey, then, had to devise a plan to ferret out which of the two was the problem, and he chose to focus his energy on the younger McIntyre after deciding the "old school" captain was less likely to rat.

Whitey created a ruse along the lines of the one he'd used with Bucky Barrett, albeit customized to fit the new target. Barrett was into jewelry, while McIntyre was into drugs. Whitey therefore sent Pat Nee to talk to McIntyre about joining Whitey in a drug-smuggling venture that Whitey guaranteed would pay off 10 to 1. The chance to partner with Whitey was a privilege, and McIntyre was told he needed to invest twenty thousand dollars. In turn, McIntyre told his customs agent about the developing deal, and the agent even fronted McIntyre the necessary twenty thousand.

McIntyre delivered the money to Nee a week after Thanksgiving. He was in now—and a meeting with Whitey was set for the next day, Friday, November 30, in South Boston. The location: 799 East Third Street, the deadly house of horrors. Whitey and Weeks arrived at about high noon. Pat Nee's brother was away in New Hampshire for the weekend. Flemmi showed up a few minutes later. He carried a duffel bag filled with tools of their trade—handcuffs, rope, chains, and firearms, including several pistols, a Mac11 9 mm submachine gun, and a .22-caliber rifle with a silencer, cut down and outfitted with a pistol grip. Nee delivered McIntyre. They walked into the house carrying a case of beer. In McIntyre's mind a party with friends was in the offing. Instead he walked into the kitchen and met the barrel of the rifle recast as a pistol. As Whitey steadied the gun, McIntyre, startled, lost his balance and fell backward. Weeks grabbed him and put him into a chair, where he was chained and handcuffed.

Whitey then lit into him. Like Barrett, a terrified McIntyre folded quickly. He confessed he had informed on them, telling customs agents about the *Ramsland*. He even admitted to Whitey that Customs had financed his stake in the putative drug-smuggling deal.

"I'm sorry," McIntyre told the crime boss. "I was weak."

The admission likely disgusted Whitey—a wretched mixture of frailty and betrayal. But the terror written all over the young fisherman's face did not surprise Flemmi.

"Look at the position he was in," he later said. "I mean, who wouldn't be under those circumstances? Of course he was in fear."

The interrogation continued through the afternoon. Whitey questioned him about the *Valhalla*. McIntyre insisted he was not responsible for the failure of the gun smuggle. He said he only began cooperating with the authorities after that. Whitey pressed hard for information about Joe Murray's drug-smuggling operation. He demanded that McIntyre reveal names of vessels, offload sites, crew members, and the amount of drugs imported and distributed. It was as if Whitey were pursuing a financial audit to determine if Murray might owe him more tribute.

The plan Whitey had originally explained to Flemmi and Weeks called for sending McIntyre away to either South America or some other faraway place—get him out of Boston until the federal investigation died down. Another possibility was crafting a script of lies for McIntyre to recite to the federal grand jury. But as the afternoon unfolded, Whitey shifted to a different course of action, one that came as no surprise to Flemmi. Flemmi knew that once McIntyre confessed—especially the mawkish way he did it—his fate was sealed.

"Bulger decided to kill him," he said.

By Whitey's calculus McIntyre had lost his right to live, to Bulger a ruling both appropriate and just—and the only outcome making sense given Whitey's obsession with self-preservation bordering on paranoia. Whitey did not want to leave anything to chance—allowing McIntyre to live would be just that. But there was something else. Whitey seemed to bring a touch of sadism to cases like McIntyre's; it was as if going face-to-face with an informant tapped into a deep reservoir of loathing—and self-loathing. Even the equally sadistic Flemmi took note of Whitey's capacity for savage pleasure when it came to terminating informants. Flemmi only had to recall Louis Litif and the thirty-eight stabs with an ice pick.

"I don't believe anybody had the stomach that Bulger had," Flemmi said.

Five hours after the interrogation began, an exhausted McIntyre had become restless and panicky. To calm him, Whitey mollified McIntyre with talk about giving him some money to hide out in South America. Whitey had McIntyre unbound and told him they were going down to the cellar to talk some more. But once downstairs McIntyre was plunked back into a chair, secured, and handcuffed again.

Whitey took the boat rope Flemmi had brought in his duffel bag and wrapped it around McIntyre's neck. He pulled the rope tight. McIntyre squirmed in his chair, struggling. He gagged for breath and made gurgling sounds. Whitey pulled harder, and McIntyre vomited. But Whitey was having trouble strangling McIntyre. The boat rope turned out to be too thick. McIntyre wouldn't die, and Whitey was tiring.

"This ain't working," Whitey said.

McIntyre was slumped in the chair. He was alive but no longer fighting.

Whitey had an idea. "Do you want one in the head?"

McIntyre just wanted an end. "Yes," he said. "Please."

Whitey aimed and shot McIntyre in the back of the head, using the rifle customized with a pistol grip and silencer. Flemmi put his ear to McIntyre's chest to check for a heartbeat. He told Whitey he thought McIntyre might still be alive. Flemmi lifted McIntyre's head by grabbing a handful of his hair. Whitey stepped close and fired several more bullets into the side of the fisherman's face.

"He's dead now," Whitey pronounced.

In the cellar the men continued exhuming McIntyre's body parts. They'd prepared McIntyre for burial just as they had Bucky Barrett—by stripping off his clothes and using pliers to rip out his teeth, although Flemmi was a little careless with the pliers and accidentally yanked out McIntyre's tongue. Whitey later gave each man five thousand dollars as their share of the twenty thousand that McIntyre had invested, noting with a smile that the customs agents had "lost their witness and their money."

They had buried McIntyre next to Barrett, which naturally was where the gravediggers found him. Weeks used a pickax to continue loosening the soil, repeatedly swinging it into the ground. At one point, he struggled to pull the ax out; it was caught on something. Weeks yanked harder. The extra effort managed to dislodge the ax, and with the ax came something else—an entire chest cavity. Weeks pulled some more and saw a body and organs that had not yet decayed. The stench overwhelmed Weeks, and he staggered upstairs, leaving Flemmi to finish the job of exhuming the body of Deborah Hussey from the grave they'd dug for her only eight months before.

When Whitey considered Deborah Hussey and Stevie Flemmi as a couple, he must have wondered what it was about Flemmi that rendered him so ineffective with certain women. Whitey could not fault Flemmi's predilection for younger women; he'd long shown the same preference. But Flemmi's choices had a way of turning out to be bad for business—Debra Davis, for example, was a problem resolved in the house Flemmi had bought for his parents just a block away on East Third Street, right next to brother Bill Bulger's house. She had required Whitey's intervention—and a grave along the Neponset River.

If so inclined, Whitey could have taken Flemmi to task about his shortcomings in women management. Because for his part, Whitey had Teresa Stanley as a long-standing example of a woman who quietly stood by her man, and by Halloween 1985 he also had the younger Catherine Greig in tow. He'd isolated Cathy Greig steadily during the early 1980s from family, friends, even geographically, and convinced her to abandon her professional ambition. In 1982 they had begun sharing a condominium in Quincy, just south of Boston, in Louisburg Square South. The deed was listed in Greig's name, but the $96,000 purchase price was paid in cash—assets Whitey possessed, not Greig. The three-story Unit 101 had a view of the Neponset River, where Whitey had buried Tommy King in 1975 and Debra Davis in 1981.

Whitey also began managing Greig's good looks; not long after Greig's thirty-first birthday, Whitey paid for her to have breast implants; it was the first in a Whitey-funded program of beauty maintenance that later included liposuction, eyelid reconstruction, and a face-lift. "Cathy had to be perfect all the time," said one Boston police investigator who tracked them. There was still residual tension, though: Greig continued to teach at the Forsyth School for Dental Hygienists and she showered her dogs with affection. Both were signs she was not fully Whitey-centric. Federal drug agents managed at one point to install a bug in the couple's windowsill and overheard the issue come up. "It was the middle of the night and Bulger had come home in a rage," recalled an investigator. "He was screaming at Cathy that she cares more about the dogs than she does about him. He says if she doesn't stop, if she doesn't pay more attention to him, the walls will be covered in blood. She yelled right back at him."

But an end to her independent kick was in sight. Greig's sister could see it happening—the way Whitey took over Cathy Greig's life. "Trips, furs, coats, I mean he bought quite a lot of things," Margaret McCusker said. Whitey, she said, had a "certain power" over people. "If he decided he wanted you to like him, you would like him. He was always in control." That control deepened after Greig suffered personal losses. Her younger brother David shot himself in the head in May 1982 in the Greig family home in South Boston. Cathy and her brother, then twenty-six, had always been close, even as David fell into heavy drug and alcohol abuse. Greig, grief-stricken, quit working at Forsyth. She turned inward—and to Whitey. "Whitey was there to take care of her, and so she just left," a coworker at Forsyth said.

The trend well under way by Halloween 1985 was irreversible. The next year, 1986, Greig's father died of alcoholism, and Whitey moved her from their condo into a tiny gray ranch in the Squantum neighborhood in Quincy, a few blocks from the ocean. The $160,000 house was bought with cash, the title again in Greig's name. Whitey renovated the house, remodeling two bathrooms and eliminating the front door near the road so that the only entrance was around back. Greig now had no brother, no father, and no job. She had her two poodles, Nikki and Gigi, and Whitey. Neighbors rarely saw her leave the house except in Whitey's company. "She was always with him," one neighbor said. "She didn't seem frightened of him. She was just never without him." In 1987 Greig even let her dental hygienist license lapse.

One regular visitor to the house on Hillcrest Road was sister Margaret McCusker, Cathy's twin sister, who took note of a globe the couple kept in the dining room. The piece was designed as a liquor cabinet, "but instead of liquor there were bills in it," she said. "You know, fifties, twenties, hundred-dollar bills, and, when she wanted, needed something, she'd just go in there and take bills. I used to be like, 'Oh, my God. Do you know how much you're spending? Do you even know?' But that was their lifestyle."

Whitey, a creature of habit in many ways, worked mostly at night, spent mornings with Greig, left in time to have supper with Teresa Stanley, and then went back to work with Flemmi, Kevin Weeks—and with FBI agent Connolly. No one could ever accuse him of being anything less than a man's man the way he juggled and controlled his women. Moreover, the ability to move so seamlessly between his women as well as his business partners—double-crossing them all—required an uncanny mastery of compartmentalization. It was the same highly tuned defense mechanism enabling him to confront challenges ranging from Richie Castucci to Debra Davis and then Deborah Hussey, oversee their ghastly executions, and then walk away calmly. Just box it away in his mind and it was finished. He'd done this his whole life, from his father through his son Douglas's death, another method to his madness.

In contrast was the tortured, bizarre relationship of Stevie Flemmi and Deborah Hussey. When Flemmi began living with Debbie's mother around 1960, Marion Hussey was a twenty-year-old with several kids, including toddler Debbie. Over the years Flemmi and Marion Hussey had three kids of their own. Then, in the mid-1970s Flemmi began having sex with Debbie; she was only sixteen, a minor, the daughter of his common-law wife, but none of that got in Flemmi's way. He carried on with her, and by the time Debbie turned twenty she was hitting Flemmi up for money, drinking heavily, using heroin, dancing in strip clubs, and getting arrested for prostitution. She came and went from the Milton home where her mother and Flemmi lived. She sometimes traveled to Florida to see her father, other times taking off for California. It all came to a head one day in 1984 when Debbie returned to the Milton house, "drugged up or drunk or whatever," Marion said.

Marion and Flemmi argued about what to do. Marion wanted Flemmi to get Debbie out of the house. "I was nervous with her being there with the other kids," Marion said. Flemmi went upstairs and found Debbie in a bed. They began yelling, and when Marion stepped into the room she saw Flemmi slapping Debbie.

Debbie noticed her mother—and then it came out. She yelled to her mother that she and Stevie Flemmi had had their own thing going for some time, that she'd been "sucking his prick." Marion Hussey stood speechless in the doorway. "I've been doing it for years," Debbie yelled. Marion Hussey left the room and returned downstairs. Flemmi got Deborah dressed and pushed her out the door.

"Ma," Debbie said, "I'm not lying."

"Debbie, I believe you."

Marion Hussey threw Flemmi out of the house that day; they never lived together again. The matter of Deborah Hussey, however, fell into the court of Whitey Bulger. The evidence was irrefutable—she had proven herself an unwanted bother beyond a reasonable doubt. When she got arrested in Boston's notorious Combat Zone for drugs or prostitution she tried talking her way out using "my name or Bulger's name," Flemmi said. Likewise she dropped Flemmi and Whitey's names when she showed up at Triple O's looking for free drinks or accosted street dealers for drugs. Reports of her misconduct got back to Whitey—reports that included particularly outrageous actions, like sleeping with black men.

"He was very upset," Flemmi said about interracial carnal knowledge.

Whitey reached a decision, which meant having Flemmi arrange a get-together with Debbie. The chosen time was a late winter morning in 1985, a few weeks after her twenty-seventh birthday. Flemmi picked Debbie up. He said he wanted to buy her a new winter coat. She said she wanted to look for an apartment or house to rent. They shopped first and then headed to South Boston to check out a house he thought she might like: Nee's brother's house, at 799 East Third Street.

Flemmi later said he wanted to send her away but had tried that already.

"I send her away, I give her money to leave, and she keeps coming back."

Whitey, Kevin Weeks, and Pat Nee were waiting. Debbie entered. Whitey was "right by the cellar door when she walked in," Flemmi said. Whitey jumped her, scissoring her neck between his forearms. Debbie, outsized and outmuscled, fought like a rattlesnake. Whitey lost his balance and they both fell to the floor. He landed on his back, with the little woman on top, but Whitey, the stronger and more experienced, quickly jackknifed his legs so that they wrapped around her chest. He regained his choke hold around her neck. He squeezed his legs as hard as he could, breaking several of her ribs. When he squeezed her neck the pressure crushed her windpipe. During the assault her nose and a shoulder blade were also broken. Debbie was overmatched.

"There was no way out of it," Kevin Weeks said. "She wasn't struggling, she was just dying."

Within a few minutes she stopped breathing. Whitey went into the living room and lay down on the couch. Weeks thought his boss was in a euphoric state—relishing, perhaps, the feeling of release that followed a task he considered entirely justified but involving plenty of tension and anxiety until completed. Flemmi thought Whitey was taking a nap—that after struggling to kill the feisty Deborah Hussey he needed to rest. But either way the point was that Whitey was done—now and forever. The killing of Deborah Hussey was of special significance—it was Whitey Bulger's last known murder. In the years to come not another homicide was attributed to him, not even after those closest to him—Kevin Weeks, Stevie Flemmi, and Johnny Martorano—became government witnesses and chronicled countless killings.

Whitey was, at fifty-five, getting on in years. His preoccupation with fitness notwithstanding, there was no way he was in the same physical condition as in 1969, when he committed his first known killing, that of Donald McGonagle. Muscle mass begins deteriorating in all humans in their mid-thirties. Whitey was also developing heart issues that would eventually require medication. It was as if going forward he'd let his prior bad acts maintain the status quo—the widespread fear in the underworld of a monstrous Whitey Bulger. Occasions certainly arose when he needed to provide dramatic emphasis. In early 1987, to drive home a point to a man named Raymond Slinger about unpaid debts during a meeting in Triple O's, Whitey pointed the barrel of a gun at Slinger's head and yelled, "I'll shoot you in the top of the head; that way there will be no blood!" Slinger began coming up with cash. The next year Whitey terrorized a mortgage broker named Tim Connolly about disputed finances. In the storage room of the variety store at the rotary near Old Harbor, Whitey pulled out a knife strapped to his leg, yelled, "You fucker, you fucker!," and began stabbing an empty box over and over again. He told Connolly he could buy his life for fifty thousand dollars. Connolly began paying.

So in the burial house following the Hussey murder, Whitey headed off to the living room while the others headed down into the cellar. He was a portrait in still life, a man in repose on the couch after his last known kill. One thing was for certain: after the first one, Whitey had learned he could kill and not lose any sleep, and in the sixteen years since he'd murdered upwards of twenty people.

Down in the cellar while Whitey rested, Stevie Flemmi stripped Deborah Hussey naked and yanked out her teeth. Weeks began digging a hole. He inadvertently disturbed McIntyre's corpse. But no one was going to get fussy about it. They pushed Deborah Hussey half on top of the fisherman's body and then covered her with the dirt and rubble.

Halloween weekend eight months later, the gravediggers were spending the day reversing course, undoing the work they'd done piecemeal over the previous three years. The stench that drove Weeks upstairs eventually got to Pat Nee, too. Flemmi worked alone, and early in the afternoon he finally rose from the dead. He stood in the kitchen gulping a glass of water, dripping in sweat, his hair mussed and wild-looking. He told Weeks and Nee the exhumation was done, and the bodies were bagged.

It was about 2 p.m. The men returned to the cellar to tidy up. They leveled the ground where the bodies had been and filled several plastic garbage bags with lime, soil, and small bones they'd missed. They showered, changed clothes, and waited. Whitey arrived at around six o'clock, backing the "the hearse" into the driveway alongside the house. They carried the body bags out of the cellar through a bulkhead. Weeks and Flemmi were lugging the second bag out when a man happened to walk by the house. The stranger concerned Weeks, but Whitey, standing by the station wagon, told him not to worry. "It's okay, it's Halloween," he said.

Whitey drove. Flemmi sat in front holding a machine gun. Weeks rode in the back of the station wagon, lying down next to the body bags. Without incident they made it to Hallet Street in Dorchester and got the corpses settled—unzipping the body bags one at a time and dumping the remains into a single grave. Flemmi used branches and twigs to cover the area when they were done. They drove back to Southie and deposited the garbage bags with bones and other detritus into a Dumpster near South Boston High School. Driving home later that night on the highway, Weeks tossed the shoes, underwear, and shirt he'd worn during the digging out the car window. For days he smelled the stink of rotted bodies.

Whitey took to calling the new site by the code name "Halloween." Once in a while he sent Weeks over to scout the area and check to see if there was any activity. But all was calm, and a relaxed Whitey liked to joke sometimes that they'd succeeded in moving the bodies "right under the noses" of federal drug agents who were trying to keep him under surveillance—obviously to no avail.

With the reburial project out of the way, Whitey could look ahead to the holidays just around the corner. Christmas was a favorite time of year for Whitey, a time he liked to say was for "cops and kids." Whitey every year put together a gift list, using drawings and code words for the names of FBI agents and other corrupt police contacts and for the amounts he was allocating to each from the "Ex-Fund." Typically, Connolly got five thousand dollars, the other agents lesser amounts.

Whitey also rewarded Connolly at other times of the year by giving the agent a cut from the tax payments the major drug traffickers paid him and Flemmi—as much as fifty thousand. When Whitey and Flemmi made one such payment to Connolly in 1983, Flemmi recalled the agent's response sounding both thankful and entitled. "Hey, I'm one of the gang," Connolly said. Over the years, Flemmi said, Connolly was paid "around $235,000, give or take."

But Connolly's spending habits at times became a concern, requiring Whitey to rein in the agent.

"FBI agents weren't making much money back in those days and he was the best-dressed FBI agent in the office," Flemmi said. Whitey, in contrast, "was a low-key person. Didn't want to appear ostentatious. He didn't want John to get to that level." In 1983 Connolly had bought a condominium on Cape Cod, with Bill Bulger's old pal attorney Tom Finnerty handling the closing. The FBI agent went too far in May 1986, however, when he bought a Sea-Ray sport boat. John Connolly, said Weeks, "was being too ostentatious, too flashy."

Whitey was mad. "He had him sell the boat," Flemmi said.

But they always worked it out. Christmas 1985 was now at hand—once again a season of giving in the unique Whitey Bulger way. His wrapped presents and cash envelopes may have seemed generous, but they were hardly that. It was the pretense of a big heart. Whitey Bulger did not give without getting something in return—and as the ground in law enforcement began to shift, by decade's end he was going to need more than ever a big return on his long FBI investment.

21

Thirty-Two Words

Fred Wyshak and Tom Foley

It was 32 words out of 22,821 about the Bulger brothers, a lean, careful statement that Whitey had a "special relationship" with the FBI that coincided with his rise to power and nary an arrest in twenty years.

The 1988 *Boston Globe* series was mostly about Bill Bulger's up-from-the-bootstraps career in politics and preeminence at the State House, but it also chronicled the remarkable ascent of James J. Bulger Jr. in the underworld and the outline of his connection with the FBI. Whitey's having no police record didn't add up.

At the outset, editors had feared starting a gang war by revealing the

Whitey liaison with agent John Connolly and the item was somewhat underplayed. But it was out there for all to see. It became the paragraph that refused to die and reverberated simultaneously in two worlds generally impervious to public opinion: Winter Hill and the FBI.

The reference was on the run-over page, terse but unmistakable: "And the Federal Bureau of Investigation has for years had a special relationship with Whitey that has divided law enforcement bitterly and poisoned relations among many investigators, the [*Globe*] Team has learned."

The FBI immediately challenged the article, dispatching the head of the Boston office, James Ahearn, to meet with *Globe* editors. He said it besmirched an outstanding agent and that the bureau would make a case in a minute against Whitey if only it had credible evidence. Ahearn leaned forward with his linebacker frame and said: "This is absolutely untrue. We specifically deny that there has been special treatment of this individual."

Ahearn, who had been Connolly's patron within the bureau for years, unsettled the editors. Some wore worried looks because this unhappy reader was, well, the FBI.

The thirty-two words in September bumped along the East Coast, too, with George Kaufman, Winter Hill's jack-of-all-trades, calling Johnny Martorano in Florida to give him a heads-up that Whitey might be an informant.

In an interview years later, Martorano recalled flatly rejecting the idea that Whitey was a snitch. "I said hold it, I wouldn't be alive if he's a rat. He'd've done me in by now."

Martorano had the Winter Hill perspective about Whitey and the FBI: Whitey had been open about dealing with Connolly since 1974, and Martorano thought that the agent was just another cop on the take, a higher-level Dick Schneiderhan, with the information coming in but never going out. But Kaufman was worried that it had become so public and wondered what that meant. So Martorano called Stevie in Boston. "I said what the fuck is this?" He said Flemmi told him "it's the *Globe* trying to stick it to Billy. Every time he runs for reelection, they try to cause him trouble. This time by picking on Whitey."

Asked if he believed the strained spin, Martorano said he bought it then because to hold otherwise was unthinkable. "I believed it. Whitey a rat?"

Flemmi later told investigators that the Mafia reached the same conclusion, that mob heavyweights Vinnie Ferrara and J. R. Russo saw it as media politics aimed at embarrassing Bill Bulger. It's also likely that concluding otherwise meant a war no one wanted with the Bulger Gang.

Whitey and Stevie had a quick meeting with Agents Connolly and Morris about their arrangement and they agreed to ride it out. They thought the *Globe* story would be a one-time thing and it was so outlandish that no one in the underworld or South Boston would believe Whitey was an informant. "Let me worry about it," Whitey said. Connolly, his payola on the line, was especially aggressive in arguing that this too shall pass. In fact, his honeymoon money might have been on the line. Connolly got married for the second time a few weeks later in November and his Christmas bonuses continued without interruption.

But if Connolly was blasé about the *Globe* and willing to let Whitey do the worrying, the thirty-two words jarred the Organized Crime Squad in the Boston office of the FBI. According to Flemmi, the paragraph and theme had a chilling effect on several agents regularly taking cash and gifts from Whitey. There were some dropouts from the Christmas club.

Slowly and surely, the Boston Organized Crime Squad had become something akin to Serpico's precinct in the Bronx, with all the drug cops on the take. With Connolly leading the way in the early 1980s, Whitey had opened the "Ex-Fund," which always had a baseline deposit of $150,000. Fittingly, it got a big boost from $500,000 extorted from one of John Callahan's accounting partners in Boston after the World Jai Alai executive was murdered. It was a classic Whitey bluff, pushing a phony debt due Winter Hill from Callahan with a death threat to a terrified white-collar businessman who knew well what could happen.

As each "cops and kids" Christmastime approached, Whitey worked meticulously with a stack of white envelopes, putting a name or code designation on it before stuffing in hundred-dollar bills.

The code name "Agent Orange," for example, stood for an FBI agent and Vietnam vet named John Newton. "Vino" was John Morris. "Z" stood for "Zip," or John Connolly, who shared a zip code with

Whitey. In addition there were Nick Gianturco, Mike Buckley, and Jack Cloherty—all FBI agents in good standing in Whitey's eyes, and eligible for holiday cheer.

Whitey ran the fund as an entitlement. "He controlled it," Flemmi said. "He could do what he really wanted. Nobody—there was no accountability." Whitey sometimes had Kevin Weeks accompany him to shop for gifts; over the years wine, clocks, knives, silver ice buckets, a jukebox, and crystal ended up in FBI hands. Or he dispatched Weeks to withdraw money from the "Ex-Fund" stash that Weeks kept in a "hide" in his house.

One Christmas, Weeks delivered the holiday cash to Connolly when Whitey was too busy to do it himself. Weeks showed up at Teresa Stanley's house to find Whitey seated in the parlor stuffing envelopes. But he and Stanley had to head out to a dinner at Stanley's daughter's house. "He gave me the two envelopes—one for John Connolly, Zip, and the one for Agent Orange, John Newton," Weeks said. "He gave me them to give to Zip."

Flemmi said each season cost up to $35,000, with Connolly at the head of the class at $5,000 and the rest going out to other FBI agents and about twenty cops in the Boston Police Department. Stevie added that only Whitey knew Connolly's total take from vacation subsidies, regular bonuses in addition to Christmas, and accessories such as a car and a cut-rate condo. Flemmi guessed it was more than $250,000.

And only Whitey knew his own net worth, perhaps even losing track with all the safe-deposit boxes in three countries and stashes around Southie. Law enforcement said the 1980s were his peak earning years and estimated his fortune was ten to twenty million dollars.

The payoffs were so routine that Connolly became the gatekeeper for much of the FBI bribes, personally passing out the Christmas "bonuses" to agents in the Organized Crime Squad, making himself the real boss no matter who else was in charge. Flemmi told investigators that the standard distribution was $2,500 each to Agents Gianturco, Buckley, Cloherty, and Newton. While he did not take any cash, James Ring, who had succeeded Morris as chief of the squad, accepted an expensive meerschaum pipe. In addition, John Morris took $7,000 in intermittent installments through Connolly or Whitey directly. In all, the tally was seven G-men on the pad.

Jim Ring may have puffed professorially on a tainted German pipe, but he could be unreliably independent about Bulger. He ran hot and cold, though his temperature seemed as tied to rivalry with Connolly as to misgivings about the dangers of having the head of a gang as an informer. Whitey was the textbook example of the downside of giving the boss de facto immunity in an arrangement unlikely to produce criminal cases.

On the one hand, as Flemmi told investigators and later testified, Ring had tipped Whitey about wiretaps on Kaufman's phone during a mid-1980s investigation by the U.S. Drug Enforcement Administration called "Operation Beans." Concerned about leaks, the drug agency had the temerity to proceed without checking with the FBI, and after the outraged bureau learned of the affront, the FBI undermined the investigation at every turn. "Beans" fell apart.

But by the late 1980s, Ring seemed to turn hostile to the "Bulger group," musing about targeting it to set the record straight. It prompted a protest from Connolly, who, according to Flemmi, said to the supervisor: "What are we, animals? We eat our young?"

While the apostasy passed, it led to some soul-searching by Whitey and Flemmi, who reflected on the hazards of being "top dog in the city." They'd never had more money; they were awash in extortions from major bookies and drug dealers that had led to special bonuses totaling fifty thousand dollars to Connolly and the state police's Schneiderhan.

And yet a spreading storm line persisted on the horizon—the thirty-two words meant public notice of a gamey deal with the FBI no matter how much it was spun. The Massachusetts State Police was probing the bookie network and two dogged Boston cops were working with DEA agents on Bulger's cocaine distribution system in South Boston. Ring had turned testy and unpredictable. After fifteen years of primacy, Whitey and Flemmi talked about getting out on top. The one insistent "no" vote on retirement was from Connolly, who urged his meal tickets to "hang in there."

Until he saw his own chance to run for it.

In 1990, Connolly had turned fifty, the age when things started to go downhill for agents and they begin checking out private employment. He had also recently lost his office patron Ahearn, who was transferred to Phoenix. And worse, Whitey was talking about retirement and taking his "Ex-Fund" with him. For all his talk, Connolly was the first one to not "hang in there."

While he had worked closely with Whitey since 1974, Connolly revered Bill Bulger for his intellect and style. And his connections as Massachusetts Senate president.

Boston Edison was a major industry in Bill Bulger's South Boston district but it had become estranged from Bulger over regulatory legislation. John Connolly became the perfect fit as head of corporate security at a time when fences were getting mended. No letters were written but nods were nodded. Connolly moved up the corporate ladder, rising to in-house lobbyist dealing with Bulger's State House and occasionally in Washington, D.C. His annual salary of $120,000 probably surpassed his FBI pay and Whitey bribes. So he was ahead of the game.

On November 30, 1990, Connolly got a memorable send-off from his colleagues and connected friends at a packed reception at Joe Tecce's, a North End restaurant that was a short distance from the FBI office and where Connolly and other agents were seldom bothered with a drink tab. At the raucous fete, Connolly stood tall on dubious laurels, leaving with a file bulging with Whitey-related commendations, hosannas to his street skills. A year earlier, FBI director William Sessions had traveled to Boston and singled out Connolly with a career award for his informant work.

Among the invited guests was Joe Pistone, the celebrity agent who had lived undercover in a New York Mafia outfit and was a featured character in the movie based on his street name—Donnie Brasco.

And at the family table was Connolly's mobbed-up brother-in-law, Arthur Gianelli, who had an interest in a Back Bay gin mill and lived side by side with the agent on a secluded Lynnfield cul-de-sac on land acquired from mobster Rocco Botta. It was more catch-me-if-you-can chutzpah at the careless corners of Connolly's world.

The party's pièce de résistance was the presence of the town's most sought-after master of ceremonies, Bill Bulger, presiding with droll asides. As was his wont, he brought the theme back to himself. When the media dared suggest that he retire, Bulger reassured them all to cheers, "I run back to my chair."

The retirement bash was almost a double billing with Bulger. Connolly talked warmly of scholarly Bill passing on the love of books to him and recalled a chance encounter on a Southie street decades earlier with Bill, as a dedicated young dad, bouncing a baby in one arm while reading the life of St. Augustine with the other. With a voice soft with emotion, he called Bulger a "special person who taught me a lot."

For his part, Whitey sent Connolly a ten-thousand-dollar retirement bonus.

Yet the early 1990s were a pinnacle that became a precipice for Whitey Bulger.

In quick succession, he lost his tenacious protector in law enforcement's top agency and the next year his lucrative drug network suffered a terminal setback when fifty-one distribution dealers were arrested in a massive DEA raid that included Irish capos John "Red" Shea and Paul "Polecat" Moore. Both were seasoned stand-up guys who would do their hard time, but Whitey's cocaine bonanza from the projects was over.

The setbacks were all the worse because Whitey had come by his first legitimate income since being a courthouse janitor a quarter century earlier. And it was more than enough to defend his low-key lifestyle if the Internal Revenue Service came after him for hiding assets and not paying taxes.

Whitey hit the lotto. But on the usual terms—what's yours is mine. Over the holidays in 1990, Whitey's variety store sold season lottery tickets to henchman Pat Linskey with a Whitey proviso—if anyone wins, I'm in, too. Six months later, Linskey's brother Mike hit it for $14.3 million. The jackpot was split up four ways—Whitey, Weeks, and the two brothers. Whitey's share converted to $120,000 a year. But the perfect cover would be wasted if he got out of the game and the money would be uncollectable if he became a fugitive.

For the last time, Connolly worked in tandem with Whitey and Flemmi with his FBI paperwork. Heading out the door to Boston Edison, he filed another cover-up 209 FBI report stating the pair were "packing it in and going into various legitimate businesses that they own." It was an advisory to all who followed that these guys had done their duty and were off-limits.

Flemmi jumped with both feet into the real estate business, staying close to home by buying up condos in high-end Back Bay, getting in early enough with a million dollars in cash to beat the price escalation of the mid-1990s. He made $360,000 on just one flip. Whitey's real estate venture was more escape strategy than investment, a follow-up to a safe-deposit box he'd opened in Dublin in 1987 and one in London in 1992.

In April 1993, Whitey paid cash for a condo in Clearwater, Florida, where he could be either Uncle Jim to winter visits from a horde of nieces and nephews or Thomas Baxter of New York if things went wrong in Boston. He also opened a deposit box there.

But what Connolly logged in as legitimate business would soon be viewed as money-laundering by new prosecutors and the latest group of state troopers who wanted Whitey bad.

Enter Fred Wyshak. Born in Boston, he came home after ten years as a prosecutor in the Brooklyn district attorney's office and U.S. attorney's office in Newark, New Jersey. In 1989, he was known as a case maker who neither suffered fools nor minced words. At thirty-seven, he could get his arms around a big case, not getting swamped by the paper chase and especially not giving an inch in court. Not everybody liked him.

For two decades, the U.S. attorney in Boston and the FBI focused exclusively on one public enemy—the Mafia. It was the sole item on the guts-and-glory agenda. Wyshak knew the drill and had just come off a major conviction in a New Jersey case in which Mafiosi had infiltrated trade unions that extorted money from contractors. His Boston colleagues kept pushing him toward Italians but he circled back to Whitey. It bugged him: How come no one cared about such a natural target?

His case-making MO was tried-and-true: Find the weak link in the cast of characters around his target and put it to him: Go to jail or become a witness. It could work with Whitey.

Enter Brian Kelly. He too was a local guy but had the Ivy League background more common in the U.S. attorney's office. Kelly was Dartmouth College and University of Pennsylvania Law School but there was nothing ivory tower about him. He became Wyshak's junior partner, wanting in on the high-profile cases and courtroom shoot-outs. He also brought some humor to leaven the full-speed-ahead Wyshak. They were an improbable pair who got on and instinctively rejected the premise that the office had but one client—the FBI.

They worked with the Massachusetts State Police detectives and

DEA and bagged the incorrigible Howie Winter, who had started dealing cocaine soon after he got out on parole from the race-fixing case. In the early 1990s, they hooked him for a ten-year sentence and then Wyshak offered his terms: Help us with Whitey or do your time. Winter thought about it but let the metal doors clank shut behind him, a wizened sixty-two-year-old looking at a decade in prison.

Howie's stoicism was a small setback, but the new team had a clear-cut victory. What's more, they got on, all members simpatico and savvy. They knew how to get around the FBI and devise a strategy for doing something no had ever done—or even tried: build a Whitey Bulger case.

Enter Tom Foley. He was a state cop to the core, up from the ranks, doing turnpike patrols for years before he got into detective work. And he too had instinctively gravitated toward going after Whitey Bulger in the mid-1980s. Repeatedly boxed in by the FBI, he concluded that the bureau was protecting Whitey.

Not everybody liked him, either. Which was okay with him, especially when the FBI gave him a joke award one Christmas as the Most Hated Man in Law Enforcement. He still has it in his den.

Foley was a working cop who piled up the arrests and engendered loyalty from colleagues. In 1984, he joined a newly formed Intelligence Unit to target organized crime and work with the FBI on Mafia cases. Given the later conflict, the irony is that the unit was the FBI's idea. Foley followed one of his mentors, Charles Henderson, up the line. Henderson became the top commander of the state police and made Foley head of the Special Service Section, a once-elite group that needed a boost in morale and redefined purpose. The new mission was "Get Whitey."

Enter Burton "Chico" Krantz: He was the underworld's version of an MIT genius who set the sports betting lines better than Vegas. Chico had become one of the biggest bookies on the East Coast, playing the odds so well he was nonchalant about million-dollar bets. He once wagered a million on a Super Bowl but fell asleep before it ended and awoke to find he'd lost. He was so good that the Mafia had him set the point spreads on games for one of its networks on Boston's North Shore, run by "Fat Vinnie" Roberto.

State police surveillance found the mother lode in the four-hundred-pound Roberto. He was the rare man in the middle who worked both for the Mafia and for Whitey through spidery connections. Staties followed him to meetings with Revere Mafiosi and then right to Chico's opulent home in Newton. Foley had a decision to make—follow Fat Vinnie up the chain for a Mafia case or see whether the Chico connection could get him to Whitey.

Foley met with Henderson and Middlesex County District Attorney Thomas Riley about which way to go, knowing that picking Whitey surely meant trouble with the FBI. They gulped and said go for it.

Foley had worked with prosecutors in the U.S. attorney's office and saw how Wyshak had maneuvered around the FBI in doing the Howie Winter cocaine case. Wyshak saw the possibilities in money-laundering's tough federal sentences to jam up bookies used to swatting away state gaming charges by paying minor fines. The premise became that Jewish bookies would never do the hard time that a Winter Hill enforcer would. Chico Krantz was the test case. And Wyshak became Foley's consigliere inside the usually hostile federal camp.

The first move was a home run. State cops raided Chico's home and found two safe-deposit keys that turned into a two-million dollar seizure of illegal cash, which immediately got Krantz's full attention.

Foley interrogated Chico at the state police barracks outside Boston.

Chico wanted to know why the troopers went to his house, which had always been off-limits. Foley shrugged.

Where's this going? Foley shrugged again.

They agreed Chico had a problem and reconvened in his Florida home for an extensive debriefing, at which he agreed to become a "CI," confidential informant. But even though Chico Krantz detested the rapacious Whitey, who had raised his monthly street rent from $750 to $3,000, he firmly declined to be an in-court witness against him, viewing it as suicidal.

Chico was about half measures and playing odds. He wanted to be half an informant and get half his money back. Foley didn't close the door to that. But Foley stipulated he needed more than just information about the Whitey Bulger network for that to happen. The game went on that way for months, until Chico made a big mistake. Old habits die hard and Krantz couldn't resist the pull of the betting game.

He not only got caught but had used his wife to deposit some of the proceeds. That was the jackpot for Foley, who handed Chico the text of a prospective money-laundering indictment against her. Krantz quickly folded and, with trepidation, agreed to be a witness against Whitey. He also got a wink and a nod on getting some confiscated money back.

Krantz pled out in 1993, the first plank in building the Whitey Bulger scaffolding. Several other bookies in the Chico Krantz network soon followed suit.

By the middle of 1993, Krantz was in hand and a grand jury was going full tilt. Indictments were in the air. All John Connolly could do was stay posted through a clueless assistant special agent in charge of the Boston office, Dennis O'Callahan. The ASAC never saw the obstruction of justice in briefing an ex-agent about a grand jury's activity.

Whitey knew there was bookie trouble involving Chico but not much else. It was still enough for him to pull Flemmi aside and suggest they both go on extended vacations. Stevie headed for Montreal, where he had hidden out two decades earlier. Whitey took a slow drive around rural America with Teresa Stanley. For a year, they were back and forth, gone for weeks and then popping up in Boston, which was still home until something definite happened. It became a taxing mind game on both sides.

Chico had been augmented by other bookies, and prosecutors lined up Polecat Moore as a witness after he decided it was stupid for him to serve five more years in prison to protect Whitey.

By the end of 1994, there was a secret multifaceted racketeering indictment in hand against Whitey and Flemmi. The plan was to get past the holiday and grab them as close to simultaneously as the edgy FBI/state police relationship would allow.

But there was covert action on the other side as well. Connolly had been gathering information from O'Callahan. Around 1 p.m. on December 23, 1994, phone records showed, Connolly called the FBI, and by 3 p.m., having failed to reach Whitey, the ex-agent held an emergency meeting with Kevin Weeks at the South Boston Liquor Mart, next to the variety store on the rotary.

An agitated Connolly insisted they go to the back of the store and into the walk-in refrigerated room stacked with cases of beer, a dank, secluded place with fan and motor noise to combat possible bugs from prying state police or DEA agents. He told Weeks that indictments were imminent and that Weeks should get word to Whitey and Flemmi right away. He made Weeks repeat the information back to him and then left in a hurry. The short conversation would send Connolly to jail.

Weeks beeped Whitey, who was with Teresa Stanley at her house. They both rushed to the variety store and Weeks jumped in the car's backseat. Whitey drove to the festive Copley Square mall downtown and Stanley made her first shopping visit to the upscale Neiman Marcus store. The men talked about Connolly's information outside the car. Whitey nodded, said to call Flemmi, and beckoned Stanley, who was standing outside the store. Weeks recalled: "That was it. He was gone."

Two weeks later Weeks bumped into Flemmi and thought, Why are you still here? Stevie had thought he'd have more time and that Schneiderhan would keep him posted on arrest plans. But he was wrong about that.

Chico, Whitey, and Stevie were the big names on the arrest warrants on January 4, 1995, when Wyshak alerted Foley that the paperwork was ready and the state police and DEA should focus on Flemmi.

Foley played a hunch again, figuring that if Stevie hadn't fled yet, he would say good-bye to his stepson Stephen Hussey, who was struggling to make a go of a restaurant/bar on the outer edge of the historic Faneuil Hall area. Stephen had just about finished renovating Schooner's when the staties staked it out. It was well past dusk as four troopers and a DEA agent anxiously circled the restaurant. There were people inside but nothing was happening. One officer radioed Foley to ask about checking some other place. Negative, said Foley. Hang in.

One of the two female troopers on the scene, Patty Gillen, who had shadowed Flemmi before, was watching the front door. Suddenly: "We think we see him. . . . Baseball cap, Asian with him." Then excitement crackled over the radio: "Oh, yeah. That's him."

Parked on a side street with a view of Schooner's, DEA agent Daniel Doherty and trooper John Tutungian raced up to Flemmi's Honda near the entrance, blocking it with a sideways screech. Guns drawn, they jumped from the unmarked car, Doherty yelling, "Steve Flemmi, do not move! Stay right where you are!" Pulling the door open, Doherty put his gun to Flemmi's temple as the Asian woman sat frozen behind the steering wheel. Fittingly, Flemmi was arrested for extorting Chico. "C'mon, man," he said meekly. "What's going on here?"

Flemmi had waited too long to head for Montreal, resting dangerously on his expired FBI connections, thinking the bureau, as it had so many times, would intervene with pesky lower-level law enforcement. But not this time. This was not Jeremiah O'Sullivan and John Connolly. It was Fred Wyshak and Tom Foley.

With Flemmi in hand, Foley turned his attention on Whitey, not trusting the FBI to do that job and unaware that Whitey was already in Florida.

Foley went first to Stanley's house in Southie, which was empty. Then to Greig's home by the water in the Squantum section of Quincy. He was greeted on the front steps by an arms-folded Greig. She knew the rules when he asked to look around. You have a search warrant? Foley shook his head. "Then go fuck yourself."

Stevie was all they had after two days of frantic searching. Flemmi thought he'd be bailed and would then slip off to Canada. But that was delusional and he was in jail for good. And he never heard from Whitey Bulger again.

Flemmi was surprised by that but shouldn't have been. They had been associates for two decades but nobody stayed close for long with Whitey, who was his own island, a one-man show in which people were used and loyalty was a twisted joke.

Stevie was windblown in Whitey's wake. They were done. As things played out without honor among thieves, Flemmi embraced his plea arrangement, which required him to help the feds catch Whitey. He was into it but had nothing to give. Whitey always kept careful compartments, even for a near equal like Stevie. Despite all their business discussions, Flemmi had no leads on where Whitey was heading or what aliases he'd be using. Whitey talked only about the here and now, never the future.

From his arrest on a winter night in 1995, Flemmi was flat out of options. He just didn't know it right away. He refused an early plea deal, thinking he could get acquitted by claiming his crimes were part of his work for the FBI, clinging to his genuine if foolhardy belief that snitching gave him immunity. The only "break" he ever got was life in prison instead of the death penalty.

Stevie had stashed most of his money in a chimney at his mother's house. Whitey had safe-deposit boxes all over the Western world. Stevie had no exit plan other than a one-way ticket to Montreal that he forgot to buy. On arrest day, Whitey had been on the road for nearly two weeks.

Part of Whitey's exit strategy was to leave behind a self-serving medical diagnosis with some truth about the dire aftermath of the LSD Project at the Atlanta Penitentiary thirty-five years earlier. He left a five-page letter in Greig's house about how badly he had been deceived by doctors who claimed to be seeking a cure for schizophrenia. Instead, he said, the experiments left him permanently plagued by visual and auditory hallucinations.

He recounted a lifelong struggle with aftereffects. "It's 3 am and years later, I'm still affected by LSD in that I fear sleep—the horrible nightmares that I fight to escape by waking, the taste of adrenalin [sic], gasping for breath. Often I'm woken by a scream and find it's me screaming."

The document seemed partly a public relations effort to blunt "monster" tales sure to follow him out of town and the beginning of a possible "LSD-made-me-do-it" defense if he got caught. He cited a medical opinion from a psychiatrist who had studied LSD and purportedly administered scans that found Bulger had been "brain damaged (physically) by LSD."

But if Whitey was beset by nightmares, they didn't cloud his strategic planning. He was clear-eyed about getting out of town. In fact, he sensed the jig was up at about the same time Chico Krantz figured out how to save half his confiscated money and became a Wyshak witness.

In June and July of 1993, Whitey and Stanley had traveled to Europe, where Whitey tended to the safe-deposit boxes he had opened earlier in Dublin and London banks.

A little over a year later, Whitey and Stanley spent nearly all of October visiting Dublin, London, and Italy. Whitey made several withdrawals from his London bank and rented an apartment and joined a health club in the Chelsea section of the city. Venice was the last stop before heading home to Boston, where the staid Stanley was in for the surprise of her life.

Shortly after their return, in November 1994, Whitey's double life with the two women was tipped over by a shrewd gambit. Catherine Greig too saw indictments coming that would put Whitey on the lam and devised a plan to hold on to him. She confronted Stanley with Whitey's two decades of two-timing her. She told Stanley her confession was the only way she could break up with Whitey, since it would be intolerable to him that she had bared secrets. But Greig's devious strategy was to make it intolerable for Stanley to stay with someone that duplicitous.

The disclosure put Whitey in a tight spot. He'd have to choose his companion for a dodgy underground life—the malleable Stanley or the calculating Greig.

Stanley said that when she had it out with Whitey about his perfidy, he became apologetic, promising to break it off with Greig, and that he would make it up to her, suggesting they go away together on yet another trip. Maybe check out New Orleans for the holidays.

What he didn't tell her was that indictments were in the air. And that their reconciliation vacation was no sojourn. They'd be gone for good.

The trip to New Orleans's French Quarter began in a rush, two days before Christmas. Stanley dutifully took her place beside her taciturn man and they spent a week, including New Year's, bouncing around Bourbon Street. Then Whitey made a dash along Route 10 across the Deep South to Clearwater, Florida. Once there, he emptied a safe-deposit box and headed back toward Boston, perhaps thinking the indictments, nearly two years in the making, were on hold again. Or perhaps with the writing on the wall, he was switching to Greig.

But on Interstate 95 in Connecticut on January 5, Whitey heard of Flemmi's arrest on the car radio and did a fast U-turn to a Manhattan hotel. Using a pay phone, he called aide-de-camp Kevin Weeks and asked him to talk to Greig, apparently to keep her on standby. Things were getting edgy with Stanley. After the indictments, Weeks met with Greig in South Boston and both were acutely aware they were under police surveillance.

By then Whitey was officially wanted as a fugitive and he began using his long-held alias, Thomas Baxter. He and Stanley headed to the Long Island home of a cousin of Weeks. They spent three weeks in the New York City area before heading out on the road again in a new 1994 black Mercury Marquis, bought with cash. At the end of January, they roamed the South and Southwest, going through Tennessee to Texas and into Arizona, where they stayed until the middle of February.

It took about seven weeks for Greig's long-range strategy to play out. Indeed, Stanley stopped being grateful to Whitey for being a good father figure to her children and focused on the bottomless betrayal and the lonely, alien life they now had. She missed her kids. Southie's familiarity. And she was tired of roaming around the barren countryside with a strange, silent man who said little and shared nothing. She had always agreed with everything he said, to avoid an argument, but now she told him, in so many words, that she was sick of his shit and wanted to go home.

Whitey called Weeks to work out an exchange plan for mid-February. He dropped off Stanley at a Chili's restaurant in Hingham, Massachusetts, near her daughter's house. He said he'd call her but never did. Earlier that day, Greig got a call to meet Weeks at Thomas Park in Southie. She left her poodles, Nikki and Gigi, with her twin sister and walked toward Weeks's car carrying a small handbag and the shirt on her back. She had a handful of friends but it was too dangerous to even say good-bye.

She and Weeks drove around for an hour to make sure they weren't being tailed. Greig seemed nervous and Weeks spent most of the ride trying to get her to relax. After the "misdirections" and "small talk," Weeks was satisfied they were in the clear and made a fast left toward Dorchester. They pulled into a parking lot at Malibu Beach near the Southeast Expressway.

Whitey emerged in the dusk from the black Mercury, embraced Greig, and shook hands with Weeks. They all got into his car and took a slow farewell tour of Southie. When they returned to Malibu, the two gangsters walked the beach. They talked about a system for staying in touch by phone, while Greig sat in the black car to ponder a new life on the run.

At nightfall, Weeks watched the Mercury disappear toward the expressway and into infamy.

22

The Band of Brothers

Bill, Whitey, and Jack

The Monday after Stevie Flemmi's arrest on January 4, 1995, Boston FBI agent John Gamel decided to begin the search for the missing Whitey Bulger by paying a visit to Whitey's brother Bill. The winter temperatures hovered around freezing but the morning skies were clear, and the agent, lanky at well over six feet tall, walked the few blocks from the FBI's office in Center Plaza to the gold-domed Massachusetts State House. With him was another agent from the Boston FBI Organized Crime Squad.

Gamel and Agent Joe Hannigan walked unannounced into the Senate president's chamber, a suite of rooms finely decorated with thick carpets, plush upholstered chairs, and polished mahogany furnishings. They found the entry room empty except for a receptionist. Bill Bulger was fresh from beating back a challenge to his presidency of the state Senate from an upstart Democratic colleague. Few had dared defy Bill Bulger during the sixteen years he'd held the post, and the challenge had proven grueling for him, lasting nearly a year. But when the votes were taken the prior Wednesday Bill Bulger crushed the opponent, 23–6.

Gamel explained the reason for the visit—he wanted to speak to the Senate president about his fugitive brother Whitey. The receptionist made a few calls. "I expected that he would at least have a face-to-face conversation with me," Gamel said. The FBI agents were then told that Bill Bulger was not available. Gamel and Hannigan sat down but after a few more minutes Gamel pulled out his business card, handed it to a staff person, and asked that Bill Bulger give him a call.

Gamel was back at his office less than an hour when his telephone rang. "Please hold for the Senate president," a voice said. The agent may have been hoping to question Bill Bulger, but the brief exchange was mostly one-way: Bill Bulger said that he'd had no contact with Whitey, was not interested in being interviewed, and would not answer any of Gamel's questions. Gamel managed to convey a couple of points—that if he learned of Whitey's whereabouts he should contact him and, if he spoke to Whitey, he should urge his brother to surrender. Bill Bulger was noncommittal, saying he would keep the agent's suggestions in mind. Then, after a less than a minute on the line, the Senate president hung up the phone.

"That was it," Gamel said.

Several weeks later the telephone rang at the home of Bill Bulger's driver, Eddie Phillips. The caller was Whitey Bulger, and standing ready to pick up the phone was Bill. The two brothers then had their first conversation since Whitey's federal indictment and disappearance. Kevin Weeks was the go-between, the one who had arranged the call. He'd notified Bill that Whitey wanted to speak to him—and that to avoid possible electronic surveillance of his home or office Bill needed to take the call at a third-party residence. Bill Bulger got back to Weeks soon afterward and said he would be at his driver's home in Quincy on the designated night.

The brothers talked for about five minutes. Whitey told Bill he was doing just fine, and he told his younger brother to let the rest of the family know that he was all right. Whitey urged Bill not to believe everything federal authorities and the news media were saying about him regarding his racketeering indictment. The comment was a variation of Whitey's lifelong refrain, "I'm no angel, but . . ." Bill Bulger told Whitey that he and the family cared about him and that he was rooting for him.

"I think I said I hope this will have a happy ending," Bill Bulger said during his testimony six years later before a federal grand jury.

In going along with preparations for the call, Bill Bulger did not take up any of FBI agent John Gamel's suggestions. He did not contact Gamel either before or after talking to Whitey. He also did not talk to his brother about surrendering. "Because I don't think it would be in his interest to do so," he testified later. Bill Bulger said that while others would likely disagree with his position, he had an "honest loyalty" to Whitey. He felt under no obligation to help in his capture.

"I hope that I personally am not helpful to anyone against him."

Bill Bulger wasn't the only family member to give John Gamel the cold shoulder. In the months to come the FBI agent made the rounds with Whitey's siblings. The contacts had a twofold purpose: to gain their cooperation and to explain the legal consequences of harboring a fugitive. It was standard operating procedure for any fugitive case. "You put them on notice so that if they do choose to aid a fugitive they can be prosecuted." The FBI agent found brother Jackie Bulger at home. "He gave his name, date of birth, and Social Security number like he was a prisoner of war or something," Gamel said. "He was not interested in talking." Gamel found older sister Jean Holland at home, too, and she "was appalled, aghast, and shocked that I was standing on her doorstep talking to her about the seriousness of possibly harboring a fugitive." Gamel had barely returned to his office when he took a call from her attorney, who gave him an earful of "how dare you talk to my client like that." Gamel missed out on any interaction with Whitey's other two sisters; they weren't home. He left his FBI business card, but never heard back. He tried Catherine Greig's sole surviving relative as well, her twin sister, Margaret McCusker, but "she was pretty hostile and had nothing to say."

The FBI agent might as well have been in a time warp wandering around Boston in the winter of 1956. Back then the FBI search for a twenty-six-year-old version of Whitey—a bank-robbing fugitive from justice—found the Bulgers "hostile" to its overtures seeking assistance. Four decades later little had changed—although, at the same time, everything had. Back then Whitey was on the front end of a criminal career. He hadn't killed anyone yet. Family and friends could cling to a slim hope that he could be reached and steered in a law-abiding direction. But by 1995 there was no hiding from the fact that Whitey, now sixty-five, was a career criminal and a crime boss. No one in the Bulger family needed to know firsthand the horrifying particulars—about the many murders or violent extortion—to know that Whitey was long set in his ways and beyond redemption.

Moreover, as a fugitive, Whitey not only arranged to talk to brother Bill, he began actively enlisting his family in what for him was the challenge of all time—a life on the run. To survive a crucial period where he scrambled to gain his sea legs, Whitey contacted family and friends to help him hide from investigators and frustrate efforts to locate him.

It meant putting family and friends in harm's way. It meant that they would all eventually pay a steep price. But Whitey Bulger on the run was counting on family, whether it was 1956 or 1995, to guard his flank. And then as now he calculated correctly—illustrating at once that indeed everything and nothing had changed. "The Bulger family to the end will not give him up, will not negotiate a surrender," said FBI agent Richard Teahan, who, several years after Gamel, took up the baton in the international manhunt for Whitey Bulger.

In late February 1995, just after Whitey traded in one girlfriend for another, Cathy Greig called her twin sister, Margaret McCusker, who was at work at a nursing home in South Boston. The call was about money. Cathy asked her sister to empty their joint bank account and to await further instructions. McCusker obeyed, withdrawing $8,000 on February 22 and two days later the remaining $7,500. Kevin Weeks then sent one of his associates by McCusker's house to pick up the $15,500 in cash.

The call was Cathy's first but not the last to her sister. Over the next eighteen months or so they talked a handful of times, including a call shortly after the bank withdrawal, in which Cathy told McCusker, "I got that package, and don't worry." Whitey often had a hand in setting up Cathy's calls to her sister or to Kathleen McDonough. McDonough was a friend who began living in Cathy's house in Squantum and was taking care of the poodles. The calls were usually placed to a neighbor or to the home of a relative or acquaintance, to elude FBI wiretaps.

McCusker wasn't the only one moving money around. Jackie Bulger and Whitey shared a bank account at South Boston Savings Bank. They opened it in 1991 so that Whitey would have an account into which his annual lottery payment could be deposited. With Whitey gone, Jackie grew concerned that the government might find out about the account and try to seize the money. He cleaned out the almost ninety thousand dollars. Then he went to a bank in downtown Boston, BayBank, where he rented a safe-deposit box and stored the cash.

Jackie Bulger took other steps to protect Whitey. Some of Whitey's mail came to his house, including utility bills and fees for Whitey's condominium in Clearwater, Florida. Jackie paid them. He also kept up the annual rental payments on Whitey's safe-deposit box in Clearwater—the box Whitey had emptied in early January. It turned out Whitey was less protective of Jackie than he was of Bill. Whitey and Jackie also talked on the telephone more than once—and they met up as well—while the single conversation with Bill Bulger was their only documented contact.

In nearly every link to South Boston, Kevin Weeks was the key—the hub in a wheel of activity during the crucial early months of Whitey's flight from justice. The two were in touch regularly, and whenever they talked, before they were done they lined up the next call. "I would give him the number, and then we had a certain time and date that he would call me back," Weeks said. Whitey used Weeks in a variety of ways; he had Weeks set up calls with other people Whitey wanted to talk to. "When he wanted to get ahold of someone," Weeks said, "I would go to the person, I would tell them, 'Get me a number where you can be,' and then I would give the number to Jim Bulger so he could call." The technique they'd used first with the call to Bill Bulger became standard procedure during Whitey's calling around.

In addition, Whitey used Weeks as his messenger—delivering news and information to brothers Bill and Jackie, as well as to retired FBI agent John Connolly. Weeks began stopping by Bill Bulger's home in South Boston every couple of weeks with Whitey updates. "To share with me whatever he was hearing or learning," Bill Bulger testified later. "For the most part he'd be telling me that he looked good, and . . . his spirits were good." (When a federal prosecutor pressed Bill Bulger during the grand jury proceedings about whether Kevin Weeks ever disclosed Whitey's whereabouts, Bulger hedged, saying he didn't think so, but then added: "There's something about New York that sounds familiar.")

By early summer 1995 Whitey heard news that made him white hot with anger—federal prosecutors were filing forfeiture papers in court in July to seize his annual lottery payment of nearly $120,000. It triggered calls and complaints to Weeks, with Whitey vowing to find a way to contest the government grab of money.

The next month, Whitey's older sister, Jean Holland, filed papers in both federal and county probate court to fight the seizure. She claimed to have a legal interest in the lottery money "in her own right as one of James J. Bulger's heirs at law, and on behalf of her brother James J. Bulger and his heirs." Given that Whitey had vanished she wanted the court to appoint her as Whitey's "absentee receiver."

Much of the legal back-and-forth involved the interpretation of the law covering absentee receivers: whether the law was meant to allow a relative such as Holland to be appointed receiver when the reason for Whitey's absence was he was a fugitive from justice; or whether Whitey was even absent, although Holland argued adamantly that Whitey had vanished. During the early days of litigation she insisted she'd not had any contact with him.

But then evidence began emerging that Whitey had slipped in and out of town and was in contact with Kevin Weeks and others. Which meant, in theory, that Whitey could appear in court on his own behalf. Over time the court rulings were consistently averse to Jean Holland's arguments, and she gave up trying to be appointed receiver of Whitey's lottery money. Eventually she withdrew her petition.

During most of 1995 Whitey and Cathy stayed on the move. In late spring they were out west, traveling through Wyoming, and by summer's end they headed to the Deep South, where they passed through the tiny Gulf Coast community of Long Beach, Mississippi. In both locations Whitey had close encounters with the law that could have proved calamitous but for his alias. While they were in Sheridan, Wyoming, a local police officer ran a routine motor vehicle check on the Grand Marquis, with its New York plates, after Whitey left it overnight in a hospital parking lot. The plates came back clean—registered to New York resident Thomas Baxter. Then one night in early September in Long Beach, Mississippi, Whitey was at a red light when a police cruiser slowed to a stop behind him. The officer, Rudy Ladner, later said he noticed right away the out-of-state plates, and that he grew slightly suspicious when the Grand Marquis did not move after the light turned green. Ladner said the car's driver was eyeing him in the rearview mirror and so on a hunch he ran the plates. But again the plates came back clean. The National Crime Information Center—which the FBI manages—had nothing on Thomas Baxter of New York.

Throughout the South, Whitey frequented a number of coin shops where he could convert cash to gold and silver, and vice versa. Piling up the miles on the black Grand Marquis, Whitey drove north again, returning to Long Island and to his pit stop in Selden, New York, at the home of Kevin Weeks's relatives. Whitey several times arranged through Weeks for Cathy to talk to her sister and friend to ask about her poodles.

The couple was posing as Mr. and Mrs. Thomas Baxter when on September 30 they checked into the Best Western MacArthur Hotel in Holtsville, New York, a tiny hamlet not far from Selden. During this stretch the well-informed Whitey was likely following a case that had gripped the nation. Television reports and front-page newspaper stories chronicled a serial mail bomber—dubbed the Unabomber—who over two decades had sent sixteen bombs that killed three people and injured twenty-three others. In June the Unabomber sent a 35,000-word manifesto to the *New York Times* and the *Washington Post* demanding they publish every word. If they did, he said, he would end his attacks; if they didn't, bombs away. The Unabomber set a three-month deadline, and so on September 18, the *Washington Post* published an insert containing the entire Unabomber screed against modern technology's dehumanizing effects.

Publication of the manifesto proved to be a turning point in the FBI's investigation. Besides a readership that likely included millions across the country, a man living near Schenectady, New York, named David Kaczynski scoured the document. To him, both the writing style and the content echoed the ideas and past work of his mathematician brother, Theodore "Ted" Kaczynski. By early 1996 he'd reported his concerns to the FBI, and then, on April 5, 1996, agents and police arrested the reclusive Ted Kaczynski at his mountain cabin in Montana. Kaczynski, called a domestic terrorist by the FBI, pleaded guilty to the mail-bombing campaign in 1998 and was sentenced to life in prison with no possibility of parole.

In later interviews, David Kaczynski, a social worker, said he'd been torn emotionally about turning his brother in but felt he had to. "He might attack someone else again," he said in an interview with MSNBC. "It was unbearable to think of waking up some morning, realizing that we hadn't done the right thing and because of it, somebody else had died." He promised to give the million-dollar reward for the Unabomber's capture—the largest in history in a domestic case—to the families of his brother's victims in the sixteen bombings.

What was right for one brother, though, was not so for the Bulgers.

While Whitey was staying again in New York, Kevin Weeks paid him a visit, and it was during the fall of 1995 that Weeks stepped up his intelligence work into the ongoing federal investigation against Whitey and his gang. Weeks moved back and forth between John Connolly and Stevie Flemmi, held without bail in a prison in Plymouth, Massachusetts, with Weeks all the while relaying information to Whitey. Most of Whitey's crime network had fallen apart, given its lean, Whitey-centric operating format, and the mission now was all about Whitey's survival.

To reach Connolly, Weeks left the message with his secretary at Boston Edison that "Chico called." When Connolly wanted to talk to Weeks he left a message with one of Weeks's brothers, who then told Kevin, "Your girlfriend is looking for you." Weeks and Connolly met at different spots—in Harvard Square, or downstairs in the pub Finnegan's Wake in Cambridge, or at the restaurant Top of the Hub in the Prudential Center in Back Bay, where Connolly's Boston Edison corporate office was located. They talked about the federal investigation, and Connolly, though retired, was a steady font of insider information. He exuded confidence, telling Weeks the "case was falling apart, that it wasn't going anywhere, that there was a lot of infighting between the FBI and the state police." Weeks then visited Flemmi in prison and passed along what Connolly told him. Over time Weeks actually tired of the running around, especially dealing with Stevie Flemmi. "He used to call me every night," Weeks complained, "so it was kind of getting monotonous taking the calls every night and then going up to see him. So I kind of stretched it out the further we went. Unless there was something important to tell him."

Mainly Connolly and Weeks talked about how to steer trouble away from themselves—and key to that strategy was to blame any wrongdoing on John Morris. For example, Connolly, through Weeks, coached

Flemmi to claim in court papers that Morris was the FBI official who had illegally leaked word of the gangsters' pending indictments. To bolster the false claim, Connolly advised Flemmi to say that Morris had learned about the sealed indictment when he got a look at the so-called prosecution memorandum. "That would give it more credence to use that terminology," Weeks said. In another instance, Connolly gave Weeks one of the tape recordings from the FBI's 1981 bugging of Gennaro Angiulo's Mafia headquarters in the North End. Weeks then delivered it to Flemmi's defense attorney, saying, "I found it in Stevie's closet—in a shoe box." The idea was to say Morris had illegally shared the tape with Flemmi, further proof of the FBI supervisor's corruption.

Morris was going to be their fall guy—and no one was more burning with enmity toward the former supervisor of the Organized Crime Squad than Whitey. He saw Morris as the originator of all the trouble that had befallen, beginning when Morris served as a key source in the *Boston Globe*'s breakout story in 1988 reporting that Whitey had a deal with the FBI. Even though Whitey had batted that story aside like an annoying gnat, he decided Morris had been trying to get him killed. Or perhaps that was what he liked to tell others as justification for his rage, when, just as likely, the thing that got Whitey so worked up was the rank betrayal Morris had shown—another in a line of informers against him. Whitey began trying to figure out where Morris, who had survived several internal FBI inquiries as a possible news leak and been transferred from Boston, was now located. He flipped through telephone books when he had the chance, and eventually, while he was staying in the Best Western, he figured out Morris was working as an instructor at the FBI's training academy in Quantico, Virginia.

He called and got Morris's secretary. He insisted on speaking to Morris, but when she asked for his name he refused to give her one. Whitey called a few more times, and the secretary told Morris about the strange calls from the man who would not leave his name. Then, on Friday, October 13, Whitey tried again in the late afternoon, this time with a new plan. He told the secretary to tell Morris that "Mr. White" was on the line, and when the secretary handed John Morris a note with the name "Mr. White" on it Morris picked up the phone. "He started to call me something. 'You fuck'—and stopped," Morris said. Whitey then identified himself, but Morris knew it was Whitey the instant he heard his voice. They talked for only a few minutes but Whitey was the one in charge. He never mentioned his brother Bill by name, but accused Morris of "ruining him and his family." He kept citing the newspaper story and warned Morris that if he went to jail "he was taking me with him." He told Morris to use his "Machiavellian mind" to undo the damage he had caused.

"Throughout the call his voice was menacing and vengeful," Morris said. "His voice expressed tension and he struggled not to lose control." Morris listened to Whitey's bill of particulars and list of demands and said, "I hear you." Then Whitey hung up on him. Later that night a shaken John Morris suffered a heart attack.

The next time Whitey spoke with Weeks, the Morris call was all he could talk about. Whitey recounted how he'd tracked Morris down to Quantico, and he loved telling the part about getting Morris to pick up. "Mr. White," he told Weeks. "I figure, you know, he would get it. Whitey Bulger. Mr. White." Weeks could tell Whitey was obsessed with Morris. "He blamed everything on Morris," Weeks said.

Weeks then met with John Connolly and told him everything Whitey had said about Morris. Connolly enjoyed the dramatic recap. "That must have been some conversation—he took a heart attack," Connolly said.

Weeks agreed. "We kind of laughed about it and that was it."

In November 1995 Whitey and Cathy returned to a tiny island ninety miles south of New Orleans they'd visited briefly earlier in the year. Grand Isle, Louisiana, had obvious appeal—small, isolated, a warm climate, and located on the water. The Gulf Coast tourist community with its roughly 1,500 year-round residents was connected by a drawbridge to the mainland. The couple checked into the Water Edge Motel on November 7 and began looking for an off-season rental. Whitey paid cash for everything, pulling hundred-dollar bills tucked alongside a pearl-handled knife in the fanny pack he wore on his waist.

They were Tom and Helen. They used several last names at different times—Marshall was one. But mostly they were Tom and Helen Baxter, a married couple from New York who spoke with an accent the locals thought was how New Yorkers talked, driving a Mercury Grand Marquis with New York license plates. They told people he was a retired real estate broker and she was a dog groomer. Whitey grew a mustache. He dressed casually in khakis and a Windbreaker during the morning walks he began taking along the beach. He was the gray-haired retiree with the receding hairline and metal-framed glasses—just another nondescript old man. Cathy was the much younger and attractive wife with the frosted blond hair who preferred contact lenses to wearing glasses. She took to going to a salon in town for a cut-and-color from a stylist who turned out to be the local police chief's daughter. Cathy often brought her own product, L'Oréal Light Ash Blonde.

During the next eight months—until July 1996—Whitey and Cathy spent about half their time in Grand Isle, divided into two extended stays. They stumbled into their first rental one day after stopping their car to watch a brushfire on property belonging to a local family named Gautreaux. Noticing the family's dogs, Whitey and Cathy fed them biscuits from a bag they kept in the trunk. The dogs led to small talk between the Baxters and the young mother, Penny Gautreaux. Whitey asked about rentals and Penny Gautreaux recommended a nearby duplex on the beach. Whitey and Cathy liked what they saw and in early December began paying the off-season rate of four hundred dollars a month for the unit with the name "It's Our Dream."

The first encounter led to others. Penny Gautreaux was thirty-one and worked as a meter reader while her husband, Glenn, was a struggling contractor. They had four kids, some from Glenn's first marriage. The island in the summer was a top fishing spot whose population tripled but had little to offer during the winter—only two restaurants and a couple of small markets—and the Baxters began enjoying dinners with the friendly local family that lived closed by. Penny Gautreaux's Cajun cooking in particular was a hit with Whitey.

It was practically instinctual for Whitey to befriend a family in his immediate vicinity, where he came across as genial and generous, when in truth he got a return on his investment—a loyalty and a kind of security knowing the family was on his side. He'd been doing it his entire life, buttering up those within arm's length, and in short order he was busy buttering up the Gautreauxs of Grand Isle. Arriving with groceries, Whitey and Cathy hung around while the food was cooking, playing with the family's Labrador retrievers and socializing with the kids and other relatives. In time, the kids began calling them "Uncle Tom" and "Aunt Helen," as Whitey showed the Gautreaux kids the same strict concern he'd given Teresa Stanley's kids during the daily dinners at Teresa's house over the years. He sometimes shut off the television while they were watching and lectured the parents about the violence on TV. Whitey also pushed Glenn Gautreaux to show some ambition about his carpentry. "He'd say, 'Get off your lazy butt; you've got beautiful kids, you need to make something out of your life,' " Penny Gautreaux said.

In January 1996 Whitey took two of the Gautreaux teens along with him and Cathy on one of their shopping trips to the Wal-Mart SuperCenter located in Galliano, Louisiana, forty miles north of Grand Isle. Whitey and Cathy went there several times a week to load up on goods but also so that Whitey could make calls. While Cathy shopped Whitey was often huddled at a pay phone using one of the calling cards he'd bought to talk to Kevin Weeks or another of his South Boston contacts. They brought the kids along after their school sent home a note saying they both needed glasses. Whitey took them to the vision center at Wal-Mart, paid for an eye examination, and then bought each a pair of glasses. Over the weeks, the gifts kept coming—at one point Whitey stopped by Island Appliance Sales and selected a new stove, refrigerator, and freezer, paying nearly two thousand dollars in cash. Whitey told the family the gifts were his way of saying thanks, and the Gautreauxs didn't question him. "He treated us like family," Penny Gautreaux said. "He was kind."

For the most part Whitey stayed in character as Tom Baxter, but there were occasions when he seemed to let his ego get the better of him. He liked to wear the belt with the Alcatraz buckle he'd bought on a visit to San Francisco, and once, as if to impress, he even told Penny Gautreaux he'd served time there. The disclosure seemed sloppy and uncharacteristic. But Whitey never let his guard down when someone in the family pulled out a camera. Even the time Cathy needled him about wanting a picture of her and the kids Whitey said no way, no exceptions, no photos.

In late February 1996, Whitey and Cathy left Grand Isle for a month or so and upon their return they rented a small two-bedroom house on a dead-end street around the corner from the Gautreauxs. The home's owners lived right next door, a retired couple named Henry and Barbara Wellman, and Whitey paid them several months' rent up front in cash. Whitey and Cathy repeated the Tom and Helen Baxter story to their new landlords. Cathy told Barbara Wellman her husband,

Tom, had worked so hard during his career that they'd never had time to travel, but now that he was retired all he wanted to do was travel and he never wanted to go home.

The couple resumed their place at the Gautreaux' table but their second stint did not go over as well as the first. The retired parents of Glenn's ex-wife had moved in, and the former father-in-law, Thomas "Black" Rudolph, was in his mid-sixties—Whitey's peer. The two began to circle one another suspiciously, a pair of wary, aging cats. Whitey may have resented Rudolph as interloping in his paternal role with his adopted family, while Rudolph did not like how Whitey made himself at home. "He had this attitude like he was the boss," Rudolph said.

That spring a tension marked the get-togethers. Rudolph found Whitey insulting in the way he praised Penny's cooking at the expense of his wife's, and Mary Rudolph thought Whitey was a jerk the way he referred to women and boasted all he had to do was clap his hands and Cathy would jump. Penny Gautreaux did her best to keep the peace, but "Black" Rudolph had no use for Whitey's gifts and his conceited manner. "I said I worked every day of my life since I was fifteen years old and he said he never had to work, he had people working for him."

The clashing machismo festered until one day Rudolph challenged Whitey to a push-up contest. Rudolph was fed up with the other man's tiresome discourse on physical fitness and his excellent conditioning. He dropped to the floor and did several one-handed push-ups without difficulty. He looked at Whitey and said he would do a one-handed push-up for each one Whitey did with two hands.

Whitey declined, going silent for once, mumbling something about being older than "Black" Rudolph. But age was not the kind of factor that would get between Whitey and a challenge. The truth was that around this time Whitey actually had more important matters on his mind than whether he could win a push-up contest.

In the spring of 1996 Kevin Weeks was trying desperately to talk to Whitey but had had no way to reach him. He was forced to wait until Whitey called him at their next prearranged time, and when they talked in June, Weeks gave him the news. The alias that so far had worked so well—Tom and Helen Baxter—was blown. Teresa Stanley's new boyfriend had persuaded her to talk to the FBI, and Teresa had revealed the alias, the Mercury Marquis, and Whitey's use of Selden, New York.

Oddly, it had been more than a year since Whitey had dumped her but FBI agents searching for Whitey had not pounced on her after her return to Boston—an omission other investigators later cited as proof of FBI incompetence or worse. Had Teresa Stanley given up the Baxter alias in 1995—and had the FBI's National Crime Information Center indicated a warrant for Baxter as Whitey Bulger—the routine motor vehicle stops in Wyoming and Mississippi might have turned out differently.

Whitey and Cathy took off from Grand Isle in early July without really saying good-bye, and their landlord found an iron and a bunch of clothes they'd left behind. It seemed as if they were in a hurry, although prior to leaving for good they made a trip to the Wal-Mart vision center, where Cathy bought a year's supply of contact lenses.

"He said they were going to San Diego," Henry Wellman said.

Eventually California, but first they were bound for Chicago. Whitey and his girl were suddenly on the road looking over their shoulders, stirring up dust rather than accomplishing what's best for a fugitive—settling down in one place. They could never again be Tom and Helen Baxter.

It was a bona fide emergency, and for the next several weeks the highest priority was establishing new identities. Before heading off for Chicago Whitey had stepped up his calls to Weeks to discuss the plan forming in his head, and he had Weeks arrange calls with the person key to that plan—brother Jackie.

Jackie took one of Whitey's calls in South Boston at the Physical Therapy Center on West Broadway. Weeks answered the telephone when it rang and handed it over. "How're you doing?" Jackie eagerly asked his older brother. Weeks left the office so that the brothers had some privacy, and when Jackie came out about five minutes later he said Whitey "sounded good." Jackie took another call Weeks had arranged for him at the South Boston home of a man who worked as an officer in Bill Bulger's state Senate. When Whitey called Paul Dooley's house Jackie was waiting, with Weeks and one of Bill Bulger's sons-in-law also standing by.

Weeks had the primary assignment of working on Whitey's new identification. Key was having a head-shot photograph of someone resembling Whitey that could be used to have phony ID cards made up.

Whitey explained that that was where Jackie's involvement was crucial—and, obeying Whitey's instructions, Weeks went out and bought a mustache, grabbed a camera, and went to Jackie's house in South Boston. "I took pictures of his brother with a fake mustache on," Weeks said. Then he had IDs made with the new photos and headed to Chicago to meet up with Whitey.

Whitey and Cathy arrived first, pulling into Chicago on July 7. In little more than a year Whitey had put more than sixty thousand miles on the Mercury Marquis. But the car had been made, and he therefore abandoned it in a downtown parking garage, never to drive it again. They checked into a hotel using the names Mark and Carol Shapeton. Then Weeks, driving from Boston with a girlfriend, arrived. He showed Whitey the fruits of his labor—a set of new IDs for Mark Shapeton, featuring a photograph of Jackie Bulger in a mustache. But Whitey could not believe his eyes. It was almost comical. "The mustache Jackie had on was too big," Weeks realized.

Whitey grew angry, unappreciative of Weeks's efforts. But under the circumstances Whitey had good reason for a quick temper. Whitey knew better than anyone that, as a fugitive, moving around and maintaining contact with people back home was the worst thing for his safety. By the next year, for example, investigators building on the information Teresa Stanley had provided were able to figure out Whitey had been in Grand Isle. "He's not doing what a good fugitive does," FBI agent Thomas Cassano told reporters in Boston. "A good fugitive cuts all ties."

Whitey needed to find a new home for himself and Cathy, a place where they could blend in and lead virtually invisible lives. Grand Isle had had many good traits, a place to practice their story line as retirees, like actors rehearsing a new play. But with the Baxter name permanently blown, there was no going back.

Whitey rejected the IDs Weeks brought as something that would not fool a ten-year-old. He took matters into his own hands and had Weeks follow him to the Bloomingdale's store in Water Tower Place, a nearby mall. He bought a blue bedsheet and a Polaroid camera and then returned to the hotel. While Cathy sat in the bedroom of the small suite chatting with Weeks's girlfriend, Whitey set up a studio in the sitting room. "We got a sheet and we hung it up and I took more pictures of Jim Bulger so it would be his picture that was on the ID," Weeks said. Whitey wasn't easily satisfied, and they worked an hour. "We took multiple pictures because we were trying to center it and get it just right so it would look like a license."

The resulting photo did not show Whitey Bulger at his best. He looked tired, worn-out even—the price perhaps of being both sixty-six years old and a fugitive, still scrambling nineteen months after he'd fled Boston.

Kevin Weeks, in addition to helping Whitey deal with the ID crisis that summer, kept Whitey posted about mounting concern on another front. Back in Boston a new federal grand jury was heating up. This grand jury was different from the one that had issued the racketeering indictment against the Bulger Gang in 1995; this new one was focused exclusively on the manhunt for Whitey and whether anyone was obstructing justice by helping or harboring the fugitive. Subpoenas were served on Whitey and Cathy's family, friends, and various other South Boston residents who'd taken calls from Whitey, including the officer in the state Senate. Margaret McCusker and Kathleen McDonough were summoned to testify about what, if any, contact they'd had with Cathy Greig. For reasons the government never explained, Bill Bulger was left alone—at least for the time being—but Jackie Bulger was served his first subpoena on September 27, 1996.

Federal prosecutors granted Jackie immunity, which meant he could not be prosecuted for anything he told the grand jury—except if he lied. Jackie Bulger testified twice that November, and then again in the beginning of 1998—and when he was sworn in each time, he knew that no cracks in the wall of silence encircling Whitey had occurred other than Teresa Stanley. He knew that just because prosecutors were forcing him to testify did not mean he had to say much.

Under questioning, Jackie admitted to harmless matters; he was paying some of Whitey's utility bills for the Florida condominium, for example. Asked why, Jackie brushed the question aside, saying that keeping up with his brother's bills was "the right thing to do." Prosecutors had learned he'd moved money from a joint account with Whitey into a new account, and so Jackie conceded he'd done that to make seizure of the money more difficult. But there was no crime in that. He feigned complete ignorance when pressed time and again about what Whitey did for a living. "I never asked him," Jackie said. Sure, he'd read newspaper stories on occasion, reporting that Whitey "was an organized crime figure or something." But he insisted he had no idea whether Whitey's work was legal or criminal. "I really don't know," he testified. "He's never told me. I never asked."

Prosecutors then probed into far more sensitive areas, and Jackie answered the questions without hesitation. Asked if he knew whether Whitey kept any safe-deposit boxes, Jackie Bulger answered, "No," despite the fact he was paying the rental fee on Whitey's box in the bank in Clearwater, Florida. Then, at his second grand jury appearance, prosecutors asked about contacts with Whitey.

"Have you spoken to him on the telephone since he was indicted?"

"No," Jackie testified under oath.

"Do you know anyone who has spoken to him on the telephone?"

"No."

"Have you received any messages from your brother Jim since January of 1995, either directly or indirectly?"

"No."

Jackie Bulger completed his testimony confident the wall of silence had held. But his lies eventually created a new complication to which the band of Whitey protectors had to respond quickly in order to extinguish it. Paul Dooley, the lowly Senate officer who'd hosted one of Whitey's calls to Jackie and Kevin Weeks, also got a subpoena to appear before the federal grand jury. Prosecutors chipping away on the outer edges of Whitey's calling campaign had learned that Whitey might have called Dooley's South Boston home. Dooley was in dire need of counsel, and Tom Finnerty, Bill Bulger's close friend and law partner, stepped up. Finnerty was not about to let Paul Dooley go before the grand jury and testify that Whitey had called his house in July 1996 to speak to his brother Jackie. That would instantly expose Jackie to criminal charges of perjury. Finnerty therefore coached his client to go ahead and admit to the grand jury that Whitey had called the house. But that would be it: he was to testify that no one else was there. Paul Dooley obeyed; he committed perjury and said he was home alone. Thanks to Finnerty, problem solved.

In late July 1996, following the crisis in Chicago with the IDs, Whitey bought two Amtrak train tickets in the names of Mark and Carol Shapeton. He and Cathy traveled to New York City via Albany. They spent the next few months, well into the fall, in New York. Whitey stayed busy, refining what, in effect, was a final exit.

He had Weeks working on even more false IDs for them, and later in the summer Weeks sent a messenger to New York City to deliver them to Whitey. Whitey and Cathy made dozens of telephone calls—to South Boston, Chicago, and even Grand Isle. Investigators later determined that the total number of calls, made with prepaid cards, exceeded fifty. Whitey knew that each call was a risk, each contact stirring a pot whose scent investigators might pick up. But he was no fool. Instead it was more like Whitey was checking off his list of good-byes. Cathy talked to her sister, Margaret. Whitey, on August 30, called a longtime Bulger family friend and asked that he tell his brother Bill he was going to be fine. The friend passed along the message not only to Bill Bulger but also to Jackie, who was "relieved to hear the news." Whitey then had Weeks set up a call with John Connolly, in which Connolly was instructed to take the call at the office of Francis X. Joyce, a former top aide to Bill Bulger who was the executive director of the Massachusetts Convention Center Authority. "Jim Bulger wanted John Connolly to come over to his office and he was gonna call there," Weeks said. "I told John Connolly the time that he was gonna call."

Then, in late November, Kevin Weeks traveled to New York one more time to see Whitey. With the grand jury subpoenas flying around, Weeks for the first time indicated to Whitey that it might be "too hot" to be in contact anymore. But Weeks wasn't telling Whitey anything he didn't already know. Whitey, with a kind of sixth sense, recognized that he'd been charmed so far as he neared two years on the run, that his trail was hottest early on with all the traveling and contacts. He couldn't keep this up. To just keep running was both expensive and exhausting. The recent ID photo taken in Chicago was proof of that, featuring a tired-looking older man. To make this work, as every fugitive knew, he and Cathy had to settle and truly start a new life.

In fact, when Weeks went to see Whitey the latter already had a major plan in the works to launch that new life, one in which he would need to draw on his self-discipline and the ability to compartmentalize that he'd relied on so successfully during a lifetime of killing and crime. But this time, instead of enabling him to murder in cold blood and then walk away, be it John McIntyre or Debbie Hussey, Whitey was going to box up and leave his Boston life.

It was a matter of survival, and in early December Whitey Bulger and Cathy Greig boarded a train. Destination: California. Not San Diego, as he'd told his landlord in Grand Isle, but not far from there. Whitey cut off any contact with Kevin Weeks—the New York visit indeed was the last one between mentor and confidant. Teresa Stanley had cracked already, and Whitey Bulger was smart enough to wonder who might be next. Smart enough to realize that eventually Kevin Weeks might be charged and that even the ever-loyal Weeks might not be able to hold up.

Whitey was right. It took a few more years, but Kevin Weeks cracked. In November 1999 he was arrested on charges of racketeering, extortion, and money-laundering. The attorney who appeared at his side during his arraignment in federal court in Boston was none other than the Bulgers' fix-it lawyer, Tom Finnerty. But by early 2000 Weeks had dropped Finnerty and begun cooperating with the government. In a series of debriefings with investigators, Kevin Weeks gave up plenty—crucial evidence about Whitey's criminal enterprise, including the Bulger burial ground. But the damage did not stop at Whitey; he brought lasting harm to Jackie and Bill.

Jackie Bulger was indicted in 2001 on charges of perjury and obstruction of justice. If the case had gone to trial, Kevin Weeks would have been the government's star witness to verify that Jackie had been in touch with Whitey and helped create false IDs. Jackie Bulger chose to plead guilty instead, and the only unsettled issue before the court was the sentence. His lawyer, conceding Jackie Bulger had chosen "family loyalty over civic obligation," said, "He lied—okay. He lied out of a desire to not aid the Government in locating his brother." The situation nonetheless warranted leniency, lawyer George Gormley claimed, because Jackie Bulger's motive "was brotherly concern and not criminal intent."

Federal prosecutor Brian Kelly argued the opposite—Jackie Bulger actively assisted in hiding Whitey from authorities at the expense of public safety—and he showed little patience with Jackie's take on family loyalty. "This notion that his loyalty to family should trump the rule of law should be rejected," Kelly said during the sentencing hearing on September 3, 2003. "If everyone were to, you know, adopt this theory, the Unabomber would still be sending bombs in the mail."

The government wanted Bulger sentenced to prison for four years.

"No one is asking him to join the FBI's Fugitive Task Force and help us capture his brother," Kelly continued. "What was simply asked of him was to testify truthfully. After he was immunized and put before the grand jury, he knowingly and willfully didn't do that. He did that to benefit his fugitive brother."

Jackie Bulger got a six-month sentence in prison, followed by six months of house arrest, and he was ordered to pay a three-thousand-dollar fine. Now a convicted felon, he was also stripped of his public pension as a former juvenile court magistrate.

Meanwhile, Bill Bulger was finally called to testify before the grand jury. He had an advantage at this point in the spring of 2001 over his brother Jackie. He was well aware that prosecutors had learned from Kevin Weeks about the telephone call with Whitey in late January 1995—and he testified about the call during a grand jury appearance that, other than the phone call admission, was marked by a forgetfulness and evasiveness uncharacteristic of the longtime political leader.

No criminal charges ever came his way, but Bill Bulger continued to face public scrutiny when ordered to testify two years later at congressional hearings examining the corrupt ties between the Boston FBI and Whitey Bulger. The experience proved humiliating for Bill, who was no longer president of the Massachusetts Senate but was still atop the state's political establishment, serving as president of the University of Massachusetts since 1996.

Under immunity, he again came across as evasive and forgetful while questioned relentlessly by committee members and staffers—although unlike the secret grand jury, the hearing was public and televised. Like his brother Jackie, he feigned ignorance about Whitey's livelihood. "I knew he was, for the most part, I had the feeling he was in the business of gaming and whatever. It was vague to me."

But for once he was forced to respond directly to the Bulger family position of Whitey being the good bad guy who was always unfairly maligned. That was the note Bill Bulger had struck over the years in his rare public comments about Whitey and, as one congressman now reminded him, was the tack taken in his memoir. The congressman picked up Bill Bulger's *While the Music Lasts* and put the matter right in his face. "In chapter nine you write: 'In the well publicized case against my brother, all of the evidence has been purchased, inducements more precious than money, release from prison, the waiver of criminal charges, have been offered time and again. Some of those who insisted they had nothing to offer at the beginning of their incarceration have had second thoughts and suddenly remembered things they could barter for advantages. Without such purchased testimony, there would be no accusations.' "

The congressman put the passage down and looked at Bulger.

"Do you still believe that to be the case?"

Bill Bulger, caught in the crosshairs of Bulger myth and present reality, replied, "No. I have a different understanding of it now."

Calls for Bill Bulger's resignation as UMass president soon followed. Massachusetts attorney general Thomas F. Reilly said Bulger was unfit to lead a public university given his failure to help authorities in the Whitey manhunt. Governor Mitt Romney followed suit. Bill Bulger at first displayed the same swagger he had shown at John Connolly's 1990 retirement party and vowed to fight his critics, but in early August 2003 he limply announced his resignation.

"You can sympathize with William Bulger over the choice he faced," columnist Scot Lehigh of the *Boston Globe* wrote during the outcry about Bill Bulger's comments to the grand jury and at the hearing. "But not over the decision he made. Instead of taking the righteous road, he chose the code of the street."

In one way or another, Kevin Weeks had brought down the band of brothers. The damage extended beyond blood kin as well. Tom Finnerty's coaching his client to lie to the grand jury came to light. Though Finnerty was never charged criminally, the state's Supreme Judicial Court disbarred him from the practice of law for his effort "to facilitate corruption and frustration of the grand jury inquiry."

Separately, Cathy's sister and friend, Margaret McCusker and Kathleen McDonough, pleaded guilty to lying to the grand jury about their calls with Cathy. Both were sentenced to probation.

But for all the damage inflicted on the house of Bulger, Kevin Weeks was unable to deliver the grand prize—Whitey. The master of the game had indeed been wise to cut off all ties with Weeks in late 1996, just before he and Cathy headed west by train for California. When Weeks folded, three years had gone by since the last contact, and the sidekick no longer had any idea where Whitey was.

23

Travesty

Debra Davis's remains

Someone didn't come home.

A headstrong daughter. A devoted father. A wayward sister. An addicted brother. A nightclub owner. A checkered accountant. A driven tycoon. A rudderless fisherman.

They were all going about humdrum life. Two stopped by a bar for a beer. Another to see a renovated house. Or to check out a new apartment. Or to invest some money. Or had just finished a round of golf. Or hitched a ride from a friend.

Then gone in brutish murders planned or perpetrated by Whitey Bulger. Some were desecrated in death, dismembered to prevent identification, with fingers cut off and teeth removed and ground into powder, and then buried on top of one another in a ghastly cellar on East Third Street in South Boston. Others were buried on the edge of the Neponset River in Quincy or in the sand of Tenean Beach in Dorchester.

In the ghoulish roll call of victims, some families had the infinitesimal advantage of knowing their loved one had been murdered, found in a car trunk in the South End or Revere or Miami. Or splayed in the front seat of a Lincoln Town Car in Tulsa or a blue Datsun on the outskirts of South Boston. Or left like roadkill in the middle of Northern Avenue. The families had the frigid comfort of knowing there had been a murder and there was a body to bury.

But nearly half the victims simply never returned from mundane errands, missing indefinitely, with families left for decades to worry and wonder what happened, slowly figuring out that there had been a deadly interaction with Whitey Bulger. But getting next to nothing from law enforcement. Local police filed missing person reports and shrugged at something beyond them. Some dazed survivors made their way to the FBI, which deflected inquiries with poker faces and even hostile asides.

After fifteen years of mystery and misery, the first breakthrough came in 1998 when a federal judge held months of hearings on Stevie Flemmi's motion to dismiss racketeering charges. While Flemmi took the Fifth on all the murders, it became clear the FBI had been protecting him and Whitey, warning them about rivals who ended up dead.

In fact, Flemmi's novel defense rested on the FBI granting him immunity from prosecution in exchange for being an informant. While that fell apart when Judge Mark Wolf ruled no agent had that kind of authority, the ripples from Flemmi's underworld treachery produced fissures in the Winter Hill Gang and starting points for victims' families who followed the hearing.

First Johnny Martorano cut a deal in 1998 to testify against Whitey and Flemmi on murders he committed with them, after realizing they had been providing evidence about him and several associates. In exchange, the government agreed to a reduced sentence of twelve years for nineteen murders.

And, most important to families of the "missing," Kevin Weeks became a government witness shortly after being charged with extortion and racketeering in 1999, from his years as Whitey's chief enforcer. In exchange for his information, Weeks served five years and his debriefings yielded the location of six grim grave sites.

Weeks blended evidence with dates and places. Once the Whitey connection arose from Weeks's and Martorano's testimony, the victims' families filed damage suits against the complicit FBI. But a new enemy arose—the murky statute of limitations, which required survivors to follow news accounts of decades-old homicides and take swift action. Timing was everything and many lost their claims because of tooth-and-nail resistance by the U.S. Department of Justice, which represented the FBI.

The unforgiving standard for filing a valid suit within two years of an "injury" was based not on knowledge of what happened but rather on having access to information available through the media matrix. It wasn't what they knew; it was what they should have known. Government lawyers showed up at depositions with stacks of news printouts that plaintiffs were supposed to have read—and tough luck if they hadn't.

While there were different starting "accrual" dates for plaintiffs with bodies found at scenes and those exhumed later, the most controlling event was testimony at a federal hearing in 1998 before Judge Mark Wolf. In general, the clock started ticking on September 2, 1998, after Stevie Flemmi finished his testimony about his relationship with the Boston office of the FBI.

Several families suffered the worst of all fates—a murder, an FBI cover-up, and a tardy civil suit for damages. It's called being "timed out," and the merits of the case count for naught. It left buckets of bile on the floor, even in the judges' lobby.

The civil suits had two things in common—the victims had crossed Whitey Bulger and all the killings were done while he was an informant for the FBI. In all, eleven murders happened on the bureau's "watch," more than half with its active complicity. Only five families received damage awards that survived appeal.

Weeks witnessed five murders and knew the location of six burial sites, all vital evidence for cases in court. No body, no murder charge.

The body count cascaded over a decade:

In October 1975, Tommy King, a Mullen gang enforcer who had recently shaken his fist in a public showing of disrespect to Whitey, thought he was part of a "hit" team when he jumped in the front seat of a car with a bulletproof vest on and was handed a gun with blanks by Whitey. It was a ruse and King was shot in the head from behind by Johnny Martorano and buried along the Neponset River shoreline. Weeks gave law enforcement the general location but it still took several days to unearth the body. King's was the first murder with Whitey officially enrolled in the FBI Top Echelon Informant Program. His family took no legal action.

In December 1976, Connolly found out that forty-seven-year-old Richie Castucci of Revere was an FBI informant who had given up the location of Winter Hill gang members hiding out in New York City. He was the first of six murders resulting from a tip-off by Connolly to Whitey about underworld rivals providing information to law enforcement. It was Connolly's "gateway" murder, which made him far more Winter Hill than FBI.

Castucci owned several clubs in Revere, including the Ebb Tide, which had such a bad reputation it had to change its name. Nonetheless, the mobbed-up strip club owner had a family and a projected income that made his wife and four children the biggest winners in the civil suit wheel of fortune—$6.25 million.

In April 1980, Whitey murdered Louis Litif, a brash forty-five-year-old bookmaker and drug dealer in Whitey's network who got too big for Whitey's idea of a subordinate. He saw Louie as a fresh, flashy bastard. Litif's body was stuffed in a green garbage bag upstairs at Triple O's and then transferred to the trunk of a car dumped in the South End. A federal judge ruled that Agent Connolly had warned Whitey that Litif, who was about to go to trial in state court on a homicide charge, was trying to implicate Whitey in drug dealing to lessen his sentence. Weeks gave prosecutors circumstantial evidence of Whitey's involvement. Litif's family was awarded $1.15 million in a civil suit that withstood a government appeal.

In May 1981, Martorano shot Roger Wheeler in Tulsa after retired agent Paul Rico convinced Whitey that the CEO was going to uncover embezzlement at his World Jai Alai headquarters in Miami. Rico promised that new ownership would pay Whitey ten thousand dollars a week skimmed off the top of the racquetball-style gambling operation. After the fact, Connolly filed a report that was a transparent alibi for Whitey being in Boston when Wheeler was shot, a strong indication that Connolly knew the murder was going to happen before it did. No matter. The Wheeler family filed suit too late for recovery in a case worth at least $200 million.

In September 1981, Debra Davis, Stevie Flemmi's longtime girlfriend, was strangled by Whitey after she was lured to Flemmi's mother's house in South Boston to check out renovations. She was buried below the low-tide line on the Neponset River shore in Quincy and found with Weeks's general guidance after a long search. Her family received $1.352 million and withstood appeal.

In May 1982, Whitey was warned by Connolly that Winter Hill mobster Brian Halloran was talking to the FBI about Whitey's role in a murder. Whitey then shot up a car outside the Pier Restaurant in South Boston, killing Brian Halloran, forty-one, and Michael Donahue, a thirty-two-year-old neighbor who was giving Halloran a ride home. Weeks acted as the lookout. Halloran's family was awarded $2.1 million and Donahue's $6.4 million. But a federal appeals court ruled both families had filed suit too late.

In August 1982, Martorano was again the hit man in another World Jai Alai murder. John Callahan, a Boston accountant who was friends with wiseguys and a driving force in the gambling business, was facing a grand jury. Agent Connolly warned Whitey of the likelihood that Callahan would incriminate everyone, information that quickly became a death sentence. But Callahan's family was timed out in its civil suit.

In August 1983, Arthur Barrett, a forty-six-year-old safecracker and bookmaker, was murdered because he was part of a major bank robbery but didn't give Whitey his cut as crime boss. Whitey shot him with a Mac 10 machine gun and Flemmi pulled his teeth to hamper identification. He was first to be buried in the South Boston death cellar. With Weeks's help, he was reburied in Dorchester. His family took no legal action.

In November 1984, John McIntyre, a thirty-two-year-old deckhand on boats smuggling marijuana into Boston Harbor, was murdered after Connolly told Whitey someone in the crew was talking to the Drug Enforcement Administration. Whitey first tried to strangle him with rope and then shot him repeatedly in the head. McIntyre was buried next to Barrett and reburied in Dorchester. His family was awarded $3.1 million and withstood an appeal.

In early 1985, Whitey strangled Deborah Hussey, twenty-six, who was both Stevie Flemmi's girlfriend and the daughter of his common-law wife, Marion Hussey. Deborah Hussey was buried on top of Barrett and McIntyre. Her family was awarded $350,000, an amount lower than other victims received, because the family dropped its loss-of-consortium claim for a wayward daughter who was a drug-addicted stripper in Boston's Combat Zone. The minor damage award for the last of Whitey's murders withstood a government appeal. Hussey the stripper got a fraction of the money awarded to Castucci the strip club owner.

After the decade of carnage ended in the mid-1980s, Kevin Weeks had a mortician's grasp of the killing fields, participating in the burials of Barrett, McIntyre, and Hussey and learning about others in idle conversation with Whitey, who relished talking about the notches in his belt.

When Weeks was arrested in 1999 and faced murder charges, his graveyard plot plans were the reason he did only short time. He flipped as a government witness and landed in lavender.

Weeks was debriefed by Tom Foley, who supervised two burial site excavations for the state police along the Neponset River. Bulger had told Weeks that both Tommy King and Debbie Davis were buried along the marshy shoreline about two hundred yards from Catherine Greig's townhouse in Quincy. But that was it. No signposts. Even with that, police found King in a matter of days, recovering the ironic bulletproof vest beside a shattered skull.

The Davis exhumation was a different matter. It took state police and forensic experts several weeks to explore hundreds of yards of waterfront. The nagging worry was that the tides had taken the bones out to sea.

After a while, the crowd of the curious on a bluff overlooking the Davis site dwindled to her three grim-faced brothers. The mainstays of the search—Major Foley, Trooper Steve Johnson, and DEA agent Daniel Doherty, who had fought off FBI obstruction for a decade—stayed with it for weeks. They had the backhoe go down two feet and then four. On an October afternoon, they were down to the final day that money and supervisors would allow.

Foley played one of his hunches and had the backhoe work below the high-tide line. On the last scoop of the last day, it came up with a green plastic bag that had a skull in it. The sad, wonderful moment left hardened investigators and the vigilant Davis brothers hugging one another. His cheeks wet, Steve Davis said simply, "Thanks for finding our sister."

Weeks's vague directions to the Neponset shoreline were the only break in the Davis case, one that had been particularly stymied by the FBI. While it was not a tip-off murder, the FBI was unhelpful beyond the usual blank stares that other families endured.

Records indicate collusion between Connolly and Whitey to thwart investigators in the murder's aftermath. After her disappearance, FBI documents corroborated Flemmi's story to Davis's mother, Olga, that he had hired private detectives, who had found Debra taken off to Houston.

After the mother reported the disappearance to Randolph police, it was registered in the National Crime Information System, which is administered by the FBI. Within six months, however, the missing-person report was deleted from the database on the basis she had been seen in Houston. Debbie Davis wasn't missing as far as the FBI was concerned. She was somewhere in Texas.

When Johnny Martorano murdered someone, there was never a long hunt for the bodies. He just shot them and left them in cars.

His cooperation with law enforcement helped solve three murders he committed at Whitey's behest and with FBI collusion. Castucci. Wheeler. Callahan.

And once Martorano decided to roll against Whitey in 1998, he was all in. His debriefing by state police was a twenty-year history of Winter Hill warfare, a litany about bodies up to the rafters, presented without emotion by the hulking man the Mafia feared.

All business. No small talk. Until the end of several days of interrogation, when Foley asked something that had been bubbling up in him for days: "Did it bother you to kill all these people?" he asked. "Just walk away and have dinner?"

Martorano looked a little confused and then looked away. "Of course I think about it," he finally said. "Do I feel remorse? Yeah, I do. Every single day." Then, looking straight at Foley: "But there's nothing I can do about it now."

Between Martorano's confessions and Weeks's road maps, the walls collapsed on former agent John Connolly.

In 2000, Connolly was first charged with tipping off Whitey and Flemmi in 1994 about imminent indictments. Then the accusation was expanded to include him warning Whitey about underworld figures

John Connolly

cooperating with law enforcement, information that resulted in the deaths of Callahan and Castucci.

Connolly took a defiant stance that has never wavered—he was a maligned hero abandoned by his government. After his arraignment, Connolly held an impromptu, fiery press conference outside the federal courthouse. Dressed in a navy blue pin-striped suit, his fist pumping the air, he indignantly proclaimed, "I am innocent of these malicious charges. . . . I would ask all fair-minded people refrain from forming a judgment until you have heard my facts and my evidence." He then refused to answer questions and jumped into a black Lincoln Town Car that sped away.

His "facts and evidence" did him little good in 2002, when he was convicted of racketeering and obstruction of justice for warning Whitey to flee. The good guys and bad guys who always swirled around Connolly were center stage at the trial. Notorious gangsters were on the stand and stymied detectives in the back row. After the guilty verdict, Tom Foley took the high road, saying there was no victory in the case of an agent convicted of corruption. But at the back of the room, there were broad grins and hands clasped among those who had pursued Whitey and been thwarted by Connolly for so long. They talked about accountability but exuded vindication.

The verdict deflated the cocky agent who had held such sway in Boston for two decades. Connolly used the same lyrics but the song was flat. At his later sentencing, the end came in a sudden rush. After being sentenced to the maximum of ten years, he was quickly surrounded by U.S. marshals, who hustled him out of the court as he threw his wife and three sons a good-bye kiss.

And it wasn't over. Six years later, in 2008, federal prosecutor Fred Wyshak stayed with the Connolly prosecution to the end, helping a state prosecutor in Florida assemble evidence and marshal a murder case. Wyshak even had to hide some of the evidence from the FBI, out of fear the bureau would have held it "under review" indefinitely. After Wyshak loaded thousands of pages into a U-Haul trailer and was high-balling it down Interstate 95 toward Miami, the FBI called him to stop the transfer. But Wyshak said too late, and no way. Connolly was con-victed and sentenced to forty years, with twelve to serve. He'd be eighty-four years old, a quarter of his life spent in prison.

The case completed his heavy fall from grace. It settled around Connolly like a demolished building. The testimony from Whitey's former cohorts was devastating. Flemmi said Connolly warned them that Callahan wouldn't stand up, and Martorano gave his monotonic account of the murder. After a seven-week trial, the jury took thirteen hours to sift through several murder counts and settle on second de-gree.

At a sentencing hearing a month later, the judge allowed Connolly to make a statement, which turned out to be a rant against Wyshak and escalated into an extraordinary colloquy. Connolly charged that the prosecutor knew about false testimony, but Wyshak countered by repeatedly asking a question that the agent could never answer truth-fully: Did you know your informers were killing people?

Of all the tragic figures in the Whitey Bulger victim avalanche of the 1980s, three stand out: the Wheelers for financial loss, the Hallorans for missing the deadline by days, and the Donahues for insult to injury.

In most of the Whitey Bulger cases, the "accrual" date was after Flemmi ended his testimony at the Wolf hearing on September 2, 1998, putting the deadline for filing suits two years later, in 2000. Plaintiffs had to know what Stevie said and when he finished saying it.

The Wheelers lost out because Flemmi testified that he was informed that Brian Halloran had been talking to the FBI about what happened to their father, and the family was required to know about it. Roger Wheeler was fifty-five years old when he was killed and making about $10 million a year. Now the businesses were gone and the workers scattered.

After being timed out, the Wheeler family withdrew from the ambush scene. But just as combat veterans struggle with flashbacks long after the fighting has stopped, the family is dismayed by the FBI's cover-up and has expressed strong reservations about some local police and prosecutors. One of the sons, Larry, wrote to the U.S. attorney in Boston to request that Whitey not be tried for the father's murder in Tulsa, to spare the family the hoopla and strain of a trial that would involve law enforcement it distrusts.

The Hallorans filed suit on September 25, 2000, three weeks too late. Brian Halloran was a leg breaker and coke dealer but still a father to two children. He had been shot ten times by Whitey in the chest and legs. The family believed his final words in the ambulance taking him from the scene, when he told police he'd been shot by Winter Hill associate Jimmy Flynn. The misidentification was caused by Whitey disguising himself to look like Flynn, who was an enemy of Halloran. Suffolk County prosecuted Flynn for murder in 1985 and the family still thought he did it even after Flynn was acquitted. They missed agent John Morris's testimony in 1998 that it was done by Whitey and that was that. Notice had been served. A $2.1 million award was overturned by the appeals court.

In 1982, Michael Donahue was a thirty-two-year-old truck driver with three sons and wanted to start his own bakery business. He left the house in late afternoon of the fateful day to do some errands, which included picking up fishing gear for a trip with his sons. He ended his day by stopping for a beer and bumping into Halloran.

An appeals court judge, who sharply dissented from overturning the $6.4 million Donahue award in 2011, said the majority underestimated the impact of the government "strategy of dissimulation," legalese for FBI stonewalling. He also revealed in his decision that when widow Patricia Donahue went to the FBI to get information about Whitey Bulger's involvement, she was not only deflected but sullied. Judge Juan Torruella wrote that the FBI was "not content with mere stonewalling, at one point FBI agents accused her of having an affair which the agents suggested was the cause of the murder." The FBI hitting bottom.

In the end, the full appeals court did a final review and split 3–3 in a controversial tie decision that still overturned the awards. The court gave more weight to a law that ensured the government would be safe from stale cases than it did to the pungent evil of what had happened. Dissenting still, Judge Torruella condemned "an unjust outcome which rewards uncontrolled wickedness."

Tommy Donahue, who grew up in Dorchester, was eight when his father was murdered. He stood on Northern Avenue near the federal courthouse and where the Topside Lounge used to be and talked about what happened. "This is like a black hole for us. It's, you know, nothing good comes out of this part of town for us. And this date is thirty years later, you know, that's a long time to be searching for justice. Now I'm a grown man with children older than what I was. I hate this part of town."

Yet the Donahues eventually got some help from that "part of town." In the fall of 2012, the family lawyers revived their suit in federal court by pursuing a different avenue of liability. The trial judge, William Young, allowed them to get around the original statute of limitations quicksand. They could seek damages from the individual agents such as Connolly and John Morris, an action with a broader, three-year window. Their hope is that the government will indemnify the agents and that, given the evidence, the U.S. Department of Justice will settle to avoid going to trial for a second time.

Paul Griffin represented the Davis family and laughed about how the anonymous plaintiff bar worked in empty courtrooms while the press and public flocked to hear reprobates like Weeks and Martorano testify in criminal cases. He shrugged at the fact of life—nothing sexy about damage suits on twenty-year-old murders.

He's a sixty-three-year-old Vietnam veteran from Dorchester and a former Boston cop who went to law school nights and tells you he's been on the wagon since 1985. He has a crew cut and wears Bermuda shorts to work in the summer.

Griffin said he feels lucky to have escaped the long haul with a viable verdict. What he remembers most about the case was the constant uncertainty about whether all the work would count for anything, that it would crash and burn in appeals court.

"Better cases than ours went down," he said. "You can't overstate how crushing it is for a lawyer to have a good case proven in court and then get timed out. We won but I'm not looking to do another one of these anytime soon.

"It's naïve now but you start out thinking the government would do the right thing on something this bad and documented. Informants killing people. C'mon. But DOJ can't wait to say too late and cheerio."

24

No Stone Left Unturned

After arriving by train in early December 1996, Whitey and Cathy holed up for a few days in a Los Angeles motel and began searching for an apartment. Whitey knew where he wanted to look—in nearby Santa Monica, the city on the Pacific Ocean with its wide sandy beach, piers, and Palisades Park, perched high on a bluff. He was already familiar with Santa Monica from a California trip he'd taken with Teresa Stanley; they'd stayed just south, in Venice Beach.

The area had left an impression. The climate and ocean were things he liked. It was also full of walkers and walking neighborhoods—another plus for him, although an oddity for the Los Angeles area, where cars dominate as self-contained worlds on wheels. The water and warm weather brought Grand Isle to mind, but with key differences. In Grand Isle there was only one way out—the drawbridge—while Santa Monica had countless potential exits if the need arose. Grand Isle was tiny in population while Santa Monica, though only 8.3 square miles, was densely populated with nearly ninety thousand residents, most of whom were renters—nearly 70 percent. In all, Santa Monica was a city with turnover—and not just renters, but people generally on the move, including young people on the rise and older people looking to retire, plus packs of vacationers, and, as Whitey was sure to note, the platoons of homeless shuffling along the beach and in the parks from Santa Monica to Venice Beach. Santa Monica had throngs of people of all ages, shapes, and sizes; Whitey could easily join them as another face in the crowd.

With one eye on apartments Whitey kept another on the homeless. He targeted a street person as his first order of business, determined to add to his hoard of phony IDs. The man, obviously alcoholic, initially wanted nothing to do with Whitey's pitch, saying he did not have a driver's license, but Whitey, ever the charmer, kept after him and came away with the man's Social Security card. Whitey, in turn, combined the number with his own photo and filled out the paperwork to score his first ID in California.

More important, Whitey played with the man's initials—C. W. G. —to invent a new name to replace Tom Baxter, which was compromised, and Mark Shapeton. The new life called for an entirely fresh identity, and Whitey came up with Gasko. He would be Charlie. Cathy would be Carol. Charlie and Carol Gasko. From Chicago.

Next, an apartment—and their timing couldn't have been better. The majority of units at Princess Eugenia Apartments, a building under rent control, were vacant after the expiration of an arrangement with the J. Paul Getty Museum. The Getty had rented apartments for their art scholars while it built a new museum complex in Los Angeles's Brentwood neighborhood. The complex was done, the scholars were gone, and the Gaskos headed over to see the newly available units.

They found the Princess Eugenia unremarkable-looking—shaped like a pillbox, three stories high, with nine or so apartments on each floor. The building's cement exterior was painted a pale lemon with green trim; the only real decorative touches were the cypress trees in front and the black iron balconies. The family that owned it also owned the grander Embassy Hotel, directly across the street, a European-style hotel built in the 1920s with a lush courtyard, a spacious lobby featuring tiled floors and dark wood trim, and suites with kitchenettes.

But Whitey was not looking for anything fancy or expensive—nothing that would call attention to him and Cathy. In that regard what might be uninviting about the Princess Eugenia to others was inviting to him—the tiny, walk-through lobby; the single, slow elevator; the long, sterile hallways; the heavy apartment doors. Neither the lobby nor the landing on each floor had an area where residents could sit and mingle, nothing like the open, elegant lobby across the street at the Embassy. The doors to the apartments, spaced along windowless corridors extending in two directions from the elevator, were like entries into private strongholds.

Little about the place was warm or welcoming—it had an overall bland feel that had to be to Whitey's liking. The apartments were rented furnished, with maid service and linens, cable and utilities. They were in clean, good shape, too; the Getty had fixed them up and hung framed prints of paintings by the European masters. With this opportunity, Whitey didn't hesitate or waste any time looking around elsewhere. Charlie and Carol Gasko, traveling light, moved in that December, paying $1,400 a month, a figure covering rent and the amenities. No lease was required.

Theirs was Unit 303 on the third floor—located to the immediate left of the elevator, meaning the elevator, rather than a person, was the abutter. It was a two-bedroom corner unit facing the front of the building onto Third Street. Inside the apartment to the left, a small hallway ran down the back, off of which were the master and guest bedrooms. Straight ahead, swinging saloon doors led to a wet bar and then into the kitchen, which was in the middle, or heart of the apartment. To the right was the living/dining area, with a Degas print and a Monet "lily pad" print that the Getty tenants left behind. (Fifteen years later the prints were still there.) Two sliding glass doors in the living room led onto a small balcony with iron railings. Partially shaded by fingers of the cypress trees, the balcony had a clear view to watch for any activity down below on Third Street and at the intersection of Washington Street.

The tree-lined neighborhood was called WilMont after the two streets marking its north-south boundary lines, Wilshire Boulevard and Montana Avenue, and it was known in the jargon of city planners as a "multifamily" area for the eclectic range of residences, from the apartment hotels built in the 1920s to the rent-controlled buildings, the bungalows, luxury homes, and newly constructed condominiums. A few doors north of the Princess Eugenia was a hospice, while a few doors to the south was a long-term residential home for the mentally ill.

Whitey and Cathy lucked out in so many ways, moving to where the living was easy, onto one of the widest streets in the area, one that, without streetlights, was also one of the quietest and darkest at night. Several blocks to the south they found the Third Street Promenade, an outdoor pedestrian mall with just about everything, from a movie theater to bookstores, from high-end chain stores to local independent retailers in clothes, crafts, and jewelry. Over the years the business trend favored national chains over local businesses—to the dismay of many longtime residents—but one of the oldest organic farmers' markets in the country continued to flourish.

Better still, two blocks away was the Pacific Ocean. It was not just any stretch of the Pacific, either, but Palisades Park atop a bluff with a spectacular view. The grassy park, with stone paths and benches set beneath towering palm trees, drew walkers of all ages, mothers jogging with baby strollers, Rollerbladers, and the homeless, all sharing the cooling breeze coming off the water. To the south were views of the Santa Monica Pier, with its iconic gateway arch and Ferris wheel ablaze at night in streams of colorful lights. Up and down Ocean Avenue along the park stood luxury homes and condos costing millions, but Whitey and Cathy had it all for the price of a rent-controlled apartment a short walk away. The beach and ocean even had an echo of Southie to it—Castle Island, mainly, where Whitey had habitually walked along the water. But Santa Monica was upscale in the extreme, an exotic version of Southie, with sunsets that tourists travel from afar to photograph. Here Whitey and Cathy began a new routine of walking in the morning and early evening around the neighborhood, to the park or the promenade or both.

During the early weeks while on their outings Whitey was on the prowl for a second target for another ID. This time he wanted to find someone who looked like him, around whom he could construct a convincing California persona, and one day he spotted a reasonably well-dressed homeless alcoholic who bore an uncanny resemblance. Same ruddy complexion and white beard, same baldness on top, and same Irish ancestry—"U.S. Army Irish" was tattooed on the man's right arm. The face was a little rounder, his eyes were hazel, and he was four inches shorter, but they were all discrepancies that Whitey could live with and resolve in good time. Whitey opened with a soft sell, not wanting to scare off the new quarry as he'd almost done with his prior target. He offered a simple greeting when he ran into the man in the park, and only after encountering each other a few times did he follow up with the actual small talk. Whitey learned the man's name—James William Lawlor—and that he was from the Lower East Side of Manhattan. Lawlor said he was an Army veteran, and Whitey told Lawlor he'd been in the service as well.

Once he established a rapport, Whitey steered into the heart of the matter. He told Lawlor he was in a bit of a fix—he was from Canada and was now in the United States illegally because his visa had expired. He wanted to stay on, and he wondered if Lawlor would do him a favor. Would Lawlor sell him his ID—his driver's license, if he had one? Lawlor had one, he said, and Whitey offered to pay a thousand dollars for it.

Lawlor took the money and Whitey took Lawlor's driver's license. The one hitch came when Whitey realized the license was about to expire, so he got Lawlor sobered up and in shape to obtain a license renewal. Whitey paid Lawlor three hundred dollars for the renewal, along with unsolicited advice that he should quit drinking. Whitey took a liking to Lawlor and was feeling generous—he added a bonus of $2,500 for the identity transaction. But Whitey rarely gave unless he got something in return, and in Lawlor he got back plenty—an authentic California identity from a look-alike. It meant he didn't have to monkey with forging documents and grafting his photograph to someone else's ID card. Whitey could easily pass for James Lawlor—the ideal situation for a fugitive from justice—and he began posing as Lawlor to meet particular needs, such as to buy the prescription medication atenolol for his high blood pressure, which had become chronic.

It didn't take Whitey long to realize he'd chosen well in picking California as the place for Cathy and him to hide. It was a land of reinvention, Hollywood, and made-up stories. It was home to the celebrity criminal—the Menendez brothers of Beverly Hills, for example, who were convicted in the shotgun murders in 1989 of their parents but once in prison attracted women who wanted to marry them. In 1994 it was O. J. Simpson; in 2001 actor Robert Blake; in 2003 Phil Spector.

The Princess Eugenia revealed itself as a good fit, too. The Gaskos met the widow who lived in Unit 103 near the elevator on the first floor, the Argentina-born Catalina Schlank, who was always friendly but not nosy. They met a neighbor, Barbara Gluck, who moved into an apartment down the hall on the third floor about the same time they did, although they didn't take to her much. But most important, the tenant interaction was the stuff of small talk—the hellos, hiyas, and how-are-yous—while passing in the hall or lobby. Nothing more. Other buildings might have a sense of community, developed at periodic meetings or social gatherings at Christmas or another time of year. Not the Princess Eugenia. Residents at the Eugenia had one basic concern—that other tenants pose no trouble to the status quo. The present, not the past, was what mattered. Said one longtime resident, "You know, it's not a community, it's a building," and it was into this dynamic that Charlie and Carol Gasko, the quiet couple in 303, slipped easily and effortlessly.

Back in Boston the FBI had not done itself any favors in 1995 when the manhunt for Whitey Bulger was assigned to the same Organized Crime Squad that had been the toxic center of corruption for so many years. Even if the roster of FBI agents had partially changed, the culture of mistrust had not, and no amount of public relations could overcome the skepticism of others in Massachusetts law enforcement.

The mistrust was deeply rooted. This was the Boston FBI whose swashbuckling Paul Rico had protected fugitive gangster Stevie Flemmi in the 1960s; the FBI whose John Connolly had taken over from Rico and protected Whitey's associates Joe McDonald, Jimmy Sims, and Johnny Martorano while they were on the lam during the 1970s and 1980s. This was the FBI that in early 1995 told state police it had Whitey "in pocket" when his indictment was ready, only to see Whitey get away. This was the FBI that saw more than a year go by in the manhunt before getting Teresa Stanley's inside secrets about Whitey the fugitive.

It was only after the bombshell in June 1997 during federal court hearings before Judge Mark Wolf—when the FBI was forced for the first time to confirm that Whitey and Stevie Flemmi were longtime informants—that FBI officials shifted the manhunt away from the dirtied Organized Crime Squad. The disclosure had meant that the mistrust of the FBI, a distrust mostly confined to the insular world of police agencies, exploded suddenly before the general public—a public left scratching its collective head in horror and disbelief, questioning how the agency that for years had coddled and protected a crime boss was the same agency leading the manhunt. The Boston FBI certainly had plenty to hide, and the capture of Whitey carried the strong possibility of a new round of devastating disclosures about sullied FBI agents. But FBI supervisors began working overtime proclaiming their determination to catch Whitey, and in 1997 officials announced the search was being taken over by a new squad trained in tracking fugitives.

Creation of a Bulger Task Force seemed like progress. But it also seemed a concession that effort to that point had been lacking—something less than a full-court press during the start of a fugitive's run, when, as was the case in any manhunt, the trail was hottest and prospects for capture most promising. It also wasn't until 1997 that the FBI offered a reward—$250,000—for Whitey, further highlighting the idea the FBI was unenthusiastic at the start. Then, that September, after the FBI announcements about investigatory upgrades and the bureau's complete commitment to finding Whitey, one Boston journalist revealed an embarrassing oversight. "The FBI has proclaimed its intent to use the World Wide Web to hunt Bulger down," began reporter David Boeri on WCVB-TV. "But today we learned that neither Whitey's face nor his name appears on the FBI website."

Boeri, one of a number of Boston reporters covering the expanding FBI scandal, began to distinguish himself by staking out a particular angle that went to the heart of journalism—challenging power and testing the official story line. The approach evolved over time but was akin to establishing a beat—in the way a newspaper assigns staff to cover city hall, the courts, or education. Boeri's beat was shadowing the FBI's effort to capture Whitey Bulger and to assess it journalistically.

His news stories about the possible sighting of Whitey and Cathy in early 2000—in Southern California, of all places—became emblematic of this brand of journalism, where he exposed a disconnect between the FBI's rhetoric about an international dragnet for Whitey and the reality on the ground. The cable television show *America's Most Wanted* had aired a piece in late January 2000 on Whitey (the third of an eventual fifteen episodes on him). The show afterward heard from a woman reporting she'd seen Catherine Greig at a hair salon called Kim's Nail Place in Fountain Valley, California—located in Orange County, about an hour south of Santa Monica. The woman was a customer at the salon and she said that Greig walked in to get her hair dyed while an older man sat waiting in a car.

The television show referred the tip to the FBI office in Los Angeles, which sent an agent to Fountain Valley, and by early April the FBI office in Los Angeles issued a statement alerting the public that Whitey Bulger "may currently be located in Orange County." It said the television show "resulted in sightings of Bulger and his companion," and that "a positive sighting of Greig was made" in the hair salon. By the end of the day, however, the Boston FBI office issued its own statement—downgrading the salon sighting to "a possible sighting" and saying there "was no confirmed sighting of Bulger" in Fountain Valley. The Boston FBI office gave no reason for backpedaling from its colleagues' findings in Los Angeles—and the public was left to wonder why the two FBI field offices were not in synch.

Then Boeri went to work. He flew to California, taking along his "Whitey bag," a collection of mug shots and photos of Whitey. He drove to the hair salon and interviewed the owner. He discovered that no one from the Bulger Task Force in Boston had been there, and while the lone FBI agent from Los Angeles had interviewed the salon owner, the agent never talked to the customer who had actually called in the tip about seeing Cathy in the salon and Whitey in the car. Boeri looked outside the salon; he saw a florist shop and a gas station across the street with a pay phone. He took out his Whitey photos and began asking merchants if they'd ever seen Whitey—and, just as important, he asked if they had ever talked to anyone from the FBI. He learned the FBI had never canvassed the area.

Boeri, while in California, kept going. He drove south with his cameraman to nearby Tijuana to show on film the ease with which he could cross the border, buy the drug atenolol that Whitey needed for his heart condition, and return to the States. Boeri interviewed immigration and border officials. He discovered they knew little to nothing about Whitey Bulger, and he saw that while fliers hung on the walls for other fugitives, Whitey's wanted poster was not there. The border officials exuded confidence that if alerted to look out for Whitey they'd capture him if ever he tried to cross to the border into Mexico to buy his heart medication.

Returning to Boston, Boeri caught FBI officials back on their heels with his findings. In interviews, the Boston officials resorted to "no comment" about a pending manhunt investigation while insisting that every FBI agent everywhere was on alert for Whitey. They also insisted the bureau had notified border officials and inundated them with Whitey fliers—and then they even tried to pass the buck. They told Boeri the FBI could not be faulted if border officials ignored the notices, failed to post them, and, in effect, had their heads in the sand regarding Whitey.

Not to be undone, Boeri went back to the border officials, who repeated that they'd never received anything from the FBI about being on high alert for Whitey Bulger. In the end, the Boston FBI's performance was flat and unconvincing. The public did not know what to make of an agency that at press conferences made it sound as if the Bulger Task Force were an army of FBI agents working around the clock to capture Whitey, when such reporters as David Boeri kept revealing otherwise and were reporting that, in truth, the task force usually consisted of a single FBI agent, who was assisted by investigators on loan from the Boston Police Department, state corrections department, and the Massachusetts State Police.

Making matters worse, around the time of Boeri's reports, word surfaced that FBI agents had begun a leak investigation to learn who in law enforcement was talking to Boeri and other reporters. "The agents even have a formal name: The Media Leak Task Force," columnist Brian McGrory wrote in the *Boston Globe* on October 17, 2000. "The bet here is that the FBI has more agents assigned to plug the leaks than to find Bulger." McGrory voiced the skepticism rampant about the FBI. "At best, the investigation represents a tin ear to the call for penance needed from the federal agency that so thoroughly and unequivocally betrayed this city. At worst, it's part of a sinister cover-up of so much that went wrong for so long."

The FBI was not about to let McGrory's words go unchallenged. Charles S. Prouty, the top agent in Boston who'd appeared in Boeri's reports, wrote a letter protesting the *Globe* column. While acknowledging "the public's trust was breached" in the Whitey Bulger scandal,

Prouty said McGrory's claim that the FBI was not trying to catch the crime boss was "absolutely untrue" and "does a disservice to the many employees who have dedicated themselves to this effort." Prouty then reiterated the FBI talking point that all hands were on deck, with "literally hundreds of agents" involved in the search. "Each of the 56 FBI field offices across the United States and many of our offices in foreign countries has committed resources."

The official FBI position: "No stone is left unturned."

The question—Where's Whitey?—was fast becoming a Boston cultural phenomenon—at once deadly serious but nonetheless tantalizing to the city's imagination as a dark, bogeyman version of "Where's Waldo?"

It was discussed at the office watercooler and across the radio dial. Popular morning disc jockey Matt Siegel on "Kiss" WXKS-FM wondered on-air about Whitey's whereabouts, as did John Dennis and Gerry Callahan on the sports show *Dennis and Callahan Morning Show* on WEEI-AM. The comedian Steve Sweeney one day interrupted his interview on WZLX-AM with Mike O'Connell of the Boston Bruins hockey team to ask the club's general manager, "Where's Whitey?"

The line had achieved that rare status of instant recognition, joining some of the city's all-time favorite phrases, such as "Curse of the Bambino," "City on a Hill," and "Havlicek Stole the Ball." "I've been around here 31 years, and 'Where's Whitey?' is now bigger than 'Curse of the Bambino,'" Upton Bell, host of a business talk show on WMEX-AM, told the *Boston Globe* for an article in the newspaper's feature section about all the Whitey talk, headlined GANGSTA RAP. "You say Whitey anytime, anywhere, and people know. You go to cocktail parties. Fancy balls. You go to bars. You go to sporting events. You go to political conventions. And all you have to do is say 'Whitey' and people know exactly who and what you're talking about."

The FBI announced in November 1999 that it was adding Whitey to its list of Ten Most Wanted. Left unmentioned was the dubious distinction that Whitey Bulger was the first FBI informant to end up on the vaunted top-ten lineup. The next November the FBI increased the reward to one million dollars, making Whitey only the seventh fugitive in the history of the FBI's list to hit the million-dollar mark. The uptick followed the unsealing of a superseding federal racketeering indictment against Whitey, charging him with nineteen murders. By now Boston reporters covering the scandal were getting calls directly about possible Whitey Bulger sightings—with many saying they'd called because they didn't trust the FBI with the tip. Just about every reporter soon had a tale about running off to Aruba, Florida, or elsewhere to follow a lead, only to discover a Whitey Bulger look-alike.

To rebut continuing news reports questioning the FBI's efforts and revealing the infighting between the FBI and other police agencies, federal officials also announced a detente at the end of 2000. The top Boston agent, Prouty, said the task force was merging with a parallel manhunt that state police had been carrying out and that the hatchet of mistrust was buried. But within months more reports surfaced revealing the truce was a public relations stunt that had never taken hold, and the bitter rivalry and "interagency feud" persisted. Top officials tried again in June 2001 to sell the idea that the era of grudges had been replaced by a united investigatory front, but once again stories revealed a contrary reality among rank-and-file investigators.

In addition, a call for the FBI to get out of the pursuit altogether was gaining traction, where the FBI would step aside and turn over the manhunt to the federal agency that had shot to the forefront in terms of skill and expertise tracking fugitives—the U.S. Marshals Service. Federal marshals, previously best known for providing courthouse security and transporting prisoners, had reinvented themselves so that "federal marshal" was now synonymous with "fugitive hunter."

"Why doesn't the FBI turn the fugitive case over to the U.S. Marshals Service, an objective agency with an outstanding reputation that specializes in the capture of fugitives?" asked Sergeant Mike Huff of the Tulsa Police Department, speaking for many in law enforcement. But the image-conscious FBI wasn't about to agree to relinquish its control. The FBI had a public relations nightmare in Whitey Bulger—as past informant and as present fugitive—and if the bureau was ever to move out from under the cloud of the worst informant scandal in FBI history, it had to be standing center stage when, and if, Whitey was captured. The only interagency talks the FBI was willing to entertain were ones by which the FBI stayed in control.

These were the themes characterizing law enforcement—mistrust, dysfunction, and failure—as the years passed and, as was done in the movies, calendar pages flipped fast from one day to the next with little to show for it. The years of "Where's Whitey?" became marked by two official status reports—at the start of the year and on Whitey's birthday in early September. The pattern was repeated year in and year out, with FBI and federal officials reiterating their pledge to catch Whitey and recapping all that was being done to accomplish that. The events were framed to reassure the public as "progress reports" but, as reporter Boeri once noted, they were actually "failure reports." Whitey remained free.

During the annual press update in January 2002, for example, officials said the 9/11 terrorist attacks had meant a reduction in manpower, but that the Bulger Task Force was once again operating on all cylinders.

"They've followed up on hundreds, if not thousands of leads," U.S. Attorney Michael J. Sullivan told reporters. "It remains a high-priority search even in light of and in spite of September 11."

The task force had investigated a reported sighting in Barcelona, Spain, where agents found a priest who resembled Whitey. They'd gotten a tip that Whitey was drinking in a bar in Weymouth, and agents had hustled to the town south of Boston only to find just another look-alike. Though investigators thought Bulger was alive they nonetheless used cadaver-sniffing dogs and ground-penetrating radar at Scusset Beach State Reservation on Cape Cod after a tipster had said Whitey and Cathy were buried on the beach.

Then came the announcement in early 2002 that had far-reaching consequences for the Bulger Task Force—and Whitey Bulger's level of comfort. The FBI in Boston disclosed the "most reliable sighting" in three years—in London, England, where a tipster had reported he'd seen Whitey in September near Piccadilly Circus. The Bulger Task Force mobilized a media blitz in London, Paris, and Bern, as the FBI announced the manhunt was entering a "new phase" with a focus that was decidedly international (and, as truth would have it, far away from where Whitey actually was). In time the tipster's credibility proved highly questionable, but that didn't change the FBI's public stance for the next several years that Whitey Bulger was in hiding overseas.

The bureau in 2003 announced it had a "positive sighting" of Whitey in Manchester, England, and in 2005 agents on the task force flew off to Uruguay to follow up a possible sighting there. "Personally, I think he is in Europe," FBI agent Kevin Kline said during a Boston radio interview in 2006. Boston FBI agent Richard Teahan, the newest supervisor of the Bulger Task Force, told reporters two years later, "We're going to continue our focus on Europe."

Even Kevin Weeks joined the conversation. The defrocked confidant might have lost access to Whitey, but that didn't stop him from offering a hunch. Weeks agreed with the FBI: Whitey Bulger was probably somewhere in Europe.

"I think he got trapped over there after 9/11 and couldn't get back," he said.

Charlie and Carol

The Gaskos' corner apartment

Kevin Weeks's comment must have been music to Whitey's ears, as he and Cathy were hunkered down for the long haul in Unit 303 of the Princess Eugenia. The twenty-first century opened with the FBI unable to decide what to make of a sighting at a hair salon only a short distance from Santa Monica. Two short years later the FBI, seemingly getting its act together, was in full agreement Whitey was hiding in Europe. What an arc for the manhunt—from too close for comfort to the other side of the globe. News about a European sighting had to be reassuring—hard to top unless the FBI announced it was switching its focus to the moon.

So they played house as Charlie and Carol Gasko. In time they dropped the maid and linen services and the rent was lowered to the even more affordable $863 a month, a figure the rent control board increased slowly over the years, to $1,165 in 2011. Whitey took to customizing the gray-carpeted unit. In the living room he and Cathy hung heavy, floor-length synthetic black drapes that deadened the bright

California sun. The top of a desk, the top of a dining room table, and the fireplace brick were painted a flat black color—also light-deadening. Whitey mostly stayed up late into the night, reading and watching television in the living room from a futon, and napped during the days. He therefore liked to keep the apartment dark.

In his bedroom, he used duct tape to cover the windows facing the building next door with sheets of reflective Mylar. The infrequent times an outsider—the manager, or a neighbor—got a glimpse inside the apartment the Gaskos would explain the darkness by saying either that Charlie's eyes were sensitive to the light or that he had a hard time sleeping at night. But this and other alterations could also be taken as security measures. The Mylar covering, for example, not only blocked out light; it could theoretically block a camera or other surveillance technology trained on the window. Then he purchased a punching dummy—workout equipment a fitness buff like Whitey hit to maintain muscle tone. But Whitey placed the full-torso mannequin in the living room near the front, and it gave the appearance of a man standing at the window. Someone on the street glancing up saw what looked like a person, and a passerby's natural response would be to look away. The punching dummy, in this way, guarded against anyone lingering and peering up at the balcony of Unit 303. Whitey also bought binoculars and not infrequently was spotted at the window with them. It was unlikely Whitey Bulger was bird-watching; more likely he was manning a lookout tower, the same kind of thing he did when he shared the condo in Quincy with Cathy, using binoculars and looking out over the marsh where Tommy King was buried in the Bulger burial ground.

The countersurveillance touches were not the only changes. Whitey set up the bank of Bulger. He sawed through the half-inch wallboard to create rectangular-shaped holes in the walls—four of assorted sizes were behind the two mirrors that hung on the wall in the wet bar, another large one was behind a print hanging in the living room, and one was in the master bathroom. Whitey had done this kind of thing before, created so-called hides; in Teresa Stanley's house on Silver Street in South Boston he hid a safe in the wall to store gold coins, uncut diamonds, and letters he'd written home as an inmate in Alcatraz. In the Unit 303 hides Whitey stashed hundreds of thousands of dollars in neat bricks of hundred-dollar bills. Ever tidy, he covered the rims of each hole with strips of duct tape to prevent gypsum from flaking off onto the carpet every time he went to make a withdrawal of cash.

Whitey also used the hides to store a growing arsenal of weaponry—the more than thirty guns, knives, and even a fake pineapple hand grenade he acquired while living in retirement. The guns ran the gamut—a .38-caliber Smith & Wesson revolver; a .45-caliber Colt Combat Commander pistol; a .223-caliber Colt Lightweight rifle; and two Mossberg twelve-gauge shotguns with pistol grips. There was also the two-shot, ivory-handled High Standard Derringer made in 1947, small enough to conceal in the palm of a hand, which Whitey likely had had for years. Most of the weapons were secreted in the walls, but he kept several in his bedroom within reach—one pistol on the shelf near his bed, three other guns behind rows of books on a bookshelf, and another Derringer inside a book he'd hollowed out.

Beyond creating a darkened after-hours effect, Whitey and Cathy filled the apartment with knickknacks in a kind of cutesy, retro cats-and-dogs decorating motif—a cat/dog kitchen wall calendar; the kitty clock on another wall; the cat/dog refrigerator magnets, including one showing a photograph of a tiny white poodle getting a haircut with the punch line: "Primping is such a pain, but it beats growing old gracefully." No pictures or photographs of themselves, family, or friends were hung anywhere in the apartment—all off-limits. Photos only of cats and dogs.

They filled storage closets with paper products, soaps, hand creams, and cleansers, preferring to buy in bulk. Food shopping involved the weekly farmers' market, Trader Joe's, and, later, Whole Foods, where a nutrition-conscious Cathy eyed fresh foods healthful for the elderly couple—low in cholesterol and high in fiber. The kitchen was stocked with such cereals as Crispix and pomegranate juice. They drank water from a pitcher with a water filter they kept on the counter, and at one point updated their galley kitchen with the cash purchase of a new stove, refrigerator, and dishwasher, and they later bought new mattress sets.

They had separate bedrooms. In contrast to Whitey's Mylar, Cathy hung light, sheer curtains in her window, placed tiny figurines around, and filled her closet with a wardrobe of modestly stylish clothes. She stored her lipstick and hair care products in her bathroom vanity. The room was simple and clean. In his bathroom Whitey kept a blue-striped terry-cloth bathrobe on a hook, and to make it easier to open his bedroom door he wrapped a sock around the knob and tied it into place. He nailed a bulky wooden crucifix over the door and also hung a print of an unfurled U.S. flag—with the words "God Bless America" streaming across.

Whitey cluttered his room with bookcases and created a library, beginning with the war histories that were always of interest to him—about the two world wars, the Korean War, and Vietnam—to which he added titles aimed at readers interested in a fugitive life, such as *Secrets of a Back Alley ID Man: Fake ID Construction Techniques of the Underground, The Worst Case Scenario Survival Handbook,* and *How to Find Missing Persons.* He saved issues of *Soldier of Fortune* magazine and eventually set aside a section for gangster lit, including the works of such former underlings as Kevin Weeks and Pat Nee—tell-all books cashing in on the years they associated with the legend of South Boston and most-wanted fugitive in America.

Whitey at one point even put pen to paper himself after watching CBS' *60 Minutes* exclusive interview with his former hit man Johnny Martorano. It was broadcast on January 6, 2008—well after the world knew Whitey was an FBI informant and well after Martorano's controversial plea bargain to testify for the government. Whitey listened as Martorano, sipping wine at dinner with correspondent Steve Kroft, referred to him as the FBI's "rat for thirty years." The natural-born killer—on national television—had this to say about Whitey Bulger as longtime FBI informant: "If I could have killed him, I'd have killed him."

Whitey, angered and inspired, went to work. "I've been driven to this by the lies of JM, and seeing his insane interview on 60 Minutes was the last straw," he wrote on the second of about one hundred single-spaced pages he produced before putting them aside. If the past provided any clue, Whitey feverishly scripted "the true story as seen through my eyes"—the words he'd used in closing his missive to Rev. Robert Drinan from the prison psych ward in 1956, the ("I am no angel, but . . .") letter where he sounded like a choirboy appalled by cell mates whose crudity interfered with his plans for self-improvement and religious study.

Indeed, one investigator, after later reading Whitey's manuscript, used profanity to describe the autobiography—"a bunch of self-serving bullshit."

Paper products and weapons were not the only items the couple stockpiled. Whitey and Cathy continued to round up IDs. They came across a woman on Venice Beach one day, struggling with a suitcase that had a broken wheel, a woman who was delusional and mentally ill. Whitey offered to buy her a new suitcase. They took her to a store along Venice Beach and bought a medium-sized suitcase on wheels for forty dollars from a Korean shopkeeper. During the encounter, they employed the supposed Canada predicament, though cast this time from Cathy's perspective—that she was from Canada and illegally in the United States, and so on. When they were done, and for two hundred dollars in cash, Cathy obtained the woman's Social Security card and birth certificate. Then there was a homeless woman who often slept in Palisades Park, an alcoholic who could certainly use the money Whitey offered, and when that deal was consummated Cathy had another Social Security number, a California driver's license number, and other personal information. In addition to making photo IDs with the aliases, Whitey ordered business cards for Cathy using the new names.

Whitey picked up a couple of new IDs as well. He bought a Social Security card from an alcoholic originally from Arizona, and another time struck up a conversation with a drug addict who happened past him and Cathy seated on a bench in Palisades Park. Whitey made small talk and learned the man was from Nevada and was carrying a valid driver's license. Whitey asked if the man had any drunk driving charges or any points against his license, and the man insisted his record was clean. Whitey cut to the chase: he offered two hundred dollars for the license. The man said he also had a Social Security card and Sam's Club membership card. Whitey offered another fifty dollars for them, and the man agreed. Whitey exchanged two hundred-dollar bills and a fifty for the three forms of ID, which he slipped into his pants pocket. The man, flush with cash, walked away saying he was going to go get a drink.

Whitey and Cathy also concocted another pair of names out of whole cloth—John and Mary—to use with a dentist in nearby Marina del Rey that Whitey began seeing through the years. The dentist was quick to note Whitey was a "high fear patient" and "hated needles"—traits Whitey was the first to admit. On one office form he described himself as the "dental chicken, from Chicago." Joking aside, Whitey hated dentists, and he needed Cathy with him during procedures, not just for comfort but also to act as a buffer on the occasions when his anxiety erupted into mistreating the staff. He fully recognized his vulnerability and actually worried that his weakened state mixed with his temper might actually put them at a risk and someday result in their arrest. It was one of Cathy's most crucial roles, keeping the true Whitey under seal during the dreaded trips to the dentist or doctor.

But Whitey's best alias remained James W. Lawlor. Whitey used the Lawlor ID for his doctor visits, and Cathy posed as Mrs. Carol Lawlor when she went to CVS or Vons pharmacy to pick up his prescribed medications. He opened a bank account using Lawlor's name at a nearby Bank of America branch office, and he was James Lawlor to use a car registered in Lawlor's name—a car Whitey bought and paid to keep insured and on the road. To repair the few physical discrepancies, Whitey submitted changes when Lawlor's license renewal came up, so that by 2003 California Department of Motor Vehicle records had Lawlor suddenly growing four inches, dropping in weight to 170 pounds, and having blue, rather than hazel, eyes—features that exactly matched Whitey's height, weight, and eye color.

To keep close track of the real Lawlor, Whitey found him a cheap one-room apartment four miles away at the West End Hotel in Los Angeles. Whitey paid the rent on room 29 for nearly a decade, dropping by to give Lawlor money and also encourage him to sober up. In the summer of 2007, after not hearing from his body double in a while, Whitey had Cathy call the hotel. She learned Lawlor was dead. Workers had found him in his room on August 8—heart failure. The last anyone saw of him was when he paid the rent on August 3. Whitey was shaken, but saw no reason to stop using the hands-down best look-alike alias he'd ever come across.

Most mornings Whitey Bulger and Cathy Greig began their day early with a walk. Cathy invariably wore white slacks and a white top, and Whitey wore light pants or jeans, a long-sleeved white T-shirt, and sneakers, preferably New Balance, a Boston-based brand. He always wore a beige, round-rimmed hat that many took for a golf or fisherman's cap.

He kept the brim pulled down over his bald head so that it practically touched the top of his large-rimmed glasses, shadowing his white-bearded face.

This was what life had come to—an ordinary life where he was a nobody. He'd managed to switch masks yet again—trading in a life-time of crime and killing for a new life as retiree. Others in his shoes—but without his makeup—might grow restless at the loss of an underworld empire. They might miss the actual exercise of power, the action of the rackets and the thrill, even, of a kill. They might become clinically depressed and, unable to cope with anonymity, require a fix of the old life that meant doing something foolish and resulted in their capture. But Whitey was different; he drew on his extreme self-discipline for survival. His life's work was certainly centered on money—the ill-gotten fortune from an underworld economy—and he'd been hugely successful. But Whitey's self-esteem always seemed based less on raw displays of money and power than on the satisfaction of being free and clear of his pursuers—of never getting caught. His genius was the ability to play out the moves, adapt to situations, and adopt various masks, from killer to the do-good bad guy to, most notably, FBI informant—and turn the situation to his advantage so that he was in control. That was more the source of his swagger—Whitey Bulger as chess master—than any pile of cold cash or ostentatious show of material wealth. The circumstances of his life might change, but the game did not, and Santa Monica was an extension of the game he'd played in Boston—and had won, by virtue of controlling John Connolly and the Boston FBI. He arrived in Santa Monica at age sixty-seven, shed one skin to become Charlie Gasko, and saw the years tick by—all the while hiding in plain sight. His raison d'être: Catch me if you can.

"We were looking for a gangster and that was part of the problem—he wasn't a gangster anymore," Boston police detective Charles "Chip" Fleming, a member of the Bulger Task Force, said years later about the failure to find him.

But Whitey was still only human, and there were times when building acquaintances did glimpse something that was not quite in character with friendly Charlie Gasko. The woman down the hall, Barbara Gluck, thought her neighbor was mean. Barbara and Cathy were exchanging pleasantries once and Whitey ordered Cathy back into the apartment. "Stop talking already, let's go!" Gluck said, imitating Whitey. Gluck decided Whitey had "a rage issue." One of the building's managers wondered about Whitey's behavior because of the way Cathy sometimes acted when she came to the office to pay the rent. "If it took too long, it was like she got really nervous, she had to go back to the apartment," Birgitta Farinelli said. While Farinelli never saw Whitey yell at Cathy, she got the sense as years passed that he was "possessive" and "a little bit controlling." Then there was the time Whitey let the Princess Eugenia's maintenance supervisor—Guatemalan-born Enrique Sanchez—know he carried a knife and that in the past he'd had a violent streak. "He said, 'I used to like weapons and I used to fight,' " Sanchez said. But Sanchez brushed aside the comment. "I just thought that was because he was in the military," he said.

Whitey was better known for his gifts and small tokens. He liked to give away tiny flashlights to other tenants and workers at the hotel, saying they were needed for safety because Third Street was so dark without streetlights. He gave an air purifier to one tenant with lung disease, a can of Mace to another, tools to the maintenance supervisor Sanchez, and other gifts to the staff at holidays. Cathy too was known for her generosity, particularly with Catalina Schlank, the longtime tenant on the first floor in unit 101. On her way out in the mornings, Cathy often picked up Schlank's copy of the daily *Los Angeles Times*, wrapped in plastic, and hung it on her doorknob so that Schlank would not have to leave her apartment. The two women exchanged small gifts and thank-you notes over the years.

"Dear Catalina," Cathy began one such note, "What a surprise! Love the pocketbook. It's lightweight, has a shoulder strap and best of all many pockets. It is great! One thing you are wrong about dear neighbor—it is I who could never thank you enough for all your good deeds. Have a good day, thank you, Carol."

With just the right touch, the couple ingratiated themselves with neighbors. "Not too friendly, but friendly enough," one of the owners of the Princess Eugenia later observed, "a way to get to know those around them superficially, get others to like them, trust them, and not suspect them." Whitey and Cathy were the quintessential retirees who stuck close to home, who spoke with a heavy accent that to some sounded like Boston but which they insisted was Chicago.

They were almost always seen together, but Cathy managed some time alone when she went out to pay their bills, shop, or get her hair done. She walked to the Third Street Promenade or to the supermarket on Montana Avenue pulling her tiny wheeled cart, her purse stocked with money from the kitchen drawer where Whitey left neat rows of bills—hundreds, twenties, tens, and fives. But even during her outings it was as if Whitey still hovered; he always seemed on her mind. "She was very worried about his health," said Cathy's hairdresser. Even when no one asked, Cathy felt a need to explain why she was out alone and Whitey was not with her, and to do that she concocted more lies—that he had a problem with his prostate, or was suffering from Alzheimer's or a bout of bronchitis, or needed to stay inside because he'd smoked heavily as a young man and had emphysema.

Cathy was in her fifties now—done with plastic surgeries or cosmetic makeovers, but always appearing fit, neatly dressed, and well groomed. She stopped coloring her hair, let it gray, and kept it short on the side and a shag in back. "Lovely-looking, but simple," neighbor Barbara Gluck said, assessing the Carol Gasko look. Suggestions about where to shop and or get her hair done were the kinds of things Cathy chatted about with building manager Birgitta Farinelli, and around 2004 Cathy became a regular client at the Haircutters on Wilshire Boulevard.

The salon became a retreat, where Cathy went at least monthly and where, over time, she and her stylist engaged in the typical hairdresser-client banter about exercise, living right—and the men in their lives. "We would talk about health. We talked about she loved animals. We talked about her husband in poor health," said hairdresser Wendy Farnetti. Most of the time Cathy seemed to direct the conversation, asking questions and enjoying hearing about the younger Wendy's world while saying little about her own. But one exchange turned out differently.

Cathy was seated in the chair and brought up the well-worn subject of Wendy's ex-boyfriend in Texas. The hairdresser, at wit's end about her love life, said she'd concluded she had the all-time worst taste in men. "I am a bum magnet," she joked. "If there's a bum in the room, I'll attract them by magnetic force."

Cathy laughed. And then she began thinking, and what she said next was not on topic about Wendy's Texas cowboy but was something else, something unexpected.

"I really love the bad boys," she confided.

And then Cathy got even more personal—adding something about her man, Whitey.

"He was a really bad boy when I married him," she said.

And lastly she bridged past to present. "He's a lot more mellow now."

Whitey Bulger and Cathy Greig—it was all there, in less than twenty-five words.

Cathy was the goodwill ambassador, functioning as Whitey's main liaison to the outside world. "Very sweet, very nice," manager Farinelli always said. Cathy maintained the household—shopped for food, paid the rent, electric, and cable television bills—in cash or with postal money orders. Farinelli said the hundred-dollar bills Cathy took from a white envelope to pay the rent were sometimes so new and crisp they stuck together when she counted them. "Did you go and rob the bank again, Carol?" Farinelli would joke, and Cathy would "laugh and explain she'd gone to the bank and done errands so got money to pay rent."

Cathy cleaned the apartment and cooked, and she did the laundry in the basement of the building, with Whitey often accompanying her. "Enrique, why don't you teach him how to do laundry," she once said to the maintenance supervisor. Whitey laughed off the playful jab. "That's why I have you."

And she got the chance finally to express her love of animals when she began caring for a tiger-striped cat from the neighborhood whose owner had died. The abandoned tabby, named Tiger, wandered between the Princess Eugenia Apartments and the Embassy Hotel across the street. It liked to lounge in the Embassy's courtyard gardens. Morning and night Cathy began leaving the apartment to feed the tabby—and, as was so often the case with everything, she did so under Whitey's watchful gaze.

It was during the care of the tabby cat that another acquaintance entered their small world in Santa Monica. Anna Bjornsdottir of Iceland had first stayed at the Embassy Hotel with her husband, businessman Halldor Gudmundsson, for a couple of weeks in July 2004. They returned the next year for a two-week stay in September and then stayed for nearly three months during the fall of 2006. The couple loved Santa Monica so much they kept returning, although no longer to the Embassy Hotel but renting an apartment just a few blocks away.

Anna had lived another life, too. In the 1970s she was a renowned blond beauty who, as Miss Iceland, competed in the 1974 Miss Universe pageant and came away voted Miss Congeniality. She was married back then to an Icelandic rock star and led an enchanted Hollywood life, called "one of the world's most beautiful and successful models" in *People* magazine, who got small parts in movies using the stage name Anna Bjorn and was featured in Vidal Sassoon and Noxzema advertisements. But by the time she began visiting Santa Monica, she, like Cathy Greig, was also leading a new, quieter life as a yoga instructor and graphic designer.

One thing hadn't changed—she'd always loved cats, and during visits to Santa Monica after 2007 Anna Bjornsdottir witnessed the way Cathy cared for Tiger. She was visiting the Embassy's manager Birgitta Farinelli, a fellow Scandinavian and friend, even though she no longer stayed at the hotel—and was impressed by Cathy's devotion to the stray tabby. She told Birgitta about watching "this lady who was so nice with the cat," and Birgitta explained the cat's caretaker was the sweet and wonderful Carol Gasko of Unit 303. Anna began chatting with Cathy and, said Birgitta, "they became little bit of friends."

"They had this cat in common."

In a way they also had Whitey in common; he was usually a fixture out on the street with them. The three carried on this way in piecemeal fashion, running into one another on Third Street on the occasions Anna was in town and Whitey and Cathy were lingering outdoors with the tabby cat.

It all went fine, this small and infrequent acquaintance, where the staple of conversation was the same innocuous small talk that had characterized all of the Gaskos' relationships during the more than ten years they'd lived in Santa Monica.

Until one day the situation soured. Somehow the subject of Barack Obama came up. Anna Bjornsdottir unabashedly expressed her admiration for the first black president of the United States. Whitey could not believe what he was hearing, and Cathy was unable to intervene in time to muzzle him. He practically exploded at the woman from

Iceland, disgusted that she could admire a black man as president of her host country.

Nothing was the same after. Whitey gave Anna the cold shoulder, would not even respond when she said hello to him. Anna Bjornsdottir, meanwhile, would not forget the old man's sudden rage—or his angry, cold glare.

The former Miss Iceland was not the only one who got the point that the nearly eighty-year-old retiree in Unit 303 hated black people. "He was definitely no fan of Obama," said Joshua H. Bond, the young man who became the general manager of the Princess Eugenia and Embassy.

Josh Bond first arrived in Santa Monica in April 2007 to take over the job of running the two Third Street buildings—and, as such, soon came to know longtime tenants Charlie and Carol Gasko. He was from the Deep South originally—born and raised in Yazoo City, Mississippi—and had headed north in 2001 to attend college at Boston University.

Inevitably, his time in Boston overlapped with plenty of front-page news about the epic saga of Whitey Bulger and the FBI—the racketeering conviction of former FBI agent John Connolly in May 2002, for example; the testimony of Bill Bulger in June 2003 before Congress and his ouster as president of the University of Massachusetts; and the sentencing of Jackie Bulger in September 2003 for obstructing justice. In fact, just weeks before Josh's class of 2005 graduated, chilling testimony was taking place in federal court in Boston about the ghoulish killing of John McIntyre and the complicity of John Connolly and the FBI. The civil case had the ring of David versus Goliath to it, called *Estate of McIntyre v. the United States of America*.

But while Josh Bond certainly became familiar with the name Bulger, he was no different from most kids flocking annually to the college town from distant points around the world. The Bulger case was background noise to their main event—college life—and for him that meant studying film, playing his guitar, and nursing dreams of someday making movies or being in a band. It also meant that when he took a job after graduating that got him nearer to Hollywood along with a steady income while he worked on his music—as well as a rent-free apartment next door to the Gaskos—he never came close to putting Charlie Gasko and Whitey Bulger together as one and the same.

Even when he detected a Boston accent in Charlie's and Carol's voices, who was he, a kid from Mississippi with his own distinct regional twang, to question their claim the sound was Chicago, not Boston.

It would all change—meaning his understanding about Charlie Gasko—but that was down the road a bit and, as it played out, involved Josh in a starring role.

For now as the unlikely friendship began between the white-bearded retiree and the aspiring musician, Josh Bond came to see his neighbor as simply a quirky old guy who just wanted someone to talk to and who "always repeated himself the way old people do," a know-it-all chatterbox who "would talk about anything" and who definitely exhibited some outmoded beliefs and prejudices.

And nothing was more evident of that than the man's attitudes about race. Even with Mississippi roots, Josh was not used to hearing the N-word in the twenty-first century, but that's what Charlie Gasko did sometimes, slipping the word *nigger* into a story he was telling.

Charlie actually took note one time of Josh's discomfort—and so he interrupted his train of thought and whatever he was saying, apologized for the racial epithet, and said he wanted to explain himself.

"I'm old-school," Whitey said to Josh, "and I don't think the races should mix."

Whitey Bulger turned eighty on September 3, 2009, an anniversary that triggered a new round of press coverage. He'd been a fugitive for thirteen years and the reward for his capture was now two million dollars. Only Osama bin Laden had a higher bounty on the FBI's Ten Most Wanted list—twenty-five million. The FBI told reporters that after years of focusing its effort abroad it was beginning to look again to warm-weather domestic possibilities, such as Florida, where they'd received Whitey tips that turned out to be look-alikes.

All along the FBI had been getting tips from within the United States, but the bureau just hadn't seemed to give them as much attention once the commitment overseas had been made. In October 2006, for example, a deputy sheriff in San Diego was convinced he'd seen Whitey leaving a movie theater that was showing director Martin Scorsese's new film, *The Departed,* starring Jack Nicholson. The movie was a remake of a Japanese crime thriller but because Scorsese set his version in Southie, most viewers concluded it was Whitey's story. The deputy sheriff followed the moviegoer but lost him on a trolley. He even went back to the theater to review surveillance tapes, but nothing ever came of the tip once he alerted the FBI, except for the FBI saying the sighting could not be corroborated. Then in late June 2008 the most tantalizing Whitey tip of all was called in to the show *America's Most Wanted* from a tourist visiting Santa Monica. Keith Messina of Las Vegas said he was reading a book near a wall on the Santa Monica Pier at about 10 a.m. on June 28 when he thought he saw Whitey Bulger walking with a woman. The "suspect" was in his "late 70s," according to a tip sheet the show kept, "wearing a hat and sunglasses, blue jean shorts." Messina, according to the sheet, said the man he thought was Whitey spotted "a couple walking and the male had on a Boston Celtics shirt, and suspect started talking to the couple and asked them did they know where Newbury Street in Boston, Ma. was." Messina provided his cell phone number, but said later the FBI never called him.

The news accounts around Whitey's birthday kept reporting that the Bulger Task Force consisted of seven investigators working full-time, but insiders knew that, again, was public relations and not reality. One federal fugitive investigator said the task force's offices in downtown Boston "had become a ghost town," and that at most one investigator was working full-time while any other investigators split time between the manhunt for Whitey and their other duties.

The trail was "really cold," said Jon Mitchell, the assistant U.S. attorney who had taken over as lead prosecutor for the task force in 2004. The last sighting he and investigators believed to be solid was ancient—back in 1996—and was from Kevin Weeks after he became a government witness. Said Mitchell about Whitey: "Here's a guy who could be anywhere in the world and fit in anywhere where Westerners lived. The possibilities were nearly endless." By 2010, it "almost became conventional wisdom in law enforcement that Whitey Bulger was dead." But without confirmation, the effort simply had to continue, although one that had devolved to chasing look-alike tips after a spate of Whitey publicity.

Whitey, meanwhile, was alive and well, celebrating his eightieth birthday with dinner at his and Cathy's favorite neighborhood restaurant, two blocks from their apartment. Michael's wasn't much to look at—a white-painted stucco exterior with narrow, uninviting windows. But the interior opened up into a stylishly decorated, softly lighted lounge and, beyond it, an outdoor dining room in a garden of plants and trees. Whitey and Cathy sat at their regular corner table, number twenty-three, and for the occasion left the staff a little extra—a 20 percent tip.

Of course Whitey had no way of knowing about the virtually moribund state of the Whitey Bulger manhunt, but the truth was he had little to worry about as he and Cathy dined, savoring his freedom in the relaxing calm of Santa Monica.

26

"Charlie Will Meet You in the Garage"

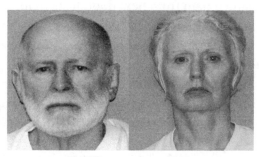

LAPD mug shots: 2011

They'd greeted each other a few times in passing, but the semi-friendship between Whitey Bulger and Josh Bond began in earnest during the summer of 2007 after Josh moved into unit 304 of the Princess Eugenia Apartments. Late one afternoon, Josh was walking around his apartment hugging his guitar while strumming a mix of blues and country. He and a musician friend named Neal Marsh were teamed up and starting a band, For the Kings, with hopes of playing in Los Angeles–area clubs and eventually recording an album.

Some of Josh's songs were original; others were by Elvis Presley, Hank Williams, the Rolling Stones, and the Band. He played hard and sang loudly, and he knew the old couple in the next apartment could probably hear him, but this was his time to practice and to recover from work. He usually came home from the manager's office, located in the hotel across the street, wiped out from talking with tenants, suppliers, staff, and guests and servicing their varied needs.

He finished playing, collapsed onto the couch in the living room, and zoned out. Then he heard a knock at the door. Josh didn't move. No one had ever knocked on his door since he'd moved in. He'd purposely avoided being neighborly with the tenants; he didn't want them thinking that just because the general manager lived in the building he was available around the clock.

Josh yelled, "Who is it?"

"Charlie."

"Who?"

"Your neighbor."

Josh reluctantly pulled his lanky frame up and sauntered across the room. He opened the door but only a crack. Standing in the hallway was the white-bearded man from next door. Josh, in his role as general manager, of course knew his name: Charlie Gasko. The man was holding a big, black hard plastic can. Josh had no idea what was in the container, and his first thought was it might be a tambourine case, and his second thought was the old guy maybe wanted to play music.

But Josh, scruffy-bearded, just stood there; he didn't open the door or invite the man in. The man, however, smiled and said he'd been listening to Josh's music and thought Josh was pretty good. "I thought you should have this."

Whitey handed the container to him. Josh opened it up. Inside was a cowboy hat. Josh lifted it out: the hat was a black wool Stetson Stallion with a leather band studded with engraved silver buttons. The man went on to say that it was an old hat of his, that he didn't need it anymore and thought Josh might have use for it.

"Oh," Josh said. He was thinking, This was weird, but said, "Cool. Thanks."

Josh took the hat and closed the door.

But Whitey wouldn't go away. He returned another afternoon, and then another, knocking on the door and looking to "shoot the shit" with "Tex"—a nickname Whitey initially gave Josh but that wore out its welcome quickly.

"If he knew I was here he'd knock on the door," Josh said.

Josh didn't want to be rude, so he let Whitey in a first time, then a second time, until Whitey was coming by to talk a couple of times a week. That was the pattern that developed—Whitey talked and Josh listened. Josh, it turned out, was a good listener. Though from Mississippi, he did not possess one of those outsized, good-old-boy southern personalities—because if he had, the odd coupling of Whitey and Josh likely would not have worked out. Whitey wasn't really looking for someone who could match his story with one of his own. He wasn't looking for a real conversation. He wanted a sounding board—not unlike the role the young sidekick Kevin Weeks had played all those years when he'd put up with the know-it-all Whitey's need to rant.

Josh, then, was yin to Whitey's yang—with a natural reserve that was actually refined as a result of working in the service industry. Josh's job required a helpful, friendly demeanor as he dealt with people all day long, but as a matter of survival he self-consciously developed the ability to smile and project the appearance of being attentive when in fact he was zoning out. Plus, he'd learned to say little and ask few questions, because that would simply extend conversations. This served Whitey perfectly—talking to someone bright and youthful but without the kind of inquiring mind that might create problems. Josh said, "It's probably why he knocked on my door and liked to talk to me. I didn't ask many questions." He'd arrive home in the afternoon—his lunch break when working the hotel desk—and then would come the knock, and in would come Whitey. "He would start talking," Josh said. "Talk about anything." Talk until Josh stood up. "Okay, I got to go back to work."

"I was someone he liked to talk to," Josh said.

Much went in one ear and out the other, but over time enough stayed with Josh that he acquired a superficial mix of Whitey personal fiction and commentary. Whitey said he was from Chicago, that he and his wife had no kids and they'd retired to Santa Monica in the 1990s. He told Josh he'd seen action in Korea. He mentioned his high blood pressure and that he sometimes traveled to Mexico to buy heart medication. There were the swipes at President Obama and opinions on local crime and public safety. Whitey sometimes circled an article about a neighborhood crime or about city legal news regarding hotels and left the newspaper outside Josh's door with the idea that, as general manager, the stories were relevant to him.

Josh occasionally partied with friends in his apartment—and he sometimes took the party up onto the roof of the building, under Santa Monica's starry night sky. The next time Whitey knocked on the door Josh braced for a complaint, but none came. Instead Josh listened to a bemused Whitey note that Josh hosted gatherings sans swearing, macho preening, and fistfights—party conduct apparently foreign to Whitey.

Josh rarely went inside Whitey's apartment, and one such time was when Whitey wanted to show him a new pair of headphones to use while watching television late into the night without waking up Cathy. Josh saw the futon bed in the living room and, except for the punching dummy, nothing seemed peculiar for a retired couple who at this point in their lives slept in separate bedrooms. Josh could tell Whitey liked his company and sometimes the sessions in the apartment weren't enough; if Josh was entering the building and ran into his neighbors, Whitey wanted to talk. But Cathy would say, "C'mon, Charlie. Leave Josh alone. He's got places to go."

Whitey had two recurring topics: music and personal hygiene. Whitey liked to critique Josh's music, opine on which songs he liked, inquire about where Josh was playing, and offer business advice. He also talked endlessly about personal maintenance and fitness. The un-solicited advice covered the gamut. Whitey observed that the bicycle Josh rode around a lot did not have a headlight. He said Josh could do a better job taking care of his scruffy beard and that he could strengthen his arms immeasurably if he used a certain piece of equipment.

Then came the gifts. The Stetson hat was the first. Then Whitey gave Josh a beard trimmer and comb, and used his own white beard as a model in urging tidier upkeep. He gave Josh a curling bar, free weights, and a stomach crunching device. Josh thought the gifts were over-the-top, even strange. When he realized many were directed at his appear-ance, he had a crazy notion that maybe the old guy was coming on to him. But Whitey never gave off a vibe along those lines, and they "were such a nice old couple" that Josh dismissed the thought. He decided Whitey was simply treating him like the son he didn't have.

Whitey and Cathy gave him gifts at Christmas, too—a decorative plate one year, an Elvis coffee table book another. Josh also learned Whitey was obsessed with mannerly protocol. One year Whitey had left a Christmas gift bag on Josh's door, and a few days later Josh ran into Whitey in the building's underground garage.

"You get the present?" Whitey asked.

Josh could tell Whitey was perturbed. "Oh, yeah. Thanks, Charlie."

"Don't you write thank-you notes?"

Josh fumbled for words. When he got home he tore out a sheet of lined notebook paper and wrote a note to Charlie and Carol thanking them for the gift and for being such terrific next-door neighbors. The next time Whitey came by he was smiling and bearing more gifts—a box of stationery and bread Cathy had baked. Carol loved the note, Whitey said. You're all set now; no need to write anymore.

Overall, Josh Bond probably got a deeper glimpse than anyone else in Santa Monica, past the eyes of Charlie Gasko and toward the heart of darkness that was Whitey Bulger. One episode involved a resident from the Ocean View Manor, the state-licensed residential facility for the mentally disabled located a few doors down from the Princess Eugenia Apartments. The manor was home to forty-four mentally disabled adults, many of whom had lived there for years, participating in programs encouraging them "to become more independent and self-sufficient in order to eventually return to the community and into society." Josh was familiar with the manor because on occasion a resident moseyed into the lobby of the Embassy Hotel and "caused a bit of trouble." Nothing huge, but incidents Josh certainly had to manage. It turned out Whitey had his own close encounter. One resident was known to hide behind a bush along Third Street and then jump out to spook a passerby. The resident just thought he was being funny, but Whitey didn't see the humor, and he told Josh that he and Cathy were on their late-day walk when the resident popped out from behind a bush. Cathy was frightened, Whitey said, and this had set him off. He kept a knife strapped to his ankle and said he'd grabbed the guy, pulled out the knife, and held the man's face close to him. "I told the guy if I ever see you do that again I'm gonna cut you."

Josh soon experienced for himself that Whitey did not like surprises. One day after work he'd changed into his running clothes, grabbed his iPod, and hustled onto the elevator to head out for a jog. In the lobby he spotted Whitey standing on the building's front stoop, his back to the lobby, hands resting on the iron railing, just looking up and down the street. Josh had already noticed that Whitey, when standing, "had this look," where his feet were planted, his arms were arched out a bit and, if not holding a railing, then arched as if he was going to rest them on his hips. It was hard for Josh to put the look into words— maybe the look of a gunfighter ready to draw his gun. Or maybe a look rooted in a past Josh knew nothing about—Whitey's body muscle memory from his days as crime boss, when he posed in the open bay at the Lancaster Garage or at some other venue projecting near-absolute power while surveying his territorial holdings. Sometimes when Josh saw Whitey posturing this way Whitey might smile and glare, and that's when Josh would notice Whitey's very white teeth and bright blue eyes, and Whitey might also chortle, where his upper body and arms shook along with the sound. "It was a weird laugh," Josh said, "a laugh with almost some anger behind it."

Whitey was ahead of him on the stoop and Josh, coming up quickly behind him, said, "Hey, Charlie, what's up?" But because he was wearing headphones it came out more like yelling, "HEY, CHARLIE, WHAT'S UP?" Whitey's hands flew up off the railing. Josh saw Whitey jump, turn, and look hard at him. Then Whitey began shouting, his mouth like an automatic weapon getting off a few rounds.

"Goddammit! Fuck! Fuck! Jesus Christ. Fuck!"

Josh was dumbstruck by the hyper-angry string of curses—something he'd never seen in Charlie Gasko, a break in character from the friendly guy next door who insisted on thank-you notes and marveled at parties where guests did not swear.

But maybe Whitey had thought he'd been ambushed—surrounded by the FBI? A Mafia hit man? Johnny Martorano? Hadn't Martorano on *60 Minutes* said, "There's a bounty on him"?

Then Whitey saw it was only Josh Bond, and he calmed down quickly.

"Jesus, Josh, don't sneak up on me like that," he said.

By the summer of 2010 a new dawn had finally come to Boston law enforcement and the Bulger Task Force. Three key federal offices in Boston now had new leaders. Carmen Ortiz was confirmed as the new U.S. attorney in Massachusetts in November 2009; John Gibbons, who'd served twenty-seven years with the Massachusetts State Police, was sworn in as U.S. marshal for the District of Massachusetts in February 2010; and Richard DesLauriers, a Massachusetts native who'd previously served in Boston, officially took over as the FBI's special agent in charge of the FBI's Boston office on July 1, 2010. Representatives from the three offices began meeting to discuss the hapless Bulger Task Force and the interagency logjam that had undermined a unified front in the hunt for America's most wanted, Whitey Bulger.

Federal marshals had been hungering for years to get involved—a new generation of proactive deputy marshals who combined street savvy with sophisticated electronic surveillance to track fugitives. "We were licking our chops," said a deputy marshal and supervisor named Jeffrey Bohn, who'd cut his teeth in Miami and had been in Boston about a decade. Many marshals viewed the FBI of the twenty-first century as institutionally hampered by two key factors—first, the bureau's phasing out of its fugitive operations, particularly after 9/11, resulting in eroding expertise, and second, its approach—seen as reactive, with FBI agents inclined to sit at desks studying computer screens rather than pounding the streets. Dating back at least a year, marshals in Boston had even put together a memorandum outlining a new task force—its manpower and strategy—that they wanted to put in play if given the chance. The marshals exuded confidence, saying Whitey would have been apprehended long ago if they had been unleashed from the start in 1995.

But the proposal required the one condition that had always stopped such ideas dead in their tracks: in the official jargon, the plan called for the FBI to "delegate apprehension" to the marshals service. In other words, the FBI would have to step aside. During meetings that spring, the FBI representatives made it clear they wanted help—that the FBI needed the marshals' expertise—but reiterated their position that the FBI had to be the lead agency, given its scandalous past ties to Whitey.

Marshal John Gibbons; his chief deputy, Dave Taylor; his assistant deputy chief, John Murray; Boston FBI assistant special agent in charge, Noreen Gleason; and representatives from the U.S. attorney's office—all wanted to get past the deeply rooted mistrust. It was 2010—meaning there were FBI agents, deputy marshals, state troopers, and federal drug agents now working in the field who hadn't been born or had been toddlers when Whitey Bulger was at the pinnacle of power in the 1980s, guarded by a corrupted FBI.

So Gibbons decided, why not? Headquarters in Washington might be against any plan that did not call for marshals to be in charge, but Gibbons had the latitude to allocate his manpower. He wanted to set a different tone, try for a new vibe. The FBI in Boston had asked for the marshals' help, and Gibbons and his deputies decided it was time. They would assign a marshal to the cause.

Gibbons chose a deputy marshal named Neil Sullivan. Sullivan had grown up on Cape Cod and became a marshal in October 1995. He had been working in Albany, New York, on the "warrant squad"—

meaning fugitive cases—and supervising a fugitive task force when he transferred to Boston in 2009. "We knew his reputation before he came to Boston as an outstanding investigator," Gibbons's chief deputy Taylor said. Just as important, Sullivan was "non-abrasive" and was known as a team player.

For the FBI's part, it was assigning an agent named Phil Torsney to work with Sullivan. Torsney was a throwback; he'd worked on fugitive cases for the FBI for more than two decades, most recently assigned to the bureau's office in Cleveland. With a career passion for working fugitive cases, some marshals considered him an FBI dinosaur, given the modern bureau's focus on counterterrorism. Over the years Torsney had been loaned for short periods to the Bulger Task Force from Cleveland, but he was now being transferred to Boston so that he could finish his FBI career working on Whitey. Torsney was known for his upbeat, can-do approach—exactly the attitude necessary for the Whitey manhunt. The task force's coordinator, FBI agent Richard Teahan, would stay in that role although continuing to split his duties with another unit. Jon Mitchell, the federal prosecutor assigned to the task force, also would continue to divide his time between the task force and other matters.

Sullivan was soon briefed on his new assignment and told he was joining a beefed-up, reconstituted Bulger Task Force. Following the necessary paperwork, he showed up for work September 2010. When he arrived at the task force's nondescript office in One Center Plaza in Boston he was slightly taken aback. The walls were covered with dozens of photographs—of Whitey and Cathy, of their many relatives, of Whitey's many associates—as well as with charts and world maps with pins stuck in various locations. Desks with computers lined the large room. But it was as if someone had yelled "Fire!" The office was empty and dead quiet, hardly the high-octane manhunt as advertised.

In reality it was going to be a task force of three—Sullivan, Torsney, and an FBI analyst named Roberta Hastings. Two investigators and an analyst. Not much in the scheme of all the resources at the disposal of the giant federal agencies. But in the context of a Bulger manhunt that was barely on life support, this was a fresh start.

During the fall Sullivan and Torsney got up to speed. The two investigators studied past strategies, assessed past alleged sightings, reinterviewed persons previous task force members had thought might have insights about Whitey's whereabouts—some who would talk only to Sullivan because they mistrusted the FBI and were convinced the bureau was protecting Whitey. They each arrived at similar positions about the state of Whitey Bulger affairs—that Whitey was alive, not dead; that the much-ballyhooed London sighting of 2002 was bogus and had steered searchers off track; that Whitey and Cathy Greig were hiding in the States; and that he and Cathy were living near the water and in a warm-weather climate.

They learned that during the previous year an effort had begun to employ new facial recognition technologies to search databases of driver's licenses. The idea was to see whether Whitey's or Cathy's face popped up on a license in the name of an alias. There was no federal database of licenses, however, which meant the process was slow and time-consuming, involving going to each state's motor vehicle registry. That initiative continued into 2011, with about half the states accounted for—California being one of the states not yet covered.

And they began brainstorming new ideas with task force prosecutor Jon Mitchell and others in a bid to revitalize the manhunt. Mitchell championed the idea of exploiting social media. He'd been fascinated by the success in December 2009 of the so-called Red Balloon Contest, where the Pentagon's research agency had offered a prize of forty thousand dollars to the first person or group to find ten eight-foot weather balloons that had been positioned around the United States. The outcome was eye-popping: a team from the Massachusetts Institute of Technology located the ten balloons less than nine hours after the contest began on December 5. Their winning strategy was to use the Internet and social media to recruit searchers by offering financial incentives—two thousand dollars to the person who spotted a balloon; one thousand dollars to the person who'd "invited" the person who'd spotted the balloon to join the challenge, and so on. The team's marketing approach had gone viral, and correct sightings of all ten balloons came flying in to the MIT team across the Internet.

Mitchell wanted to create a similar contest to find Whitey. He and members of the Bulger Task Force met with Pentagon researchers and the MIT team during 2010, and they even began roughing out a plan. Mitchell had the idea of enlisting actor Matt Damon—a friend of Mitchell's college roommate—to advertise the contest when it came time to market it. The competition would have been the first-ever application of social networking in a fugitive manhunt.

"It would have been cool to see this thing roll out," Mitchell said. But the proposal faltered when the estimated budget turned out to be about $250,000. "Basically we could not get the FBI to fund this," Mitchell said.

The task force turned more fully, then, to a different initiative— one that was less expensive but new nonetheless. The idea was to put the spotlight on Cathy Greig, using new photographs that the task force had obtained. The photos were of Cathy before she fled with Whitey, but they were fresh, enhanced images the public had not yet seen. The task force started small with this new Greig-based publicity campaign, taking out advertisements in two trade journals, *Plastic Surgery News* and the American Dental Association monthly newsletter, in the spring of 2010.

"The thinking was anyone who had plastic surgery in her thirties would have more, not less, as time goes on," Mitchell said, "and anyone as fastidious about her teeth would stay that way."

But, as with every other publicity campaign to catch Whitey, nothing came of the trade journal ads. Even so, as Sullivan and Torsney teamed up during the fall of 2010 they liked this idea-in-progress—of paying more attention to the woman in Whitey's life. It hadn't really been tried before, and it made common sense. Cathy was attractive and more social, and anyone encountering the couple might well remember her better than the bearded man with glasses and hat pulled down.

The next spring, on May 1, 2011, U.S. Navy SEALs descended stealthily into a private compound in Abbottabad, Pakistan, where they shot and killed Osama bin Laden. The raid brought an end to the leader of al-Qaeda, who had been the mastermind behind the September 11, 2001, attacks in the United States.

And it dislodged bin Laden as the most notorious entry on the FBI's Ten Most Wanted list, making room at the top for the legendary Boston fugitive Whitey Bulger.

In Santa Monica, in the wake of the news about bin Laden, Whitey Bulger cum Charlie Gasko hunkered down in Unit 303, becoming even more reclusive.

Whitey posted a note on his apartment door, hand-printed in thin block letters: "PLEASE. Do Not Knock On This Door At This Time. Thank You." Cathy Greig began telling other tenants her husband's Alzheimer's disease was worsening.

Whitey once had had a talk with Cathy about options if he should die—she could either go home to Boston or stay on as Carol Gasko in Santa Monica, living off the cash he'd stashed in the walls.

But Whitey was of sharp mind and good health in May 2011—and as he withdrew further into his tiny world at the Princess Eugenia the reason had nothing to do with failing health. He might be eighty-one but he was nowhere near death's door. Instead, it was as if Whitey sensed a change in the wind, a possible storm brewing.

And staying by his side was Cathy Greig, who'd made her choice long ago.

"Wishing You a Valentine's Day That's Tail-Waggin' Fun," read the card she'd gotten for him on the day devoted to sweethearts, a card showing a Jack Russell terrier and a big heart on the front. Inside Cathy wrote in her cursive style that Whitey was her "Valentine."

She signed it simply "C," which could stand for Cathy or Carol.

Either way worked, and it was "Love Always," followed by, "XXXXOOOO."

The same month that bin Laden was killed, the Bulger Task Force in Boston applied the finishing touches for a June launch of its latest publicity campaign targeting the fugitive couple. Neil Sullivan, Phil Torsney, supervisor Teahan, and prosecutor Mitchell were taking the next step in the Greig-angled strategy—going big, a campaign plastering Greig's face before the general public and, in particular, the mostly female audience watching soap operas and other daytime television shows. The heart of the campaign was a thirty-second spot with photographs of Cathy and Whitey along with information about the international manhunt to run during commercial breaks. Cathy's reward was being doubled to $100,000 while Whitey's was still $2 million, tops on the FBI's Ten Most Wanted list.

They bought time on stations in fourteen cities—but skipped Los Angeles and New York City, in part because the TV ad rates in those markets were budget busters for the campaign's fifty-thousand-dollar fund. Ads were scheduled to run during such shows as *Live with Regis and Kelly, Ellen,* and *The View.* To maximize the publicity push, they also arranged to feature Whitey and Cathy on digital billboards in about forty states as part of the FBI's fugitive billboard program, where billboard owners donated space to the FBI. Finally, a press release was drafted explaining the new initiative in hopes that the media would run news stories about Whitey and Cathy.

Neil Sullivan and Phil Torsney got ready for the start of the new publicity campaign on June 20. Sullivan planned to oversee the morning/afternoon shift while Torsney would cover the afternoon/evening shift. Extra analysts were deployed to their office to handle the surge in telephone calls.

The whole idea behind this and any other publicity campaign was simple—to get lucky. To reach that one person who, seeing the ads or spin-off news media coverage, recognized Cathy or Whitey or both—a person who'd been in the right place at the right time to cross paths with the fugitive couple. That was what the manhunt for years had been all about—luck—and, after so many luckless years, the karma this time was going to be different.

On a Friday two weeks before the new campaign was scheduled to start, Cathy Greig, out doing errands, stopped at the local pharmacy to pick up a refill of Whitey's heart medication. She signed for the prescription using Whitey's main alias, James W. Lawlor. Her entering and leaving the store were captured on the store's security camera.

On a later June weekday Cathy walked into the Haircutters on Wilshire Boulevard—her last haircut, it turned out, before the start of the media blitz. Hairdresser Wendy Farnetti was glad to see her. Cathy had missed a previous appointment. "She sort of disappeared, and I was worried," Wendy said. "I thought, where did she go?"

Cathy settled into a chair. "Her hair was a mess," Wendy said. "It was long." Cathy wanted the usual—cut short on the top and sides, shaggier in back. The hairdresser noticed she seemed "really distraught, really nervous."

Wendy asked, "What's wrong?"

"You don't know," Cathy said. "You don't even know."

Wendy Farnetti wasn't alone noticing something different. Josh Bond didn't make much of it but one day he realized the knocks at his apartment door had stopped. He might see Carol Gasko heading out to do an errand, but it had been more than a month since Charlie Gasko had stopped by.

"Probably the longest I went without seeing him," he said.

The launch of the new Whitey and Cathy media blitz on Monday, June 20, 2011, went smoothly. FBI officials and federal prosecutors held a press conference in Boston to unveil the latest publicity campaign. The thirty-second commercials began appearing on daytime television in fourteen cities, and the news media, especially cable networks CNN and Headline News, gave the new Cathy Greig angle plenty of coverage that aired around the globe.

The two most interested viewers in the world caught the news while watching TV inside their rent-controlled apartment at the Princess Eugenia in Santa Monica, California. The end of bin Laden, and now the new focus on Cathy—Whitey had always wondered why they hadn't focused on Cathy; she was the more social of the two, circulating in the world while he was largely a shut-in. She was more memorable.

Whitey later said he had a hunch and turned to Cathy, saying, "This is it," although investigators doubted the claim of clairvoyance. They saw the claim as another example of "Whitey ragtime"—his need to seem all-knowing. If Whitey had truly had a hunch he should have cleared out for a few weeks, just in case.

The next day, Tuesday, Deputy U.S. Marshal Neil Sullivan and FBI agent Phil Torsney thought they had something. Seven or more tips reporting possible Whitey sightings came in from Biloxi, Mississippi, and the surrounding area. The team began to get pumped up—a cluster of calls was the kind of thing you looked for, plus the Deep South was historically a location Whitey was known to inhabit—Grand Isle, Louisiana, being the most notable. But as quickly as the barometer of excitement had risen, it had fallen. By day's end none of the tips had checked out—the information too vague, inconsistent, unverifiable. Sullivan and his colleagues concluded that the handful of calls from the same geographic area had been an odd coincidence.

Under rainy skies Wednesday morning Sullivan arrived to work at the task force office in Boston around six o'clock, wondering what this day, the third of the new Whitey media blitz, would bring. During the first forty-eight hours they had received more than two hundred calls, and Sullivan saw that some of the extra analysts brought on board were already going through voice mails left on the task force's toll-free 800 number during the early-morning hours when the office was not staffed.

It took time for the analysts to go through them, in part because some of the messages were difficult to follow due to a speaker's accent or syntax. For each, the analysts wrote up a tip sheet summarizing the information. Then they put them in a pile. They didn't prioritize them—assessments were Sullivan and Torsney's job.

Sullivan ordinarily would listen to the voice mails, too, but instead began going through the stack of tip sheets. The phones were continuing to ring, with analysts busy writing down information from new tipsters who thought they had a bead on the whereabouts of Whitey Bulger and Cathy Greig. Sullivan reviewed the tip sheets when one caught his eye—a sheet summarizing a predawn voice mail left by a woman, a woman with an accent who said she was calling from Europe to report that Cathy Greig and Whitey Bulger were living in Santa Monica, California.

The caller had even provided an address—an apartment on Third Street. That was the detail that grabbed Sullivan's attention. Most common were tips along the lines of Whitey was spotted in such-and-such a town at a convenience store at such-and-such a time—fleeting information that wasn't really helpful in that there was no meat, nothing that could really be followed up on. But a detail like this—a specific address—was exactly what a deputy marshal was trained to spot in a pile of tip sheets, most of which signified nothing. Sullivan continued working his way through the other sheets but he put this one aside.

Then, shortly after 9 a.m., the task force got a call from the FBI office in Los Angeles, referring a tip it had received the previous night about a possible Whitey sighting in Santa Monica. Sullivan right away saw that the tip was from the same woman from Europe who'd called Boston and left a message. Then around 11 a.m. an analyst handed Sullivan the sheet from a tipster he'd just finished talking to on the phone. Sullivan saw why—it was the woman again, reporting that she was calling from Europe and had seen the news on CNN about the media blitz and that she was certain Whitey and Cathy were in Santa Monica posing as the couple Charlie and Carol Gasko.

Sullivan quizzed the analyst. How did the woman sound? Sane?

Believable? Crazy? The analyst told him she sounded solid. The tip was radiating heat—the specifics combined with the caller's persistence—leaving a message in Boston, calling Los Angeles, then calling Boston back. Sullivan put everything else aside, took the tip sheet, and tried calling the woman on the telephone number listed on it. He had in hand a lead gaining traction, and his intensity was building. But something was wrong. The call went nowhere—no voice mail, just noise and static. He tried using a different landline in the office, thinking maybe something was wrong with the first phone he'd used. The call still didn't go anywhere. He tried his cell phone—still nothing. The number simply wasn't a good one, and Sullivan realized that the analyst must have written down the number incorrectly. Luckily, however, the analyst had gotten her email. Sullivan sent the woman a message on his BlackBerry asking her to contact him immediately.

Thirty minutes later—about noon on Wednesday in Boston—his cell phone rang. The caller was Anna Bjornsdottir, and for the next twenty minutes Sullivan talked with the woman who'd been calling Boston and Los Angeles about the manhunt for Whitey Bulger and Cathy Greig.

Sullivan could tell from the start she had it all—their height, weight, and mannerisms. She gave a specific address at the Princess Eugenia Apartments in Unit 303, and she mentioned the couple's heavy accents, which they'd told her were New York accents. She talked about the couple's daily walks, their affection for dogs and cats. She described a particular stray cat named Tiger and explained the friendship that had developed with Cathy because of Cathy's care for the animal. She included that Cathy was nice while Whitey, ever present during their encounters, could be nasty, and she described the hard feelings following a discussion of President Obama. The woman was 100 percent certain about the Gaskos' true identity.

Sullivan knew she was right, too, and the deputy U.S. marshal was now in full operational mode. He told her they were going to move on the lead as quickly as possible and then, as was standard operating procedure, he issued a series of warnings—that she was not to discuss the manhunt with anyone, not her husband, a friend, a relative, no one; that a dangerous fugitive, a killer, was at stake, as well as a two-million-dollar reward. She promised to cooperate and await further instructions.

Once the call ended, Sullivan got on to the computer to run some quick background checks on Charlie Gasko—looking for a Social Security number, a date of birth, a credit history, anything that would indicate an official existence. He confirmed that a Charles Gasko lived at the same Third Street address the woman tipster had provided, but nothing else showed up. Not even a date of birth, and without a date of birth he could not continue to search for any state licensing information, such as a California driver's license, a car registration, even parking tickets. In Boston he did not have access to the California database that allowed searches using only a person's name. He turned to an FBI staffer to call an FBI bureau in California to quickly run a motor vehicle and license check on both Charles and Carol Gasko. Once again nothing turned up. This, Sullivan knew, was not typical, a red flag indicating the persons in question were trying to go undetected.

It was early afternoon now in Boston. Sullivan's instinct was to contact his fellow marshals in Los Angeles to deploy a team to capture their man, but this was the FBI's task force. He notified the task force's supervisor, FBI agent Richard Teahan, about Anna and the background search, saying, "This tip needs immediate coverage." Teahan listened and tried to contact the FBI office in Los Angeles but left a message when the agent he called did not pick up. Sullivan watched this unexpected pause and grew antsy—everything about the tip screamed this was Whitey Bulger. Sixteen years after he fled Boston. Sixteen years on the run.

Twenty minutes went by, and Sullivan went back to Richard Teahan, diplomatically mentioning that time was of the essence and urging him to call Los Angeles again. "We can't wait," he said. Teahan, agreeing with Sullivan's sense of urgency, called the Los Angeles bureau a second time, this time getting through to another agent, an agent named Scott F. Garriola. Garriola did not work on a fugitive squad—he was a member of the Violent Crimes Task Force—but the minute Sullivan began working with him he could tell Garriola got it. Sullivan briefed Garriola and brought him up to speed about the Gasko tip from Anna Bjornsdottir and the apartment location in Santa Monica. Then Sullivan played the middleman, sending a text message to Anna and arranging for her to talk to an FBI agent in Los Angeles. The direct connection made, Sullivan stepped aside so that Garriola and Anna spoke directly. By this time it was about mid-afternoon in

Boston, midday in Los Angeles. FBI agent Scott Garriola, after his own conversation with the tipster, informed Boston he would immediately "get eyes" on the apartment—and that he would take it from there.

Josh Bond had been working extra-long hours for more than a week while the other manager, Birgitta Farinelli, was away on vacation, but this day, Wednesday, June 22, he was cutting himself some slack. He'd bought tickets with bandmate and buddy Neal Marsh to see a favorite band, My Morning Jacket, that night at the Pantages Theatre in Hollywood. He'd arranged with an assistant manager, Thea, to cover the desk starting at 1 p.m. He was going to crash on his couch for a solid nap, head to Hollywood late in the afternoon, meet his friend for some drinks, and attend the concert.

Josh was asleep when his phone rang about 3:30 p.m. He fumbled to answer the call. It was Thea, from the office across the street at the Embassy Hotel Apartments. She explained there was an FBI agent standing in the office who said he needed to talk to him. She said it was about one of their guests.

Josh, groggy, struggled to get his bearings. Thea's voice sounded different, and he wondered what this could be about—an FBI agent?

The agent got on the phone and identified himself as Scott Garriola. He asked Josh if he was the manager of the building. Josh said yes, he was. The agent said he needed to come to the office. They needed to talk.

Josh couldn't believe it. He asked, Can't this wait until tomorrow?

No, the agent said.

Josh noted firmness in the voice—no room for negotiation. He pulled himself to his feet and headed across the street into the hotel. He crossed the tiled lobby floor and went up the three steps to the tiny office on the left side. Thea, looking anxious, was in the office with FBI agent Garriola.

The agent had a manila folder. He told Josh he was there to check out a tip—a tip about a man who was possibly living in the Princess Eugenia, a man without a Social Security number, a bank account, and other identifying information. The agent then opened the folder to reveal the FBI's fugitive flier for gangster James J. "Whitey" Bulger and Catherine Greig.

Josh stared at the two faces side by side. "Holy shit," he said.

Josh had recognized Carol/Cathy Greig first. "I knew she was her immediately, she was first, and then I knew it was him," he said.

The agent's interest was clearly heightened. "That's them?" he asked.

Josh looked at him. "What's my reaction tell you?"

The agent ignored Josh's comment. "How sure?"

"Ninety-nine-point-nine percent sure." The moment the words came out of his mouth he realized he was being ridiculous trying to account for some kind of cosmic philosophical truth that nothing was ever absolutely certain. He amended his answer. "I'm one hundred percent sure," he said.

He looked at the flier, stunned—the Bulger name racing around his head, as he remembered random news during his time at Boston University: Bill Bulger, a politician, and then Whitey Bulger, a criminal who was wanted for something. But he knew very little beyond basic name recognition.

The agent immediately made a call. Josh couldn't overhear exactly what was said but got the gist of it—the agent told another FBI agent, This kid here thinks it's him, and I think we got him, so let's not fuck this up.

Josh also noted the agent's calm, in contrast to his own condition—heart pumping, mind racing with half thoughts, things like, Whitey Bulger—he's been wanted for a long time for a lot of crimes. I know him, I'm living next to him.

The agent got off the phone, and suddenly a second FBI agent stepped into the office, and Josh quickly got the sense there were more agents where that one had come from, agents out on Third Street and in the alley behind the Princess Eugenia.

Garriola said he wanted a view of Whitey's Unit 303, so Josh took him to an empty room upstairs in the Embassy Hotel. The room briefly became what felt to Josh like a command center of sorts, with Garriola making lots of calls.

Between calls Garriola asked Josh if he had any plans. Josh replied, yes, as a matter of fact, and he explained about the My Morning Jacket concert that night.

Cancel, the agent said.

For the next hour he and Agent Scott Garriola were seemingly joined at the hip, as Garriola worked the phone and radio, talked to other agents, and talked to him. The agent at one point asked Josh for the keys to Whitey's apartment, and Josh, wondering about privacy rights and his responsibilities as manager, said he wasn't sure he could do that. But the agent basically ordered him to hand over the keys and said if he didn't they would break down the apartment door.

Josh gave him the keys. He also began to realize the agents did not have a plan for what they were going to do next, that as the minutes ticked by they were making it up as they went along, and what seemed like the initial idea of raiding the apartment was fast losing altitude—at least until they confirmed positively that Whitey Bulger was actually at home.

That's when the agent had the idea of asking Josh to go knock on Whitey's door. Knock on the door, find out if Whitey was inside. Josh told the agent he'd never knocked on their door. Never. It would be weird, suspicious. What if Whitey figured something was up and pulled him inside? What then? Garriola pushed him; Josh needed to help them out, and the agent even mentioned a possible share in the reward, but Josh was actually thinking what he wanted most was to go to the concert. He'd called his friend Neal and said he probably wasn't going to make it, and his friend had gone, What the heck, why? and Josh had only said he couldn't say.

Garriola decided next he wanted to move in closer to Unit 303—and Josh became his guide. Josh led him out of the hotel and into the alley that ran behind the Princess Eugenia. He led the agent through a rear door, up the rear stairs to the third floor, and into his apartment, next door to Whitey's. Once inside, Garriola continued conferring on the phone, and Josh was alarmed at the noise the agent was making standing in his living room. He motioned to Garriola to move back into the bedroom, explaining Whitey heard a lot of what went on his apartment.

Josh could tell that agents at this point had confirmed Cathy Greig was home; she'd appeared on the balcony, where they'd made a positive identification. Garriola's phone and radio crackled with updates, and Josh thought the voices on the radio were getting tense—even jumpy, especially after a man was spotted on the balcony. The voices competed as they tried to determine if the man was Whitey. Who is it? Is it him? What do we have? But the man wore some kind of light shirt with a hoodie, and no one could tell positively whether it was Whitey.

Then, after the man went back inside, the heavy black drapes were pulled shut, and that set off a cacophony of voices worrying that the couple in the apartment had made the surveillance and knew investigators were watching.

It was clear to Josh the tempo had picked up. It was also clear Garriola had decided that instead of a raid they now wanted to lure the man they believed was Whitey Bulger out of the apartment. Josh offered an idea: he told Garriola he could go onto the roof and walk around, that he sometimes hung out and partied on the roof, and that Whitey and Cathy heard him. He could go up there, stomp around, and Whitey would probably come out.

Garriola listened, but rejected the idea. The agent then asked Josh a question about the parking garage in the basement of the building. Did Whitey have a car there?

No, Josh said. But they did have a storage unit. Every tenant had one.

Then Josh had a new idea: what if he notified Whitey his storage unit had been broken into? Whitey would want to come down to check it out.

Garriola liked this idea. He spoke with his colleagues, and the plan was hatched. Josh and the agent left the bedroom and walked down the rear stairs into the basement garage. The agent instructed Josh to stay put, saying he'd return in a few minutes. Left alone, Josh called his brother in Mississippi on his cell phone and told him the most bizarre story he'd ever heard, and then said he had to go. Garriola was knocking on the garage door. Josh let him in. The agent had bolt cutters.

They returned to Josh's apartment after Garriola had cut the lock on Whitey's storage unit. Garriola issued marching orders: he was going to leave, head back down to the garage, get the arrest team in place, and then call Josh on the cell phone. Josh would then walk down the hall, knock on Whitey's door, tell Whitey about the storage locker, and bring him down into the basement garage.

No way, Josh said. No way. He couldn't believe the agent was asking him again to knock on Whitey's door. He told the agent he had a better idea—he would go back to the hotel office and call Whitey about the storage unit. The FBI agent concurred, and they left the apartment to take up their respective positions.

When Josh walked into the office, Thea was still there, waiting. She was mostly in the dark about the events that were unfolding, and Josh filled her in. Waiting for Garriola's call, they sat together at the computer, looked up Whitey on Wikipedia, and began reading. Josh suddenly felt the full force of a hurricane-like blast of information, where all he could think was, "This guy has killed a lot of people."

Thea told Josh he looked all white. "Take a deep breath," she said.

The phone rang. It was Garriola; they were ready.

Josh said, "Look, man, I'm not sure I want to do this."

Garriola coached him, calmly telling him he was just making a telephone call, that everything would be okay, that he would take it from there. Josh said, "Okay, okay." He got off the call and began dialing the number on the tenant sheet for the Gaskos, knowing once he dialed he would have to go through with it.

But no one answered. The phone rang and rang, then just stopped ringing. There was no sound at all. Josh hung up. Now what? He called Garriola and told the FBI agent there was a problem—no one had answered. Garriola's response was that it was white-knuckle time—Josh was going to have to go to the apartment, knock on the Whitey's door, and escort him down to the garage. No way around it.

Josh recoiled—after reading about Whitey online he was more freaked-out than ever. What if Whitey pulled a knife on him? Or a gun? The agent offered advice Josh thought was insane—if Whitey drew a weapon Josh could act both cool and perplexed, say something like, "Hey, man, what's going on?"

The standoff ended abruptly. The office phone rang and Thea was holding the phone waving at Josh to indicate Carol Gasko was on the line. Josh hung up on the FBI agent and picked up the other line.

"Hey, Carol," he said.

She asked Josh if he'd just called. Josh said he had. He explained several storage units had been broken into, including theirs.

Josh could hear her relaying the information to Whitey. "Charlie, someone has broken into our storage unit," she said.

Josh couldn't hear what they were saying next. He asked, "You want me to call the cops, or meet me there?"

He could tell they were conferring some more. Then she got back on the line.

"Charlie will meet you in the garage."

Josh told her, Fine, he'd head over after finishing up with a guest. He called Garriola to say that Whitey was on his way down. Garriola told him to sit tight, but Josh's nerve endings were on fire. He couldn't stay in one place so he walked outside and began pacing around the front courtyard. He saw it was almost 6 p.m., and he called his friend with the weird thought he might be able to make the concert after all.

It was while he was talking on the phone that he happened to look up and notice Carol Gasko—he meant Cathy Greig—stepping out onto the balcony. She spotted him, too, and their eyes locked. Then she leaned over the railing to look down at the front entrance to the basement garage. Then she looked back at Josh.

Josh was supposed to be meeting Charlie in the garage. He raised a hand and waved awkwardly. Then he turned around and hurried back inside the hotel. Josh was convinced she knew something was up, something was not right.

Riding down the elevator to the basement garage, Whitey Bulger likely sensed something might be afoot. His reaction to the killing of Osama bin Laden in May. His further seclusion and then seeing the coverage of the new media blitz on Monday. His mind was busy churning everything over, studying the possible action on the grand chessboard.

If so, once the doors opened and he walked into the garage he knew he'd guessed correctly. Because waiting for Whitey Bulger was FBI agent Scott Garriola and a team of agents and police, all with their handguns drawn and trained on the elderly, nondescript-looking old man.

The agents began yelling at Whitey, ordering him to get down. Down on his knees. Get down, or else. "They threatened to shoot," Whitey wrote later in a letter. "It was a tense scene in the garage."

Whitey would not budge. The mask of Charlie Gasko had melted away, and it was Whitey Bulger who next looked down at the cement floor, saw that it was filthy with oil, and decided he was not going to kneel in an oil puddle. The crime boss who'd always hated messes was not about to be taken in with oil stains on his pants.

Facing a phalanx of guns Whitey announced he was going to take two steps to his right. The agents screamed at him not to try. Whitey said he was taking the first step, and then he stepped slowly to his right. The agents yelled at him to stop and ordered him again to get down. Instead Whitey told them, Here was the second step. "More threats. Loud. Guns shaking a bit," Whitey wrote afterward.

"When I took step two I figured they would kill me."

The curtain was dropping on a lifetime of crime and Whitey

needed to impose his personality, his signature strut—some indication that he would not go down without demanding at least an iota of control.

But for all the yelling and shouting, the agents weren't going to fire away on a weaponless old man. Instead they let Whitey Bulger have his way and remain standing—allowing him a fleeting moment of his old self—before swarming in and easily taking him into custody. The arrest took seconds.

Whitey's final gesture was small, however, almost pathetic. He might summon a dose of swagger from his eighty-one-year-old frame for the final scene, but in truth the end had come quickly and quietly, no fireworks. He'd made history—a feared killer and crime boss who amassed millions while turning the Boston FBI into his palace guard—but no amount of attitude changed the fact that, finally, he was finished. Sixteen years on the run, and decades of crime and underworld glory before that. Finished. Done in by Cathy Greig and Tiger the cat. What if Cathy hadn't been so fond of stray cats? What if she hadn't cared for Tiger? Who knew?

EPILOGUE

Back in Boston

Josh Bond's cell phone rang within minutes of Whitey's capture.

"We got him," FBI agent Scott Garriola told him. "Go to your concert."

Josh hurried to his apartment, changed his clothes, and jumped into his car. He made three calls—to the building's owners, his family in Mississippi, and his pal Neal. What's going on? they asked. Josh gave them a brief recap of what still felt surreal: "I just helped the FBI arrest the most wanted man in America."

Garriola and police also began alerting colleagues, so that word of the arrest raced through the law enforcement world. FBI agent Phil

Torsney, working the late shift at the task force in Boston, woke up Deputy U.S. Marshal Neil Sullivan at home with the news. Federal prosecutor Fred Wyshak was awakened just before midnight. Caught who? he asked the coworker who'd said they got "him." Then it sank in. My God, he said. It took Tom Foley a moment as well to work through the fog of sleep. "Whitey Bulger, Tommy," repeated the woman who'd succeeded him as head of the state police. "He was captured in California." The details came in a rush. Santa Monica. Fourteen years. Two blocks from the beach. With Catherine Greig.

In the basement garage of the Princess Eugenia police now had Whitey Bulger safely in handcuffs. More FBI agents and Los Angeles police continued arriving to secure the building and surrounding area. "What are you doing?" resident Janice Goodwin yelled when she happened upon the commotion in the garage and saw Charlie Gasko, shoulders slumped, in handcuffs.

"He's sick," the third-floor neighbor shouted. "He's got Alzheimer's." FBI agents calmed her, pointing out that the huge display of police firepower meant the situation was serious.

Once in custody, Whitey was surprisingly submissive. Following FBI orders he called Catherine Greig and told her to stay put. "I've been arrested," he explained. FBI agents soon brought Greig down to the garage. Next Whitey not only consented to a search but acted as their guide around Unit 303, as if proud of his precautions and the various hiding places he'd created for cash and weapons. But, ever calculating, he tried to insulate Greig from future illegal weapons charges. He told Garriola, "Catherine has never held a gun in her hands."

Teams of agents conducted the first of several searches of Whitey's apartment. They saw the pistol and cash in plain view on a night table in his bedroom. They found a pile of his phony IDs, including ones Kevin Weeks had provided that dated back to 1996. They also came across the unfinished memoir Whitey had begun in 2008 as an angry rebuttal to comments Johnny Martorano had made on *60 Minutes*.

"Shit, you found it," Whitey said when Garriola mentioned the discovery.

Whitey looked to Greig. "Did I name names?" The question seemed to suggest he hadn't worked on the memoir in a while and wasn't sure what was in it.

Greig was reassuring; she didn't think so. But officials who read the manuscript later wondered why Whitey was acting worried—unless it was just that: an act. Maybe Whitey had planted the document, a stratagem similar to the exculpatory LSD document he left behind in Greig's condo in 1995. Because Whitey's latest writing exercise was another self-serving manifesto in which others, such as Johnny Martorano, were to blame, not him.

Within hours the news of Whitey's capture went viral around the world. It made the front page in all the major U.S. papers—the *Los Angeles Times,* the *Chicago Tribune,* the *Washington Post,* the *Wall Street Journal,* the *New York Times,* and, of course, the *Boston Globe* and *Boston Herald.* The *Globe*'s bold banner headline kept it simple: WHITEY BULGER ARRESTED, while the *New York Times* splashed an eye-catching 1953 mug shot of Whitey wearing a fedora above the fold. England. Australia. New Zealand. Scotland. Belfast. Dublin. The story was everywhere. It even dominated the *Telegram,* the online newspaper in Whitey's ancestral homeland of St. John's, Newfoundland. Most reports identified Whitey as an FBI informer, and some included the angle that the FBI was long suspected of not looking hard for him. Even on its day of glory, the FBI's possible dereliction continued to haunt.

The next morning, Thursday, June 23, Whitey seemed to enjoy the spectacle created by his surfacing. Reporters filled the federal courtroom in Los Angeles, many of whom had taken overnight flights from Boston in hopes of making the proceedings. The first public glimpse of the legendary crime boss revealed a fit-looking and tanned eighty-one-year-old man with a neatly trimmed white beard. He wore blue jeans and wire-rimmed glasses, and stood in a holding area along with Catherine Greig. The couple chatted and, on occasion, shared a laugh. Whitey even mocked his news chroniclers when he mimicked them scribbling notes.

The hearing lasted just long enough for the judge to order Whitey and Greig returned to Boston. Ready to accompany the couple the very next morning were the last men standing on the much-maligned Bulger Task Force. Deputy U.S. Marshal Sullivan and FBI agent Torsney, joined by FBI supervisor Rich Teahan, had flown out for the honor. And once Whitey was aboard a private jet for the cross-country flight on Friday, June 24, he waived his rights and continued the nearly nonstop banter with his captors that he'd begun soon after his arrest. He told Torsney and the others a bit of the Charlie Gasko narrative—about his arrival in Santa Monica in 1996 and the move into Unit 303. He shared his technique for acquiring aliases, particularly his exploitation of James Lawlor, which had lasted until Lawlor's death.

It was as if Whitey were holding court, steering the conversation by deflecting some questions while answering others. He bragged about traveling to San Diego and crossing the border easily into Tijuana, Mexico, to buy his medication, and said he also traveled to Las Vegas to play the slots—winning more than he lost, of course. He said, too, that he'd returned to Boston in disguise a few times, "armed to the teeth," to take care of some "unfinished business." But he gave no specifics, and investigators were left to wonder whether Whitey was playing them.

In the end, the Whitey monologues included no bombshells or admissions but they did feature a tantalizing aside when he invoked his brother Bill. Whitey said that "his brother" might be able to pay for Catherine Greig's defense. Whitey was using Bill as his go-to guy once again—just as he'd done during his prison years; or when he sold the John Connolly alliance to the Winter Hill Gang in 1974; or when he needed legislation to slow down the state police in 1981. Bill Bulger was well positioned financially; he had received a $960,000 severance package in 2003 after resigning as UMass president, and his annual pension for the decades he'd served in public office exceeded $200,000.

When Catherine Greig did retain Kevin Reddington, one of the higher-profile criminal defense lawyers, the media immediately speculated that Bill Bulger was likely footing the bill. Federal prosecutors certainly thought so, saying in court that Whitey had a motive for wanting to keep his companion quiet and in good lawyerly hands. "She could cause legal headaches for those close to him who were helping them remain fugitives," one prosecutor said.

Shortly after noon the next day, Friday, a motorcade of police cars and black government SUVs carrying Whitey and Greig left Boston's Logan International Airport and headed into the city to federal district court. The John Joseph Moakley Courthouse on South Boston's waterfront—located a few hundred yards from where Brian Halloran and Michael Donahue had been gunned down on May 11, 1982—did not even exist when Whitey was last in town. Indeed the fan pier area was, in

Whitey's time, mostly a no-man's-land of empty lots, dive bars, and the fishing docks. It was now the city's prime location for redevelopment, with luxury hotels, restaurants, and office buildings rising all around.

Had Whitey been able to charm his police escorts into touring the old neighborhood he would have found many other changes. The folks walking down Broadway and living in the housing projects—once nearly all white—were now a diverse mix. Triple-deckers had been bought up, renovated, and converted into pricey condominiums for the young professionals who'd discovered the convenience of living just across the Broadway Street Bridge from the financial district. The story of the massive gentrification was told in the U.S. Census figures: the population ranging in age from twenty-four to twenty-nine in Southie had doubled in a little more than a decade.

Triple O's, Whitey's barroom of terror, was long gone, although some other sites had survived. The South Boston Liquor Mart, which Whitey once controlled, was still at the rotary. The house atop Telegraph Hill at 78 Thomas Park, where John Connolly had hosted him, was unchanged, as was the house at 799 East Third Street, which Whitey had used to bury bodies. But the properties had been sold more than once, a process that moved them out from the underworld and into the civilian. One thing had stayed constant, though. Bill Bulger still lived farther down East Third Street at number 828, across the yard from where Stevie Flemmi's mother once lived.

But this was a day for justice, not a ride down memory lane. The motorcade headed straight to a courthouse that for Whitey's return had been converted into a high-security stronghold. Coast Guard boats, mounted with machine guns, patrolled the harbor, while heavily armed Boston and state police surrounded the premises on foot. Bulky television trucks carrying satellite dishes on top were lined up outside the front entrance. Inside, court officials opened up two courtrooms and a jury assembly room and brought in video monitors. The extra room was set aside to handle the overflow of hundreds of reporters and onlookers who began arriving at 8 a.m. to see what the *Boston Globe,* a newspaper hardly known for hyperbole, had described as "perhaps the highest-profile court appearance in the city's history."

That appearance formally began at about 4 p.m. when a rear door in Courtroom 10 creaked open. Bill Bulger, seated in the second row with

Jack Bulger and Bill Bulger

two of his sons, quickly looked up. Whitey Bulger entered, his hands in cuffs, escorted by two deputy marshals. Bill offered his older brother a smile.

Whitey scanned the standing-room-only courtroom. He found Bill. Whitey nodded slightly and mouthed, "Hello." It was a moment loaded with subtext, an exchange full of what some later described as the epitome of Bulger smugness, as if the brothers, one to the other, were quietly acknowledging that the run might be ending here but look, just look, how long it had lasted. There had been slights and nicks along the way to be sure, but they could look back across the many decades and realize they'd not only proved durable in their respective careers—careers known generally for short life spans—but had prospered beyond the wildest dreams of two boys from Old Harbor. Most important, they'd done it on their terms.

The principals were all seated at the oak table in the well of the courtroom. Whitey, in the same white pullover shirt, jeans, and running shoes he'd worn in Los Angeles, was at one end with his temporary court-appointed attorney. At the other end sat the two prosecutors who'd been after him for two decades, Fred Wyshak and Brian Kelly—although, consistent with the investigation's fractious history, the pair had to fend off a backstage move by the FBI to replace them. The FBI sniping was the usual—that the two prosecutors hated the bureau. It wanted a different lawyer, more inclined to minimize bad publicity for the bureau, its first criterion in all things. But the U.S. attorney leadership refused to budge. This case was Wyshak and Kelly's to finish.

Magistrate Judge Marianne B. Bowler explained to Whitey the charges he faced—racketeering, extortion, and nineteen murders—and Kelly recited the penalties for each. Whitey listened intently, evincing none of the fuzzy thinking Greig, as Carol Gasko, had talked about with neighbors in Santa Monica to ward off their curiosity about her reclusive husband. Instead he displayed swagger. When asked if he could afford counsel, Whitey quipped, "Well, I could if you gave me my money back." The one-liner evoked muted chuckling in the audience, which stopped suddenly when the crowd realized who had thought it was funny. "You'll have to talk to Mr. Kelly about that," the magistrate responded, and Whitey kept his jocular tone: "I don't think he wants to." Kelly objected to the idea Whitey was indigent while Wyshak, arms clasped behind his head, said nothing and was unmoved.

The magistrate scheduled new court dates to address the issues of bail and the appointment of counsel, and suddenly the initial court proceeding was over. Whitey was approached quickly by fit young men in black mesh tops that had U.S. MARSHAL stenciled on the back in white block lettering. He was cuffed behind his back and escorted out. He threw a departing look to his brother, and Bill nodded his good-bye. The brothers had had their moment, sharing warm smiles, but others in court were disgusted. In addition to reporters, curious attorneys, and many of the investigators who'd hunted for Whitey, relatives of his victims were also on hand. "It was a sickening feeling in my stomach, seeing him, the guy who murdered my father," said Tom Donahue, whose father was an innocent victim in Whitey's hit on Brian Halloran. "Whitey stood there with his punk smirk, his wiseguy remarks."

Outside the courtroom the media besieged Bill Bulger as he made his way to the elevator. His two sons ran interference, which included one son shoving a reporter out of the way. "Will you pay for Whitey's defense?" someone shouted. Bill looked straight ahead. The questions and microphones came from all directions. He said he had no comment beyond a prepared statement he'd issued.

Continuing down the long hallway, Bill Bulger looked frail and

seemed off his game, the way he leaned on his sons and refused comment. Over decades he'd created for himself the image of erudite law-
maker with a sense of history, always ready to toy with reporters, chide
them for never giving Southie a break, and summoning the words of a
Greek philosopher to fit the moment. This time it was as if he was overwhelmed by history—Whitey's deadly legacy.

"Perhaps later I'll make a statement," was all he kept saying.

But one reporter's comment finally got through: "You seem emotional right now."

Bill Bulger began to answer, "No—I . . . ," but then he stopped.
After a pause he resumed, his voice low and sounding far away. "It's an
unusual experience," he said.

Whitey, meanwhile, was en route to the Plymouth County Correc-
tional Facility in a caravan of three black SUVs that included Catherine
Greig, whose brief court appearance came after Whitey's. The first government vehicle carried state police and U.S. marshals, while the middle vehicle held Whitey and Greig. They were not permitted to sit next
to each other but were free to chat during what amounted to their last
ride together. The drive south took about forty minutes, and at 6:15
p.m. the motorcade pulled into a parking area next to the administrative complex that, with its two large garage doors at each end, was ten-
derly known as the "vehicle trap."

Whitey and Greig were manacled federal prisoners now. There was
no *Casablanca* moment ("We'll always have Santa Monica") and no
long good-bye. Whitey was ushered inside for processing into a wing of
the county facility devoted to federal prisoners, while Greig was driven
to a women's prison in Rhode Island to await her trial.

They would never be together again.

By the end of June federal prosecutors had completed some legal
housekeeping. They dropped the original 1994 racketeering case
against Whitey to focus on a second and more explosive racketeering
indictment from 2000. Critics accused the government of "judge shopping," of wanting to get away from the exacting U.S. District Court
Judge Mark L. Wolf, who, in adjudicating Stevie Flemmi's part of the
1994 case, had overseen the historic 1998 hearings exposing the depths
of FBI corruption. But the government insisted they wanted to proceed

in the 2000 case before Judge Richard G. Stearns, a former federal prosecutor, in part because of the victims' families. The 2000 indictment was the one containing murder charges that Whitey had participated in nineteen killings—eleven while an FBI informant—as so-called predicate crimes in his racketeering enterprise.

The June 30 court hearing featured another key development. Prominent Boston attorney J. W. Carney Jr. was appointed by a federal magistrate to defend Whitey. The bespectacled attorney, who, like Whitey, sported a neatly trimmed white beard, embraced the challenge. "Jay Carney," he said as he vigorously shook Whitey's hand in court. Carney said afterward he planned to assemble a team of investigators, paralegals, and other attorneys to work on Whitey's defense. He immediately began meeting with his famous client and soon enough seemed charmed. "I feel like I'm talking to a historical figure," Carney said. "He's very smart. He's got a great memory and he's a voracious reader, like his brother."

For this second hearing the federal courthouse was once again in a virtual lockdown. Whitey arrived at Logan International Airport aboard a U.S. Coast Guard Jayhawk MH-60 helicopter that had flown him from the Plymouth County prison facility. From there he was driven to the courthouse. It cost the government $7,500 for the forty-minute helicopter service—as well as a flood of negative public reaction. The video of Whitey, shackled and wearing a radiant orange prison suit, disembarking and being escorted to a waiting SUV, was broadcast around the country.

"Enough already of the helicopters and the jets and the caravans that make Whitey Bulger look like he's the exiled president of a developing nation," began the *Boston Globe*'s Brian McGrory in his column headlined WHITEY, STILL FLYING HIGH.

The question of preferential treatment was further inflamed when Bill Bulger, accompanied by brother Jack, walked down the fifth-floor corridor. Court officers cleared the crowd to allow the brothers to enter the empty courtroom and get settled in the front row before anyone else, including the contingent of relatives of Whitey's victims. Steven Davis, the volatile brother of Debra Davis, lost his cool. "I don't give a shit if he [Bill] was the president of the United States!" he shouted. "They had no business putting him in front of the victims' families."

The government did not repeat its helicopter mistake, and the circus atmosphere was replaced by the grind of pretrial legal wrangling between prosecutors and Whitey's defense team. In the months to come, Carney's refrain centered on the herculean task of mastering the mountain of evidence the government was required to turn over so he could prepare for trial. Prosecutors, Carney argued, were not making the task any easier. "The government's landfill of discovery is so poorly compiled and presented," he complained in one court filing. "The government has produced over 500,000 pages of discovery, hundreds of photographs and videos, and 921 cassette tapes of audio recordings without accompanying transcripts or an index of the speakers." Carney eventually won a postponement of the initial November 5, 2012, trial date to early March 2013, and later won another postponement to June 2013.

Throughout, Carney made a point of saying Whitey was eager. "James Bulger is looking forward to his trial. He is physically in good health. Mentally, he is sharp, focused, candid, and effusive, with an excellent memory of events. His assistance to prepare for trial is essential, especially to dispel the lies advanced by cooperating witnesses when they thought they would never encounter him again."

Carney's assurances that Whitey was fully functioning came as welcome news to one key Bulger loyalist—Whitey's former G-man, the imprisoned John Connolly. Ever since his 2008 conviction in Miami for the John Callahan murder, Connolly, seventy-one, had refused the occasional request for an interview. But he broke his silence now to announce Whitey was coming to his rescue. "My lawyers have information that since Bulger was brought in, he spoke to the FBI agents and told them I had nothing to do with tipping him off," he told the *Daily Beast*. Investigators scoffed at the idea—Whitey Bulger as an alibi witness? They also noted it would be in Whitey's interest to dangle a possible lifeline to the agent who'd served him so loyally, given that Connolly, if he ever wanted to talk, likely had plenty on all the Bulgers.

No peep about exoneration, however, was ever heard from the other law enforcement mole who'd served the Bulger Gang on a tier lower than Connolly's vaunted FBI. Richard Schneiderhan, the state police detective who Flemmi said traded information for cash for two decades, had gotten tripped up in the late 1990s trying to warn Bill and Jack Bulger that their telephones were tapped. He was convicted at trial in 2003, served sixteen months in prison, and faded from view.

Meanwhile, the FBI was left to deflect some flak about the historic arrest. Instead of an afterglow of praise the bureau faced widespread skepticism that the capture had happened as quickly and cleanly as reported. It had a hard time selling the idea that its "Greig strategy" had worked in three days after sixteen years of nothing. Given the decades of complicity and protection, the FBI had such an enduring credibility problem with Whitey that even when it did something right the public reaction was that something was wrong somewhere. To blunt the negative fallout, FBI officials released a few telling details about the capture, including a key one—that a woman from Iceland who vacationed in Santa Monica had provided the tip. But that only sent reporters out to hunt down the woman's identity. The *Boston Globe* broke the story that Anna Bjornsdottir was the tipster and had received the two-million-dollar reward. The news buttressed the FBI's account but then led to a fresh round of criticism from U.S. marshals and others in law enforcement that the FBI had failed to protect a source in a fugitive manhunt. More rancor in the ranks.

Then came trouble on another front. Not long after Whitey's capture it was revealed that the Boston FBI had had a more recent informant relationship with a high-level mobster engaged in violent crime. The FBI's ties to Mafia boss Mark Rossetti of East Boston seemed like Whitey redux, albeit on a smaller stage. State police had wiretapped Rossetti's phones and figured out he was working with the FBI, even though Rossetti was near the top of the New England Mafia, directing extortion, drug trafficking, loan-sharking, and gambling—and was a suspect in six homicides. In short, he was the definition of a career criminal who should not be in the informant program. That was the supposed lesson of the Whitey Bulger scandal. But there he was. Congressman Stephen Lynch of South Boston, a member of the congressional panel that in 2003 examined the FBI's unholy alliance with Whitey, concluded the FBI could not be left on its own to decide whether an informant had gone too far. Lynch seemed a man alone, but before 2011 was over he filed legislation to give Congress a direct oversight role to mend the FBI's broken system.

Held in Rhode Island since her capture, Catherine Greig, turning sixty-one and gray-haired, gave every indication she would stand by her man. Her lawyer, Kevin Reddington, had advised her not to write letters but she wrote to her twin sister, Margaret McCusker, and others anyway, notes in which she described how much she missed Whitey and that she would never cooperate against him. She was inundated with movie and book offers to tell all about Whitey, but she refused.

Her sister became a regular visitor, although Greig never had the pleasure of Bill or Jack Bulger's company. Instead Greig maintained contact with the Bulger family through one of Bill's nieces. Indeed, that contact became the way Whitey managed to get messages to her. Through the niece Greig received photographs that contained something personal from Whitey written on the back—brief expressions of love and affection, such as "Those were the best years of my life." Prison officials and prosecutors became aware of the ruse to get around the ban against inmate-to-inmate contact, but they allowed it to continue in the event that down the road they needed evidence to show Greig's ongoing culpability.

They wouldn't. In March 2012 Greig said she would plead guilty. The plea meant she faced a maximum of five years in prison and a $250,000 fine for each of the three counts—conspiracy to harbor a fugitive, conspiracy to commit identity fraud, and identity fraud. Prosecutors recommended a ten-year sentence, while Greig sought a much shorter term of twenty months. Her argument for leniency wasn't that she was a clueless partner of the most-wanted man in America, bumping along for the ride in oblivion. Rather it was a choice she'd made and stuck to—blinded by a love for the ages and the wonders of Whitey Bulger. She and her lawyer spun it into a Shakespearean sonnet in their bid for mercy from the court.

It was a tough sell. On June 12, 2012, Greig was sentenced to eight years. "This is not a romantic saga," U.S. Attorney Carmen M. Ortiz told reporters afterward. Greig was taken to Waseca, Minnesota, to a low-security federal prison. She'd thought she would serve a total of three years with time served, but the new reality was she'd be behind bars for about six and a half years with good behavior. She'd also hoped she'd be nearby in a Connecticut prison. In November 2012, her attorneys filed an appeal to shorten the prison term. Greig claimed that relatives of Whitey's victims should not have been allowed to deliver "inflammatory" remarks about her to the judge.

Then there was Whitey's other significant woman—Teresa Stanley. After her three decades with Whitey, and a short stab at the fugitive life, she'd made the deliberate choice for her hometown and family. She had arrived home in early 1995 nearly penniless, taking on the demanding job of banquet waitressing, hauling heavy trays and getting up at four-thirty in the morning. Over the years she came to exult in her grandchildren and especially her two great-grandchildren. For the first time she enjoyed a social life with girlfriends that was impossible to maintain with the controlling Whitey. In the end, she broke his spell and was happy to be the woman left behind, appalled by the gory details of Whitey's murders as they became known. Her choice brought ostracism from the Bulgers, with Jack berating her on the street one day for disloyalty and being shunned by Bill and his family. In early 2012 Teresa Stanley was diagnosed with lung cancer and in August, at the age of seventy-one, she died at her home on Silver Street, surrounded by family.

Throughout 2011 and 2012, Whitey occupied Cell 108 in the G-Unit of the Plymouth County House of Correction—an area for pretrial federal prisoners segregated from the general population. It was similar to his days in Alcatraz—kept in a single cell, with only an hour a day outside for exercise and fifteen additional minutes for a shower and shave. Not every cell in G-Unit had a surveillance camera on the wall, but Whitey's did so that guards could watch him around the clock from the control room. His cell opened into a "day room" that had a pay telephone and enough space to walk in small circles. That room opened to a small outdoor recreation area with a basketball hoop, a breath of fresh air, and a sliver of sky. In his cell, the narrow slit for a window made it hard to keep track of day and night. To help pass the hours he had a portable audiocassette player and earphones. Like other prisoners held in Administrative Segregation he wore an orange prison suit, while inmates in the general population wore green. Breakfast came at 6:00 a.m. sharp, lunch at 11:30 a.m., and dinner at 4:30 p.m. The menu for Christmas Day 2011 featured blueberries for the breakfast pancakes and a roast beef dinner. But Whitey was not impressed; he was said to be generally unhappy with the food.

The number of conferences with attorneys was not limited, but other visitors were restricted to two a week. Both Bill and Jackie Bulger came to see him, escorted to the visiting room adjacent to G-Unit, where they sat on one side of a large plate glass window and talked to Whitey over telephones that were monitored.

Whitey rejected every request for an interview, but media interest hardly flagged, with just about any Whitey tidbit or rumor either published or broadcast. One report said Whitey was reduced to wearing diapers due to an illness. Untrue. Another said he was reading romance novels. Untrue. As in Alcatraz, he read voraciously, with his brothers and attorneys making sure his taste for World War II histories and biographies was met, given that the prison's nonfiction collection was thin. He wrote, too, using the "safety pen" issued to inmates that was made soft and flexible so that it could not be used as a weapon. Whitey corresponded with folks from Santa Monica whom he'd known as Charlie Gasko. The mostly chatty letters were noteworthy for the fact that when he did refer to his capture and his true identity he never showed any remorse. Instead, once he got onto the subject of Whitey's World he urged them not to believe everything reported about him in the media, and then he complained about former associates who'd turned on him, especially Johnny Martorano. Whitey was obsessed with Martorano, denouncing the fact that the hit man had confessed to killing more than twenty people but was out of prison, a free man, seen dining at Daisy Buchanan's in Boston's Back Bay.

How just was that?

The implication was clear. What about him—the good bad guy?

But no matter what Whitey wrote he could not alter the new reality: he was no longer in charge of his legacy. He'd lost control of that long ago, ever since the federal court hearings in 1998, the congressional hearings, and the many federal civil trials that followed, and especially with the fall of the FBI's John Connolly, who for so many years spun the myth of Whitey Bulger as Southie's Robin Hood.

During the early 1930s, J. Edgar Hoover's FBI had coined the term *public enemies* to describe targets of its War on Crime—gangsters like John Dillinger, Ma Barker, and Machine Gun Kelly. James J. "Whitey" Bulger, it turns out, has been the biggest public enemy of them all. That's Whitey's legacy—he was a monstrous killer and mob boss whose star in the constellation of crime burned hot for decades, in contrast to the meteoric careers of the gangsters from an earlier time. This longevity resulted from his criminal genius and cold-blooded savagery—and also because of his unrivaled mastery of a corrupted FBI, the very federal police agency whose original purpose was to protect Americans from their public enemies.

None of this, however, was going to stop Whitey from insisting otherwise—in letters, in an unfinished memoir, or, as he announced midway through 2012, at his federal racketeering trial. Whitey said he was going to testify. "He is going to tell the truth, if the judge permits him to," his attorney, Jay Carney, told reporters in early August. Moreover, Carney said, he and his client were developing a defense to beat the charges—Whitey had an agreement with the FBI authorizing his crimes.

Stevie Flemmi had previously attempted a so-called immunity defense, a claim that he could not be prosecuted for crimes committed while an FBI informant. The courts had soundly rejected the notion, ruling no FBI agent had the authority to make such a devil's deal. But Carney insisted his claim would be different, contending that years ago Whitey had reached an understanding with higher-ups in the U.S. Justice Department. In October 2012, Carney asserted in a court filing that Jeremiah T. O'Sullivan, the former head of the Organized Crime Strike Force who had dropped Whitey and Flemmi from the 1979 horse race–fixing indictment, was the one who had promised Whitey protection. O'Sullivan, who died in 2009, was unavailable to respond to Carney's bombshell claim.

Whitey Bulger was saying O'Sullivan had given him a license to kill. The defense was the ultimate in legal swagger—capturing a sense of entitlement rooted in a long, charmed life of crime, interrupted by only one stretch of hard time. Legal observers were astonished. "There's no such thing as a license to kill, and that's what he's claiming," one prominent Boston defense attorney told reporters. Said another, "None of us have ever heard of immunity to commit murder."

In unison, they asked, What could Whitey possibly be thinking?

Likely, that there was always a first time.

After all, he was Whitey Bulger.

ACKNOWLEDGMENTS

Over the many years we've written about Whitey Bulger, John Connolly, and the FBI we've had the help and support of so many people from our professional and personal lives that there is no way to acknowledge everyone. This is a partial list aimed at thanking those who pitched in to help tell the life story of James J. "Whitey" Bulger.

We'd like to thank a number of friends and colleagues at Boston University. Tom Fiedler, the dean of BU's College of Communication and previously an award-winning reporter and editor at the *Miami Herald*, provided continuous support, as did Bill McKeen, chair of the Journalism Department. Susan Walker, Chris Daly, and Bob Zelnick were regular cheerleaders. Dorothy Clark introduced us to her friend Paul Horan, who shared his photographs and Santa Monica contacts. Jon Surmacz provided technical support and Ken Holmes helped in countless ways that kept us humming along. We'd also like to thank journalism students Carly Geslinger and Max Lewontin for their research assistance in locating historical court and Bulger family records.

We'd especially like to thank Mitch Zuckoff, a BU colleague whose friendship dates back years and includes working side by side with us at the *Boston Globe*. For *Whitey*, Mitch was there at the start, helping to brainstorm the book's outline and overarching themes, and all along the way he served as a valuable resource.

We thank Tom Mulvoy, another former *Globe* colleague, a talented editor who did it all during his years at the newspaper, for his careful reading of the manuscript. His edits and suggestions were a big help and improved the book.

We'd like to extend our gratitude to Dr. Alison Fife, a leading forensic psychiatrist, who generously gave us many hours of her time, serving as a sounding board for our findings and steering us in important directions in terms of our research and analysis of a criminal mind like Whitey's. Quite simply, her guidance was crucial in the development of our psychological take on Whitey.

Marie Daley and Rhonda R. McClure at the New England Historic Genealogical Society were valuable resources for our historical and archival research. Marie Daley is the NEHGS expert on Irish ancestry who discovered the Bulgers' roots in Ireland by locating records in Newfoundland establishing that the great-grandfather emigrated from County Wexford. John Mannion of Memorial University in St. John's, Newfoundland, an expert on the Irish immigration there in the early nineteenth century, helped with various records on Whitey's great-grandparents and grandparents. We'd also like to thank Marta Crilly, an assistant archivist at the City of Boston Archives, a division of the Boston City Clerk's Office, who provided information on Whitey's father's employment in two city departments and his home addresses while a city employee.

We'd like to acknowledge Vita Paladino, director of the Gotlieb Archival Research Center at Boston University, whose passion for archival research is infectious, as well as Sean Noel, the Gotlieb's associate director, and Alex Rankin, the associate director of acquisitions, who were always ready to provide a helping hand.

We thank archivist Charles Niles for locating the proverbial needle in the haystack—an exchange of letters between Bill Bulger and John W. McCormack about Whitey, written in the 1960s, that were buried in McCormack's papers.

At BU's Mugar Memorial Library, we thank librarians Diane C. D'Almeida and Donald Altschiller for their research assistance; and at BU's Education School Pickering Library, we thank Sean Giere for pulling historic newspaper clips about Whitey and his associates from the *Boston Traveler* newspaper archive.

In addition, we'd like to acknowledge George Cully, Air Force historian; Bill Talent at the Air Force archive at Maxwell Air Force Base in Montgomery, Alabama; archivist Joseph Sanchez at the National Archives in San Bruno, California; Robert J. Sampson, Henry Ford II Professor of the Social Sciences at Harvard University; Sonia Barbosa and Dwayne Liburd at Harvard University's Murray Research Center; Susie McIntyre, Head of Information Services at the Great Falls, Montana, Public Library; Judy Ellinghausen at the County Museum, Great Falls; reporter Kimball Bennion at the *Great Falls Tribune;* Dave Easley, a base historian at the Air Force base in Great Falls; Mary Curry, Public Service Coordinator and Research Associate at the National Security Archive; Dr. Colin Ross of Richardson, Texas; Elizabeth Bouvier of the Massachusetts State Court archives; Beverly Mahan, assistant clerk at the South Boston District Court; Margaret Sullivan, Boston Police Department historian; Elaine Driscoll, spokesperson for the Boston Police Department; and Angelene Richardson of BPD's media relations unit, who provided several cross sections of Boston crime data from 1960 to 2011.

We thank Lindsey Cyr for sharing personal information about life with Whitey and the anguish of their son Douglas's death.

We'd also like to acknowledge several journalists who over the years have become Bulger experts—namely David Boeri, Dan Rea, and Fred Rothenberg, at NBC's *Dateline,* and Howie Carr, author of *The Brothers Bulger* and *Hitman.* We'd like to point out that when all of us were working the "Whitey beat" for our respective media, the idea of sharing materials was out of the question given the competitive nature of journalism. It's refreshing that when a project is noncompetitive and the context is entirely different from the daily news scrum, they did not hesitate to share their perspective or records, primary source materials, and photographs. We'd also like to acknowledge the first-rate work of friends and former colleagues at the *Boston Globe* who have continually advanced the public's understanding of the epic Bulger story—Kevin Cullen, Shelley Murphy, Ralph Ranalli, Patricia Nealon, Brian McGrory, and, more recently, Maria Cramer and Milton Valencia. In California, we thank Lynda Gorov for her help in mapping out the lay of the land, and at the *Boston Herald* we acknowledge Peter Gelzinis's contributions.

There are a number of lawyers serving in varying roles in the Bulger case over the years whom we would like to thank for their input and assistance —Anthony Cardinale, Paul Griffin, Michael J. Heineman, Edward Berkin, Robert Sheketoff, and Jon Mitchell, a former assistant U.S. attorney and now the mayor of New Bedford, Massachusetts. In addition, there are many local and federal investigators, as well as various public officials, who have helped us, some of whom wish to remain anonymous. We'd like to acknowledge Scott Keller, U.S. Marshal John Gibbons, supervisory Deputy U.S. Marshal Jeffrey L. Bohn, retired Chief Deputy U.S. Marshal Dave Taylor in Boston, and retired Deputy U.S. Marshal Arthur Roderick. We'd like to thank John Birtwell, the public information officer at the Plymouth County House of Correction, along with Sheriff Joseph D. McDonald Jr. and his staff.

We would be remiss if we overlooked the defining work of a handful of federal judges sitting in the District of Massachusetts who made critical contributions unraveling the scope of Whitey Bulger's carnage. Their monumental work began with Judge Mark L. Wolf, who first presided over months of public hearings in 1998 that blew the cover off the toxic secrets involving Whitey and the FBI. Too often judges seem to opt to keep their heads down, looking for reasons, oftentimes procedural, to avoid the most vexing challenges. Not Judge Wolf. His willingness to pursue a big dig into Whitey and the FBI seemed to set a tone for other federal judges who followed—most notably the late Reginald C. Lindsay, Nancy Gertner (retired), and William G. Young. In their handling of wrongful death and wrongful conviction claims that came before them they seemed at once horrified by the depths of wrongdoing and determined in their extensive fact-finding and rulings to not turn away from any of it. The public owes them thanks.

Our agent, Richard Abate, came to us after Whitey's capture in June 2011 and told us we weren't done writing about Whitey until we wrote the full life story, and we thank him for teaming us up again and matching us with Sean Desmond, our editor at Crown. Sean, always enthusiastic, oversaw our work with patience and a keen eye for story and detail. We also want to thank Stephanie Knapp, a Crown assistant editor, and the entire team at Crown who helped us bring the book to the finish line.

Then there are our friends and family who keep us going day in and day out. We thank Jon Tisch, Dave Holahan, and Kyn Tolson for their friendship and support.

Janet O'Neill was a terrific first reader. Shane O'Neill shared a writer's insight. Nick and Christian Lehr read large chunks of the work-in-progress. Their edits were a big help, and their interest in the story always worked as motivation. Holly and Dana Lehr were cheerleaders of a younger kind, curious (and sometimes complaining) about the amount of research, writing, and time—*so much time*—that goes into a project like this. Karin Lehr somehow kept everything going, seamlessly filling so many roles: wife, mother, running coach, editor, and inspiration.

SOURCES

To research the life of Whitey Bulger we have built upon the years of reporting for our two prior books and for articles we wrote for the *Boston Globe* about Whitey, the FBI, and the Boston Mafia. We have added to more than one hundred interviews, and to thousands of pages of court records, criminal and civil case files, sworn testimony, depositions, grand jury testimony, and investigatory reports. Much of the material we have relied on for this book is new— material that was only recently made public or material that remains sealed but that we obtained through sources. Of all the previously unexamined material, we want to single out Whitey's vast federal prison file from the 1950s and 1960s. The file, running more than five hundred pages, was a rich and untapped treasure of information about Whitey, his entry into the criminal life, South Boston, and his family. In the file were numerous letters Whitey and others had written, including his brother Bill. The file contained extensive, previously undisclosed information about Whitey's participation in the LSD Project at the Atlanta Penitentiary (including the contract he signed as an LSD "volunteer") and about his suspected role in breakout attempts. It was also filled with periodic conduct reports that prison officials had prepared, as well as lengthy federal probation reports containing new information about the Bulger family, Whitey's boyhood, and his strained relationship with his father. The file is held at the National Archives in San Francisco, cited as "Inmate Case File AZ-1428, BOLGER, James Joseph Jr., Comprehensive Inmate Case Files, 1910–1988 (ARC Identifier 622809) US Penitentiary, Alcatraz, Record Group 129 The National Archives San Francisco."

Examining the life of Whitey as a boy in South Boston during the late 1930s and 1940s was a challenge, and we came across a resource that allowed us to infiltrate that period in ways not previously accomplished. We were granted access to a landmark study of juvenile delinquency in Boston conducted by the husband-wife academic team of Sheldon and Eleanor Glueck. The Gluecks' voluminous fieldwork, held in the archives of Harvard University, gave us a window into the everyday life of Southie boys, especially juvenile delinquents. The files were filled with the original handwritten field notes of social workers' interviews with the subjects and their parents. Reading the interviews, we were able to travel back in time, learning how the boys hustled and spent their days, discovering the colorful names of the various street corner gangs—many of which had been lost to time—and even the unique way they talked to one another. Several of the researchers noted that in conducting interviews they had to adjust to the boys' unique street jargon. One social worker, in his summary of one interview, seemed to marvel at the boy's manner of speech, noting that he "talks in his own colorful action-packed idiom." The researcher continued, "when the boy is talking freely one has all he can do to understand what he is saying."

The following is the study's official citation at Harvard:

Sheldon Glueck (aka the "Glueck Study"), 1986, "Crime Causation Study: Unraveling Juvenile Delinquency, 1940–1963," http//hdl.handle.net/1902.1/00896 UNF:3:R/WVfEEDsx1R+V6uFQAn/w==Murray Research Archive (Distributor) V2 (Version). We zeroed in on case studies of nearly one hundred South Boston boys, learning about life on the streets mostly from boys numbered 34, 82, 286, 379, and 452.

To research Whitey's entry into the federal prison system in 1956 we relied extensively on the inmate quarterly magazine the *Atlantian,* maintained in bound volumes at Ohio State University and obtained through Inter-Library Loan. We read volumes 14, 15, 16, 17, 18, and 19, covering the years 1957–59. The articles and photographs provided an up-close look at the prison and prison life during Whitey's time there—the physical plant, the cell blocks, the eight-man cells that Whitey detested, the meals, daily schedule, activities, work, and sports. Inmate-authored articles described the quarantine experience, how to do time, even participation in such prison experiments as the LSD Project.

Specific articles of the *Atlantian* are cited in the chapter notes.

To flesh out the LSD Project at the Atlanta Penitentiary in the late 1950s we drew on a variety of source material, much of which had not been consulted previously in connection with Whitey's participation. The source material includes unclassified CIA documents about LSD experiments conducted at the prison under the auspices of Dr. Carl C. Pfeiffer of Emory University, which was known as Subproject 47 of MK-ULTRA. We obtained various CIA records from the National Security Archive's eleven-box unpublished collection, "CIA Behavior Control Experiments," also known as the "MK-ULTRA Collection," which the author John Marks donated to the archive. We found material in Box Nine especially helpful.

We obtained additional CIA records and materials about the LSD Project from Dr. Colin Ross, author of the book *The CIA Doctors.*

We also found invaluable a federal civil rights lawsuit that several of Whitey's fellow inmates who also participated in the LSD Project had filed in 1979 against CIA director William Casey, the director of the Federal Bureau of Prisons, and U.S. attorney general William French Smith. Using the Freedom of Information Act, we obtained access to the case's original papers and depositions from the National Archives and Records Administration. In them we discovered unprecedented detail about the LSD Project conducted in the prison's Ward F, in documents that included the original complaint filed in U.S. District Court for the Northern District Court in Atlanta, dated Feb. 17, 1981, docket number C81–291A; the "Outline of Plaintiff's Case"; a 114-page transcript of the sworn deposition of Dr. Carl C. Pfeiffer, taken on June 26, 1982; and the seventy-one-page sworn deposition of plaintiff-inmate Don Roderick Scott, on March 12, 1982. The lawsuit was dismissed on procedural grounds on April 29, 1983, when a federal judge ruled that the inmates had failed to file their lawsuit within the two-year statute of limitations.

To further develop the context for the experiments, we found helpful the testimony of former CIA director Admiral Stansfield Turner on August 3, 1977, at a joint hearing before the Select Committee on Intelligence and the Subcommittee on Health and Scientific Research of the Committee on Human Resources in the First Session of the Ninety-Fifth Congress, a panel on which U.S. senator Edward M. Kennedy of Massachusetts served. The committee's investigation included MK-ULTRA, the CIA's program of research in behavioral modification.

Other specific citations to LSD source material are in the chapter notes.

Legal and Congressional Proceedings

A complete listing of the past court cases and documentary sources that we consulted in researching *Whitey* can be found in Lehr and O'Neill, *Black Mass*. Other court cases, either newly discovered or more recent, include:

- *Don Roderick Scott, et al. v. William Casey, et al.* Civ A. No. C81–291A. U.S. District Court, N.D. Georgia, Atlanta Division. (*Scott v. Casey*, 562 F.Supp. 475 [1983].)
- *United States v. John V. Martorano*, U.S. District Court, District of Massachusetts, criminal docket 97–10009.
- *United States v. Margaret McCusker, Kathleen McDonough*, U.S. District Court, District of Massachusetts, criminal docket 98–10148.
- *United States v. John J. Connolly Jr., James Bulger aka "Whitey," and Stephen Flemmi*, U.S. District Court, District of Massachusetts, criminal docket 99–10428.
- *United States v. James J. Bulger*, U.S. District Court, District of Massachusetts, criminal docket 99–10371.

- *United States v. Stephen Flemmi,* U.S. District Court, District of Massachusetts, criminal docket 99–10371.
- *United States v. John P. "Jackie" Bulger,* U.S. District Court, District of Massachusetts, criminal docket 01–10409.
- *Emily McIntyre and Christopher McIntyre, as co-administrators of the Estate of John L. McIntyre v. United States of America, et al.,* U.S. District Court, District of Massachusetts, civil docket 01–10408.
- *Estate of Brian Halloran v. United States of America, et al.,* U.S. District Court, District of Massachusetts, civil docket 01–11346.
- *Estate of Michael Donahue v. United States of America, et al.,* U.S. District Court, District of Massachusetts, civil docket 01–10433.
- *Peter J. Limone, et al. v. United States of America,* U.S. District Court, District of Massachusetts, civil docket 02–10890.
- *Estate of Richard J. Castucci, et al. v. United States of America, et al.,* U.S. District Court, District of Massachusetts, civil docket 02–11312.
- *Anna M. Litif, et al. v. United States, John Morris, John Connolly, James Bulger and Stephen Flemmi,* U.S. District Court, District of Massachusetts, civil docket 02–11791.
- *Estate of Debra Davis v. United States, John Morris, John Connolly, James Bulger and Stephen Flemmi,* U.S. District Court, District of Massachusetts, civil docket 02–11911.
- *Marion Hussey v. United States, John Morris, John Connolly, James Bulger and Stephen Flemmi,* U.S. District Court, District of Massachusetts, civil docket 03–10087.
- *Commonwealth of Massachusetts: In Re Thomas E. Finnerty—Judgment of Disbarment,* Supreme Judicial Court for Suffolk County, no. BD–2008–055.
- *State of Florida v. John J. Connolly Jr.,* Circuit Court of the Eleventh Judicial District in and for Miami-Dade, Florida, criminal docket F01–8287D.
- *United States v. Catherine Greig,* U.S. District Court, District of Massachusetts, criminal docket 11–10286.

We have also relied on the extensive debriefings of three key Bulger Gang members conducted after they became witnesses for the federal government.

- John V. Martorano: a twenty-two-page summary of July and November 1998 debriefings.
- Kevin P. Weeks: a ninety-two-page DEA-6 Report of Investigation dated January 18, 2002.
- Stephen Flemmi: a 146-page DEA-6 Report of Investigation dated November 19, 2003, and a 62-page DEA-6 Report of Investigation, titled "Corruption," dated November 22, 2003.

We also relied on testimony taken during congressional hearings examining FBI corruption in the FBI's use of informants, formally called the Hearing Before the Committee on Government Reform, House of Representatives, One Hundred Eighth Congress, First Session, chaired by Representative Tom Davis of Virginia.

Of particular interest was the testimony of Bill Bulger on June 19, 2003.

The committee issued a report in November 2003 in two volumes, titled *Everything Secret Degenerates: The FBI's Use of Murderers as Informants.*

Archival Materials

The John W. McCormack Collection: Howard Gotlieb Archival Research Center, Boston University.

Theses and Journal Articles

Chafe, Edward-Vincent. "A New Life on 'Uncle Sam's Farm': Newfoundlers in Massachusetts, 1846–1859." A.M.A. thesis, Memorial University of Newfoundland, 1982.

DeMaar, Edmund W. J., Harry L. Williams, A. I. Miller, and C. C. Pfeiffer. "Effects in Man of Single and Combined Oral Doses of Reserpine, Iproniazid, and Lysergic Acid Diethylamide." *Clinical Pharmacology and Therapeutics* 1, no. 1 (1960).

Dishotsky, Norman I., William D. Loughman, Robert E. Mogar, and Wendell R. Lipscomb. "LSD and Genetic Damage." *Science* 172, no. 3982 (April 30, 1971): 431–40.

Halpern, John H., and Harrison G. Pope Jr. "Hallucinogen Persisting Perception Disorder: What Do We Know After 50 Years?" *Drug and Alcohol Dependence Review* 69 (2003): 109–19.

Kerstein, Milton Lewis. Thesis about Old Harbor housing development. University of Massachusetts, Boston, 1981.

Mannion, John M. "Old World Antecedents, New World Adaptations, Inistioge (C. Kilkenny) Immigrants in Newfoundland." *Newfoundland Studies* 5, no. 2 (1989): 103–75.

———, ed. "The Peopling of Newfoundland, Essays in Historical Geography." *Historical Atlas of Canada,* vol. 2, *1800–1891.* Toronto: University of Toronto Press, 1993.

Miller, I. A., Harry L. Williams, and H. B. Murphee (introduced by C. C. Pfeiffer). "Niacin, Niacinamide, or Atropine Versus LSD-25 Model Psychosis in Human Volunteers." *Journal of Pharmacology and Experimental Therapeutics* 119 (1957): 169–70.

Murphee, Henry B., Roy H. Dippy, Elizabeth H. Jenney, and Carl C. Pfeiffer. "Effects in Normal Man of Methyltryptamine and Ethyltryptamine." *Clinical Pharmacology and Therapeutics* 2 (November–December 1961): 722–26.

Selected Books

Bruce, John Campbell. *A Farewell to the Rock: Escape from Alcatraz.* New York: McGraw-Hill, 1963.

Bulger, William M. *While the Music Lasts: My Life in Politics.* Boston: Houghton Mifflin, 1996.

Burrough, Bryan. *Public Enemies: America's Greatest Crime Wave and the Birth of the FBI, 1933–34.* New York: Penguin Books, 2004.

Carr, Howie. *The Brothers Bulger: How They Terrorized and Corrupted Boston for a Quarter Century.* New York: Warner Books, 2006.

————. *Hitman: The Untold Story of Johnny Martorano: Whitey Bulger's Enforcer and the Most Feared Gangster in the Underworld.* New York: Forge, 2011.

Cleckley, Dr. Hervey. *The Mask of Sanity: An Attempt to Clarify Some Issues About the So-Called Psychopathic Personality.* 2nd ed. St. Louis: C. V. Mosby, 1950.

Dorchester Streets: The Story of the Sheehan Family in Dorchester, 1921–1943. Boston: Dober Dan Press, 1999.

Fitzpatrick, Robert, and John Land. *Betrayal: Whitey Bulger and the FBI Agent Who Fought to Bring Him Down.* New York: Forge, 2012.

Foley, Thomas J., and John Sedgwick. *Most Wanted: Pursuing Whitey Bulger, the Murderous Mob Chief the FBI Secretly Protected.* New York: Simon & Schuster, 2012.

Glueck, Sheldon, and Eleanor Glueck. *Delinquents in the Making: Paths to Prevention.* New York: Harper & Brothers, 1952.

Gregory, George H. *Alcatraz Screw: My Years as a Guard in America's Most Notorious Prison.* Columbia: University of Missouri Press, 2002.

Handlin, Oscar. *Boston's Immigrants, 1790–1865: A Case Study.* Cambridge, MA: Harvard University Press, 1941.

Hare, Dr. Robert D. *Without Conscience: The Disturbing World of the Psychopaths Among Us.* New York: Pocket Books, 1993.

Laub, John H., and Robert J. Sampson. *Shared Beginnings, Divergent Lives: Delinquent Boys to Age 70.* Cambridge, MA: Harvard University Press, 2003.

Lehr, Dick, and Gerard O'Neill. *Black Mass: Whitey Bulger, the FBI, and a Devil's Deal.* New ed. New York: PublicAffairs, 2012.

Marks, John. *The Search for the "Manchurian Candidate": The CIA and Mind Control.* New York: Times Books, 1979.

McCarthy, Michael. *The Irish in Newfoundland, 1600–1900: Their Trials, Tribulations and Triumphs.* St. John's, Newfoundland: Creative, 1999.

Nee, Patrick. *A Criminal and an Irishman: The Inside Story of the Boston Mob–IRA Connection.* Hanover, NH: Steerforth Press, 2006.

O'Connor, Thomas H. *South Boston, My Home Town: The History of an Ethnic Neighborhood.* Boston: Quinlan Press, 1988.

O'Neill, Gerard, and Dick Lehr. *The Underboss: The Rise and Fall of a Mafia Family.* New York: St. Martin's Press, 1989.

Ranalli, Ralph. *Deadly Alliance: The FBI's Secret Partnership with the Mob.* New York: Harper Torch, 2001.

Sammarco, Anthony Mitchell. *Dorchester: A Compendium.* Charleston, SC: History Press, 2011.

Sampson, Robert J., and John H. Laub. *Crime in the Making: Pathways and Turning Points Through Life.* Cambridge, MA: Harvard University Press, 1993.

Schroth, Raymond A. *Bob Drinan: The Controversial Life of the First Catholic Priest Elected to Congress.* New York: Fordham University Press, 2011.

Shannon, William. *The American Irish: A Political and Social Portrait.* Amherst: University of Massachusetts Press, 1963.

Shea, John "Red." *Rat Bastards: The Life and Times of South Boston's Most Honorable Irish Mobster.* New York: William Morrow, 2006.

Trout, Charles H. *Boston, the Great Depression, and the New Deal.* New York: Oxford University Press, 1977.

Vale, Lawrence J. *From the Puritans to the Projects: Public Housing and Public Neighbors.* Cambridge, MA: Harvard University Press, 2000.

NOTES

This is a work of nonfiction. The use of dialogue is based on at least one participant or taken from sworn testimony or recorded transcript. In those instances where sources' accounts differed we went with the weight of the evidence. We have elaborated further in some instances about conflicting accounts, in chapter notes that follow. These notes contain a more detailed listing of source material, often using an abbreviation. For example, a reference in a note to the investigatory report of the debriefing of Kevin Weeks will appear as Weeks's DEA-6 debriefing.

Chapter 1: September 17, 1981

Main sources:
U.S. District Court Judge William G. Young's 56-page "Memorandum of Decision and Order for Judgment" (Jan. 29, 2010) in the Davis family's civil action against the federal government. In his Findings of Fact, Judge Young ruled: "Flemmi lured Davis to Bulger's mother's house in South Boston. Bulger, lying in wait, grabbed her and scissored her neck between his forearms in order to crush her windpipe" (p. 19). Judge Young ordered the government to pay the Estate of Debra Davis a total of $1,352,005.60 for conscious pain and suffering, for loss of consortium, and for funeral expenses (p. 50).

Also from the Davis civil lawsuit, the sworn depositions of Olga Davis (Sept. 21, 2004); of Kevin Weeks (July 13, 2006); and of FBI agent Matthew Cronin (April 9, 2005); the sworn testimony at trial of Eileen Davis (July 12, 2009); of Kevin Weeks (July 1, 2009); of Stephen Flemmi (July 9, 2009), along with his hand-drawn floor plan of the Flemmi house; of Stephen Johnson of the Massachusetts State Police (July 13, 2009); of Daniel Doherty of the federal Drug Enforcement Administration (July 13, 2009, July 20, 2009).

In the state of Florida's murder case against John J. Connolly, the trial testimony of Kevin Weeks and Stephen Flemmi (September/October 2008); the

DEA-6 debriefing reports for Kevin Weeks (January 2002) and Stephen Flemmi (November 2003).

Davis v. Flemmi, No. 01–282 (Norfolk Superior Court, Judge Brady's ruling, September 11, 2009); City of Boston property records for 828 and 832 Third Street.

Interviews:
Lindsey Cyr (September 2011 and after); attorney Paul J. Griffin (September 2011 and after).

Books and articles:
Bill Bulger's memoir, *While the Music Lasts;* Bryan Burrough's *Public Enemies* (pp. 2–6); Dr. Dominick J. Di Maio and Dr. Vincent J. M. Di Maio, *Forensic Pathology* (Boca Raton, FL: CRC Press, 2001), ch. 8, "Asphyxia."

Notes:
According to many accounts, Debbie Davis's relationship with Stephen Flemmi lasted for nine years, but they overlook the simple math showing Debbie and Stevie were involved for seven years, from 1974 until her murder in 1981.

Regarding the specifics of where Whitey Bulger strangled Debbie Davis, U.S. District Court Judge William Young gave more credence to Flemmi's account that Whitey killed Davis upstairs and then dragged her body into the cellar. But we have found the confederate Kevin Weeks's account more credible—that Whitey killed her in the cellar after Flemmi gave her a kiss. This was a version also accepted by Judge Brady in the Norfolk County Superior Court. Our analysis for going with the Weeks version is that Flemmi would want the world to believe the killing was quick. He had set it up and then stood by as it happened. "I didn't do anything," he admitted during his trial testimony. Whenever he testified about the murder he became anxious and talked about the killing being "traumatic" for him, as if he sensed its extreme depravity. But once pushed, Flemmi ended up saying things that actually suggested that the truth about the manner of Debbie's death was closer to the Weeks version. For instance, when attorneys pressed Flemmi in court, he conceded that Debbie might have been in a chair in the cellar. And while denying he said anything to her about going to a better place, he said something that implied she was still alive in the cellar. He said he told Whitey: "I did make the point, I said, 'Let her pray.' "

Chapter 2: Riverhead and Chapter 3: Old Harbor

Main sources:
In addition to the books and periodicals cited in Sources, we worked with Marie Daley and Rhonda R. McClure at the New England Historic Genealogical Society to research the Bulger family tree.

Regarding the research into the Bulger family in Newfoundland and later in Boston, one key document was the birth certificate for Whitey Bulger's grandfather James. James Bulger's birth record for August 25, 1844, was located for us in the Mormon Church Family History Library in Salt Lake City, Utah, by the NEHGS.

The discovery of that birth record allowed further research of the grandfather's parents in Riverhead, Newfoundland, because it identified his parents, William Bulger and Mary Myer, Whitey's great-grandparents. Their obituaries were then located in Newfoundland publications, with Mary Myer's death notice stating her deceased husband immigrated from County Wexford in Ireland.

Other important materials documenting when the Bulgers arrived in Boston in the late nineteenth century were records of Whitey's father's naturalization papers in 1895, his first marriage in 1916, his divorce in 1925, and his second marriage in 1928. Also, the father's work history with the city of Boston obtained from the city's archives.

We made extensive use of the U.S. Census for Boston in 1930 and 1950.

Key dates in the Bulger family chronology
from Ireland to Newfoundland to Boston:

1799: Whitey Bulger's great-grandfather William Bulger is born in County Wexford, Ireland, according to an obituary in Newfoundland.

1812: Whitey's great-grandmother Mary Myer is born, likely in St. John's, Newfoundland. Her family is from southern Tipperary, a location near Waterford Harbor. Her father emigrated from Ireland to Newfoundland during the early 1800s.

1825: William Bulger likely arrives at St. John's, Newfoundland.

1833: On Nov. 20, William Bulger marries Mary Myer at the Old Chapel in St. John's.

1844: On Aug. 25, Whitey's grandfather James is born.

1854: Whitey's grandmother Alice Gardiner is born in Harbour Grace, near St. John's.

1875: On Nov. 25, James Bulger marries Alice Gardiner. They move in with his parents at 128 Lazy Bank Road in St. John's.

1877: On May 4, Whitey's grandfather James's first child, a son, William, is baptized at St. Patrick's Church in St. John's.

1879: On April 15, Whitey's great-grandfather William's death is recorded in the Catholic burial register for St. John's, 1871–79.

1881: On July 22, Whitey's grandfather James's second child, a daughter, Mary Maud, is born.

1883: On July 6, Whitey's grandfather James drowns in a fishing accident in

L'Anse-au-Loup, Labrador, according to records of births, deaths, and marriages in Newfoundland newspapers, 1810–90. On Nov. 25, Whitey's father, James Joseph Bulger, is born.

1884: On July 14, Whitey's great-grandmother Mary Myer Bulger dies at 72, according to vital statistics from a Newfoundland newspapers database.

1889: Whitey's widowed grandmother Alice Gardiner Bulger immigrates to Boston, leaving her son James Joseph and daughter Mary Maud behind in Newfoundland.

1892: Alice Gardiner Bulger marries Michael Kelley in Boston. Like her, he was born in Harbour Grace in Newfoundland.

1895: On July 4, 12-year-old James Joseph immigrates to Boston and joins his mother and stepfather in Charlestown. Two years later, his mother and Kelley have a son, Brendan.

1899: Fifteen-year-old James Joseph runs away to Rhode Island. The next day, he tries to hop a freight train home but falls between cars, crushing his left arm, which has to be amputated, according to a Boston Globe article.

1900: James Joseph lives with his mother and Kelley in Charlestown, according to a 1900 census.

1905: James Joseph's naturalization papers list him at 22 Unity St. in Boston's North End.

1911–18: James Joseph works as a messenger and clerk at Deer Island House of Correction and then at the horseshoe division of the South Stable on Albany St., according to the City of Boston employment archives. He is off the city payroll by 1919.

1913–16: James Joseph lives at 47 Snow Hill in the North End, according to city directories.

1916: On May 7, James Joseph Bulger marries Ruth I. Pearce of Boston in front of a justice of the peace and moves to Melborne St. in Dorchester near Codman Sq.

1917: City employment records list James Joseph Bulger at 908 Harrison Ave., a boardinghouse in the South End.

1918–22: James Joseph Bulger lives with his mother at 91 Eustis St. in Roxbury. According to a city directory, she works as a janitor at 91 Eustis St. According to the 1920 census, Michael Kelley had died.

1925: James Joseph Bulger and Ruth Pearce get divorced.

1923–27: James Joseph Bulger lives in Everett and Revere near the town where Jane "Jean" McCarthy resides.

1928: On Jan. 10, James Joseph Bulger and Jean McCarthy are married in New York City in a civil ceremony at the Somerset Hotel. On May 15, daughter Jean Marie Bulger is born, according to records in Boston and Revere.

1929: James Joseph Bulger lives at 10 Yeamans St. in Revere and works as a clerk at a sand and gravel company. On Sept. 3, James J. "Whitey" Bulger Jr. is born in Boston, and the family is listed as living in Everett.

1932: Whitey Bulger's grandmother Alice dies at Long Island Hospital, a facility operated by the city of Boston.

1933: The Bulgers live at 28 Bay Rd. in Revere for part of the year. Whitey's father's occupation is listed in the city directory as clerk.

1933–38: The Bulgers live in three apartments in Dorchester, going from 92 Florida St. to 13 Centre Ct. and 61 Crescent Ave. Whitey's father is still listed as a clerk.

1938: The Bulgers and five children move to 41 Logan Way in South Boston's Old Harbor project.

1940 and 1941: Whitey's father is listed as a foreman at the Navy Yard in the city directory.

1961: Whitey Bulger is in prison. The family moves within Old Harbor to 252 O'Callahan Way.

1964: Whitey's father, James Joseph Bulger Sr., dies.

1980: Whitey's mother, Jean Bulger, dies.

Chapter 4: "Where's Jim?" and Chapter 5: The Smile and Swagger

Main sources:

For Whitey Bulger's criminal history we relied on his official criminal record, including his juvenile arrest record, obtained from a variety of police sources, including a document dated October 17, 1973: "Personnel Identification Division, Boston, Massachusetts Police Department, record of James J. Bulger Jr., address 41 Logan Way, South Boston, Massachusetts." We also reviewed historical dockets from the South Boston District Court at the archives of the Massachusetts Supreme Judicial Court; and we reviewed Boston police arrest logs from various police districts from the 1940s and 1950s, obtained through a Freedom of Information Act request to the Boston Police Department.

For information about Whitey Bulger's academic performance we relied on a copy of his school record, and for information about his enlistment in the Air Force we relied on a copy of his application form. Author Howie Carr provided both documents. For additional information about Whitey's academic record and his relationship with his father, including the fact that his father beat him, we relied on a lengthy federal "Presentence Report" prepared in 1956 in anticipation of Whitey's sentencing for bank robbery. The report was found in Whitey's prison record, which consists of hundreds of pages and is held in the National Archives.

For South Boston crime statistics we referred to annual reports of the Boston Police Department, and for a sense of the residential makeup of the Old Harbor project we relied on the Commonwealth of Massachusetts Thirty-Third Annual Report of the Police Commissioner for the City of Boston for the Year

Ending November 30, 1938; Ward 7—Precinct 1 (South Boston), City of Boston, List of Residents 20 Years of Age and Over as of January 1, 1939, Joseph F. Timilty, chairman, City of Boston Printing Department.

For an in-depth look at juvenile delinquency in 1940s Boston, particularly in South Boston, we relied on the 1952 Glueck study at Harvard, *Delinquents in the Making*. We zeroed in on case studies of nearly one hundred South Boston boys, learning about life on the streets mostly from boys numbered 34, 82, 286, 379, and 452.

Interviews:
In 1988 with Bill Bulger, Will McDonough, George Pryor, Kevin Joyce, Father Thomas J. McDonnell, Sally Dame, William Monahan, and Joseph Quirk for stories we wrote about the Bulgers in the *Boston Globe;* in 2011–12 with Lindsey Cyr, Kevin Healey, and Dr. Alison Fife.

Books and articles:
Bill Bulger's memoir, *While the Music Lasts* (pp. 2, 3, 20, 31, 32, and more).

John H. Laub and Robert J. Sampson, "Crime and Context in the Lives of 1,000 Boston Men, Circa 1925–1955," a chapter in *Current Perspectives on Aging and the Life Cycle: Delinquency and Disrepute in the Life Course* (Greenwich, CT: JAI Press, 1995); Sheldon Glueck and Eleanor Glueck, *Delinquents in the Making: Paths to Prevention*.

News articles:
Articles in the *Boston Globe* about the drowning of youths in South Boston on the ice floes, dated Jan. 16, 1940, Jan. 17, 1940, Jan. 18, 1940, Feb. 23, 1940; articles in the *Boston Globe* about Whitey's arrest on a rape charge, dated May 31, 1948, and June 1, 1948.

Miscellaneous:
Copy of Air Force recruiting poster from 1948, titled "This Is the Life of an Aviation Cadet."

Notes:
For more evidence of Whitey's strained relationship with his father we also relied on excerpts from letters Whitey wrote to Bill Bulger. The letters, written when Whitey was in federal prison starting in 1956, were obtained by WBZ-TV Channel 4 in Boston. The station broadcast several stories based on its scoop, and the stories included sharing the letters with law enforcement and mental health experts to gauge their assessments. But the station never made the letters public in full. It never posted the full content of the letters on its website—an

oddity given the letters' historical value and the trend in media to tap the benefits of the Internet and disclose online all kinds of records and documents. The station refused our request to disclose the full contents of the letters. "Everything is competitive," the news director, John Verrilli, said. He said he wanted to maintain exclusive control for possible future use on his TV station. We, of course, differ with his perspective.

Chapter 6: AWOL: 1949–53

Main sources:
Whitey's Air Force military record, which included his USAF assignment history, was obtained from the National Personnel Records Center, Military Personnel Records, through a Freedom of Information Act request; Whitey's enlistment, discharge, and a letter regarding his alleged fraudulent enlistment (dated June 22, 1949, and authored by Dale C. Smith, 2nd Lt. USAF, Personnel Officer) were provided by author Howie Carr. We also obtained the records and histories of units in which Whitey served at bases in Texas, Illinois, Kansas, Louisiana, California, Montana, New Jersey, and Bermuda. The unit histories are kept at the Air Force Historical Research Agency at Maxwell Air Force Base in Alabama. Military historian George Cully of Montgomery, Alabama, provided invaluable assistance in locating and analyzing the unit histories.

For information about Whitey's arrests in 1951 while he was stationed at Great Falls Air Force Base we relied on Complaint No. 110 in Police Court, Great Falls, Montana, *City of Great Falls v. James Bulger,* dated March 19, 1951; Complaint No. 116 in Police Court, Great Falls, Montana, *City of Great Falls v. Grace Box,* dated March 20, 1951; the Register of Prisoners Confined in the County Jail of Cascade County, Montana, showing the following entry: "June 12, 1951—ID 3786—James J. Bulger, 21, 5' 10", blond, blue, 160, Complexion—light. By What Authority Committed—Police. Original Charge: Hold for County Attorney. Date Released—6–19–51. Released to East Base by order of County Attorney." The police court complaints and the sheriff's jail records were found in the History Museum of Great Falls, with the help of archive administrator Judy Ellinghausen. We would also like to acknowledge reporter Kimball Bennion of the *Great Falls Tribune* for providing us with additional research information about Great Falls in the early 1950s, particularly information about conditions at the city jail and about the area in the city where Whitey was arrested while on leave from the base.

Books:
For background on psychopathy we relied mainly on Hervey Cleckley's *The Mask of Sanity* and Robert Hare's *Without Conscience.*

News articles:
Articles about Whitey's arrest on assault charges in March 1951 in Great Falls, Montana, in the *Great Falls Leader,* Mar. 19, 1951; about Whitey's arrest on a rape charge in June 1951 in Great Falls, in the *Great Falls Tribune,* June 12, 1951, June 13, 1951, and the *Great Falls Leader,* June 11, 1951, June 13, 1951, June 21, 1951, June 24, 2011; about Army Lt. Joseph D. Toomey missing in action in the *Boston Globe,* Jan. 27, 1951.

Chapter 7: Packing Heat: 1953–56

Main sources:
Whitey's criminal history covering arrests for tailgating; our review of Boston police district arrest logs. To reconstruct Whitey's bank robbing spree, we consulted numerous government records and media accounts, many of which were not previously public. In the Castucci estate's federal civil action, we relied on Exhibit V (B): "Bank Robbery File on James J. Bulger," which includes internal FBI investigatory documents from 1956 describing Whitey's bank robberies; agent Paul Rico's use of informants to capture Whitey; internal FBI memos and letters praising Rico for his work in arresting Whitey; a June 1956 report by U.S. Attorney Anthony Julian in which Whitey's cooperation was outlined. From Whitey's prison file, we relied on the numerous FBI and other official records, particularly the five-page "Presentence Report" prepared for Whitey's sentencing in June 1956, which included a detailed biography and family and criminal history.

In addition, we reviewed the federal jury indictments of Whitey, Ron Dermody, and Carl Smith Jr. in the Rhode Island bank robbery (Indictment No. 6512); the federal indictment of Whitey and Richard Barchard in the Hammond, Indiana, bank robbery (Hammond Criminal No. 2692).

Other source materials include the FBI's press release on Feb. 21, 1956, announcing the arrest of Whitey's partner Ron Dermody in the Rhode Island bank robbery; the stenographer's transcript of Whitey's sentencing in U.S. District Court, District of Massachusetts, before Judge Sweeney, in June 1956 (Criminal No. 56–89, 90, 113, 130).

Regarding Carl Smith, we obtained an FBI report dated April 17, 1956, describing Smith's role in bank robberies, his guilty plea, and the assistance he provided the FBI, including his informing on Whitey; Smith's fifteen-page "Presentence Report," prepared by chief U.S. Probation Officer Anthony S. Kuharich, dated March 31, 1956, which described in detail Smith's crimes and cooperation against Whitey.

In addition, "FBI Record Number 1 950 456," dated Jan. 11, 1972, contained Smith's complete criminal record; various prison records for Smith, including a memo dated May 29, 1956, by the warden at the Atlanta Penitentiary recommending Smith's transfer to Alcatraz; a memo dated Oct. 10, 1957, by the warden at Alcatraz to the director of the Federal Bureau of Prisons about Smith; a report by the chief medical officer about Smith to the Alcatraz Classification Committee, dated Dec. 3, 1957.

Regarding Richard Barchard, we obtained from his prison files a four-page "Report of the Probation Officer," written by U.S. Probation Officer John J. Gildea and dated June 21, 1956, that was filed in connection with Barchard's sentencing in federal court in San Francisco in *U.S. v. Barchard* (No. 8038-Misc) for the Indiana bank robbery.

Books:
The quote about psychopaths comes from the preface in Robert Hare's book *Without Conscience.*

Interviews:
Will McDonough in 1988; Lindsey Cyr in September 2011 and after.

News articles:
Article in the *Boston Globe* on July 1, 1953, covering Whitey's arrest for tailgating along with Richard Kelly.

Articles about the Pawtucket, Rhode Island, bank robbery, in the *Pawtucket Times* on May 17, 1955, and May 18, 1955; the Associated Press teletype of Feb. 27, 1956, reporting the grand jury's indictment of Whitey; and the *Boston Globe* on Feb. 27, 1956.

Articles about the Melrose, Massachusetts, bank robbery, about Whitey and Richard O'Brien in the *Boston Globe* on Nov. 18, 1955, Nov. 20, 1955, May 4, 1956, and May 5, 1956.

Articles about the Hammond, Indiana, bank robbery, about Whitey, Richard Barchard, and Carl Smith in the *Hammond Times* on Nov. 23, 1955, Nov. 25, 1955; the Associated Press teletype of Jan. 9, 1956, reporting that a warrant was issued in Indianapolis for Whitey's arrest; in the *Boston Globe* on Jan. 7, 1956, and Jan. 21, 1956.

Other *Boston Globe* articles about Whitey's bank robberies on Feb. 9, 1956, Feb. 28, 1956, May 4, 1956, and *Boston Herald* articles on Jan. 7, 1956.

Articles about Whitey's arrest in Revere in March 1956 included the Associated Press teletype of Mar. 4, 1956; *Boston Globe* articles on Mar. 4, 1956, Mar. 5, 1956, Mar. 6, 1956; and a *Boston Herald* article on Mar. 5, 1956.

Article on the sentencing of Whitey in the *Boston Globe* on June 22, 1956.

Articles about Ron Dermody in the *Boston Globe* on Nov. 19, 1947, Feb. 9, 1956, Apr. 21, 1956, Sept. 6, 1964, Sept. 7, 1964, Sept. 9, 1964, Sept. 27, 1964, Dec. 12, 1964, Jan. 13, 1965, Feb. 1, 1965, Nov. 17, 1965, Feb. 13, 2004.

Articles about Carl Smith Jr. in the *Boston Globe* on Oct. 19, 1951, Oct. 20, 1951, Oct. 24, 1951, Nov. 27, 1952, June 26, 1953, May 19, 1954, Sept. 17, 1954, Nov. 17, 1954, Nov. 18, 1954, Dec. 17, 1954, Jan. 27, 1955, and Jan. 21, 1956; in the *Vidette-Messenger* (Valparaiso, Indiana) on Dec. 10, 1955, and the *Hammond Times* on Nov. 4, 1956.

Articles about Richard Barchard (and his wife, Dorothy Barchard) in the *Boston Globe* on Jan. 31, 1950, Dec. 5, 1956, Jan. 25, 1957, Apr. 2, 1957, Apr. 9, 1957, Apr. 12, 1957, and Jan. 28, 1965; and the *Hammond Times* on June 22, 1956, and Sept. 5, 1957.

Articles about the increase in bank robberies and law enforcement's response in the *Boston Globe* on Mar. 16, 1956, Mar. 28, 1956, Apr. 15, 1956, and Apr. 18, 1956.

Chapter 8: The Informer: 1956 and Chapter 9: "I'm No Angel, But..."

Main sources:

Proof that Whitey turned informant following his arrest—and also had Jacquie McAuliffe cooperate with the FBI—is found in three reports that Boston FBI agent Herbert F. Briick prepared at the time. The first, a four-page, single-spaced report dated March 5, 1956, was prepared for FBI Director J. Edgar Hoover and was marked "personal and confidential." In it, Briick described how Agent Paul Rico led the way in Whitey's capture in Revere. This report was found in Exhibit V (B): "Bank Robbery File on James J. Bulger," in the Castucci estate's federal civil action. The second Briick report, an "FBI Form No. 2," was dated July 5, 1956, and prepared for Whitey's sentencing in federal court. In it, Briick described Whitey's cooperation and his persuasion of Jacquie McAuliffe to cooperate. The third Briick report, another "FBI Form No. 2," was dated July 13, 1956. In it, Briick provided more detail about Whitey's bank robberies and cooperation. The second and third Briick reports were found in Whitey's prison file at the National Archives in San Francisco.

We again relied on the five-page federal "Presentence Report" prepared for Whitey's sentencing in June 1956, which included a detailed biography and family and criminal history. The report is contained in Whitey's prison file.

For information about FBI agent Paul Rico's raise and praise from J. Edgar Hoover following the capture of Whitey in March 1956, we relied on government documents and Hoover's letters contained in Exhibit V (B): "Bank Robbery File on James J. Bulger," filed in the Castucci estate's federal civil action.

For his transit from Boston to Atlanta, we relied on Whitey's file from the Federal Detention Center at 427 West Street, New York City, and for information about his arrival in Atlanta we relied on his prison file, specifically records covering his admission, his quarantine, and his "Classification Study." For information about Whitey's breakdown we relied on his letter to Rev. Robert Drinan and medical notes and records of the prison's psychologist.

Regarding Richard Barchard, we obtained from his federal prison file an eight-page, handwritten "Motion to Vacate Judgment," which Barchard filed, pro se, on Aug. 31, 1957, in San Francisco in U.S. District Court for the Northern District of California, Cr. No. 35113, while he was an inmate at Alcatraz. In the motion, Barchard described how FBI agents convinced him to plead guilty in 1956 because Whitey Bulger, already in custody, had informed on him and detailed his role in the Hammond, Indiana, bank robbery. (Note: In his motion Barchard further argued that he was innocent, and that Carl Smith, not he, had robbed the bank with Whitey. U.S. District Judge Edward P. Murphy dismissed Barchard's motion on Sept. 9, 1957.)

Books and articles:
Bill Bulger's memoir, *While the Music Lasts,* the quote about loathing informers.

Winfield Burdette, "Medical Research: Lysergic Acid," *Atlantian,* Summer–Fall 1956.

Eugene Campbell, "Medical Research: Anectine," *Atlantian,* Summer–Fall 1956.

Bill Parker, "Code of the Convict: Manifest or Myth," *Atlantian,* Fall 1958.

H. Lee White, "The Glare of Sunlight: Inside Prison," part one in a series about prison life in the Atlanta Penitentiary that appeared in the Fall–Winter 1959 issue of the *Atlantian.*

News articles:
Article about Whitey being held in the Milk Street police station and about his arrest in the *Boston Herald American* on Mar. 5, 1956.

Article on the sentencing of Whitey in the *Boston Globe* on June 22, 1956.

Articles on the Brink's trial in the *Boston Globe* on Aug. 6, 1956, Aug. 28 1956, Aug. 30, 1956, Sept. 1, 1956, and Oct. 6, 1956. Article on J. Edgar Hoover's statements on the need for confidential informants in the *Boston Globe* on Jan. 1, 1956.

Chapter 10: Acid Head: 1957 and Chapter 11: Ringleader

Main sources:
Whitey's prison records from Atlanta, including his LSD contract to volunteer for the LSD Project, his periodic classification reports where prison officials assessed his status, his disciplinary reports, the correspondence of the prison chaplain, Father John J. O'Shea, Whitey's visitor and correspondence

lists, Whitey's work and other records, correspondence of Bill Bulger and John McCormack.

Whitey's five-page, single-spaced handwritten account of taking LSD while in prison, titled "LSD," written in the early 1990s and discovered by investigators conducting a search of Whitey's belongings after he fled Boston in 1995.

The sworn deposition of Dr. Carl C. Pfeiffer (June 26, 1980) in the federal civil rights lawsuit inmates filed against the federal government's LSD Project. In addition, plaintiff inmate Don Roderick Scott's deposition (March 12, 1982).

Biographical information about Dr. Carl C. Pfeiffer, including a list of his medical research, was found in the Historical Collections, Health Sciences Library, Emory University, Atlanta, Georgia. We also relied on medical journal research articles about LSD that Pfeiffer coauthored in the late 1950s and early 1960s.

The sixty-three-page transcript, along with supporting materials, of the August 3, 1977, U.S. Senate hearing on MK-ULTRA, a panel on which Senator Edward M. Kennedy (D-Mass.) served and at which CIA Director Stansfield Turner testified.

Books and articles:
John Marks's *The Search for the "Manchurian Candidate"* about the CIA and LSD; John Campbell Bruce's *A Farewell to the Rock* about the escape from Alcatraz; Bill Bulger's memoir, *While the Music Lasts,* about Whitey's time in prison.

Anonymous Atlanta Penitentiary Inmate, "S Is for Sanity: They Go Insane Voluntarily," *Atlantian,* Fall–Winter 1960.

Winfield Burdette, "Medical Research: Lysergic Acid," *Atlantian,* Summer–Fall 1956.

Dr. Robert H, "I Went Insane for Science," *Man's Magazine,* August 1956.

Michael J. Karabelas, "Prison Medicine: The Prisoner and the Doctor as a Team," *Atlantian,* Summer–Fall 1957.

News articles:
Articles about the LSD Project at the Atlanta Penitentiary and about Dr. Carl Pfeiffer in the *Atlanta-Journal Constitution* on Jan. 13, 1957 (by Katherine Barnwell), Mar. 17, 1959 (by Edwina Davis), July 13, 1962 (by Edwina Davis), Aug. 10, 1975 (by Fay S. Joyce); in the Associated Press on Jan. 26, 1958.

Articles about the CIA's role in administering LSD to mental health patients, Harvard students, and prisoners in the *Boston Globe* on Jan. 4, 1994, Jan. 13, 1994, and in the *Boston Herald* on Jan. 13, 1994.

Chapter 12: The Rock: 1959–62 and Chapter 13: The End of Time

Main sources:
Whitey's prison files from Alcatraz, Leavenworth, and Lewisburg, including his periodic classification reports, disciplinary reports, work reports, official and personal correspondence with Father John J. O'Shea, the correspondence of Bill Bulger, John McCormack, federal Bureau of Prison officials, federal Parole Board officials; the prison chaplain's notes and records regarding the death of Whitey's father; records covering Whitey's parole applications; Whitey's later diary writings about taking LSD in Atlanta; excerpts of letters between Whitey and Bill Bulger as broadcast on WBZ-TV in Boston.

In addition to the correspondence between Bill Bulger, McCormack, and federal officials found in Whitey's prison file, we discovered correspondence between Bill Bulger and McCormack covering the days leading up to Whitey's parole in the McCormack Papers at Boston University's Gotlieb Archival Research Center.

In the prison file, we found Richard Barchard's four-page, handwritten letter to prison officials at Alcatraz in which he admits he concocted the story that Whitey and others had killed someone in connection with the Hammond, Indiana, bank robbery in 1955.

The prison files of Carl Smith, Richard Barchard, and Frank Lee Morris.

For a summary of the Boston gang war in the early 1960s, we relied, among other sources, on U.S. District Court Judge Nancy Gertner's ruling in the *Limone et al.* lawsuit against the federal government involving the murder of Teddy Deegan.

Interviews:
Will McDonough (1988); John Connolly (1988 and after); Richard B. Sunday (April 8, 2012, and after); Lindsey Cyr (2011 and after).

Books:
John Campbell Bruce's *A Farewell to the Rock* on the escape from Alcatraz; George H. Gregory's memoir, *Alcatraz Screw,* on working as a guard at Alcatraz; Bill Bulger's memoir, *While the Music Lasts,* about Whitey's time in prison.

News articles:
Article about Boston police cruisers being painted in the *Boston Globe* on Apr. 28, 1963.

Article about the Boston gang war in the *Boston Globe* on Sept. 6, 1964.

Articles about the Red Sox road trips to Kansas City in the *Boston Globe* on

May 5, 1963, May 6, 1963, May 8, 1963, July 14, 1963, July 17, 1963, July 18, 1963, July 19, 1963, Sept. 14, 1963, and Sept. 15, 1963.

Articles about House Speaker John McCormack's work with newly elected President Lyndon B. Johnson in the *Boston Globe* on Jan. 21, 1965, and Feb. 3, 1965.

Miscellaneous:
The full text of the poem "The Ballad of Billy the Kid," a favorite of Whitey's and written by his inmate friend in Atlanta and Alcatraz, Richard B. Sunday. The poem is included with permission from Sunday.

The Ballad of Billy the Kid
Most of the town was sleeping that day,
When the stranger happened to pass its way.
It was siesta time in the little Mex town, "high noon,"
As the rider hitched his horse, before the Golden Saloon.

He shouldered his bat wings, open wide,
Then the stranger entered, stopping just inside.
And while his eyes adjusted to the gloom,
A quiet fell over the crowded room.

He was just a boy, of maybe seventeen,
But his steel blue eyes, flashed real mean.
And not till every man there had felt his gaze,
Did his eyes lose some of their blaze.

His gear was Mex from boots to hat,
Cruel Mex spurs, spiked, like claws on a cat.
The big pair of colts on his hips hung low,
And the tied down holsters, were not for show.

But still the guns looked out of place,
So small was the owner and so young of face.
Yet, while he was covered with dust from the trail,
The guns were clean, so as never to fail.

He checked his surroundings, then stepped to the bar,
His dust-caked clothing, showed he had traveled far.
When the wisecracks aimed, at the boy began,
He acted the sport, taking it all with a grin.

A couple of beers, is all that he had,
Before some gunslinger got him mad.

A local gun-slick, already of some fame,
Began to play his deadly game.

With two of his pals, he set the boy up for the kill,
Planning to send him on his way to "Boot Hill."
When the boy kept right on drinking his beer,
The gunman mistook, his silence for fear.

When the gun-slicks called for the boy to draw,
He let them know they had pulled the last straw.
It was then, that they saw in his youth,
Only too late, the deadly truth.

From the look in his eyes, they all could tell,
That this was Satan's son, straight out of hell.
With lightning speed, each went for his gun,
To this kid, this was his own game of fun.

Across his face there spread a smile,
This he had waited for all the while.
But the odds were against him, one to three,
A pretty tough spot for the boy to be.

Then the smile twisted to a sneer on his lips,
As the kid's hands snaked, to the colts on his hips.
Forty-fours roared, the devil's call to the dead,
Death's cold hand reached out, fingers of hot lead.

When the saloon cleared of the heavy gun smoke,
Three once upon a time lay twisted, torn and broke.
With eyes glazed over, faces etched in pain,
Three men went down, with nothing to gain.

Already their blood is drying in the noon day heat,
Three more fools, lay dying at his feet.
Fast guns these three, a few of the best,
But the kid pulled their life, through holes in their chest.

And this boy went on to kill many more,
Till he himself died, by the Colt forty-four.
His name lived on, long after he was dead,
For the baby faced boy was . . . "Billy The Kid."

Chapter 14: Chandler's Summit

Main documents:
Stevie Flemmi's DEA-6 debriefing in 2003 on Whitey's job as a janitor at the Suffolk County courthouse and on Tommy King killing Billy O'Sullivan in 1971. Agent Dennis Condon's FBI 209 memorandum on his unsuccessful recruitment of Whitey as an informant in 1971.

Books and articles:
Bill Bulger's memoir, *While the Music Lasts,* on getting Whitey a job as courthouse janitor. Howie Carr's *Hitman* on John Martorano's account of murdering Tony Veranis in 1966 and Whitey seeking assurances from Mafioso J. R. Russo that the first Chandler meeting wasn't a trap.

The *Boston Globe* in 1971 for an account of the murder of Billy O'Sullivan. The *Boston Herald* in 1987 for court official John Powers's account of firing Whitey from the custodian position.

Interviews:
Lindsey Cyr on several occasions in 2011 and 2012. John Martorano in 2011, which covered two underworld meetings at Chandler's in 1972 on peace with Mullen gang members and gambling expansion of Winter Hill. Also, an excerpt from Cyr's interview with Northern Light Productions as part of a documentary on Whitey. Will McDonough in 1988 and Old Harbor resident Sally Dame in 1988, both as part of a *Boston Globe* series on the Bulger brothers.

Notes:
Firing Whitey (page 172): Whitey kept the janitor's job for a decade until he was fired in the 1970s by the elected clerk of the Supreme Judicial Court, John Powers, who was also from South Boston and a former president of the Massachusetts Senate. Bill Bulger took revenge by freezing Powers's pay for five years. Powers said there was a confrontation about him dismissing Whitey and that Bill claimed Powers was saying "bad things" about the Bulgers "but for Chrissakes, I didn't rob a bank."

Trap insurance (page 178): To make sure he wasn't walking into a Mullen trap, Whitey asked one of the North End Mafia leaders, J. R. Russo, to get assurance from Winter that the parley would be a gun-free zone and peace terms the only agenda.

Chapter 15: Go and Talk

Main documents:
Peter Limone et al. v. USA decision in 2007 by Judge Nancy Gertner on Stevie Flemmi manipulating government witness Joseph Barboza and FBI agents Paul

Rico and Dennis Condon suborning perjury from Barboza in a murder trial of four wrongly convicted men.

The papers of Congressman John McCormack at Boston University on sponsoring John Connolly's application to the FBI.

John Connolly's FBI file on seeking a "hardship" transfer to Boston from New York in 1973.

Marion Hussey testimony in the *Davis Hussey Litif v. USA* civil suit on throwing a homecoming party for Stevie Flemmi after fugitive charges were dropped against him in 1974.

John Martorano's 1998 debriefing and testimony at John Connolly's 2008 murder trial in Miami on Winter Hill's hunt for rival bookie "Indian Al" Notarangeli.

Stevie Flemmi's DEA-6 debriefing in 2003 on his homecoming from Canada at Chandler's in 1974; on him and Whitey threatening a bookie with an ax; on the murder of Eddie Connors in 1975; on Agent Condon huddling with Howie Winter at Marshall Motors in Somerville; on widespread police payoffs in Roxbury in the 1960s; on his service as a paratrooper; on his various businesses in Roxbury; on working with Agent Rico in hunting down Edward "Punchy" McLaughlin in 1965; on Whitey killing Paul McGonagle in 1974; on Joseph McDonald and Jimmy Sims's murder of a West Coast arts dealer in 1976; and on Howie Winter's shortcomings as boss of Winter Hill.

The Davis Hussey Litif suit documents for the text of J. Edgar Hoover's teletype to the Boston FBI office in 1961 to make cases against the Mafia the FBI's top priority.

Interviews:
Johnny Martorano in 2011 on the McLaughlins spreading rumors that Agent Paul Rico was gay; on his impressions of Whitey when he first teamed up with Winter Hill in 1972; and on Stevie Flemmi's enhanced underworld reputation after killing Punchy McLaughlin.

Books and articles:
Lehr and O'Neill's *Black Mass* on conversations between Stevie Flemmi and Whitey on dealing with FBI agent Connolly.

O'Neill and Lehr's *The Underboss* on police corruption in dealing with the Mafia in 1960s and 1970s; on Joseph Barboza's background; on Larry Zannino's praise of the hit on Barboza in 1976 in San Francisco.

Howie Carr's *Hitman* for detail on the first unsuccessful murder attempt on Punchy McLaughlin.

The *Boston Globe* in 1998 on Stevie Flemmi's juvenile crime record and military service. And a 1983 *Globe* obituary on John Connolly's father, "Galway John."

Notes:

Deegan contradictions (page 190): More than three decades after the Deegan trial, and when the walls were caving in on the Boston FBI office and Congress was investigating the long suppression of exculpatory documents, the agent in charge still held to the party line. In 2001, Charles Prouty told the *Boston Globe:* "The FBI was forthcoming. We didn't conceal the information. We didn't attempt to frame anyone." Months later, in congressional testimony, FBI director Louis Freeh was more "forthcoming." He said the case is "obviously a great travesty, a great failure, disgraceful to the extent that my agency or any other law enforcement agency contributed to that."

Barboza trial (page 191): Barboza's perjury had the compromised FBI endlessly over a barrel. Agents Rico and Condon appeared at the California trial as character witnesses for the defense, firepower that gave the local district attorney little alternative but to accept Barboza's plea to a reduced sentence.

Chapter 16: My Own G-man

Main sources:

For the murders of Tommy King and Buddy Leonard, we relied on Stevie Flemmi's confession, or "Agreed Upon Facts," in his plea agreement in his federal criminal case; Flemmi's DEA-6 debriefing; Flemmi's testimony at the Davis federal civil trial; Johnny Martorano's confession and plea agreement in his federal criminal complaint; Martorano's state police debriefing; Martorano's testimony at the John Connolly murder trial.

For the alliance forged between Whitey and John Connolly, including their meeting at Wollaston Beach, we relied on Stevie Flemmi's DEA-6 debriefing; Flemmi's testimony at the McIntyre federal civil trial; Flemmi's testimony at the Connolly murder trial; Johnny Martorano's state police debriefing; and Martorano's testimony at the Connolly murder trial. In addition, we examined numerous internal FBI documents, known as 209's and 302's, some of which were written by Connolly, describing the recruitment of Whitey during 1974 and 1975. The batches of internal FBI documents included a number from the 1974–75 period quoting underworld sources that Whitey was a ruthless, murderous gangster.

In his ruling in the McIntyre family's federal civil lawsuit, Judge Reginald C. Lindsey provided a detailed, authoritative summary of the FBI's Top Echelon program, including an explanation of the correct way to run it. His analysis was instructive.

Biographical details about John Connolly, particularly his FBI career, were contained in records and FBI documents found in Exhibit II (C), "Reports of Agent Performance and SA John Connolly's Personnel File," in the Castucci family's civil lawsuit. In his ruling in the McIntyre case, Judge Lindsey found as fact that Connolly took more than $200,000 in payoffs from Whitey, and the judge gave a blistering summary of Connolly's motives: "I find that Connolly was motivated in part by greed and his friendship with Flemmi and especially Bulger."

For detailed examples of Connolly protecting Whitey and his cohorts, and for examples of ways Connolly padded Whitey's FBI files with fabrications and embellishments, we relied on our own past analysis of internal FBI informant reports; the findings of Judge Mark Wolf in the so-called Wolf hearings of 1998; Flemmi's DEA-6 debriefing; Flemmi's testimony at the Davis civil trial; Flemmi's testimony at the Connolly murder trial.

For information on the murder of Richard Castucci as the "gateway killing," or murders resulting from Connolly tips, a key source was U.S. District Court Judge Reginald C. Lindsey's ruling on March 31, 2008, in the Castucci family's federal civil lawsuit. Lindsey, issuing findings of fact in granting the plaintiff's motion for summary judgment, said, "Castucci was the first of four FBI informants killed by, or at the behest of, Bulger and Flemmi after the disclosure of his identity to them by Connolly." In addition, the judge ruled, "Connolly (who is a defendant in this case), Bulger and Flemmi were co-conspirators in the murder of Castucci." The judge also said this about Flemmi: "Flemmi testified extensively about many events relevant to this case. As should be clear from these findings and conclusions, I understand that Flemmi is a violent criminal who callously participated in countless acts of cruelty and violence, including numerous murders. However, I found his testimony in this case generally to be credible."

We also relied on Flemmi's confession, or the "Agreed Upon Facts," in his federal criminal case, which contained the following about the Castucci murder: "Bulger was informed by FBI agent John Connolly that Castucci was an informant for the FBI and that Castucci had disclosed the existence of the Greenwich Village apartment to the FBI. Bulger told defendant Flemmi, Winter and Martorano about Castucci and they decided to murder Castucci." We also relied on Flemmi's testimony in the Connolly murder trial; Flemmi's testimony at the Davis civil trial; Flemmi's deposition and testimony in the McIntyre civil lawsuit; and Martorano's testimony at both the Connolly racketeering trial and the Connolly murder trial. We also relied on many internal FBI reports, known as 209's and 302's, about Castucci's service as an FBI informant, the Castucci murder, and the FBI investigation afterward.

We also relied on Bill Bulger's sworn testimony on June 19, 2003, at a congressional hearing examining FBI corruption regarding Whitey.

For Paul Rico's comment about how best to target potential informants, we relied on an FBI 302 dated March 21, 1997, that Agent John Gamel wrote based on his interview with Rico. For comments from Connolly's first wife, Marianne Connolly, we relied on a 1997 FBI report based on an interview agents conducted with her.

Interviews:
John Connolly (1988 and after).

Books and articles:
Lehr and O'Neill, *Black Mass;* Howie Carr, *The Brothers Bulger.*

News articles:
Article on the death of Francis X. (Buddy) Leonard, *Boston Globe*, Nov. 7, 1975.

Chapter 17: Wild West Broadway

Main documents:
Boston Police Department crime data from 1960 to 2011, including separate figures for South Boston and arrest statistics, South Boston and city-wide, for the busing years of 1974 and 1975.

U.S. census data for South Boston in 1970 and 1980 to trace "white flight" there.

Johnny Martorano 1998 debriefing on Whitey firing shots at the *Boston Globe* building during the first year of busing.

Stevie Flemmi's DEA-6 debriefing on police corruption concerning Whitey's weekly payments to James Kelly while he headed the antibusing South Boston Information Center.

Books and articles:
J. Anthony Lukas, *Common Ground: A Turbulent Decade in the Lives of Three American Families* (New York: Knopf, 1985), on the prospect of Mullen gang members arming teenagers in the first week of busing in 1974.

Thomas H. O'Connor, *South Boston, My Home Town,* on Southie's view of minorities, and James Kelly's commentary after the racial incident at Carson Beach in 1975.

The *Boston Globe*'s coverage of Carson Beach in 1975 and its 2007 obituary of James Kelly and then his services in South Boston.

Interviews:
Christopher Lydon in 2012 about his television interview of Kevin White when the mayor thought the mike was off and he talked about the possibility of being assassinated by Bulger during busing.

William Bulger in 1988 about his clash with Boston Police Commissioner Robert diGrazia after a busing protest outside a South Boston school in 1975.

Brian Wallace of South Boston in 2001. Wallace, a longtime supporter of Mayor Raymond Flynn, said he was threatened by Whitey for being critical of William Bulger in 1975.

Chapter 18: Whitey Rules

Main sources:
Transcripts from the Aug. 3, 1977, hearing about the CIA's secret LSD Project known as MK-ULTRA, at which Ted Kennedy and Stansfield Turner testified. In addition, we relied on Whitey's writings from the early 1990s about his LSD use.

Regarding the 1979 federal horse-race-fixing case and the gang's breakup meeting afterward, we relied on extensive court and investigatory records, including new information about the June 1977 FBI debriefing of government witness Anthony Ciulla, as well as an FBI report (302) of an interview conducted on March 27, 2000, with Jeremiah T. O'Sullivan, the federal prosecutor in the race-fixing case. Both documents were found in the Castucci family's lawsuit against the federal government, Exhibit VII (D), "Race Fix Case." We also relied on more new information in Stevie Flemmi's DEA-6 debriefing; Flemmi's testimony at the John Connolly murder trial; Johnny Martorano's state police debriefing; Martorano's testimony at the Connolly murder trial; Kevin Weeks's testimony at the Connolly murder trial; and John Morris's testimony at the Connolly murder trial.

For information on Whitey's control of drug trafficking and his arsenal of weapons, we relied on Flemmi's DEA-6 debriefing; Flemmi's "Agreed Upon Facts" in his guilty plea agreement in his federal criminal case; Flemmi's testimony at the John Connolly murder trial; Weeks's testimony at the Connolly murder trial; and case records from the federal criminal case against Michael Flemmi. In his 111-page ruling in the McIntyre civil lawsuit against the government, Judge Reginald C. Lindsey ruled that "Bulger and Flemmi were involved in the drug trade from approximately 1981 to 1990. Bulger required all of the drug traffickers in South Boston to pay tribute to Winter Hill, and he and Flemmi often obtained a share of the profits from drug shipments brought into South Boston" (p. 65).

For information on Connolly's idea to keep Martorano as a fugitive we relied on Flemmi's DEA-6 debriefing and his testimony at the Connolly murder trial. For information on how Whitey ran his gang enterprise, along with his travels with Connolly, we relied on Flemmi's DEA-6 debriefing; Flemmi's testimony at the Connolly murder trial; Flemmi's testimony at the Davis civil trial; Weeks's testimony at the Connolly murder trial. For information on Connolly's spending habits, which concerned Whitey, we relied on Flemmi's testimony at the Connolly murder trial; Weeks's testimony at the Connolly murder trial; and Morris's testimony at the Connolly murder trial. For information about Whitey, Provincetown, and his rumored homosexuality, we relied on Flemmi's DEA-6 debriefing and Flemmi's testimony at the Connolly murder trial and the Davis civil trial.

For information about Catherine Greig we relied on her federal criminal case file and the hundreds of pages of government exhibits in the case. For information about Kevin Weeks we relied on his DEA-6 debriefing; his testimony at the Connolly murder trial; and his interview with NBC's *Dateline* for its 2009 two-hour special about the Connolly murder trial, *Crossing the Line*.

We also relied on the testimony of Teresa Stanley during the 1998 Wolf hearings and at the Connolly murder trial in 2008.

Throughout the period covered in this chapter, circa 1980, we also relied on numerous internal FBI reports (209's and 302's), particularly one written in late 1980 by the new special agent in charge of the Boston office, Lawrence Sarhatt, about his four-hour meeting with Whitey and John Connolly, as well as one written on March 15, 2000, summarizing an interview with retired FBI agent James C. Crawford in which he described the "C-3 mentality" in the Boston FBI office in the 1980s.

For the murder of Louis Litif, we relied on Weeks's DEA-6 debriefing; Weeks's deposition in the Davis civil lawsuit; and, most important, the Litif family's federal civil lawsuit against the federal government, FBI agents, and Whitey. In his fifty-six-page "Memorandum of Decision," U.S. District Judge William G. Young ruled that Litif "sought to cooperate with the authorities by informing on Bulger and Flemmi. The pair murdered Litif before he could make any sort of deal with the government." The judge described how Connolly was present at a meeting during which Litif's decision to cooperate against Whitey was discussed. "Three weeks later, Bulger and his accomplices murdered Litif," the judge ruled. The judge further ruled: "The Court infers that Connolly leaked to Bulger Litif's willingness to incriminate Bulger." The judge found that "Litif was lured to the Triple O's bar where Bulger and an associate ambushed him," and he noted that Litif had been "stabbed dozens of times with an ice-pick-like implement before he was shot in the back of the neck."

Interviews:
John Morris (1988 and after); Bill Bulger (1988 and after); Lindsey Cyr (2011 and after); John Connolly (1988 and after).

Books and articles:
Lehr and O'Neill, *Black Mass;* John Shea, *Rat Bastards.*
   Peter Manso, "Out on the Cape," *Boston Magazine,* May 2006.

News articles:
Articles about Senate hearings about the CIA's MK-ULTRA LSD Project in the *Boston Globe* on Aug. 3, 1977; Aug. 4, 1977; Aug. 5, 1977; and Aug. 10, 1977.
   Articles in the *Boston Globe* about Staniford A. Sorrentino, co-owner of the Crown and Anchor Motor Inn in Provincetown, and his friendship with

Whitey, on Aug. 31, 1981; Sept. 3, 1981; Dec. 12, 1982; Feb. 4, 1983; Feb. 10, 1983; Feb. 14, 1983; Feb. 18, 1983; Mar. 22, 1983; Feb. 2, 1989.

The obituary for Whitey's mother, Jean Bulger, in the *Boston Globe* on Jan. 3, 1980.

In-depth article about Catherine Greig in the *Boston Globe* on Nov. 20, 2011.

Notes:

In his memoir, *Rat Bastards,* John Shea wrote at length about working for Whitey as a dealer in Whitey's South Boston drug operations. He also mentioned that his uncle Richie Kelly was Whitey's old tailgating partner from the early 1950s, and that his uncle's name came up the first time he met Whitey. "Now, that guy had a ton of balls," Whitey said about Kelly. Wrote Shea, quoting Whitey: "I'd go over to your uncle's house in the morning and wake him up so we could go out to work. Your uncle and me, we'd go out stealing and robbing anything not tied down."

Chapter 19: Categorical Bill and the Tulsa Trilogy

Main documents:

Stevie Flemmi's DEA-6 debriefing on the move from Marshall Motors in Somerville to the Lancaster Street garage in Boston's West End.

Flemmi's DEA-6 debriefing on police corruption concerning leaks within law enforcement to Whitey and Flemmi about bugs being placed at Lancaster Street; on state police detective Richard Schneiderhan's long tenure as a paid double agent for Winter Hill and Flemmi's tally on payments to Schneiderhan.

The 2003 congressional testimony and report by the House Committee on Government Reform concerning William Bulger's role in Massachusetts legislation that would have required the ouster of a commander investigating Whitey.

Flemmi's DEA-6 debriefing contradicting Bulger's congressional testimony that he had no role in the legislation.

Testimony in 2008 by Flemmi and Johnny Martorano in Connolly's Miami murder trial about the effort to wrest the World Jai Alai business away from Roger Wheeler of Tulsa and the decision to murder him when he refused to sell. Flemmi's testimony about Connolly warning Whitey and him about Brian Halloran cooperating with the FBI concerning the Wheeler murder.

Martorano's 1998 debriefing and court testimony in 2008 on his murder of Wheeler and Callahan.

Kevin Weeks's 2001 debriefing on Whitey's 1982 murder of Brian Halloran and Michael Donahue.

A 1999 FBI memo by Boston agent Matthew J. Cronin about his unsuccessful effort to get Brian Halloran into the Witness Protection Program to stop Whitey from killing him.

A 1982 FBI memo by Sean McWeeney, director of the Organized Crime division in Washington, on the stormy aftermath within law enforcement about the World Jai Alai murders of Roger Wheeler, Brian Halloran, and John Callahan.

Testimony by retired agent Paul Rico in 2001 before the House Committee on Government Reform evincing indifference to the plight of four men convicted by the false testimony of FBI informant Joseph Barboza.

Books and articles:
Howie Carr's *Hitman* and Foley and Sedgwick's *Most Wanted* on Martorano and state police officer Schneiderhan becoming friends and then the detective taking money from Winter Hill.

Hitman for Martorano figuring out Rico's real motivation for having Wheeler killed and for an account of Rico's arrest in the Wheeler murder in Miami.

Lehr and O'Neill's *Black Mass* on the cast of characters in and out of the Lancaster Street garage; on Tulsa detective Mike Huff closing in on Callahan in Miami the day after Callahan was murdered by Martorano.

For Rico's imprisonment and death in January 2004, articles from the *Boston Herald, Oklahoman, Boston Globe, St. Petersburg Times.*

For Rico's autopsy in April 2004, articles prepared by the Associated Press and *Tulsa World.*

Notes:
Connolly's Tulsa role (page 244): While Rico had provided minute details on Wheeler's car and location information, he was not the only agent with Tulsa blood on his hands. According to court testimony, Connolly had warned Bulger that the FBI knew where Martorano was living in Florida. In fact, Flemmi gave Johnny two heads-up, one in 1979 and the other just before the Wheeler murder in 1981. Martorano reluctantly shifted locations and lifestyles, giving up living large in Miami to tone it down some in Ft. Lauderdale and then get properly anonymous in Boca Raton. But without Connolly's intervention, Martorano would not have been at large to lie in wait for Roger Wheeler in the Tulsa country club parking lot.

Congressional hearing (page 242): Bill Bulger was questioned by Congress in 2003 on other issues besides the punitive legislation aimed at the Massachusetts State Police. One of these issues was his involvement in major development at 75 State St. in Boston. Bill Bulger's law partner, Thomas Finnerty, who also grew up in a Southie project, demanded a percentage of the project that converted to $1.8 million. But the firm did no work in getting state or city approvals for the skyscraper. They split a down payment of $500,000, but the developer refused to pay the balance and Finnerty sued for it.

It became a cause célèbre in 1988 but the same FBI agents who took care of Whitey—John Connolly and John Morris—worked to deep-six the case. Morris took a $5,000 bribe from Whitey Bulger while supervising the 75 State St. investigation. Another Bulger partisan, Jeremiah O'Sullivan, acting as interim U.S. attorney, formally exonerated Bulger in an unprecedented press conference called to expound on an *unsuccessful* investigation. O'Sullivan said there was influence-peddling by the firm but no extortion, and handed it off to state prosecutors. They later reported to Congress that they could not make a case. Ultimately, Congress took no action against Bulger.

Chapter 20: Gravediggers

Main sources:

For the murders of Bucky Barrett, John McIntyre, and Deborah Hussey we relied on Stevie Flemmi's "Agreed Upon Facts," in his guilty plea agreement in his criminal case; Flemmi's DEA-6 debriefing; Flemmi's testimony at the McIntyre civil trial against the federal government; Flemmi's testimony at the Davis et al. civil trial against the federal government; Kevin Weeks's DEA-6 debriefing; Weeks's testimony at the McIntyre civil trial; Weeks's testimony at the Davis et al. civil trial; Marion Hussey's testimony at the Davis et al. civil trial; the legal brief prepared by the Hussey family's attorneys in connection with the Hussey civil lawsuit.

Most important, we relied on the rulings of federal judges in federal civil lawsuits against the federal government.

In his 111-page ruling in the McIntyre case, Judge Reginald C. Lindsey ruled in his "Findings of Fact" that "McIntyre was murdered by Bulger and Flemmi on November 30, 1984, after they learned he was cooperating with law enforcement" (p. 73). In addition, Lindsey ruled that John Connolly "disclosed to Bulger" that one of the *Valhalla* crew was cooperating with law enforcement and that "the information Connolly conveyed was sufficient to identify McIntyre" (p. 79).

In his fifty-six-page ruling in the Litif, Davis, and Hussey civil lawsuits, Judge William Young ruled that Whitey and Flemmi murdered Hussey: "They murdered her in much the same way they murdered their other victims, by luring her into a house and strangling her. Here again, Bulger grabbed Deborah Hussey from behind and scissored her neck between his forearms to crush her windpipe. Hussey fought desperately for her life and knocked Bulger over. When the two fell to the floor, Bulger jack-knifed his body to work his legs around Hussey's body to crush her torso" (p. 22).

Regarding the murder of Deborah Hussey, we would like to note the disparity in testimony between Kevin Weeks and Stevie Flemmi. Weeks said he saw Flemmi choke Hussey after her body was dragged down into the cellar. Flemmi denied that account, saying she was already dead and that he was pulling off her tight sweater in preparation to bury her.

We also relied on city property records for 799 East Third Street, South Boston.

For the FBI bugging at Mafia headquarters in Boston's North End we relied on O'Neill and Lehr's book *The Underboss;* Flemmi's DEA-6 debriefing; Flemmi's testimony at the Davis et al. civil trial; and John Morris's testimony at the Connolly murder trial, in which Morris testified that Whitey and Flemmi were not necessary to include in the FBI's affidavit in order to win court approval for the bugging operation. For information about John Connolly's spending habits and Whitey's "Ex-Fund," from which he made payoffs to FBI agents, we relied on Flemmi's DEA-6 debriefing; Flemmi's testimony at the Connolly murder trial; Flemmi's testimony at the Davis et al. civil trial; Flemmi's deposition in the Rakes' civil lawsuit; Weeks's testimony at the Connolly murder trial; Morris's testimony at the Connolly murder trial. For a description of other illegal gifts, plane tickets, and money John Morris accepted from Whitey, see Lehr and O'Neill's *Black Mass.*

For information about Catherine Greig, we relied on property records about Whitey and Catherine Greig's condominium in Quincy, Massachusetts; Greig's twin sister Margaret McCusker's testimony before a federal grand jury on Feb. 9, 2012; a letter McCusker wrote June 4, 2012, to the federal court in connection with Catherine Greig's sentencing; FBI records on Catherine Greig's cosmetic surgeries.

For information on the extortion of Raymond Slinger and Tim Connolly we relied on Flemmi's DEA-6 debriefing; Weeks's DEA-6 debriefing; other government records; and Lehr and O'Neill's *Black Mass* and the sourcing therein.

News articles:
Articles about the *Valhalla* in the *Boston Globe* on Oct. 17, 1984, and Nov. 13, 1984.

In-depth article about Catherine Greig in the *Boston Globe* on Nov. 20, 2011.

Article about Halloween 1985 in the *Boston Globe* on Nov. 1, 1985.

Chapter 21: Thirty-Two Words
Flemmi's DEA-6 and his testimony at John Connolly's 2008 murder trial in Miami on Agent James Ring warning Flemmi that a Winter Hill underling's telephone was tapped as part of a DEA investigation. Flemmi told investigators in his 2003 debriefing that in November or December of 1984 he was called by Ring and told "don't be talking on George's phone." Flemmi further said Ring

and other agents were out to embarrass the DEA because it failed to notify the FBI about the investigation before it began. At the murder trial, prosecutor Fred Wyshak asked Flemmi about the George Kaufman wire. Flemmi testified "supervisor Jim Ring had contacted in *(sic)* my mother's home and said that— there was a tap on George Kaufman's telephone . . . actually the words he said were 'Don't speak on—on—George Kaufman's phone.' I knew what he meant obviously."

Main documents:

Flemmi's DEA-6 debriefing on consensus among John Connolly, Bulger, and Flemmi to "ride out" the *Globe*'s revelation about Whitey's relationship with the FBI; on the chilling effect the disclosure had within the Organized Crime Squad in the Boston office of the FBI.

Flemmi's testimony at the 2008 Connolly trial in Miami on the 1982 extortion of a Boston accounting partner of John Callahan and it being used to start the slush fund for police payoffs.

Weeks's 2001 debriefing on bribes to FBI agents in the Boston office and their nicknames; on details about splitting up the proceeds of a winning lottery ticket.

Flemmi's DEA-6 debriefing on corruption, on payments to FBI agents in Boston. On Whitey giving Connolly a $10,000 retirement bonus; on Bulger and Flemmi talking about retirement.

Weeks's testimony in the 2008 Miami trial about picking up Catherine Greig in South Boston and bringing her to meet Bulger, who took her on the road.

A chart prepared by the U.S. attorney's office in Boston about Whitey's travels and finances.

Flemmi's and Weeks's debriefings and Weeks's 2008 testimony on Connolly's tip-off about imminent indictments in 1994. And Weeks's testimony about his surprise that Flemmi didn't leave immediately after the tip-off.

Whitey's five-page letter about dealing with the aftermath of the deceptive LSD Program at the Atlanta Penitentiary, posted on *Boston Herald* columnist Howie Carr's website.

Books and articles:

A 1988 *Boston Globe* article on the FBI and Whitey as part of a series on the Bulger brothers.

A 1993 *Boston Globe* article on Stephen Flemmi's real estate investments in Boston.

A 2011 *Boston Globe* article on Catherine Greig informing Teresa Stanley of Whitey's two-timing them both, and details on Whitey's switching from Stanley to Greig for his road companion.

Articles in the *Boston Globe* and *Boston Herald* on John Connolly's 1990 retirement. Plus, a partial video of the party featuring Connolly and William Bulger.

Lehr and O'Neill's *Black Mass* for FBI agent James Ahearn's response to the *Globe*'s revelations about Whitey being an informer. On John Connolly getting a job at Boston Edison.

Foley and Sedgwick's *Most Wanted* on state police commander Thomas Foley's clashes with the FBI and on dealing with bookie Burton "Chico" Krantz; on the arrest of Stephen Flemmi and his questioning of Catherine Greig at her home in Quincy.

Interviews:
Johnny Martorano about his reaction to the *Globe*'s disclosure of Whitey's relationship with the FBI.

A background interview with an attorney about Flemmi's working with law enforcement to capture Whitey and his turning down an earlier plea bargain that would have meant a lesser sentence.

Chapter 22: The Band of Brothers

Main sources:
For information on the FBI's efforts in early 1995 to enlist the assistance of Bill Bulger and the Bulger family in the capture of Whitey, we relied on an FBI report (209) that agent John Gamel prepared regarding his interaction with Bill Bulger on Jan. 9, 1995; Gamel's testimony and supporting materials before the 2003 congressional inquiry into the FBI's corrupt informant practices; and Bill Bulger's 2003 testimony before the same congressional inquiry on June 19, 2003.

For details on Whitey's fugitive activities in 1995 and 1996, his secret contacts with his brothers Bill and Jackie Bulger, his and Catherine Greig's contacts with others in South Boston, particularly with Kevin Weeks, we relied on Weeks's testimony at the John Connolly murder trial; case records from Catherine Greig's 2011 federal criminal case, including the "Statement of Facts," in her plea agreement, the government and defense sentencing memorandums, the testimony of FBI agent Michael Carazza and Kevin Weeks at Greig's federal detention hearing on July 11 and July 13, 2011; case records from Jackie Bulger's federal criminal case, including his four-count indictment on Nov. 8, 2001, the government and defense sentencing memorandums of Aug. 20, 2003, a memorandum and order by U.S. District Court Judge George A. O'Toole Jr., dated Dec. 31, 2002, and a transcript of Jackie Bulger's sentencing hearing on Sept. 3, 2003; the federal government's civil forfeiture actions against Whitey and his lottery winnings, docket number 95-cv-11513; the sworn affidavit of Boston police officer Charles "Chip" Fleming, dated Mar. 13, 2000, filed in Norfolk County Probate

Court in connection with the lottery winnings forfeiture proceedings; the federal criminal case records of Greig's sister, Margaret McCusker, and friend Kathleen McDonough; maps and timelines developed by the U.S. Justice Department; an FBI report (302) prepared by agent Lisa M. Horner and dated Sept. 10, 1997, based on interviews the FBI conducted with residents of Grand Isle, Louisiana, regarding interactions with Whitey and Catherine Greig; the testimony of Bill Bulger before the 2003 congressional hearing, specifically the exchange he had with Massachusetts congressman John Tierney when Tierney read an excerpt from Bill Bulger's memoir about Whitey; the disbarment case records and rulings against attorney Thomas Finnerty at the Board of Bar Overseers and the Massachusetts Supreme Judicial Court, including Finnerty's sworn affidavit of May 1, 2008, in which he confessed he advised a client to lie before the federal grand jury investigating the whereabouts of Whitey and Catherine Greig.

For information about Whitey's call to FBI agent John Morris we relied on Weeks's testimony at the Connolly murder trial; Morris's testimony at the Wolf hearings on April 30, 1998; Morris's testimony at the Connolly murder trial; an FBI report (302) that Morris wrote after taking the call from Whitey on Oct. 13, 1995.

Interviews:
FBI agent (retired) John Gamel (May 23, 2012).

News articles and broadcasts:
Article on Bill Bulger's defeat of William Keating in a contest for the presidency of the Massachusetts Senate in the *Boston Globe* on Jan. 5, 1995.

Article in the *Boston Globe* on June 28, 2003, about FBI agent John Gamel's interaction with Bill Bulger.

Article about Bill Bulger's testimony before a federal grand jury regarding his telephone call in January 1995 with Whitey and his meetings with Kevin Weeks to get updates on Whitey while Whitey was a fugitive in the *Boston Globe* on Dec. 3, 2002, Dec. 4, 2002, and Dec. 5, 2002.

Article about Whitey and Greig in Grand Isle, Louisiana, in the *Boston Globe* on Jan. 4, 1998.

Television broadcast about two 1995 police encounters with Whitey or his car in Sheridan, Wyoming, and Long Beach, Mississippi, on the WCVB-TV Channel 5 show *Chronicle* in Boston, Jan. 2005, reporter David Boeri.

Articles about John "Jackie" Bulger's criminal case in the *Boston Globe* on Nov. 10, 2001, Apr. 11, 2003, Sept. 4, 2003, Apr. 2, 2004.

Articles about the Unabomber in the *Washington Post* on Sept. 19, 1995, and in the *New York Times* on Apr. 5, 1996, Jan. 5, 1998, and Aug. 21, 1998.

Articles about Whitey the fugitive and the FBI's search for him in the *Boston Globe* on May 13, 1998, Feb. 23, 1999, May 28, 1999, Apr. 4, 2000, Jan. 5,

2006, Jan. 5, 2007, June 13, 2008 (quoting FBI agent Richard Teahan); and in the *Boston Herald* on Mar. 5, 2000.

Chapter 23: Travesty

Main documents:
The summary of the eleven Bulger victims murdered while an FBI informant is drawn from federal district and appeals court cases; articles about the murders in the *Boston Globe* and *Boston Herald;* law enforcement debriefings of Johnny Martorano, Kevin Weeks, and Stephen Flemmi.

The 2012 decision by federal judge William Young allowing the Donahue family to go forward despite an earlier adverse appeals court decision by suing individual FBI agents. Also, the *Boston Globe* article on Young's decision.

Books and articles:
Foley and Sedgwick's *Most Wanted* on exhumation of the bodies of Tommy King and Debra Davis and on the debriefing of Johnny Martorano in 1998. *Boston Globe* articles in 2000 on exhumation of the bodies of Tommy King and Debra Davis.

Davis et al. v. USA civil suit about Davis missing person report being deleted from a database controlled by the FBI.

Boston Globe article in 2000 about John Connolly's press conference after arraignment on racketeering charges.

Boston Globe articles on John Connolly's convictions and sentencing in 2002 on racketeering and 2008 on second-degree murders. And NBC's *Dateline* video of the 2008 exchange between Connolly and prosecutor Fred Wyshak.

Interviews:
Northern Light Productions' 2012 transcript of Tommy Donahue and Patricia Donahue.

Notes:
The first victim (page 307): The body of the "twelfth" man, Paul McGonagle, was recovered on Tenean Beach in Dorchester with Weeks's help. He was murdered in November 1974 before Bulger was formally in the FBI's Top Echelon Informant Program.

Chapter 24: No Stone Left Unturned, Chapter 25: Charlie and Carol, and Chapter 26: "Charlie Will Meet You in the Garage"

Main sources:
For information about Whitey and Catherine Greig's life in Santa Monica from 1996 until their capture in 2011 we relied on the records in Catherine Greig's

criminal case, including many of the about one hundred government exhibits unsealed at her sentencing in June 2012, among them photographs taken by investigators of the interior of the couple's Unit 303 in the Princess Eugenia Apartments, of their money and arsenal of weapons and where Whitey hid both, of the furnishings, books, and decorations and foodstuff in the kitchen, etc.

Other exhibits that proved particularly helpful were the sworn affidavit of FBI agent Philip Torsney, which described Whitey's arrest and his return to Boston; the grand jury testimony of Joshua Bond, the resident manager of the apartment building, on July 21, 2011; two FBI reports (302's) prepared by agents who interviewed Bond on July 6 and July 8, 2011; the grand jury testimony of Birgitta Farinelli, another manager, on Aug. 8, 2011; the FBI report (302) of an FBI interview with Farinelli on July 5, 2011; the grand jury testimony of Greig's hairdresser, Wendy Farnetti, on July 21, 2011; the FBI report (302) of an FBI interview with Farnetti on July 5, 2011. We also relied on Greig's "Statement of Facts" dated Mar. 7, 2012, as part of her guilty plea in her criminal case; the federal government's sentencing memo dated June 8, 2012; and the testimony of FBI agent Michael Carazza and of Kevin Weeks at Greig's detention hearing in federal court in Boston on July 11 and July 13, 2011. We also relied on many other government records, including maps and timelines investigators prepared, as well as our own interviews with government officials, some of whom requested anonymity.

In addition, we relied on the work of photographer Paul Horan, who gained entry into Whitey's apartment shortly after his arrest and took a series of his own photographs of the location and neighborhood. We relied on a copy of the tip sheet, which we obtained, that was prepared on June 30, 2008, when a viewer called *America's Most Wanted* to report he'd seen Whitey in Santa Monica.

We also relied on a written "Statement of Purpose" and other materials from Ocean View Manor, a residential facility for developmentally disadvantaged adults located down the block from where Whitey lived in Santa Monica.

Interviews:
Michele Nasitir (Jan. 18, 2012), Barbara Gluck (Jan. 18, 2012), Catalina Schlank (Jan. 19, 2012), Joshua Bond (Jan. 19, 2012, and after), Joe Clarke (Jan. 19, 2012), former assistant U.S. attorney Jon Mitchell (Feb. 22, 2012, and after), David Boeri (July 6, 2012, and after).

News articles and broadcasts:
Articles about Whitey and Catherine Greig's life as fugitives and the FBI's manhunt in the *Boston Globe* on Jan. 4, 1998, Mar. 5, 2000, Oct. 17, 2000, Nov. 6, 2000 (Letter to the Editor by Boston FBI Special Agent in Charge Charles Prouty), Jan. 23, 2001, Mar. 3, 2001, Jan. 5, 2002, Sept. 5, 2002, Dec. 5, 2002, Jan. 3, 2003, Jan. 4, 2003, Jan. 2, 2004, Jan. 3, 2004, Jan. 4, 2004, Sept. 9, 2004, Dec. 19, 2004, Dec. 22, 2004, Aug. 4, 2005, Jan. 5, 2006, Jan. 18, 2006, Nov. 16, 2006,

Jan. 5, 2007, Sept. 15, 2007, Sept. 28, 2007, Jan. 4, 2008, Jan. 5, 2008 (quoting FBI agent Richard Teahan on focus of manhunt in Europe and quoting Kevin Weeks saying Whitey stuck in Europe after 9/11), June 13, 2008 (quoting FBI agent Richard Teahan about lack of cooperation from Bulger family), Sept. 4, 2008, Oct. 25, 2008, Aug. 26, 2009, Apr. 21, 2010, June 10, 2010, Oct. 8, 2010, and Jan. 5, 2011; in the *Boston Herald* on Feb. 7, 2000, Nov. 14, 2000, Nov. 30, 2000, Mar. 16, 2001, Mar. 27, 2001, June 4, 2001, June 7, 2001, July 27, 2001, Sept. 3, 2001, Sept. 5, 2002, Dec. 2, 2002 (column by Peter Gelzinis quoting Tulsa, Oklahoma, investigator Mike Huff), Dec. 6, 2002, Dec. 12, 2002, Jan. 4, 2003, Jan. 10, 2003, June 20, 2003, Sept. 4, 2003, Oct. 19, 2003 (column by Peter Gelzinis), and Jan. 2, 2004; WCBV-TV Channel 5's news report on Sept. 11, 1997; New England Cable News broadcast Mar. 23, 2006, with Jim Braude (quoting FBI agent Kevin Kline).

Articles about the sighting in February 2000 of Greig at a hair salon in Fountain Valley, California, in the *Boston Globe* on Apr. 5, 2000, Apr. 6, 2000, in the *Boston Herald* on Mar. 6, 2000, along with press releases from the FBI offices in Boston and Los Angeles issued on April 5, 2000. In addition, WCBV-TV Channel 5's news reports by reporter David Boeri about the sighting.

CBS News' *60 Minutes* interview on Jan. 6, 2008, with John V. Martorano.

Article about the balloon contest sponsored by DARPA, the Pentagon's research agency, in the *New York Times* on Dec. 1, 2009.

We consulted multiple articles covering Whitey's capture and the aftermath, notably in the *New York Times* on June 24, 2011, June 25, 2011, June 26, 2011, June 29, 2011, July 1, 2011, July 15, 2011, editorial Oct. 24, 2011; in the *Boston Globe* on June 23, 2011, June 24, 2011, June 25, 2011, June 26, 2011, June 27, 2011, June 28, 2011, June 29, 2011, June 30, 2011, July 1, 2011, July 2, 2011, July 3, 2011, July 4, 2011, July 7, 2011, July 12, 2011, July 12, 2011, July 13, 2011, July 14, 2011, July 17, 2011, July 19, 2011, July 24, 2011, July 27, 2011, Aug. 2, 2011, Aug. 19, 2011, Aug. 21, 2011, Sept. 15, 2011, Sept. 24, 2011, Oct. 7, 2011, Oct. 9, 2011 (quoting retired Boston Police Department detective Charles "Chip" Fleming and Enrique Sanchez), Oct. 11, 2011, Oct. 13, 2011, Oct. 28, 2011, Nov. 2, 2011, Nov. 3, 2011, Nov. 5, 2011, Dec. 29, 2011, Jan. 2, 2012, Jan. 12, 2012, Mar. 10, 2012, Mar. 14, 2012, Mar. 15, 2012, May 15, 2012, May 31, 2012, June 9, 2012, June 12, 2012, June 13, 2012, June 26, 2012, and July 18, 2012; in the *Boston Herald* on June 25, 2011; in the *Boston Phoenix* on Oct. 5, 2011; in the *Los Angeles Times* on June 16, 2012.

Epilogue

Main sources:
For information about Whitey's return to Boston, his federal racketeering case, his incarceration, and Catherine Greig's case and her incarceration, we relied

on our own coverage of the events, including interviews with a number of attorneys and law enforcement officials and investigators, and a June 26, 2012, tour of the Plymouth County House of Correction. We also relied on the many legal filings made in connection with both Whitey's and Greig's federal criminal cases. In addition, we relied on several FBI reports (302's) that were filed in Greig's case.

The material and prosecutor's quotation regarding the possibility of Bill Bulger paying for Greig's defense came from a transcript of her detention hearing, held on June 25, 2011.

News articles and broadcasts:
We consulted many articles covering developments in Whitey's case throughout 2011 and 2012, including the *New York Times* on June 25, 2011, June 29, 2011; the *Boston Globe* on May 21, 2011, June 25, 2011, June 26, 2011, June 27, 2011, June 28, 2011, June 29, 2011, June 30, 2011, July 1, 2011, July 2, 2011, July 7, 2011, July 15, 2011, Sept. 15, 2011, June 12, 2012, June 13, 2012, June 18, 2012, June 26, 2012, Aug. 7, 2012, Aug. 8, 2012; the *Boston Herald* on June 25, 2011.

Notes:
Following Whitey's arrest in June 2011 the new watercooler query replacing the long-standing "Where's Whitey?" was "Where's the money?" Law enforcement has estimated his fortune peaked circa 1990s at about $20 million, an era when the FBI had his back. Only $822,000 was found hidden in the walls in his Santa Monica apartment. A shackled Whitey told investigators on his plane back to Boston that he had spread much of it around to people who owed him favors, but then he shut up about it. The questions that remain, which are much speculated about, include how much is still out there and how Whitey will get it now that he is imprisoned.

PHOTO CREDITS

INDEX

About the Authors

DICK LEHR is a professor of journalism at Boston University. He is the author most recently of *The Fence: A Police Cover-up Along Boston's Racial Divide,* which was a finalist for the Mystery Writers of America's Edgar Award for best nonfiction. Lehr is a former investigative, legal affairs, and magazine writer for the *Boston Globe,* where he was a finalist for the Pulitzer Prize in investigative reporting, and he has won numerous national and regional public service journalism awards. He lives outside Boston with his wife and four children.

GERARD O'NEILL was editor of the *Boston Globe*'s investigative team for twenty-five years before retiring to teach graduate courses in journalism at Boston University. With Dick Lehr, he coauthored *The Underboss* in 1989 and *Black Mass* in 2000. *Black Mass* was a *New York Times* bestseller and number one on the *Globe*'s bestseller list for a year. He has won several regional and national reporting awards over several decades, including the Pulitzer, the Associated Press Managing Editors Award in 1977 and 1998, and the Loeb Awards for business reporting in 1991, and was a Pulitzer finalist in 1997. He holds a master's in journalism from Boston University and lives in Back Bay with his wife, Janet. He has two sons.

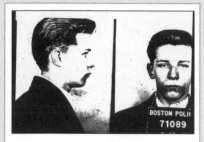

Whitey Bulger

Great Falls

Boston 1953

in custody 1956

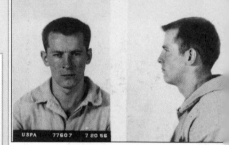

Atlanta

Alcatraz

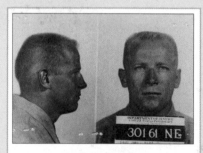

Lewisburg

Deb Davis exhumation

Whitey